An Inside Job

An Inside Job

Policing and Police Culture
in Britain

MALCOLM YOUNG

CLARENDON PRESS · OXFORD

1991

Oxford University Press, Walton Street, Oxford OX2 6DP
Oxford New York Toronto
Delhi Bombay Calcutta Madras Karachi
Petaling Jaya Singapore Hong Kong Tokyo
Nairobi Dar es Salaam Cape Town
Melbourne Auckland
and associated companies in
Berlin Ibadan

Oxford is a trade mark of Oxford University Press

Published in the United States
by Oxford University Press, New York

British Library Cataloguing in Publication Data
Young, Malcolm
An inside job: policing and police culture in Britain.
1. Great Britain. Police
I. Title
363.20941
ISBN 0–19–825296–X

Library of Congress Cataloging in Publication Data
Young, Malcolm, Dr.
An inside job: policing and police culture in Britain.
Malcolm Young.
Includes bibliographical references and index.
1. Police—England. I. Title.
HV8196.A2Y68   1990   363.2'0942–dc20   90-39318
ISBN 0–19–825296–X

Set by 10/12 pt Plantin by
Graphicraft Typesetters Ltd., Hong Kong
Printed in Great Britain by
Biddles Ltd
Guildford & King's Lynn

Preface

I joined Newcastle upon Tyne City Police in the mid-1950s direct from school. I was 16. By the early 1970s I was a detective inspector and had been with the Criminal Investigation Department (CID) for some ten years. For most of this period and throughout the era of 'flower power', I had been with the first drug squad in the North-East of England, created in 1967. During this time I became increasingly involved in a somewhat unsystematic analysis of the controls we were imposing. In an unschematic way I was becoming aware of the ambiguities which permeate police society, but which the imbued nature of our task-orientated world rarely provides time to reflect upon.

In 1974, as a number of smaller units in the area melded into the amalgamated Northumbria force, I was awarded a Home Office scholarship after my Junior Command Course at the national Police Staff College at Bramshill and I chose to read Social Anthropology at Durham University. The experience was a turning point. I was then half-way through the usual thirty-year police career when the opportunity occurred to pursue the theoretical ideas of Lévi-Strauss, Mary Douglas, and the like, which were revealed to us by lecturers of the calibre of Judith Okely and above all my tutor David Brooks. Visiting lectures given by such inspirational anthropologists as the late Edwin Ardener and his wife Shirley, as well as pilgrimages made to hear Sir Edmund Leach discourse eloquently on a structuralist interpretation of the Cistine chapel paintings, gave me an incentive to examine new ways of looking at the social condition; so that I determined to make time in the following years to pursue a reflexive anthropology, as I wrestled with the practice of carving out the remainder of a police career. The anthropological mode seemed to provide the tools to enable the complexity of policing to fall into place as a structured whole, exhibiting patterns of meaning and making more human what can be a difficult occupation. I am therefore grateful for the Home Office scholarship scheme which provided this opportunity to make such a personal journey in which the serendipitous nature of the anthropological experience could occur. It undoubtedly changed my way of looking at the world.

Above all I am indebted to the hundreds of men and women in Northumbria Police and those in West Mercia Police where I finished my career. They and their clients—the 'villains'—provided me with the most extensive field experience possible. Few had any real idea that they were contributing to the 'thick description' which provides the basis of this ethnography, and I humbly acknowledge their practical mastery in living what is always a tense and charged existence; for the extremes of human behaviour and experience do occur at the sharp end of policing on the streets. These 'real policemen' constantly walk a tight-rope in the inexact social conflicts with petty offenders, bloody-minded criminals, and those in their own administrations and the many critics of policing who lie waiting to pounce on any mistake.

In all references to fieldnotes and case studies, I have changed the names of individuals and some locations to avoid identification. To prevent those still serving in the police from pointing the finger at colleagues over certain revelations I have used techniques of 'displacement' in an attempt to draw a veil over who actually did what to whom and when. However, in an ethnography based on an anthropology 'right at home', this may not always succeed, for much of the data obviously derives from those I worked closely with over the years.

Full-time work in the pragmatic world of policing while pursuing academic research has often been a conflicting and paradoxical existence. Life with one foot in both worlds is not easy and the experience of continually living within the field with one's own 'natives' is an uncommon (if not unknown) situation for anthropology, criminology, and sociology.

From day to day for over a decade I moved between the two camps of the practical police world and the academic universe. This has become part of my anthropological experience and I am grateful for the support and friendship of many anthropologists who recognized the tensions this can create. I am indebted to my fellow postgraduates at Durham for their inspiration and help over these years. Allison James, Marie Johnson, Jenny Hockey, Brendan Quayle, Bob Simpson, Ian Whitelaw, Iain Edgar, Joan Knowles, Jane Szurek, and many others were part of an active and stimulating group who made my split existence more tenable.

This 'Durham School' of anthropologists were in the vanguard of semantic studies in the late 1970s and helped coax this book towards completion.

To David Brooks I am extremely grateful, for he pushed my ideas much further and into areas I might not otherwise have pursued. He stimulated and encouraged me to develop research papers and seminar material which led me to publish articles which might otherwise have remained unwritten. To the many individuals from academic institutions who have invited me to give papers over the years, I give thanks. For they helped me to refine ideas and kept me going when the research process seemed more than arduous. I am especially grateful to the late Edwin Ardener and his wife Shirley and the members of the Centre for Cross Cultural Research on Women at Oxford University, for they have been particularly encouraging.

Finally to my wife Dorothy who helped, threatened, and cajoled a completed text out of me and who proof-read various drafts on many occasions I dedicate the finished result. Any mistakes or omissions now are purely mine.

Contents

List of Figures

1

Participant Observation of Police Practice

AN ARM OF EXECUTIVE POWER

For over a century the control of certain aspects of British social life has rested in the hands of the police forces of England and Wales. However, these increasingly centralized and expensive units only enforce control over a very narrow range of public or 'street visible' acts of social disorder.

This system of power and control has primarily been directed towards the protection of property and to prevent assaults on the individual, but only in very specific situations. These aims have gained a high symbolic place in the public imagination and the institution has set out to prevent and detect acts which are usually subsumed under a generic (but simplistic) classification of 'crime'. To a less immediately visible extent the institution of policing is also set up to control those who would publicly demonstrate against the state and its executive powers. It is in relation to this area of activity that recent moves towards systematic amalgamation, centralization, and mutual aid seem to have been made.

Cohen (1973) describes how, at specific times, certain public crimes generate 'moral panics' directed at 'folk devils' or scapegoat groups. Pearson (1983) further showed that the identification of these groups as 'the dangerous classes' manifests itself as a continuous historical phenomenon. Tracing this back to the seventeenth century, he points out that in such times, it is 'always those crimes that are associated with the materially disadvantaged underclass which have provided the continuing thread within this history of respectable fears ...'. Prior to the establishment of the modern police system, the control of this underclass was the responsibility of the army working for the monarch or government. Foucault (1980) details the move away from the army, to control by the civil police; describing how the judicial control and surveillance systems emerged. He suggests the army could no longer be used to drain off the unemployable proletariat by conscription, nor could the newly independent colonies be used to dump the troublesome of society (see also Hughes 1987). In consequence, the burgeoning nineteenth-century penal and criminal justice system was aimed at these socially 'dangerous classes' simply because of their potential for contesting the power of the state and those in control. Foucault (1980: 17) suggests:

the bourgeoisie erected an ideological barrier around those who went to prison . . . [an ideology] about crime, criminals, theft, the mob, degenerates, 'animals' . . . which was in part linked with racialism . . . The Army can't play the same role as it used to. As a result we have a reinforcement of the police and an overloading of the penal system . . .

He goes on to argue that the bourgeoisie have always used sections from within the 'dangerous classes' to control those who are overtly troublesome, perhaps following the maxim that 'it takes a thief to catch a thief', when he argues: 'for one and a half centuries the bourgeoisie offered the following choices: you can go to prison or join the Army; you can go to prison or go to the colonies; you can go to prison or you can join the police' (ibid. 23). This somewhat idiosyncratic interpretation is no doubt coloured by the specificities of French history, yet there is little doubt that the British police system is also a political construction of the nineteenth century, created to contain the potential in the newly urbanized working classes for mob disorder, which the excesses of the military had seemed likely to exacerbate rather than disperse. Furthermore, a fear of revolution on the lines of that which had occurred in France still loomed large in the minds of the new English bourgeoisie, underpinning the demand for an organized police system geared to the protection of the life and property of the ruling classes (Reiner 1985). This fear of the mob has continued to haunt the executive, who saw that control could best be determined by the installation of a professional police organization formulated on strict hierarchic, semi-militaristic lines, and possessed of discipline, obedience, and loyalty.

Today, police forces pursue the control of the 'dangerous classes' by employing a crucially important range of ritual metaphors of negation. The police world is one of preventing, detaining; arresting, stopping, containing, denying, and rebutting; it is a world of diffused and hidden versions of reality where deflection is a prominent tool of the trade. Moreover, it has a culture which is built on a history of defensive skirmishes and has generated a metaphorical language of warfare which looms large in all of its structures of significance. In addition, it often seems that police culture possesses a dramaturgical or melodramatic inflexion, as the increasingly autocratic operational style is brought to bear in contests with new generations of dissenting workers, political radicals, and the largely dispossessed criminal underclass.

Police methodologies of controlling the dangerous classes may well reflect that we are in a period which Foucault (1980) has described as the 'end of an historical epoch'. This, he suggests, is a time when we have witnessed the ending of the construct of what he calls, 'the homogeneity of man' which was a product of a special political climate that has now passed. Leach (1982: 57) has suggested that if Foucault's assertion is correct, then this demise will undoubtedly enhance the separation of man by man into categories of 'inhuman', 'subhuman', and 'animal'. Such classificatory techniques and use of social binaries seem all too obvious in police practice and undoubtedly enhance ideological barriers and present further opportunities for the powerful to encourage their agents in the police to pursue bigotry and authoritarian measures in their contests with the dispossessed.

If the philosophical discontinuity Foucault describes is truly occurring, then an inside or reflexive exploration of police practice should reveal the strength of these divisive classificatory techniques, for any binary separation of man by his contemporaries into the non-human categories suggested by Leach (1982) is the very stuff of anthropology. And if such a classificatory system is a major feature of the way the police control their fellow citizens, then it seems essential it should be identified, assessed, and described.

Foucault (1980), like Thompson (1980), asserts that the criminal justice system is increasingly becoming an arm of the state apparatus, with the institution of policing beginning to wield expanding socio-political power. In a liberal democracy this needs to be scrutinized constantly, and herein lies the first problem for the researcher. For how can one really study a system of state control without acknowledging that such an activity itself is antithetical to the direction of power? Indeed it reverses the direction, as we shall see.

If the British system of policing is a social construction geared to the maintenance of élitist power and is primarily concerned to keep control over a materially disadvantaged underclass, then these same 'dangerous classes'[1] seem to have willingly entered into this game of power-relations with their masters; and by doing so they have deflected attention away from their own lack of privilege and power. Never having shown the same propensity as the French for violent revolution, the dispossessed have entered into a complex ritual of action within the processes of the criminal justice system, and in doing so have encouraged those tasked with their containment to consider them as being less than human and therefore needing further control and discipline.

As Wilson (1981), Reiner (1985), and others have clearly identified, policing is basically a socio-political tool of the state and government. It is sustained by an intimate knowledge of its 'enemy'—the underclass of society—and exemplary use is made of this knowledge to produce the technological and structural means for the continuity of this system of power.

As we shall see, there is now a specifically created police culture of the dramatic, which incorporates illusion, praxis, and imagery as part of a well-directed social production. It rejoices in an enhanced belief in Manichaean and mythological archetypes of good and evil which are made manifest in exaggerated games of 'cops' and 'robbers'. Series of interlinking metaphors of chaos and inhumanity are generated to maintain this dramatic mode and ensure that the agenda for control remains firmly with the system, and already I have used such metaphorical terms as 'animals' and 'enemies' to indicate some of the ways in which those in power make use of the rich imagination contained in everyday language. As Lakoff and Johnson (1980: 157) remind us: 'whether in national politics or in everyday interaction, people in power get to impose their metaphors'. So when the police declare (as they do) that they are non-political institution, this can only be a partial truth. For a co-ordinated system of mutual police aid is now one

---

[1] Thorpe *et al.* (1980) also uses this term when he correctly asserts: 'the law weighs most heavily upon the most defenceless and is hardly brought to bear upon the illegalities of the powerful and well-connected'.

of the primary tools for repressing expressions of political discontent, as the miners discovered during their disputes with government policy in the mid-1980s; and the chief constables of the forty-three forces in England and Wales now form a powerful cabal for co-ordinated action against any political or moral dissent. In the main, however, policing continues to be publicly concerned to prevent and detect individual attempts to steal the property of the citizen and it suits the police's purpose for their community role to be well broadcast, for on those rare occasions when they have expanded their controls to include the activities of the middle classes, they have found themselves on less certain ground. These groups, like all élites, have no previous perception of themselves as belonging to the troublesome classes, and it does not do for the police to remind them that the application of control can be redirected depending on who is defining the 'illegalities'.

If the police are to continue to exercise control over an increasingly pluralist society, which is better educated and less willing simply to accept any version of events handed out by the powerful, then it seems essential they should avoid scrutiny yet suggest they are totally accountable to the democratic ideal. In order to achieve this they seem certain to continue to deny close analysis of their practices, for exposure could well generate the potential to contest the system by releasing knowledge to those the system was set up to control. It is really one of the foundations of any executive power group that it maintains secrecy about its activities and avoids the possibility for its antagonists to subsume that power. As Arendt (1958) indicated, the more public a group, the less power it is likely to have. Real power, she clearly demonstrates, begins where secrecy exists.

It should come as no surprise, therefore, to find that detailed ethnography of police social practice is antithetical to the philosophies of control by which they operate. Yet in a liberal democracy, such a declaration cannot easily be made; indeed the opposite must be proclaimed. To carry out participant observation into the minutiae of police practice might be theoretically approved in any statement made for general consumption, but in the cold light of institutional reality it will most likely be thwarted or subverted even as it is being agreed.

In the remainder of this chapter I will explore some of the ambiguities and problems which face those who set out to research the police and assess some of the fears of the academic incursion into police society. They illustrate some of the problems the policeman/anthropologist faces when he sets out to describe and interpret police culture, for he must—if the ethnography is to count—reveal hidden aspects of the relationships of power which are an integral aspect of this institution of state.

THE POLICE OFFICER AS ETHNOGRAPHER: ANTHROPOLOGY AT HOME

Traditionally in anthropology, the ethnographer has studied a social system or culture through a period of intensive participant observation in the field. This has generated considerable concern about the ethnographic experience itself, and specifically about the subjective nature of the process.[2] Unlike the natural sciences, where discussion often starts with the results and ignores the methodology of the research, the social sciences—and increasingly anthropology—have developed an elaborate argument about the practices of doing research. The interpretation of culture and even the ability to understand what is happening in the society under scrutiny as well as the need to grapple with political or ethical questions are all endless and fundamental problems of the moment (Phillips 1973: 78).

Mere observation and reporting is inadequate, given the limited scope of things which can be truly observed (Holy 1984: 25). Rather an alternative and extra dimension to the observation is required if the deep structures and meaning inherent in any arbitrarily constructed social world are to be understood. Analysis of any construction of meaning from which social practice is derived has to be part of the participant ethnographer's cognitive processes, replacing the notion of simple observation as the main data-yielding technique. This role as observing participant reverses the emphasis of traditional fieldwork, so that the researcher is required to participate actively in the social life studied and thus consciously eliminate the distinction between the observer and the observed phenomena (ibid. 29).

This can create something of a dilemma for the anthropologist

---

[2] See, for example, the enormous bibliography on methodology and the dilemma of the research process in Ellen (1984).

and for the discipline itself, for one of the tenets of social research is that it requires detachment. However, even at the same time as this controversy continues the discipline has not only come to recognize the influence of the self, but has urged that we use it as a scientific construction (Okely 1975*a*).[3]

Analytic detachment is an elusive construct of the intellect. As Cohen (1984: 227) points out: 'by detachment I do not mean we have to distance ourselves emotionally; that I think would be perverse. But we do have to attempt to maintain some intellectual detachment'. In consequence it is becoming increasingly accepted that not only does the anthropologist have his own social history and subjective stance, but more importantly, that those accounts which ignore this seem to lose something in the telling.

For my contemporaries in the postgraduate school at Durham in the early 1980s, the inclusion of the scientism of the self (to use Okely's phrase) became part of 'doing the business' (to move to the jargon of my contemporaries in the detective departments). The ethnography we pursued and the seminar papers we created all tended to include the subjective 'I' as part of the discourse, and we were encouraged to explore the effects of our history, our social, political, sexual, and economic influences and include our vision of what we had experienced during the fieldwork situation. For as Crick (1982: 16) has suggested, doing anthropology is inherently autobiographical.

It is by making use of this complexity of an extended *observing participation* I believe anthropology can edge beyond its contemporaries in the other social sciences, so that the 'thick description' which Geertz (1975) urged us to use, takes on the 'finer grain and detail' necessary for an anthropology at home (MacDonald 1987: 120) where access to the social group or community studied is readily available to any demand for analytic reassessment.

Furthermore, the political implication of becoming an observing participant in an institution such as the police is immense, both for the group studied and for the ethnographer. To a unit of executive power, any analysis of how that power is maintained

---

[3] Well over a decade later, in 1989, Judith Okely was one of the organizers of the annual conference of the Assoc. of Social Anthropologists, where the theme of 'autobiography' and inclusion of the self into the account still seemed to pose problems and qualms for some members of the discipline, who enjoyed the accounts 'with the same guilty feeling they got from reading novels' (Young 1989).

and used must be uncomfortable; while the 'insider' had no means of retreating across some geographic boundary or vanishing like the traditional anthropologist, back into academia. The researcher who is really at home as one of the natives must seek inside himself to create his 'remote areas' (E. Ardener 1987). He must, as Ardener demonstrates, seek to sow 'semantic grain and grow theoretical crystals' which he may well appreciate no one is asking for. His ethnographic boundaries cannot be described as being geographically to the north of anywhere,[4] for they are around him and within. The insider who studies his *own* society is really the 'anthropologist at home' and he cannot move away.

Much of the recent writings on anthropology at home remain largely concerned with temporary visits by the academic to what is still the 'exotic' world of 'out there'. Usually the field trip is still an episodic visit to somewhere else, geographically to another culture from which the analyst can take leave or bring visitors too. Returning to academia he can recall the spatial remove as being 'out there in the field'; so that much of the current anthropology at home may still only be practising in its own backyard, pursuing an exploration of 'exotic cultures at home' rather than looking into its own front room (Cheater 1987: 166). Sarsby, (1984: 130–1) echoing Cheater, points out that 'anthropologists have tended to study people whose values and life-styles are different, even in their own society . . . [seeking] the unfamiliar at home as well as abroad'. An assumption remains inherent in the literature that anthropology is academically based, funded by some research organization, presented in seminar, taught to students, and then written up and published. It exists largely as a product of the institutions of higher education (Sarsby 1984: 132) and has only recently begun to surface in policy and practice. As Okely (1987: 67) observes, the urge to create publications is not always as crucial to others as it is to the academic. Indeed for those insiders living in Cheater's metaphorical front room—such as in the police—the need to obscure and seek a degree of anonymity from the analytic gaze can be described as a major principle in the preservation of power, ranking highly in the structures of significance.

Yet there are those of us who, although firmly based inside such an institution, have undertaken anthropological training and have

---

[4] MacDonald (1987: 122) reveals this 'spatial otherness' when describing the 'thrill of crossing into territory north of Birmingham to attend a conference at Keele on anthropology at home'.

subsequently developed the academic wish to be discursive. Our interpretation of the field situation therefore becomes a specific and unusual type of 'anthropology at home', for it is not out there in the exotic or even in the backyard. It is neither here nor there, but is everywhere. It is all around, all of the time, and not even an interpretation of another but similar society, 'at home' in what Hastrup (1987) has called a 'parallel culture'.

This research at home is primarily about the society of the self and the self in that society. It encompasses an internal exploration of a personal history within a culture and inevitably differs in scale from much of the 'anthropology at home' which has become one of *the* genres of the 1980s. Inevitably it has qualitative differences and is not easily written or smoothly integrated into the 'isms' or historical categories of the discipline.

Material obtained in such circumstances inevitably contains the seeds of a special inside knowledge, avoiding problems described by Liebow (1967: 232–56), who was still separated by cognitive barriers while pursuing research in what was ostensibly his own society, and who found an insider's language, education, and 'social membership' all helped to retain boundaries he was unable to penetrate. The semantic ability of the insider to translate the hidden and the unspoken aspects of the cultural agenda which occur in any society should be especially productive in any analysis of the police, where a massive visibility at one level is matched by a secretive, hidden side to institutional practice.

Furthermore the ethnography must contain a recognition that the anthropologist within is stepping outside himself to describe how and why he performs within his own culture. This requires a detached intellectual process to illuminate how the culture is constructed and how modes of thought are translated into organized beliefs and action. He must understand how these are taught to the neophyte and inculcated into the consciousness to be transmitted across time. It requires a conscious act of experiencing a reflection of yourself and of how you have become what you are! It can be quite painful, for the insider is studying his own social navel, with the potential always present that he will recognize this to be only one of a number of arbitrary possibilities and perhaps also find that many practices are built on the flimsiest of moral precepts.

Such special knowledge holds further difficulties, for it highlights the specifically political nature of any ethnographic account of such an institution, bringing to the forefront those expectations of loyalty which the executive demands of any individual who has hold of the account. Ethical problems will surface, for no power-based organization likes to have its idiosyncrasies made public, and the anthropologist who is a member of the family and not merely a temporary visitor to the 'backyard' exotica can find that writing anything at all becomes crucially problematic. Expectations of confidentiality and silence prevent many accounts from reaching fruition, for as the revelations of *Spycatcher* (Wright and Greenglass 1986) revealed, it is not necessarily what is written which causes the pain; rather it is the breach of the convention which requires members in various arms of the executive to say nothing about their practices.

This returns us to Arendt's observation that secrecy is a prerequisite of totalitarianism, for those involved in the executive use of power know that to reveal is antagonistic to its maintenance. The insider/anthropologist is therefore somewhat schizophrenic, something of a Jekyll and Hyde, for he knows that publication and explication might be career-suicidal but are necessary intellectual tasks.

One result of this constant paradox is that while the police make statements welcoming research and applaud intellectual debate, they strive to impose rigid control over a system of preferred rules and regulations to negate open enquiry, so that systems are quietly but firmly deployed to deny the critical approach—as we shall see. The observing participant insider is consequently torn between self and scientism, for he knows the strengths of an inculcated approval for quality of restraint which sustains the police mind.

It should come as no surprise, therefore, to find that most insider participant observation of policing is almost always confined to discussion on management techniques and to the implementation of new systems. Philosophical reflexivity is not high on the agenda and in an organization which makes much of the concept of loyalty but really means subservience, the insider can find it hard to bite the hand that feeds and reveal any unhealthy aspect in the agenda. When the research is carried out by academics from outside, critical analysis creates enormous tensions. Barrie Irving, director of the Police Foundation, indicated this antipathy in his title to a paper given to the British Psychological Society,

'Research into Policy won't go' (1983). He told his audience that 'C.I.D. officers use deception, trickery and psychologically oriented persuasive tactics amounting to threats and inducements, in order to obtain confessions; and this process is potentiated by the custodial environment'. Of course, insiders are well aware of the drama which surrounds interrogation and do not need to be reminded or really welcome such information being made public, for as a detective colleague pointed out after reading Irving's paper, 'if we don't use fear, force, fraud or the promise, how do they think we are going to clear up the crime and get the coughs the system needs to survive?' Irving had studied the 1984 Police and Criminal Evidence Act proposals to legislate for interrogation and prisoner control. He concluded the bill was a legislator's attempt to 'assume institutions work on the kind of rational and ordered basis which they outwardly pretend'. In this he recognizes the same problem which faces the insider/ethnographer, for he clearly understands that pretence, deception, and bizarre social drama play a large part in police culture and accepts this will be difficult to research. However, he is optimistic (as any professional researcher must remain!), for he cites Sir Kenneth Newman's efforts as the new commissioner of the Metropolitan Police to 'make police ethics a major issue, so that performance assessment, promotion criteria etc., will take integrity and professional conduct more and more into account'. With hindsight it seems that the prevailing structures of police practice will remain as powerful as ever, for at a conference on policing at Bristol University (1988), the newly retired Sir Kenneth admitted that police culture had defeated many of his attempts to bring a new ethic to the managerial style during his reign as commissioner of the metropolis.

ANTHROPOLOGY FOR THE POLICE

It seems relevant that anthropology be used at this time to contribute to the debate on policing, for since the 1964 Police Act and the preceding Royal Commission which was generated through concern over police practice, the organization has held an increasingly central place in the public imagination.

Policing issues are never long out of the headlines (Chibnall 1977), and this media obsession has been transmitted into a wealth of analyses of policing—which have mostly been carried out by outside observers.[5] Indeed insider accounts have largely consisted of bland reminiscences in the style of 'my greatest arrests and cases' and it has been left to investigative journalism to redress some unacceptable police activity, by calling attention to the limits and abuses of police authority, power, and accountability.[6]

Concern also continues to be expressed in some quarters over the increasingly authoritarian attitudes and methodology which surrounds some police practices and there is a commensurate fear about the growth in policing and the exercise of their extensive powers, which look set to become increasingly centralized and wieldy. Thompson (1980) has warned of the potential danger of a strong police autocracy, conscious, no doubt, of the slim line which exists between the democratic use of power and its subversion by a more centralized totalitarianism. And the forty-three forces in England and Wales now contain some formidable units, amalgamated out of the small borough, city, and county forces of the pre-1960s, many of which were prone to the whims of corrupt local politicians (Simey 1988).

Some of the forty-three police units now have visibly autocratic chief officers who consistently spell out their public accountability yet pursue very personal perceptions of what they consider to be disorderly and what needs to be controlled,[7] and such constructions of reality generate systems which enforce power differently from force to force. For example, James Anderton, the chief con-

---

[5] Ben Whitaker in an appendix to *The Police in Society* (1979), has a selected bibliography on the police which contains nearly 200 publications of recent work. Since then, with the Brixton riots, the miners' strike, the Confait case, the Stalker affair *et al.*, the number of works continues to proliferate. See, for example, the highly recommended bibliography in Reiner (1985).

[6] See, for example, Cox, Shirley, and Short (1977).

[7] Chief constables belong to ACPO (the Association of Chief Police Officers). On my Intermediate Command Course at the Police Staff College in 1987, during a seminar on the role of ACPO, one of their members told a crowded lecture theatre that 'ACPO found it very difficult to agree on a national drink/driving campaign at Christmas . . . for they couldn't agree on Christmas!' 'But, of course', our speaker continued, 'when one gets his instructions *from* God, and his next door neighbour thinks he *is* God, can you be surprised?' No names were given in the account, but the audience of superintendents and chief superintendents, with their practical mastery of the politics of the world of policing, were clearly aware of the internal antagonisms referred to here and duly supplied audience laughter at the right place.

stable of Greater Manchester, pursued a drive against pornography in the early 1980s which was not imitated by other chief officers. Pornography—like homosexuality, which he has similarly crusaded against—is an ambiguous activity and creates very marginal offences in any standard police hierarchy of crimes. Thus, the use of anthropological ideas of social marginality and the construction of gender and masculinity are of primary use in the analysis of such actions, revealing the depth of concern with bodily form which structures considerable areas of police thinking. For a fear of pollution and impurity in the body physical is constantly and easily transposed to create controls in the body social.

Disquiet over deaths in police cells, to take one further example, is another area in which anthropology seems well placed to make some comment. Statistically these deaths largely occur as a result of the inhalation of vomit and alcoholic poisoning, and it therefore seems somewhat bizarre for the police to be in charge of those suffering in such a way. More often than not the victims have serious medical problems, show a long history of social inadequacy, or are clearly suffering from mental illness. At the 1987 annual ACPO conference, chief officers complained they were still having to deal with this illness and asked why do people still need to die in cells from inhalation of vomit?

In Chapter 3 I will describe in detail the culture created to deal with these 'street-visible' offenders in a cell-block situation, but suggest the inertia surrounding the whole problem is more easily understood when we consider the social history of such illness (Foucault 1967), and see how the executive has always allocated the control of such 'drunken dossers' to the police. As 'social dirt' they become an affront to purity and possess the danger of the contagious and impure (Douglas 1966), requiring their removal from the public vision. As yet there is no other body to undertake this task, and even tentative moves to remove the problem from the cell block and into the detoxification centre foundered in the entrepreneurial 1980s; for there is little immediate profit to be made from reclamation of this kind of scrap material (although the long-term value of a humanitarian return might be thought to be well worth pursuing in a civilized society!).

The argument is therefore not about police control or a utopia without controls, but to explore why some cultural behaviour has a history of police action and to discover where that behaviour fits into police ideology. Its status or (as importantly) its lack of value creates complex systems of meaning which are rarely articulated; for the police world has similar strictures to that which Benedict (1967) described in her attempts to understand the rigidities of Japanese culture:

men who have accepted a system of values by which to live, cannot without courting in-efficiency and chaos keep for long a fenced-off portion of their lives where they think and behave according to a contrary set of values.

Anthropological modes of enquiry are therefore programmed to steer us through the assumptions of police society, so that contradictions no longer remain incomprehensible. The cultural baggage which any social group, tribe, or institution such as the police acquires over time can thus be translated to reveal just what sustains it, and furthermore reveal what the society itself may not even have understood.

Where there does exist a genuine public expression of concern about the way the police operate this cannot just be dismissed as a matter of misunderstanding or be written off as the foolish ramblings of that police 'folk devil' the 'loony left', who would dismantle the system for their own political ends. Such a mood of concern has existed now for more than a decade and seems to mirror uncertainties of role occurring elsewhere in society. For example, it can be argued the expansion into amalgamated police units has enlarged the organization to a point where it is no longer accessible to the man in the street; alternatively, it may be that the use of a centralized computer and complex technical aids has alienated the public even at the same time they are increasingly fed a diet of violent news snippets which reinforce a fear of crime and generate another 'folk devil' of criminal menace, which demands the impossible: a policeman on every corner.

In nightly theatrical TV rituals of social order and chaos, a stream of hero-policemen stand at the symbolic crossroads between peace and mayhem, and the detective and the chief officer now operate at the point where once the church and its priests declaimed on categories of good and evil and the resulting binary codes they produce. Inevitably, as a secular interpretation of morality has superseded that of established religion, so the activities of the social controller have become increasingly important in the drama. It can be no accident that the opinion of the police officer is now sought on matters which once would have remained the province of the archbishop and his clergy. The immediate result is that alongside a few major clerics such as Runcie and Jenkins, we find that Stalker, Sampson, Anderton, Alderson, Newman, Imbert, Dear, Oxford, and Hermon are national personalities, while a second division of chief officers regularly proclaim on a range of subjects which at other times would lie outside the province of the police.

Yet Robert Reiner (1989), writing on the collective culture of chief constables, is the first to explore their extraordinary place in modern society, simply because as an élite among the powerful in society they have had little need to reveal how they operate, link together, or reveal what structures of significance guide their actions. Across the history of policing their need has always been for the light of research to illuminate the activities of the underprivileged and the powerless, rather than focus upon the élite themselves!

Analysis of police culture is therefore particularly suited to the anthropological method, for it requires an extended field study to reveal much about the unspoken agenda which determines many aspects of police practice. These are governed by an often unwritten series of transformations, creating homologies which reaffirm operational practice and which are determined by a definitive, but rarely acknowledged rationale. For, as Benedict (1967: 12) implied, reflexivity in any dogmatic culture always presents the possibility that the whole scheme of things will simply fall to pieces. In consequence, there is always a careful code of practice, elaborated in Force Orders to suit the legalistic need to define. In addition the system also has a range of unwritten rules about such aspects as loyalty and the way activities should be handled in practice. These are taught to the initiate to show him the accepted response to the vagaries of order, disorder, ambiguity, and ambivalence which lies in the complexities of social behaviour.

As Crick (1976: 123) has argued, 'criminology (like anthropology), is largely concerned with systems of classification'. In consequence, police modes of thought build up into classifiable systems of praxis which are the product of dealing with the extremes of social experience. These in turn become massively overdetermined, regenerative and self-justifying, creating an institutional mind which, although allegedly acting on behalf of society and the majority population, comes to regard that same group as outsiders and potential antagonists who are never to be accorded easy access to the processes of the organization.

Such a world view is the product of a perception conceptualized to contend dramatically with the instant experience of dealing with highly emotive, personal conflicts at street level, or the tensions of ritual 'battles with criminals'. Inevitably in such circumstances, the detail of practice suffers a reduction to enable these charged and emotional situations to be handled more easily and to allow the complexities of social events to be reduced to the simplicities of narrative necessary for the file of evidence. In such a situation, action becomes more easily defined if it runs along well-known lines, following precepts which have status and acceptability. Such compression into a carefully managed logic allows policemen to deal quickly with what are intensely charged and often dangerous situations, best resolved with the minimum of introspection or self-analysis.

Not unnaturally one consequence of this reductionism is that action and pragmatism take on an extra dimension in the police mind, holding a special place in the institutional imagination. While any analytic appraisal or reflexivity on this rationale is never given much credibility in the structures of significance.

Anthropological analysis of these beliefs, I believe, should add a crucial semantic dimension to compliment the many non-qualitative enquiries into policing now in progress. For example, the Police Foundation is only one of the bodies publishing indices of current research on the police. Their 1986/7 register of police research (Bird 1987) contains over 200 pages of police-related projects, yet only one item in the index specifically relates to police culture. This is being conducted by Simon Holdaway, an ex-police officer turned academic, with whom I discussed the anthropological potential for police studies at a 1988 conference we both attended. He agreed there was little in an anthropological vein and deplored the current lack of funding available for cultural or qualitative research into the semantics of policing.

Much of the work which is being undertaken is dependent on government funding and, of necessity, is required to provide material which fits current political philosophy. As a result, the bulk of research listed in the Police Foundation Register, or outlined in a Home Office Research and Planning Unit 1987/8 'Research Programme' document, is concerned with managerial effectiveness, workload assessments, resource deployment measurements; evaluation of neighbourhood watch or victim support schemes, or the analysis of the effectiveness of enforcement programmes. All are described pragmatically (ibid. 21) as measures 'to aid decisions as to how police manpower can most usefully be deployed'. In their own research departments the police continuously attempt to measure aspects of their activity, largely to demonstrate cost effectiveness in line with criteria imposed by the limits on public spending (HO Circular 114/83) and the prevalent socio-economic world view of society.

This has meant that many studies tend to concentrate on the objective assessment of a fiscally quantifiable reality. For example, the Audit Commission (an arm of the treasury) spent some time in 1987/8 with myself and others in a police research department assessing an OSU (Operational Support Unit) administrative system which they claimed had 'revolutionized police decision making' and released manpower for patrol equal to £6.358 million. However, a colleague looking at these OSUs in relation to their cultural impact, saw there were many aspects of a qualitative nature which could not easily be expressed in fiscal terms (Adams 1988: 11):

direct submission of reports to the O.S.U. was to be encouraged, eliminating chains of assessment and decision making which had lain within the purview of the superintendent. A central decision making process involving Inspectors and civilian decision makers was established and developed. . . . Its early implementation met with a degree of resistance, [for] the new system fundamentally dislocates the well established and cultural preferences of the service. Inspectors can no longer 'hide behind a paper managing a desk' (quote from a Chief Superintendent).

Then again for reasons of established cultural preference we had to go back to the Audit Commission and ask them to translate £6.358 million into 'real men', for we had difficulty in trying to sell such an alien concept to the police mind. In effect their fiscal mandate meant their version of reality failed to synchronize with the police world view.

Constantly the symbolic or qualitative nature of police culture slips through the grasp of the researcher or the audit analysis, simply because of its ephemeral potential for statistical assessment. At a 1988 Police Foundation Conference 'Coming to Terms with Policing' (ed. Morgan and Smith 1989), where I had had the discussion with Simon Holdaway mentioned above, the symbolic nature of police culture consistently surfaced to confound the economic assessment of good practice which the Home Secretary had set in his opening address to the participants. All too often the outside researcher pursues lines of enquiry which the prevailing culture manages to encompass and nullify. For example, Christine Horton (1989) told the conference she regretted that many aspects of policing had a symbolic role which were not conducive to quantitative measures and were difficult to present with absolute objectivity. Others described problems in dealing with the influences of culture and the ingrained systems of status attributed to 'real police work'. Shapland and Hobbs (1989) consider many low status activities are effectively invisible, while Chatterton and Rogers (1989) acknowledge many cultural inhibitors, ranging from a lack of trust between the ranks to a 'number of deeply rooted myths about the existing police systems which protected it from criticism and disguised its deficiencies'. Chatterton told the conference: 'regretfully there is a considerable amount of material which is unrecorded and unavailable to the researcher locked away in the constable's heads'. This troublesome invisibility in the material record is often inversely related to its semantic value, and activity which may well have a central place in the police model of reality can well remain beyond the grasp of the outsider. Often a priority given to some activity in this police hierarchy of meaning has been laid down from a constable's first days as a probationer and now lies beneath the immediate consciousness, so that any calls for a change in direction of police response may well be defeated by an unspoken semantic value which the institution gives to that activity. For example the considerable criticism of the police response to domestic disputes 'mainly related to their failure to take effective action by arresting men who assault their wives and girl friends' (Shapland and Hobbs 1989) is largely determined by wider social factors pertaining to the historical role and place of women in society. Systems will simply not change as easily as Shapland and Hobbs seem to hope; for police society is extremely conservative and masculine in outlook, and has long reflected the low esteem women are given in wider society, as I will describe in more detail in Chapter 4.

In consequence the wealth of research contained in the bibliographies I have mentioned often fails to follow through the deep structures of police culture or establish the ways in which the culture is self-sustaining even in the face of calls for social change. As long ago now as 1974, Michael Maguire argued a need for a semantic ethnography of police systems and the criminals they pursue; and there has been a subsequent trickle of attempts to carry out participant observation inside the world of 'cops and robbers'. Ditton (1979) was said to have carried out 'a *unique* situational ethnography in a bakery', when he set out to assess fiddling; while Holdaway (1979, 1982, 1983) has pursued aspects of police culture, using his previous insider's knowledge to peel away some of the layers of obfuscation. Dick Hobbs (1988) lived with thieves and detectives as they set out to 'do the business', and perhaps one of the most effective pieces of participant observation in recent times has been the four-volume Policy Studies Institute work on the police in London (1983). Robert Lustig (1983), writing in the *Observer* (20 November 1983) called it:

the most detailed examination of the relationships between police and public ever conducted. Every statement is based on observation; every conclusion is supported by evidence; every judgement is carefully weighed. Two of the institute's researchers spent the best part of two years observing.

Its analysis of police culture was certainly incisive and accurate, as can be judged by its wholesale condemnation. Sir Kenneth Newman, to whom the report was presented, candidly admitted he would not have commissioned it in the first place (it was commissioned by his predecessor, Sir David McNee), while the official Police Federation magazine (*Police*, December 1983) concluded in an editorial:

the report is certainly not a definitive and unchallengeable portrait of the Metropolitan police. In later, calmer moments, those conclusions which are not based on published research material need to be contested. There is a world of difference between research findings based on safe academic principles and methodology, and those produced with graphic literary phrases, but based upon anecdotal heresay, recorded by listeners blessed with total recall.

This attack was repeated again in 1987 in the Federation magazine, for the report had obviously hit a very raw nerve. Its frenzied rejection was very different to that of the many projects listed in the Police Foundation or Home Office Registers of Research mentioned above, most of which are simply ignored and never ever receive any review. I believe the denial of the PSI report and the furore it caused occurred precisely because it managed to get beneath the surface of police culture to explore the deep structures of belief and to comment adversely about their influence on police activities.

The invisibility in the written record, which Shapland and Hobbs (1989) observed, and the unrecorded information which Chatterton told the conference remained hidden in the heads of the constables are the result of cultural values, which are then brought to bear to deny validity to these agendas. It is worth noting the language in the Federation rebuttal of the PSI report, for it illustrates how the culture is programmed to sneer at the 'graphic literary phrase' and dismiss the use of 'anecdotal material' as unscientific: while participant observation is considered to be a world away from 'research based on *safe* academic principles' (my emphasis).

Police culture is omnipotent is structuring such views of critical research. Historically it has homed in on sociology as the generic symbol of reformatory zealousness, regarding its practitioners almost as 'folk devils' or bogeymen. Such a view of 'sociology' sets up another binary derived from the police preference for a Manichaean world created on homologies of 'good ∼ evil', and further reflects the ferocious resistance to and fear of change which permeates the organization (see for example Weatheritt 1986, Butler 1984, and Adams 1988). Certainly the social sciences are seen to be the arbiters of revolutionary change which might somehow dismantle the police institution and its processes, and this has led it to negate the reforming social scientists, keeping them as outsiders beyond the system.

A further example from the Police Foundation Oxford Conference gives some indication of the different perspectives which exist for the analytic researcher and the practical policeman:

Barrie Irving, the Police Foundation director has presented a paper today outlining research into the Police and Criminal Evidence Act (PACE).

Having some 1979 data on custody practices and prisoner interviews he sought to replicate the study in 1986/7 to assess the influence of the legislation on police practice. Claiming significant differences in post-PACE activities he suggested these showed the need for legal measures to impact upon police practice and influence change. His observational sample of prisoner interviews, although small, had found the PACE codes of practice were followed to the letter and he argued this showed that it required the sanction of the law to effect changes in interview and interrogation techniques. A detective inspector shrugged this off, arguing from 'practical mastery' and 'insider's' knowledge, that the practices of 'doing the business' remained undisturbed outside of the PACE interview. He accepted there was no question that the PACE interviews Irving had witnessed would have been carried out with exactitude, but was certain that the negotiation of justice could easily continue outside of the world of the written custody record or file of evidence. The fact that a sociologist was witnessing the interviews make it all the more certain they would be conducted with scrupulous care, but there was no way he would be given access to the extra-legal deals which may well have gone on outside the interview room or later during a prison visit for 'write-offs'. As the detective cryptically pointed out:

> I could make up the detections that his presence lost me in a matter of days, and if he thinks he is going to see any wheeling and dealing when he is sitting in, well he's naïve! As a working detective, it would take six months of living with a mate to trust him and know that when it came to the Crown Court appearance he would know exactly what to say. (From fieldnotes.)

This distrust of the social scientist is so deeply ingrained that when I was reading anthropology as an undergraduate and I was asked by my colleagues what subject I was reading, I knew that I would have to prevaricate or face problems. Usually I was challenged as to why I was not reading law, which was always quoted as the 'proper' subject for a police officer. I eventually described the discipline of anthropology to certain colleagues as 'the study of old bones, prehistory, and human evolution you know; David Attenborough and all that'. I had taken two classes in physical anthropology and felt less guilty because of this and they were satisfied; although they would have preferred I had chosen to read law. But as one said, 'so long as you're not reading that bloody sociology'. In 1987 I worked with a chief inspector who had just returned from university having read for a Bramshill scholarship in what he called 'black letter law'. He described the study of precedent and case law as being 'real academic activity' for police officers, thus supporting my contention that research into the philosophy of control is 'unreal' or polluting. He spoke revealingly about the problems he had had with jurisprudence, bemoaning the fact that it was ambivalent and undefined, concerned primarily with the ambiguity which sustains the anthropologist by revealing the centralities of a system: 'it was all grey areas; no black and white certainties or decisions; no precedent or case law giving the definitive interpretation'. At the Police Staff College shortly before I was offered the scholarship to university, I had listened as lists of degrees obtained by previous scholars were read out. The majority were for law and were greeted by applause in an assembly of the staff and students. Later on, however, the names of those who had graduated in the social sciences and especially sociology were greeted with hissing disparagement and barely concealed denigration.

Greenhill (1981), then a lecturer at the college, discussed this history of police/sociology antagonism in detail, arguing a tendency in each side to discredit the other; resulting in a situation where 'the number of published British texts and research studies on the sociology of the police may be numbered on the fingers of both hands'. I suspect Greenhill was referring specifically to a dearth in the cultural analysis of policing, while his use of the duality of 'sides' reveals another parallel binary to that of 'cops and robbers', with the police and sociology arraigned against each other in yet another of the wars which the police wage against those who defile the sanctity of their definition of the concept of order.

Constant separations between the two categories are promoted, producing a dichotomized vision of left-wing, radical reformists, antagonistic to the 'right-minded' 'boys in blue' and includes a wealth of negative imagery of sociology which is lodged deep in the collective consciousness of the police mind. The sociologist, as I shall illustrate, is the despised, hairy, intellectual subversive, who is set against the 'clean and ordered British bobby'.

To reinforce a belief in their own omnipotence and popularity, the police have made increasing use of market research to show they are well liked; especially by that important category 'the silent majority'. The findings have tended to support the view that the police are held in relatively high esteem, although those polled have invariably had little or no contact with the police in any capacity. Although such findings are not in dispute, and of course are rarely undertaken in areas where public antagonism to the institution is known to run high, there is continual pressure to replicate them and repeat the consoling message. For such results show the police to be 'on the side of righteousness', arraigned with the numerically superior forces of goodness and order in their fight against darkness and the void.

This tendency to dichotomize policemen against the social reformer even led the ex-police liberal John Alderson uncharacteristically to describe the historian E. P. Thompson as being 'an unfair critic of the police' (*Public Office*, Granada TV, 20 June 1980); and this at a time when Thompson (1980) had just pointed out that most policemen are 'ordinary blokes, and no society could do without them in dealing with many of its sordid realities'. And sordid behaviour does exist, for even without the labelling techniques beloved of deviance theorists and favoured by the police, there remains the grim fact that such activities would not cease to occur (Maguire 1974). Thompson (1980) has further suggested that many of these analyses are designed to present some utopian vision of a police-free world, but often include 'the soppy notion that all crime is some kind of displaced revolutionary activity'. This perspective, he contends, is a particularly sociological construct, implying criminal activity is some kind of pure or moralistic behaviour. If Thompson is correct, then such presentations are as simplistic as many of the police images which imply that society is consistently under attack from rampaging and ubiquitous criminal enemies, and which (it follows) only they can fight off and defeat.[8]

In the light of these partial versions of reality, I suggest there is a need to look beyond the surface presentation, whether handed out in the form of a press release or in the crime statistics which senior officers consistently use as an indication of social mayhem. It is essential to look beyond the public utterance dressed up in

---

[8] Police language is full of metaphoric references to such militaristic activities. Terms such as 'vandals', 'assault', and 'crime fighting' all help sustain the military image and reinforce the belief that secrecy is a necessity as the 'troops' set out to 'defeat the enemy'. Lakoff and Johnson (1980) explore these metaphors in depth and argue that such use is central to human thought and experience. Salmond in 'Semantic Anthropology' (1982) has a similarly useful essay in which she considers the ideological and structural value which metaphoric language possesses.

these metaphors of battle, and seek the structural forms which determine the ideological base. It is here that an anthropological observing participation comes into its own, for in living with the semantics of the system the analyst has the potential to undertake a rarely used method of social research. This contains the experience and depth of the insider's knowledge, which Holdaway (1979) recognizes is unlikely to become readily available, simply because 'there is a lack of impetus within contemporary sociology to spend lengthy periods of observation in what may be uncomfortable research situations [with the police]'. And here the problem really begins, for the ethnographer must explore beyond the public presentation of self, to seek the underlying discourses of police reality. Inevitably this takes the researcher beyond the press release, the statistical return, or the 'folk explanation' and into an interpretive framework, perhaps to seek how these presentations are used (often unconsciously) as part of a well-constructed formula to replicate positions of power and support the ideology and practices of the institution.

Immediately the police officer/anthropologist sets out to undertake research or record fieldnotes he is forced to confront a moral dilemma. This exists simply because he must necessarily reveal aspects of a closed and somewhat secretive society to the outside if he is to pursue any ethnography at all. Furthermore, he will know that his contemporaries are not really too keen on its revelation: indeed they may well argue that the police have research facilities of their own which are geared up to the internal needs and interests of the institution (Benyon 1988: 21). He becomes crucially aware that they have little need of any critical analysis, for as Benyon (ibid. 23) goes on to point out,

historically, the powerful have encouraged hagiography, not critical investigation. . . . And they have been in a position to determine the way they are investigated and the manner of their public exposure. They have also, when confronted with [any] critical research findings, been quick to use this power to neutralize the critical impact . . .

Yet in such circumstances the insider's account has a potential to combine 'action anthropology', 'applied anthropology', and 'pure anthropology', to create a fully semantic analysis; and this raises the question of whether it will then be possible to publish and be damned? For such special knowledge holds the potential for an ethnographic interpretation of police culture which incorporates aspects of 'practical mastery' (Bourdieu 1977) and to enlarge on what Kuper (1973: 238) has somewhat critically dismissed as 'the prissy sterility of much of the methodological or reformist sociology'. Such an insider's account will therefore hopefully achieve the 'finer grain and detail' MacDonald (1987) demanded of postmodern 'anthropology at home', while 'practical mastery' of the ethnographic field should reduce the problems faced by McCabe and Sutcliffe (1978), who set out to pursue participant observation on the police and found that 'it would be necessary for anyone wishing to fully understand the process of policing to take into account the difficulties in gaining access and an understanding of just what was going on'. Seeking to unravel police decision-making in relation to the classification of crimes, McCabe and Sutcliffe (ibid.) admitted that as outsiders they were usually not quick enough to grasp the nuances of what was taking place before them. They went on to suggest that where complex insider activities are being carried out in a sub-language designed to exclude the uninformed, the best ethnography would probably be carried out by the insider/ethnographer.

That this will require some radical reflexivity on the part of the insider is obvious, for it is almost inevitable that his revelations will not only create some discomfort for himself, but will almost certainly be unwelcome. Even the research listed by the 'independent' Police Foundation or undertaken at the University Centres for Criminological Research (and largely dependent on government grants and funding by such bodies as the Economic and Social Research Council) often comes up against the anti-intellectual bias which permeates all levels in police thinking (Lewis 1976). This facet of the culture is perhaps the reason why the British administrative and academic élites have obliquely indicated to the police that they do not consider them fit to be allowed to take charge of police research. It may also be the reason why, in its forty-year history, the Police Staff College has never achieved any real academic status; for, as Lewis (ibid. 183) also points out:

there is a deep feeling that academic training gets between a policeman and his knowing and getting the respect of the crude masses of a very crude, very egalitarian and anti-intellectual European race ... the police have indeed a general belief that they know more psychology than academics.

Always the demand is for 'practical' skills, while academic analysis remains a despised pastime, so that even the Superintendents' Association (the equivalent of the Police Federation for the lower ranks) has similarly denied any place for intellectualism for its members. At their 1974 conference they decided: 'It is time to end the service's love affair with education'. Although this conference comment is now well over fifteen years old it still holds good. In 1987 when I attended the Intermediate Command Course at the Police Staff College with some thirty-five other superintendents from around Britain, I found that my Ph.D. was the source of extreme curiosity and even some apprehension, and I watched (and recorded fieldnotes) as my new colleagues sparred warily with the 'Doctor' in their midst. I realized I would need to convince them at the first opportunity that I was primarily a practical policeman and not an academic; and I also noted that while the college was keen to list the academic qualifications of those on the course, the participants quickly justified Lewis's assertions by playing them down to emphasize their history of praxis and practical mastery.

AN ANTHROPOLOGY OF THE SELF: PARTICIPANT OBSERVATION OR ESPIONAGE

Any insider who sets out to pursue a reflexive anthropology of policing eventually has to face difficulties which arise when he reaches an objective and analytic understanding of his society and its own specific versions of reality. He must come to terms with living with this consciousness and with the inherent problems he will face in revealing this knowledge to the outside in an ethnographic account. Moreover, he must come to terms with a new awareness of what he has previously accepted, perhaps without thinking, which under the intense microscope of social enquiry may well seem to verge on the ludicrous or to be morally indefensible. And having long been supported by the institution he will be crucially aware that it expects a degree of loyalty verging on deference or acquiescence.

In such an archetypal world, where 'good' is constantly and insecurely balanced in an eternal struggle against 'evil', the objective explication of the rituals and symbols which surround and mystify police work can seem tantamount to a treasonable act. In 1979, James Anderton, the Christian moralist chief constable of Greater Manchester, described the greatest threat to law and order as stemming from 'seditionist . . . interested groups who do not have the well-being of this country at heart and who mean to undermine democracy' (Thompson 1979: 380). In the light of such a polemic stand, it begs the question whether the revelation of how crime figures are manipulated by the police to sustain institutional beliefs (see Chapter 5) could be said to undermine democracy or be classified as sedition. For Anderton vehemently rejects the idea of any internal evaluation which might explore the moralities or philosophies of policing: 'there is simply no room in the management and organization of police operations for vague, academic dissertations' (*Police Review*; 90, 19 November 1982: 4684). In his 1977 annual report, Sir David McNee, then commissioner of the Metropolitan Police, urged that 'the libertarian should beware'. In due course, his successor, Sir Kenneth Newman, echoed this anti-intellectual stance, when he warned insiders that 'policemen must remember that they are practitioners, not crusaders; theirs is to do, not to righteously philosophise' (*Police Journal* 56, No. 1 (1983)). Such pronouncements implicitly acknowledge police structures to be a logic upon which rationalizations, justifications, and systems of protection are built up. To reveal these is to peel back a curtain and show this version of institutional order is only one social possibility, and furthermore is a continually manipulated experience. For the insider such an exploration of the secular rituals and social constructs which govern police practice will hold what Myerhoff and Moore (1977: 18) have described as 'the possibility that we will encounter ourselves making up conceptions of the world, society, our very selves. We may slip into that fatal perspective of recognising culture as our construct, arbitrary, conventional, invented by mortals'. Inevitably this perspective will create problems for the insider as he now comes to recognize the arbitrarily constructed nature of his universe. For over a decade I lived with this new knowledge and with the ethical dilemma surrounding my own pursuit of insider research. During the creation of a doctoral thesis and preparation of papers for seminars, I had to face the conscious problem of writing about a system which I know prefers silence and links such reticence to ideas of 'respect', 'order', and 'discipline' in an all-encompassing paternalism. And of course I knew that this hierarchical organization offers the possibility of reward and incorporation into the highest ranks to those who conform to such dictates. The dilemma followed me through the publication of a few accounts of my researches.

This loyalty to the family (or force) is another lived quality which is imbued at every turn by practice and example. Although rarely defined, it is often on the lips of the members, so that the phrase, 'I don't want to seem disloyal, but . . .' will often preface even the mildest internal criticism of any of the systems of policing. This total reverence to the group binds ideas of silence, loyalty, and reticence together to create a positive category for belief and action and, in turn, links silence to other concepts of respect for the order of the institution. In consequence, even the publication of an academic seminar paper carried out without formal approval could form a breach in the regulated structures of police existence and be subject to disciplinary control. In such a world, the easy resolution of the ethical dilemma remains problematic, for as Anne Akeroyd (1984: 134)[9] recognizes 'there is not, nor ever likely to be any definitive agreement about the nature of either the problems or solutions [facing the social scientist and the question of ethics]'. I have never completely resolved my own dilemma, for I do not think it has a simple resolution. Unlike the natural sciences, which deal largely in results, the social sciences are rightly concerned for practice, perhaps because results are rarely possible in an exact mathematical sense. Consequently, this ethnography will continually raise such matters simply to illustrate the dilemma as it arises, for I have consistently had to contend with the nature of an insider's breach of social boundaries. Asked to comment on the publication potential of my Ph.D. thesis (Young 1986), Mike Chatterton (1988) rightly homed in on this question of ethics, saying: 'there is reference here to the moral dilemma(s) posed by "insiders" using their access to do ethnography and what that entails regarding betraying confidences etc. . . . The way the writer resolved them is not adequately addressed . . . the issues are raised, but no explanation [is given] of

---

[9] Akeroyd explores the ethical problems surrounding social science research in some depth, culling material from an enormous bibliography, and showing the variety of ways in which the research is undertaken and the problem approached. Almost regretfully she concludes that compromise seems inevitable.

how they were resolved in practice.' Of course there is no perfect solution. I had the easy choice of remaining silent, or the more difficult one of addressing the problem at some length in various publications; which is how I resolved the practical difficulties. This ethnography is therefore an attempt to meet the dilemma, for the problem of revelation and betrayal continues to surface and can only be resolved, at best, by overcoming these subjective feelings and pursuing compromises (Barnes 1981: 2). Indeed, I believe, along with Akeroyd (1984: 154) that:

In a pluralist world and an increasingly pluralist discipline, consensus about ethical behaviour and research practices is unattainable and compromise seems inevitable . . . The social researcher must make compromises . . . between roles as scientist and citizen; between commitment and impartiality; between openness and secrecy, honesty and deception; and between the public right to know and the citizen's right to privacy and protection . . . the onus for making decisions in practice rests with the individual researcher.

In the light of these points and Benyon's claims mentioned above, it seems inevitable that any insider analysis of policing seems destined to alarm. To suggest from within the institution that these influential and powerful units of control are essentially ephemeral and arbitrary constructs, involved in very limited and narrow areas of practice, will almost certainly lead to a rejection of the account; and the findings are more than likely to be attributed the same metaphorical rejection as the activities of the villains and criminals, as was illustrated in the response to the study undertaken by the Policy Studies Institute outlined above. For in a similar vein to the criminal 'enemy', the researcher's activities are across the bounds, a challenge to be taken on, attacked, and, destroyed or at least to be denied. As Chatterton (1973: 107) has written:

on more than one occasion . . . senior ranking officers have made no bones about the fact that they attribute many of the problems of contemporary police work to the pernicious influence of the media and sociology! Such people are radically opposed to the idea of sociologists conducting research on the police and long for a return to a 'golden age' when the proverbial veil of secrecy surrounded police work.

When the research is experiential, carried out by an insider, the publications can prove emotive and will almost certainly be career-problematic for the author. Usually policemen know the limits allowed by the organization and play safe. Harry Templeton (1980), a police officer in North Wales, suggested:

when you read in Police Review that an officer has been awarded an M.A. after post-graduate study, it will probably be in a 'safe' subject such as business management. Few officers who continue their academic studies ever consider sociological study of their own job. Serving officers who attempt constructive criticism of the police, risk being labelled traitors and put their promotion prospects in jeopardy. If internal criticism is unwelcome, the views of outsiders are even more likely to be seen as hostile and derogatory.

This risk to promotion chances is well understood and can be clearly illustrated. In his Durham Business School M.Phil. thesis, 'Communications in a Disciplined Society', a sergeant (Wilson 1978: 6) explained why he had chosen the Royal Navy in preference to the police in which to carry out his research: '[I] considered incompatible a progressive career within the police force, and the implications of carrying out research within that organization'. In other words, Sergeant Wilson (who has since left the force) agreed to compromise to enhance his career opportunities rather than present any challenge to the system. Obviously concerned that his analysis of the negative influence of discipline on the efficiency of systems of communication might offend or incite displeasure, he avoided confrontation; but he need not have worried. For it received the neglect that a great deal of insider research achieves and was channelled (unopened) to me, accompanied by a two-line memo from a senior officer which suggested, 'I understand you are doing some research; you may find this useful'. In the following three years the thesis remained on my desk, unrequested by anyone else. Any suggestions for improvements in communications or any critical findings it may have contained were negated by institutional neglect and the 'silence' which Arendt (1958) argues is a primary tool of authority operated to effect!

The police, of course, can never really be geared easily to incorporate structural challenge to their existing concepts of order and control, for they are set up to maintain the symbols and practice which has sustained the status quo. It would be paradoxical for them to be in the vanguard of social change, for as Templeton (1980) points out, they are 'there to preserve the structure; to uphold the state of play'. But there are a few who *are* questioning the state of play, and who agree with Ben Whitaker (1979: 312) when he urged 'that police thinking would profit if it more often came out of its shell and concerned itself with wider questions about the role of the police and human relations'. However, this is not always easy to achieve, as I found out when I first returned to work in 1977 after my degree course. In order to continue post-graduate studies I had applied for some financial assistance for part-time fees, under a scheme created by the Home Office and set up specifically in recognition of a lack of higher educational qualifications in the police service (HO Circular 29/74). This directive encourages officers to research and study in their own time and lists suitable subjects, which include 'public administration, management studies, economics, law, criminology, social sciences, youth work, English language and literature and relevant modern languages'. The circular goes on to point out that the list is not exhaustive and suggests other courses may be appropriate. I had applied to continue full-time research following my degree course, but this had been turned down by my chief officers; however, I had been told that assistance for part-time study would almost certainly be approved in view of the national policy of encouraging officers to extend their educational qualifications. I then found my application for financial assistance for part-time study had been rejected 'because anthropology is not on the approved list of subjects (in the Circular)' (Memo from HQ 1977). Eventually I was able to convince my senior officers that anthropology *was* one of the social sciences, perhaps only because I somewhat sardonically returned a memo which asked 'why, if anthropology is not approved, have I just been allowed to read the subject on a Bramshill Scholarship, on full pay and allowances?'[10]

Just over a year later, at a 'Career Appraisal Interview' with the chief constable, I was asked: 'tell me, how did you find the law course at the polytechnic?'[11] I pointed out that I had not been to the polytechnic, but had been to Durham University on a scholarship—only the second the force had been awarded. I was then

---

[10] The Bramshill Police College Scholarship scheme is discussed at length by Smith (1978). The author found that scholars, by and large, do not reach senior rank, but opt for personal job satisfaction.

[11] Northumbria then had a small number of places booked each year in the law department of the local polytechnic. Smith (ibid. 147–8) also mentions these local arrangements.

asked: 'what's the difference between a law course at polytechnic and at the university?' This assumption that policemen study law becomes axiomatic. As Smith (ibid.) indicates, the cost of one scholarship (when he was writing in 1978) was about £30,000 and by the late 1980s this had risen to well over £100,000. Yet some twelve months after I had graduated, I was now having my first interview with my chief constable who had no idea what I had studied or what result I had achieved. This tendency to ignore those on scholarships is mentioned by Smith (ibid. 154):

with one exception, all [scholars] contacted have expressed strongly that the service did not appear to see the practical relevance of university training, did not know how to exploit the benefits gained by the individual and in many cases showed noticeable coolness to those who were part of it.

This 'coolness' is something other scholars have experienced. An inspector reading humanities at Oxford, told me: 'I felt cut off, with no contact back at work. No one wished to know me, I was away and forgotten.' Another inspector from Merseyside, reading social studies at Liverpool, said: 'I felt isolated, not just ignored, but socially dead' (personal communication). Smith (ibid. 157) also touches on the crucial feeling of potentiality which the university experience can produce in the individual, but which the police are generally unable to incorporate. Yet another inspector returning to Leicester with a degree in psychology was set to work in the force vehicle store counting tyres. Like many graduates stimulated by their experiences, he discovered that although he had been of sufficient calibre to acquire the offer of the scholarship in the first place, he now faced the inevitable service obsession with a rejection of academic prowess in preference for 'practical skills in the real world' (ibid. 157):

the greatest problem with the current working of the scheme appears to relate to 're-entry' into the Service ... The impact upon the personality expectations and the way of life of a mature scholar by the University experience is not appreciated by many of the police ... It is therefore difficult for him to appreciate the general view of the Service, that, on his return ... he must re-establish his professional standing, even though a few years earlier the Service had sent him to University because he had proved himself to be a good, practical policeman.

For those who go on to read postgraduate studies, there is the further problem of publishing any research findings. A police graduate I met at a seminar on 'Research into the Police', which we had both attended in a private capacity and without force blessing or financial assistance, later wrote to me:

there are always strong moves to keep studies under wraps. There is a tendency for senior officers to suppress research findings and to advise those who see it as useful and important, to desist. Usually career coercion will suffice to ensure that any troublesome thesis stays unpublished and out of the public eye.

In the late 1970s another insider academic experienced this autocratic preference for silence when he was served a notice under the Official Secrets Act. He had proposed to publish his Ph.D. thesis, and although apparently not very controversial, it invoked such extreme measures simply to ensure it remained under wraps. It would, of course, have revealed some aspects of the variable world of police culture to the outside and this was unacceptable.

Another writer on the police met similar problems when he wished to write and publish. I had discussed the problems of insider analysis with him at a 1988 Police Conference, where he described how, on return to his force after his undergraduate degree, he had asked for permission to publish research material. His request was refused in a written memo from HQ, but no reason was given. Unwilling to accept this constraint, he went on to ask 'why not?' (again in written report) and was informed reasons were never given; the official line was simply to refuse all such requests. Not unexpectedly, this officer left the police and moved into academic life.

Even the simple article sent to the magazine *Police Review* can be subject to vetting and many Force Orders demand this privilege. Another inspector I know had problems with an innocuous piece written in a mildly conversational style. This was put up for vetting to a nominated superintendent whose instinctive response was to deny its submission, suggesting it 'looked as if it would be editorially unsuitable'. He had come up against sterner stuff, however, and an assistant chief constable was called in to mediate and eventually agreed to send it on after the author urged that the editor of the magazine be allowed to decide (fieldnotes 1988).

Even a letter to the *Police Review* can be regarded as a form of indiscipline:

Writing to the Police Review

In a duty report to my chief constable I mentioned I had written to *Police Review*. He sent me a memorandum directing me to inform him in future before I write to any newspaper periodical on matters appertaining to the force. Do you consider that I may have committed a disciplinary offence?

Answer

A chief constable is perfectly entitled to insist on being informed when a member of his force writes to the press on matters appertaining to his force. The Disciplinary Code in Schedule 1 to the Police (Discipline) Regulations 1985 contains an offence of 'improper disclosure of information', which is committed where a member of a police force without proper authority communicates to any person, any information which he has in his possession as a member of a police force. This does not apply to matters of general interest, although some senior officers appear to have strange interpretations of their own. (*Police Review* 26 August 1988: 1797)

Of course, the desire to obtain control of the written word has always been one indication of the autocratic mind. This fear of open debate continues even when the publication is by a retired officer and when control is less easy for the chief officer to enforce:

Sir Peter Imbert, the Met Commissioner, has written to Met officers warning that he would take proceedings under the Official Secrets Act against police who break an internal discipline code which prohibits 'improper disclosure of information'. The step follows the newspaper serialisation of former D/Chief Supt. Drummond Marvin's account of sensational cases he handled as deputy head of the force's Serious Crime Squad. (*Police Review* 26 June 1988: 1779)

There are shades of Peter Wright and *Spycatcher* here, with the warning to stay silent extending to ex-members of the 'family'. It is a salutory lesson on the stability of this precept to see Sir Peter following the precedent set by his predecessors in Sir David McNee and Sir Kenneth Newman, both of whom, as I have indicated above, rejected the internal desire to philosophize or be discursive.

In West Mercia, there have been regular reissues of Force

Orders to remind members to be circumspect in their dissertations and essays prepared for part-time diplomas in Management
Services or the NEBS[12] qualification which is now an integral part
of inspector training. The fear is always that the outside will be
presented with the chance to gain knowledge and power at the
expense of the institution; although this is often only obliquely
implied:

Persons Undertaking Outside Study: Disclosure of Information

From time to time, and particularly in connection with external courses,
police officers and civilian employees may have cause to write articles,
dissertations, essays, etc., which require them to research information of
a privileged nature. It may not be . . . prudent for such information to
be then read by other than police personnel. Such information may not
necessarily carry any security classification within the Service, but may
simply reveal dispositions, working arrangements etc. When such
information is submitted to tutors or course directors etc., there is no
guarantee of its circulation or copying. All personnel who undertake
external study or produce articles should be mindful of the dangers of
revealing privileged information and should:

   a) Use their own discretion on the use or reproduction of such informa-
      tion.
   b) If in any doubt, seek the advice of a senior officer of the rank of
      Superintendent or above.
   c) If it is considered imperative that such privileged information
      should be included on the paper and which [sic] falls within the
      terms of the concern expressed above, then the whole should be
      submitted for approval by a Chief Officer . . . who will give a ruling
      as to its use and circulation.

Nothing in this order changes the already existing practices exercised in
connection with courses or papers overseen by the Regional Inspector
Training Unit or Police College. In these cases a Senior Police Officer
has 'first read' of any papers and all other personnel involved have been
required to enter into an undertaking to respect the security of the
information. (Force Order w/e 28 November 1987).

In effect, such an order intends that all dissertations and papers
will be submitted for vetting. Any criteria for defining 'privileged
information', or what the 'dangers' are in revealing such matters
as dispositions (of manpower) are so vaguely incorporated as to

[12] NEBS = National Examination Board for Supervisory Studies.

ensure that few will risk submitting an essay without approval, which might later be assessed as an 'improper disclosure'.

The creation of this order at the time a new Official Secrets Bill was being pushed through Parliament by an increasingly interventionist government is significant, and the idea of a senior officer's having 'first read' of any essay to maintain the integrity of the institution manifests the importance of the legalized surveillance of allegedly dangerous material and enhances the separation of the world of control from that academic enquiry; although its implementation is only randomly applied. Just as Sgt Wilson's thesis was channelled to me because I was known to be interested in research, so many police research departments now get allocated the task of reading the essays submitted by sergeants and inspectors for NEBS or DMS qualifications. In 1988 a visiting colleague from the Royal Ulster Constabulary asked if it was part of my role in Systems Development Department to comment on such essays. He told of his own difficulties in finding time to read all the variable essays submitted and knew of many that were never sent in at all. For although Force Orders inevitably direct that such material will be submitted for assessment, it is typical that in a task-orientated institution which gives low priority or credence to the academic tome, the systems to ensure submission of the essays, or the ability to make much use of any useful ideas they contain, often remains sketchy.

As the director of the Police Foundation, Barrie Irving (1984: 4) commented, 'Unlike their American counterparts, the British police community, together with their administrators, do not devour large quantities of written material [and] if a research project does not produce results which can be acted upon . . . no amount of careful editing and dissemination will make an impact.' Research in the police, Irving further asserts, is a matter of pragmatics, eliminating philosophical enquiry into systems of belief, or how the knowledge of an ideology is transformed into action. In the end, only the action is viable, so that all these essays tend to match the inside ethnography and are nullified by neglect or have any contentious matter treated as 'privileged information', for as Templeton (1980: 904) argues 'the police fear that if you have a better understanding of society, you are in a better position to change it—the very exercise [they] are reluctant to engage in'. Those who do go public are disloyal and there are thinly veiled attempts to dismiss the value of any revelation they make, for they are expected to remain silent and uncritical. When Ronald Gregory, the ex-chief constable of West Yorkshire, said little or nothing new about the 'Yorkshire Ripper case' in a series of newspaper articles, he was castigated in *Police Review* (1 July 1983) and they republished a 1979 photograph of him when 'his loyalty was unquestioned'. John Alderson, the ex-chief constable of Devon and Cornwall has suffered even more from his subsequent public persona, because of a move into academia, some critical publications, and a flirtation with the political life. *Police Review* (18 February 1983) has an article on him by a superintendent, which is full of graphic metaphors clearly illustrating this idea of 'traitors to the service'. Alderson is revealingly described: 'poor old John Alderson [has] gone careering off the rails, [and is] now shacked up with the liberal party . . . an intellectual liberal reformer with radical ideas [whose] philosophical mumbo jumbo, often incomprehensible, and not very original, did nothing to impress'. Furthermore, 'there have been questions about his loyalty', for Alderson has had the temerity to caution the service about an apparent drift towards paramilitarism.[13]

Needless to say the revelations made by John Stalker (1988) were also less than welcome to the service, and all around I heard my contemporaries condemn the fact that he had gone public. Inevitably, I noted these criticisms were rarely in relation to what he had said (few had actually read the book), but rather were expressions of shocked outrage that he had failed to keep silent and say nothing at all. Indeed, the fact that he had apparently used an editor from a Manchester newspaper for some of his purposes was latched onto and quoted as a sign that he was 'suspect' and 'disloyal'.

One consequence of these modes of thought is that the service has to live out a continuous and enormous paradox. Even at the same time as it publicly commends higher education, seeking out the graduate entrant, spending large sums on publicity to this

---

[13] Crick (1976) suggests everyday language is the most social of all institutions, providing the anthropologist with a firm basis for understanding any field situation. Here, Alderson has metaphorically gone 'off the rails' and is 'shacked up' with that despised enemy, the liberal, practising 'philosophical mumbo jumbo'. In this graphic everyday language, we have intimations of all the bogeymen and folk devils which haunt the institutional police mind.

end, and funding access to degree courses on scholarships, it also holds to a central ethic of distrust of the academic. Whitaker (1979: 229) clearly understands the way this rejection of training and education operates within the service:

at present good recruits often have to be chased to Bramshill [on the lengthy command courses], because chief constables are not anxious to spare able men, and officers themselves are reluctant to be separated from their families and homes, as well as having a fear that they might lose from being 'out of sight, out of mind' for promotion.

And although always implied rather than broadcast, this rejection of intellectualism is so well understood throughout the service that it has even affected those to whom Bramshill scholarships to University have been offered, and many turn them down. I know several inspectors who have refused a college scholarship, arguing that the time spent away from the force was time spent in structural limbo, and it has become almost a common adage that time away is time lost in 'the promotion stakes'. All that is required, they feel, is the offer of a scholarship from the Police College, for it serves the same purpose on the c.v. and reduces the need to spend time in limbo or the need on re-entry to re-establish oneself. Furthermore, it reduces the risk of being labelled with the derogatory term of 'academic'.[14]

This marginality of academics continually comes to the fore and my fieldnotes are full of examples. In 1987 at one of the regular meetings of superintendents, I listened as the deputy chief constable talked his way through a potential problem for the increasing numbers of graduates in the service, who 'obviously cannot all make it to the top'. Of course this has always been the case for all entrants, for there are only forty-three chief constables and the same number of deputies, so few have a chief officer's truncheon in their knapsack (to paraphrase an old army chestnut). The inference in this was not really about the career chances of the still tiny percentage of graduates (who are obviously well aware that their chances of reaching the highest echelons are constrained by the limitations in the numbers of top posts), rather it was a reassertion

---

[14] On a promotion board in 1982, the first question I was asked by my deputy chief constable, was 'Does it worry you that you are considered to be something of an academic?' As I was then deep into the creation of a doctoral thesis, I replied that 'I would be worried if I was not'.

that those with a degree are almost a different species and remain a threat to the stability of the institution.

It is not uncommon for the police magazines to feature this antipathy to the academic, and especially the social science researcher:

When you take away all the sociological *clap trap* which is fashionable in some circles, policing is all about dealing with folk. At the end of the day we must concern ourselves with the practicalities and not philosophies of dealing with everyday problems. (*Police Review*, 18 May 1983)

now 'body language' has to be dressed up with a lot of sociological *clap trap* and paraded as some marvellous new technique, aimed at revolutionising police relations with the public. If you believe that not only will you believe anything, you'll probably end up as a Doctor of Philosophy. (*Police* magazine, May 1981; my emphases)

Inevitably those few insiders who do undertake postgraduate research in the social sciences are aware that they are involved in the creation of 'clap trap', and must know that this denigration stems from the implicit threat they pose to the structures of pedagogy and institutional power. Those who pursue explication can expect to be seen as suspicious, for they embody the marginality of the anthropologist, described by Lévi-Strauss (1973: 67) as being someone who is 'psychologically speaking maimed, an amputee'. This maimed psyche, according to Francis Huxley (1970: 62), creates a specific concept of the self and makes the inside anthropologist 'a mutilated man . . . in curious revolt against his own society'. In such a world many graduates learn to play down their qualifications, for they know the hostility which exists towards academia and realize the significance of 'practical ability' gained in 'the university of real life'. Furthermore the graduate recruits can judge the derisory attitude to academics for themselves, simply by picking up most editions of *Police* magazine. One example (September 1980) headed 'University Challenge' exemplifies this antipathy, with a full page of cartoons on graduate candidates illustrating a range of negative symbols. These graduate applicants are shaggy, long haired, and bearded, reflecting a direct binary to the approved short back and sides. Their need for thick-lensed 'John Lennon' spectacles implies they are physically imperfect as they slouch or lean against props; for these lazy, untidy creatures have techniques of the body which reveal major structuring principles of police thinking. Their clothes are bedraggled in a clear symbolic indication of bodily order and its antithesis, and illustrate a microcosmic representation of police values. Bourdieu (1977: 94–5) describes these as a means by which

all totalitarian institutions (in Goffman's phrase) embody their principles in an inexplicit way, beyond the grasp of consciousness and exhort the essential by an implicit pedagogy, capable of instilling a whole cosmology, an ethic, a political philosophy through injunctions as insignificant as 'stand up straight'.

It is little wonder then that social research is equated with 'clap trap' in police magazines, for they aim to support the beliefs of those who have taken on this unconscious cosmology, and for whom as Bourdieu (ibid.) indicates, such challenges would defy 'the most natural manifestations of submission to the established order [and abolish] lateral possibilities'.

In consequence of this acquired system of generative schemes, an imbued belief is implanted in the institutional mind which verges on 'the natural', while Huxley's 'mutilated man' pursuing his insider's reflexivity seeks out the lateral possibility, and makes gestures against the principles of the organization. In doing this the anthropologist 'at home' quickly comes to understand why he must always stand on the margins of structure. For it is one of the dictums of the discipline of anthropology that it will reveal unwelcome truths:

the anthropologist is committed not simply to description, but to analysing and questioning the definitions and assumptions on which social groups base their existence and predicate their activities, and to unveiling that which may be concealed or unrecognised. This makes the anthropologist at the least an uncomfortable associate, at the worst seem 'dirty', 'dangerous' or even 'subversive'. (Akeroyd 1980: 6)

Anthropology has been prominent in showing how the marginal in any society tends to pose problems for state institutions and governments; and the insider must anticipate that his conclusions might well be

frequently uncomfortable [and] may well challenge the assumptions of the institution. Anthropological knowledge can seem, and often is, dangerous and subversive—not because we are good at digging up dirt (we are), nor simply because we document what 'actually happens' rather than what is supposed to happen, but because our ways of defining situations and problems often raise questions in our minds about the fundamental assumptions on which any institution bases its own definitions, and indeed the assumptions on which it rests as an institution. They get far more than they bargain for. (Grillo 1980: 3)

In effect, the insider who reveals the structural formations of a system of power inverts that power and the revelation creates a situation where elements of 'anti-structure' (Turner 1969, 1974) now present a version of how things might be constituted; and what has been seen as solid reality begins to be identified as only one social possibility. In this observing participation, the 'thick description' which Geertz (1975) argued for comes hurtling at the ethnographer, so that the classic use of an 'anthropological informant' is hardly necessary. Rather it will be a case of the researcher finding a means of recording and sorting the mass of detail which continuously bombards him and presents him with the lateral possibilities which make the discipline potentially dangerous.

He will have little opportunity to stand back and examine the data in the cool light of the academic 'ivory tower'. Nor will he be able to take a sabbatical to formulate the complex structures of meaning lodged deep in the empirical material, which Lévi-Strauss (1976: 80) has argued are capable of linking together symbolic and metaphoric programmes to 'reveal properties not immediately accessible to the (empirical) observation'. To coin another military metaphor, he must 'soldier on' knowing that all of this activity might well smack of sedition. Even the fact that someone inside is writing fieldnotes will produce unease, as I have experienced; and their collation can almost certainly be tantamount to something akin to espionage; for as Sean Conlin (1980) observed: 'often our work can seem "political" rather than scientific'.

WRITING THE 'ESPIONAGE'

Because of this insider's knowledge, I chose to record my fieldnotes surreptitiously and with much burning of the midnight oil. My practical mastery had made me acutely aware of the boundaries which separate those inside the institution from those excluded from the specialist knowledge of 'doing the business' and I was more than ever aware of the suspicions which would have been aroused if I had introduced questions of an academic nature, or had distributed questionnaires. Like Powdermaker (1967), who recorded fieldnotes in Mississippi only when she was away from her field data, I found I only took notes at the time if I was willing to risk begin interrogated about what I was going to do with the information I was recording. Webb *et al.* (1966: 72) recognized such unobtrusive measures have found favour in field-work and I discovered at an early stage that the problem remains one of revealing the structural warts of the system while somehow indicating that this need not be seditious; and indeed might even be of some value.

As it is, when I showed close colleagues my first working paper (Young 1979*a*) on experiences in a police bridewell (see Chapters 2 and 3), they were alarmed. I was told on more than one occasion, that I should not really let outsiders see this sort of thing, even though it was agreed that what I had written was an accurate analysis of events. In some respects, I think it was the detail of the ethnographic 'thick description' which most alarmed them; for as almost all of them wistfully pointed out: 'it shows exactly how we do the business'.

In effect the insider who questions the gross systems of classification which define police practice seems set to join those deviants or criminals who contest the system of law and order by breaking its rules and regulations. Any challenge to what is an almost xenophobic and dichotomous world of 'order' and 'disorder' casts the social analyst and the critical criminologist onto the dark side of the binary. To some extent these academic outsiders are 'the enemy' of police society, whose training and class aspirations makes them supporters of the status quo and resentful of liberal ideas or academic intrusion (Reiner 1978*a*). When Sarah McCabe (1980) queried the logic of why just one police system should be entrusted with the control of crime, law, order, and social assistance, pointing out, 'there is some disagreement about the use of the criminal law—unease about control of the streets . . . [which poses the question] who will be controlled and [who will be] assisted', she found the tenor of her 'thoughtful and moderate examination of the police role . . . was too much for the senior officers to whom it was presented, and they set out to discredit it with a will' (Greenhill 1981: 98).

It seems most likely then, that the increasing police budgets (up from £3.35 billion in 1988/9 to £4.1 billion in 1989/90), which have risen by over 50 per cent in real terms since 1979, will be used to maintain, defend, and expand on this hegemonic style. For who within the service is seeking or is willing to dismantle these units whose power and autonomy has been growing in strides since the Royal Commission of 1960 and the subsequent Police Act of 1964 first created the amalgamated giants? Today, in the early 1990s there seems to be every possibility their taste for autocracy and power might persuade the police that secrecy should take on a new dimension, so that sedition could acquire new status as a deviance, while even the 'espionage' of ethnography could well become actionable.

In this situation, research into the police could well become increasingly difficult and even less welcome than it was a decade ago. At that time, Punch (1979) pointed out (in a comparison of facilities in Britain and Holland) that research into the police in Britain is not easy and

I think it would be more difficult to gain access and get co-operation [from a British Force]. Also there is more hostility towards academics than in Holland where their status is higher. In the U.K. academics tend to be denigrated ... In practice some areas of police work are unresearchable, but in principle they shouldn't be. If research can be done in Holland and the USA, I don't see why it shouldn't be done in Britain, except I suspect that some British police forces are just hostile to outsiders. I think this is probably true of the Metropolitan Police; they have never really allowed any fundamental research on any sensitive issue. You get people like Belson who was allowed to do a survey research of public opinion. Few people have been allowed to do any extensive fieldwork.

Since this condemnation of reseach opportunity, few studies have penetrated deeply beneath the sensitive skin of 'police culture', and even though Chatterton in his notes to my thesis argued there has been a considerable amount of 'participant police research', I would question whether many of these inquiries achieved 'the finer grain and detail' of the insider's account, for they can never really know or tell if they have been excluded from the inner workings of police practice or prevented from gaining access to the hidden realities 'contained inside the heads of the constables'.

Because of the élitism which such an organization of control wields, it is not surprising there is difficulty in incorporating the outside researcher, or in accepting his critical findings. And

certainly that other main arm of executive control—the army—
seems little better at this than the police, for the number of participant accounts of their deep structures remains negligible, supporting McCabe's (1980) contention that we should be asking of
all of these costly institutions, 'who is to be controlled by whom
and for what reasons?'

Meanwhile, as Reiner (1985) suggests, the politicization of the
police has proceeded at a pace, and can be illustrated by their
growing willingness to respond to political dissent as a form of
'crime' or deviancy. This trend is further displayed in their growing tendency to agree to be used as a pseudo-military arm of
government in its socio-economic and industrial/political disputes
with whole sections of society. In 1985, Cressida Dick, a probationary constable, wrote a prize-winning essay which clearly
showed an awareness of this politicization, and asked the sort of
questions which few senior officers seemed to be thinking or
voicing. In her essay 'Implications of the Miners' Strike', she
pointed out that:

the Government's seeming indifference to the effect of the dispute on
police public relations, [should entitle the police] to wonder whether it is
being used to preserve law and order or to implement government policy.
This view of the use of the police as agents of government economic policy was shared, frequently with concern, by much of the public . . . The
miners' strike marks a set-back for those who argue that police and politics don't mix . . . for the discussions generated will serve to accelerate
the politicisation of the police . . . [and] has highlighted the presence of
ACPO and the NRC [the co-ordinating National Reporting Centre],
as bodies, set up without the authority of Parliament, of apparently
unquantified and unaccountable power.

Such expansions of police power were forecast by E. P. Thompson
(1980), who considered this to be a period which has no equal. He
argued, historically, that he knew 'of no period in which the police
have had such a loud and didactic public presence, . . . [or] when
they have offered themselves as a distinct interest as one of the
great 'institutions' and perhaps the first in the realm'. In such a
climate it seems even more suitable to pursue the creation of a
radical, insider ethnography and in the not too distant past this
even seemed to have official support. Writing in a more liberal
decade, the commandant of the Police Staff College (Lamford un-
dated—but probably in the late 1960s) suggested:

it would seem desirable to encourage individual police officers to come [to the college] to do research on their own account. The Staff College should be a place where serving officers have the opportunity to contemplate society as a whole and in particular to study and consider those liberal and humane values which are central to our society. The college should have as its prime concern the nurture of ethics and integrity; they are the core of any professions.

Such a proposal is now of another era, however, and I was present when an ex-Dean of Academic Studies at the college presented a paper (Stead 1980) attacking the trend to expensive, amalgamated police units which had grown up in the previous two decades. The appetite for power these immense forces display worried Stead, and he argued their style could only lead to an autocratic national system with a minister of central government at the apex. His fears seem to be well founded, for a move towards regionalization is now occurring, with a proposal that the forty-three forces disappear into perhaps eight or nine giant regional units.

Stead argues that only constant inquiry (for which I could substitute 'inside ethnography') can prevent such an unacceptable trend, and it is some comfort to see a probationary policewoman, such as Cressida Dick (1985), pointing out the political compromises such autocracy can produce, but which few of the chief officers seem willing to admit or even acknowledge. However, I am not hopeful that her example will force the institution to reassess its attitude to the critical account, for even the fears of someone like Stead, which came from a central location of police power at the Staff College at Bramshill, seem to have largely fallen on stony ground.

In the main, the college has produced little radical comment or research of note during the four decades of its existence, for the various chief officers have jealously ensured that any consolidation of ideological excellence at this location has been neutered, and under Home Office direction its senior courses have primarily been used to provide a stream of suitably acquiescent candidates for the ACPO ranks, who readily take on the symbols and metaphors of dominance which feed the appetite for power Stead warns against.

In 1987 I spent the summer at the college on the Intermediate Command Course and found it depressing to see just how little research was being sponsored or carried out there. The vast library on police matters was clearly under-used and there is obviously a need for a critical ethnography of the college itself, for it takes in numbers of senior and middle police managers each year, maintains a considerable staff of academics and visiting lecturers, but has singularly failed to provide an academically stimulating 'university of policing'.

Even the civilian academics at the college seem to be nullified by the overriding police desire for circumspection in the written account and the preference for academic silence. It could be anticipated that the college would have seen the creation of a continuous stream of books and papers generated by the rich source of material which pours through its gates, but this has hardly been the case. Two books in the recent past (Pope and Weiner 1981 and Thackrah 1985) both contain veiled indications of the problems these civil service academics encounter when they write about the police. In a forward to *Modern Policing* (Pope and Weiner ibid.), Sir Kenneth Newman—then commandant—suggests that the book's claim to attention is that its contents are contributed by insiders; while in their introduction, the authors claim it goes some way to challenging Holdaway's claim (1979) that 'research from the Police Staff College has not resulted in a major project on the police'. However, an anonymous reviewer of the Pope and Weiner edition (*Police Journal* 1982), seems to disagree with their claims:

there is a consistent air of frustration in the writings of some of the social scientist contributors ... it is almost as though they wish they were in closer touch with the operational side of the service. Certainly the absence of contact is noticeable.

Furthermore, as these college-based insiders stress, their essays do not represent police college views or those of the Home Office; and both Thackrah (1985) and his publisher, James Tindall, take pains to ensure from the outset that we are aware than any views expressed in the book are 'those of individual contributors, and not those of the college, the Home Office, or [even] the police service'. One might suggest then that the 'major project' Holdaway recognized was missing from the college inventory is still to come! Indeed the anonymous reviewer of the Pope and Weiner edition went on to propose that 'if the police staff college is to fulfil its task [of producing a major project] with any credibility, it must encourage its academic staff to go out into the field to study policing at first hand'. Other challenges to social researchers to pursue a form of participant observation are to be occasionally found in the journals:

questions were being raised about what the police were doing, what they ought to be doing and how they ought to be organised and accountable. The fact that these questions are being raised has significance for the authority of the police . . . and it is the single most important determinant of the style of policing. Thus we need to explore in more concrete terms the operational aspects of the questions and the dilemmas they produce. (Manning and Butler 1982: 338)

But if attempts to produce this concrete research are doomed to neglect or derision or to be defined as 'espionage', then what can be achieved? The answer must be 'not a great deal'; for none of the portents of success are immediately apparent. WPC Dick's salutary essay (1985) changed little and generated few ripples on the ACPO pond, while one of the most powerfully critical books on policing in recent years (Jones 1980) seems to have had little effect on the structures of the organization, except, perhaps, to help draw its author—then a chief inspector—into the ACPO ranks.

Mervyn Jones (ibid.), in this book on organizational behaviors, presented some glaringly uncomfortable findings. Critical of the way that status is attributed by the institution, his thesis was that even as the service proclaims 'beat patrol work' to be the basis of all good policework, it penalizes and stigmatizes those who remain there. The young officer, he concluded, must escape at the first opportunity or risk being classified as an unambitious 'no hoper' at an early career stage. A keenly stated desire to move into some area of specialization is a necessity, and, as a result, uniform patrol work becomes synonymous with failure and punishment. Men get sent *back* from specialist posts to uniform duties as a punishment and the strength of this metaphorical move downwards or back-wards (you can never move 'up' or 'forwards' into uniform) is not lost on young officers. Few prior to Jones had cared to admit this seditious point except in the columns of the *Police Review*, where disgruntled beat officers (often anonymously) indicate the paradox of being the revered and reviled base on which all the hierarchy is built.

Jones's book remained untouched on the shelves of Northumbria's modest library in its first two years, even though it had good reviews; and the influence of his research has been all but negligible. For even though some attempt to give status to the 'community or home beat officer' has been made following Lord Scarman's (1981) report on the Brixton riots which gave something of a 'slap on the wrist' to the service, the deference accorded to specialist posting or to detective work remains untouched. In effect Jones's book revealed an unwelcome truth which no one really wanted to hear and which the service was able easily to diffuse and ignore.

Indeed when I was at the police college in 1987 and Jones was on the Senior Command Course prior to taking up a position as assistant chief constable, I took a straw poll among my immediate colleagues to see what influence such books achieve. None had read the book or knew its detail, although one or two knew he had written something.

The real problem is that such research reveals modes of thought and practice which are well known and constituted, but which are necessarily concealed. For who inside the system needs to be told what is well understood? Silence continues to sustain the hegemony, and social change only occurs when irresistible and more powerful forces are brought to bear from outside (see Adams 1988). Furthermore, such pressures are limited, thus creating a situation where

there has been hardly any research on the police compared with the large output of critical scholarship on industry, commerce, the civil service, the health service and education . . . what little direct research there has been on the police has scarcely begun to ask such fundamental questions as what is the police force and what is it doing.

This point (Wojtas 1982) occurs in a description of a new research centre for Police Studies at Strathclyde University, which is 'to ask whether anyone is doing research on the police, what degree of co-operation they have met . . . and to encourage research by the police themselves'. Once again, however, defensiveness won the day and when the Strathclyde Centre circulated forces asking them to co-operate in the venture, a decision was taken to withhold co-operation and a circular went round to this effect, suggesting the existing Home Office funded PRSU (Police Research Services

Unit) and the Home Office Research and Planning Unit were adequate for the needs of the service. This latter unit (formerly the HO Research Unit) does provide some research material for those who seek it out and its bulletin is a reference source to recent government funded research, which is largely concerned with operational systems and the tools of policing. However, I have never seen a copy of this circulated at the subdivision level at any location I have worked; and outside force HQ the availability of any research or analytic literature on policing falls off dramatically.

HO Circular (194/78) describing British and American research literature on policing is another typically apologetic, anti-intellectual document, for within its first few paragraphs it admits:

the implication of attempting to establish a central research information centre to give advice to chief officers about research findings, [or] collect, collate and distribute research of interest to the police service, and maintain an up-to-date index of research would be very considerable. There are no plans to establish such a centre.

No one seems to have asked whether the Staff College could have taken on this job, but then again such anti-intellectualism is apparent even in the Bramshill Scholars' Association. In 1985, they proposed to extend their role beyond that of an annual dining club for officers who had taken a degree through the police college scheme. It was mooted the association

could offer a unique police view of current problems. We could host University seminars to which speakers of note could be invited to attend. In this way the Association could counter the Left Wing Type Seminars [*sic*] which were often very one sided and misrepresentative of current Police views ... The Chairman also suggested that the membership could publish papers.

This narrow academic proposal for a one-sided, right-wing debating group was circulated in August 1986, with options for the future of the association. These were to be considered at the AGM on 20 September 1986 when the association would seek to create 'a blend of social and professional academic pursuit'. The options never reached a vote, however, as the meeting was cancelled for lack of support! Perhaps in the light of the somewhat narrow academic bias outlined by this cream of police studentship, it is just as well the college was not allocated the task of collating and circulating research to chief officers!

In the early 1980s, many forces had reduced secondments to universities or polytechnics, for these had been somewhat unprogrammatic. By 1987, the Home Office Research and Planning Unit Programme was indicating, 'now that resources are more constrained, more stringent criteria of relevance must be applied to the funding of research for the Home Office'. Four years previous, Northumbria decided to reduce the numbers allowed a secondment. An assistant chief constable told a conference of senior officers: 'with future recruitment, the number of graduates will increase'.[15]

The conference was also told that as an alternative to the expense of sending officers to university, it was proposed to '*direct* officers to research a particular problem . . . and give them a short period to carry out intensive research'. The emphasis on 'directed' research is mine and indicates the reduced potential for any ethnographic sedition, for which force would seek to direct officers to the critical analysis of its subcultural idiosyncrasies? Furthermore, such short periods of 'directed' research can be shown favourably as a saving over any extended degree course in the budgets. The emphasis of this 'directed' (or controlled?) research, it was announced, 'is to be on pragmatic, problem-solving enquiries' (i.e. policy-orientated research), which, it was explained, 'would be of cost-effective advantage to the force'. There seems to be little chance of any philosophical, unprogrammatic enquiry here which might be critical of the system; and no 'espionage' from within!

This cost-effective nature of a scholarship was a matter I had been asked to justify when I first asked my new assistant chief constable about the potential of postgraduate research as an 'observing participator'.[16] I had mentioned the unquantifiable public relationships which could be generated during a secondment and argued for the intangible value of the many hundreds of contacts I had made which could not easily be costed in purely fiscal terms. He dismissed this as irrelevant and his use of metaphor, in what

[15]   In this he echoes Alderson (quoted in Flaher 1982), who had sensed a change from a time 'when few graduates would even consider the option (of joining the police)'. However, even in a decade when high unemployment has been consistent, the percentage of graduates in the police has only just reached double figures after remaining constant at 2% for years.

[16]   This was the same senior officer who in 1982 was to ask if I was worried about being considered an academic.

turned out to be an eighty-minute interview, was most revealing. I later recorded he invariably used the idea of an 'escape from real work' to describe any research secondment; in doing so he embodied the common institutional fear of uncontrolled social movement across a divide or boundary into another society such as academia. This is part of the ideological pedagogy which the institution uses to create and maintain defensive boundaries against the outsider or those who might produce a critical analysis of its systems; it is one major strength of the organization.

Again, as I recorded in a fieldnote, this assistant chief exhibited aspects of what I could only then describe as 'institutional paranoia', when he went on to deride an unnamed social scientist who had been allowed research facilities inside a police force (unspecified). He dismissively described how this man had 'come in, taken the material provided, and then had written a childish and critical book on the police, out of which he got a Ph.D.' Again a metaphorical breach of a sacred boundary has occurred and an 'enemy' made a gain at the expense of the integrity of the inside! It is this logic of practice which effectively negates most research and is perhaps the main reason that between 1979 and 1988, only one of the research papers I have compiled has been looked at by senior officers.[17] Neglectful silence is, of course, the most perfect means of maintaining the powerful integrity of the institutional boundaries against any criticisms.

During this period I have given readings and seminar papers at various academic centres, including the universities of Oxford, Durham, Edinburgh, Essex, Manchester, Lancaster, Newcastle, Sussex, and East Anglia, and have written a number of unpublished papers which I have given in seminars at other similar establishments. On more than one occasion, I have included a bibliography when submitting a c.v. to my senior command and in 1986 I informed my chief officers of the acceptance of my Ph.D. thesis, in accordance with the directive laid down by Force Orders. No one, of course, has asked to read it, for—if my argument is correct—the service has no need of any reminder of how

---

[17] These have included papers published in university journals (Young 1979*a* and 1979*b*), but it was only in late 1984, when I informed my command that a paper I had given at Oxford had appeared in a book (Callen and Ardener 1984) and had been reviewed in *New Society* and *The Times Literary Supplement* that I was requested to submit a copy.

the ideology works or how to implement the paradigms which support their cultural norms. Nor do they need their daily practice to be exposed to the analytic eye of anthropological 'thick description', for in their task-driven world there is little to be gained by reflecting on what they already live and understand. Any need to analyse the ways in which the multi-variant police world forms a coherent and self-sustaining whole is material for the social scientist and not the practitioners, for they already live the system as a matter of course. The police, therefore, have little to gain in promoting any exploration of their modes of thought, for analysis can only hold the possibility that the whole intricate system, to paraphrase Lévi-Strauss (1967), will be revealed 'as an immense disorder [which] is organised in the form of a grammar'. In consequence, police ethnography remains largely unwritten simply because it is unlikely the organization will be keen to reveal the ways this 'immense disorder' is constructed, for it is not in their nature to allow other individuals to create their classifications for them. Indeed, institutional ideology sets out to 'strait-jacket minds and bodies and overcome individual thought' (Foucault 1970). Mary Douglas (1987: 92), in her analysis of *How Institutions Think*, pursues Foucault's argument a stage further to show that:

Institutions systematically direct and channel our perceptions into forms compatible with the relations they authorize. They fix processes that are essentially dynamic, they hide their influence ... Add to all this that they endow themselves with rightness and send their mutual corroboration cascading through all levels of our information systems. No wonder they easily recruit us into joining their narcissistic self-contemplation. Any problems we try to think about are automatically transformed into their own organizational problems. The solutions they proffer only come from the limited range of their own experience. If the institution ... is one that depends on participation, it will reply to our frantic questions: 'more participation!' If it is one that depends on authority, it will only reply: 'More authority!' Institutions have the pathetic megalomania of the computer whose whole vision of the world is its own programme.

This extremely perceptive analysis of the institutional mind fits the police world like a glove, and recent elaborations in policing, along with its growth in the mainstream of the daily social process, supports Douglas's contention (ibid.) that an institution which is dependent upon authority can only demand more of the same. In such ontological circumstances this allegedly public service must be singularly unsuited to objective assessment of any external demands for a reduction in its power or to encompassing any critical analysis which might cause loss of prestige.

Given this premiss, we should not be surprised to find the police are in the forefront of support for proposals such as the introduction of identity cards; it was not surprising to find the 1988 Superintendents' Association conference not only supporting this motion, but arguing for the creation of twenty-four hour armed patrols throughout the country and making a plea for a national motorway squad. Always the call will be for more power to the organization, so that the 1989 cry of alarm from the Police Federation conference about private security firms is based more on a fear that areas of influence are being taken from the institution than on beliefs that such groups are incompetent. In a similar fashion, all the representative bodies of the police—ACPO, the Superintendents' Association, and the Police Federation—were outraged at the creation of the Crown Prosecution Service in the Prosecution of Offences Act in the mid-1980s; for one area of police power in the courts had been removed at one fell swoop and given to another arm of the executive.

So although in a liberal democracy it would seem practical and even suitable for the police to have a say in the way order is defined and maintained, as Foucault (1970) and Douglas (1987) have shown, this will inevitably take on an expansionist line; for anything other than bland support of the proposals of the institution will present a challenge or pose a threat. This dilemma generates the paradox I have outlined above, where intellectualism and graduate recruitment become prized commodities and are publicly sought after as the organization seeks to elaborate its professionalism, but are simultaneously denigrated. In such a world the very idea of research and academic prowess becomes charged with structural ambiguity simply because it creates the potential for outsiders to bring challenging concepts across boundaries which, at other times, are sacrosanct.

So what then is the position of the police practitioner who becomes an anthropologist? He is unable to 'switch off' his analytic mind, for he becomes possessed of something which can best be described as 'special knowledge'. On the one hand he can support his understanding of the institutional expectations by simply repeating those inculcated practices he has learned as a neophyte from the 'stories of the great days of policing', which are interminably repeated 'at the charge room desk' or 'taken on at Nellie's knee'. Alternatively he can use his understanding of the way the metaphors and structures of significance are used to sustain the institution, and thus reveal the system to be the product of a specific mode of thought, which is only one possibility among many. He must be aware, however, that any antagonistic or critical assessment will not only be unwelcome, but coming from an insider will smell of blasphemy.

Anything other than an uncritical acceptance is a direct challenge to the idea of the rule of law which has sustained the police since their inception and which argues that the replication of a known system of order is the best means of containing those who need to be controlled. Alternative readings or critical analysis of this entrenched reverence for a rule of law (which at times may well be out of step with a wider interpretation of ambiguous social behaviour) smacks of subversion simply because it denies the primacy of the institutional framework. And surely, it can be argued, the understanding of what is to be ordered and who is to be disciplined has long been defined and subject to the practical mastery of the controllers.

In consequence, even when the insider retires and ostensibly leaves the family, he will be expected to maintain his silence, and although bland hagiographic biography has been acceptable in the past, there has been no place for the espionage of critical ethnography. And even as the unlamented Official Secrets Act of 1911 groaned in its death throes in the late 1980s (to be replaced by an even more constraining measure), officers about to retire in West Mercia were presented with an official force form and asked to sign a 'Declaration' under the Act. This reiterates the whole catch-all section 2 of the Official Secrets Act of 1911, as well as the scale of punishments laid down by the Official Secrets Act of 1920 for those who

possess any secret official code word, or password, or sketch, plan, model, article, note, document or information which relates to or is used in a prohibited place or anything in such a place, or which has been made or obtained in contravention of this Act, or which has been entrusted in confidence to him by any person holding office under Her Majesty or which he has obtained or to which he has had access owing to his position as a person who is or has been employed under a person who holds or has held such an office or contract—[and who]

(a) communicates the code word, pass word, sketch, plan, model, article, note, document, or information to any person other than a person to whom he is authorised to communicate it, or a person to whom it is in the interest of the State his duty to communicate it, or

(aa) uses the information in his possession for the benefit of any foreign power or in any other manner prejudicial to the safety or interests of the State, or

(b) retains the sketch, plan, model, article, note, or document in his possession or control when he has no right to retain it or when it is contrary to his duty to retain it, or fails to comply with all directions issued by lawful authority with regard to the return or disposal thereof, or . . .

The form continues, listing other sections of the Act. It makes it abundantly clear that even the *possession* and academic presentation of information necessary for an ethnography could be actionable. For a considerable amount of inconsequential information owned by the institution is classed as confidential, even though its release could only be considered prejudicial to the safety and interests of the state by the most bigoted autocrat. The need to get the retiring member to sign such a document indicates the institutional fear of the outside lying behind the threats which Sir Peter Imbert issued to those who would write controversial memoirs (*Police Review*, 26 August 1988); for the 'family' demands silence unto death from its members!

And even if an uncommissioned but critical ethnography is not considered to be in breach of the Official Secrets Act, it will most likely be construed as structural espionage and lie in breach of the Police Discipline Code as set out in Police Regulations. Any internal disciplinary measure to contain such an account is much less likely to become of public concern in the way that the Clive Ponting or the Cathy Massiter prosecutions became notorious *causes célèbres*.

As a result of this all pervading desire for reticence it is possible to suggest that the presentation of research papers in seminars, the creation of an undirected thesis, not to mention the production of a book, could easily have placed me in breach of Regulation 6, which outlines the disciplinary offence of

Improper disclosure of information, which offence is committed where a member of a police force

(a) without proper authority communicates to any person, any information which he has in his possession as a member of a police force . . .

That I avoided such a course of action is because of my own understanding of what the institution would allow before it swung into action. In effect, I kept a suitable silence and avoided direct confrontation, for I was well aware that the ultimate punishment under the regulations is expulsion or dismissal from the force, forfeiture of a considerable salary and pension, and, of course, the resulting immediate acquisition of true outsiderhood!

2

A Police Career Explored

INTRODUCTION

In this chapter I propose to link the idea of subjective knowledge to an exploration of the insider's personal history. I have mentioned aspects of the debate on the inclusion of the subjective self into an ethnography; now I hope to weave aspects of this subjective self into a scientific construct, revealing something of police culture along the way as I briefly explore some of my own early career moves.

'SPECIAL KNOWLEDGE': THE SUBJECTIVE FACTOR

In a seminal article, Pocock (1973) set out parameters for a personal anthropology. He suggested personal meanings, cultural roots, and the historical equation inevitably means that any true translation of the field experience cannot avoid including a personal interpretation. Inevitably this leads to the question of injecting matters of a subjective nature into the account. Okely (1975) suggests:

the participant observer does have a problem of subjectivity. This cannot be resolved by distancing, repression and short cuts ... the specificity and individuality of the observer are ever present and must therefore be acknowledged, explored and put to *creative use* [my emphasis].

In the accounts of 'anthropology at home' currently being produced, the potential to include the personal is unlike that which exists here, for only rarely does the research material contain an account in which the analyst is the subject as well as the researcher. Most fieldwork is simply episodic, made by an outsider moving in for a period to assess observed social behaviour. In this case, however, I have been unable to make the separation and the fieldwork is both empirical and continuous; it is diachronic and retrospective, taking in the historical with the contemporary. And as Mary Douglas (1973: 15) had pointed out, 'if we cannot bring the argument back from tribal ethnography to ourselves, then there is little point in starting it at all'. Like Douglas, I see no point in setting up a false theoretical dichotomy between 'us' and 'them', creating separate realms and polarities of modern and archaic thought, for I anticipate my inclusion of the concept of self can help link the tribalism which haunts the police defensiveness to an understanding of their 'modern' beliefs, modes of thought, and action. Hopefully this will allow the ethnography to extend on the interpretive analysis which Kuper (1973) termed 'neostructural' and which has since combined aspects of a feminist, semantic, and symbolic framework to generate what may well be a short-lived disciplinary 'ism' of 'post-modern' anthropology (Young 1989). As an inside exploration of culture this might also be considered to be a 'liminal' or 'liminoid' phenomenon (V. Turner 1974, 1977), for as it delves beneath the surface phenomena, the subjective analysis can reveal unconscious categories and transformational operations which lie between the dual poles and such exclusively preferred categories as 'cops and robbers'. It should then contain a generative formulation which cannot easily be suppressed or denied (T. Turner 1977), for such domains of power lying between functional systems of control and disorder are, as Victor Turner (1977: 45) reminds us, 'not merely reversive, they are often subversive, representing radical critiques of the central structures [of a system]'. Inside analysis incorporating a subjective 'special knowledge' should therefore inevitably encompass aspects of the 'liminoid' and present a radical critique simply by revealing hidden structures to the outside. The effect of living with this knowledge and using this skill raises the consciousness of the insider, perhaps giving him his most effective methodological tool. For as a member of the institution, the insider/anthropologist is uniquely situated to move across the interfaces of his society. He is qualified to think the unthinkable and to pose those questions which in normal circumstances would go unasked. Because of his understanding of practice, he is able not only to show how police ideology is maintained, but even propose alternative models by merely writing down and presenting his knowledge. For, as Gramsci pointed out in respect of those institutions of the establishment, 'hegemony . . . is not universal and 'given' to the continuing rule of a particular class. It has to be won, reproduced and sustained' (taken from Hebdidge 1979: 16). The way the police sustain this ideology of action to maintain their hegemony becomes clearly apparent to the researcher, and he in turn stands revealed. To have advanced within the job and achieved rank means he is likely to have followed and supported institutional precedents without question, and to have unwittingly accepted and been involved in the reproduction of the narrow modes of thought and practice demanded by the culture.

It is this special knowledge, or gnosis, which hopefully can make the inside ethnography so different and illuminating. Burridge (1969) has written most persuasively about the effects which fieldwork can have on the anthropologist, describing the prophetic experience this can produce. He links this to the act of consciousness raising, which I consider presents the greatest problem for the insider who cannot leave the field or return to academia.

The insider/ethnographer can turn his understanding of an interpretive methodology to an assessment of his own actions, and see connections as if scales had been removed from his eyes. However, he cannot always escape the results, or move away; and may not be able to use this newly acquired knowledge to amend much within the institution. Yet I believe this new understanding must be included in the account, for as Blacking (1977: vii) pointed out in his preface to the *Anthropology of the Body*:

one solution . . . is to use subjectivity rather than try to push it aside . . . and [so] it might well be included in analyses and used consciously as a research tool. If I understood him correctly, this is an aspect of what David Parkin described at the 1973 Association of Social Anthropologists Conference as Personal Anthropology.

By consciously using subjectivity as a research tool, the insider is peculiarly placed to generate what Geertz (1976) described as 'an inward conceptual rhythm', moving between the particular and the general. Hopefully, he can use the creativity which exists between the experiential inside view and observational outside view of a cultural system to formulate an ethnography which incorporates 'a continuous dialectical, tacking between the most local of detail and the most global of global structures in such a way as to bring them into simultaneous view' (Geertz ibid. 235). But it is not just how the new consciousness is to be used which produces problems in handling this new-found wisdom; it is the very acquisition of knowledge itself which makes the concept of self so dynamic. This structural awareness can be as hard to handle as any decision to try to publish the account, for what has happened in the past and what is expected now from the insider is tied up with an understanding of how the institution of policing prefers to present a restricted image for outside consumption, as I have described above. It all becomes uncomfortably apparent and that which had been lived and accepted is opened up in a revelatory manner, so that the vice of being caught up within the hegemonies of such a system designed to control a powerless underclass can become overbearing. In such a situation, the necessary intellectual detachment often becomes difficult to sustain.

In extreme cases anthropologists have found such a role impossible to live with, for the field situation was beyond their previous imaginations. Castenada (1970), for example, found he was dealing with new events and totally new ways of understanding. As a result, he necessarily developed a new self-image, and took on a new social personality in the process. In Castenada's case, he 'enters a world so different that he comes to accept reality itself as nothing but a social construct, with effects so devastating . . . that ethnography becomes mysticism' (Goward 1984: 90). For Jeanne Favret-Saada (1980), who set out to study witchcraft in the French Bocage, the only means of moving in on the discourse she hoped to understand was to become part of it. Her involvement in the process of witching and un-witching was the single path to obtaining any information on the subject, for she found she was unable to operate 'in the standard situation in which information is exchanged and where the ethnographer may hope to have neutral knowledge . . . about beliefs and practices' (ibid. 11). In some ways I feel her peculiar dilemma parallels my own for she described her stance as one which distanced her from the classical anthropological mode, creating a 'memorable adventure', which she claims, 'has marked me for life' (ibid. 22).

Favret-Saada's unique analysis (ibid. 1–28) of the bizarre subjective position she found herself in is a masterful assessment of the difficulties which arise when the ethnographer seeks to gain knowledge of a social group which depends for its existence on 'misknowledge' or silence:

For anyone who wants to understand the meaning of [such a] discourse, there is no other solution but to practise it oneself, to become one's own informant . . . and to try and make explicit what one finds unstatable in oneself. For it is difficult to see how the native could have any interest in the project of unveiling what can go on existing only if it remains veiled. (ibid. 22)

In succumbing to 'the temptation of subjectivism' (ibid. 23), she recognizes that it becomes impossible to put any distance between oneself and the 'native', or more importantly between oneself and oneself in such a situation. In the world of an inside ethnography as Favret-Saada identifies, 'one is never able to choose between subjectivism and the objective method as it was taught' (ibid. 23), so long as one wishes to find out answers which, in traditional ethnography, are often missing from the finite corpus of empirical observation. This transformational stance, she goes on to argue, allows the ethnographer to have a personal discourse on aspects which are outside the usual limits of the body or corpus of collected material. In my own case I had been taught by Okely to avoid the split between subjectivism and an objective reality, but I had no preparation to contend with the changes which the field experience created in me. That which had been so familiar to me and accepted almost without thinking now took on a new and almost bizzare aspect. My own 'tribe' became as foreign as those isolated, 'primitive' pre-industrial societies which the traditional anthropologists sought out.

Once the semantics of police experience were revealed, I had to live with the problems experienced by both Castenada and Favret-Saada, although I demur from casting myself into their intellectual companionship. Reality itself then became a construct of knowing and being known, and of living with the alternative possibility. For personal transitions made across physical and psychic boundaries during the subjectivity of the field situation can produce disjunction; indeed they can paralyse.

In such a situation it is therefore all the more necessary to recognize the unique place the ethnographer holds and to capitalize on it. During this time of subjective observing participation, the policeman/insider moves to the margins, to a point where analysis negates automatic approval or predisposition for a world of known categories and classifications. His inquiries and interpretations will inevitably draw polluting and contaminating ideas to the surface, for they are a result of his place as an 'institutional shaman' and mirror his position as a liminal mover in the organization.

By definding this insider fieldwork (and the university experience which generated it) as a liminal situation, I am extending the Turnerian concept (1969, 1974) in which the individual moves temporarily into an unstructured and somewhat ambiguous state, during the initial process of passing through a *rite de passage* before returning to structure. Here the marginality is less transitory and occurs in the post-tribal situation where the concept of liminality is less familiar to the discipline, even though transitions across spatial and temporal boundaries still create epistemological changes of the kind Turner describes. In my own case, the model of transition through liminality might still produce a recognizable replication of the move through a *rite de passage*:

policeman → student → new policeman

But there seems more to it than that! It is the total change in perspective and new semantic outlook which ensures that the subjective nature of the liminal journey can be used as an essential part of the analysis; for it can produce a dynamic simply because it incorporates aspects of a newly created ideological disjunction, as some classic accounts have shown.[1] So that now, with the dubious benefit of hindsight[2] and a keen awareness that memory and retrospective versions of reality are often skewed, I feel the subjective account must of necessity become part of the ethnography

[1] Some of the best criminological studies have been carried out by those insiders who have moved into a kind of liminality, on a journey to individuation. Genet's *Thief's Journal* (1967) and Jimmy Boyle's *A Sense of Freedom* (1977) are subjective accounts surpassing many other analyses of crime and criminality. It is crucially important to note how established society finds such difficulty in handling the change of status which the Boyles of this world undergo when they move out of the criminal world and 'go straight'. For this reminds us that criminality has no inherent base but shows that it can become its creative antithesis; and moreover implies that the reverse situation is always possible.

[2] One highly desirable piece of equipment that policemen often talk about having is 'the hindsight-ometer'. With that in the armoury, some of the many ambiguities of behaviour and classification which they would prefer to avoid could be removed.

in which I play all of the parts. I am the institutional member as well as the marginally moving player. I am the anthropologist and the field of study. Burridge (1979) writes of fieldwork:

> every anthropologist has experienced 'culture shock'; a temporary inability to grasp and act and think in the terms of the assumptions upon which the newly entered culture is based. Not only is this shock experienced in fieldwork, while one learns the ways of a new culture, but it is experienced even more disconcertingly when one returns to one's own culture . . . two different worlds have met in the same person. One alternative is insanity. Another is to comprehend one world in terms of the other . . . In this restricted sense, every anthropologist has some share in the experience of the prophet.[3]

To weld the subjective with the objective, my personal anthropology includes material culled from various observational and ranked positions within the institution of policing and from across the years. I have woven into the account experiences ranging from a reflection on uniform patrol work, to CID and specialist squad work; from the marginal world of a 'punishment posting' in a bridewell or prison, to the centrality of knowledge gained by spells in the centrality of headquarters postings. The analysis spans a period when technology and communication techniques transformed the outward face of policing. Hopefully the resulting ethnography will generate a new and clearer understanding of the nuances and specificities of police reality, incorporating what Bourdieu (1977) has called 'a practical mastery built upon objectivist knowledge'.

A subjective element in the account provides a better potential to unravel the semantic patterns which structure the maintenance of this executive unit of power. It introduces knowledge of the cultural metaphors and the symbolic capital by which the constantly changing gradations of disorder, order, crime, and social sin are determined and acted upon, or are ignored.

IN THE PAST: THE PERSONAL EXPERIENCE

During the period 1955 to 1978 I moved across classificatory police boundaries on more than one occasion. After three years as

---

[3] The section of Burridge's book (pp. 153–64) which contains this quotation is a very persuasive description of the gnosis, or self-knowledge, which can result from a reflexive anthropology.

a cadet carrying out basic police tasks around the station, I was sworn in as a constable. I joined the uniform branch on foot patrol in the city centre division of Newcastle upon Tyne City Police. Immediately I was instructed that I had had the good fortune to be posted to 'the division where real polising is done . . .'[4]

There were only three divisions in the city—east, west, and central—and each of us in our own division knew we were the élite; for just as the men in the west were certain they were best, so the men from the east remained convinced of their own superiority. And together we were emphatically co-operative that neighbouring forces were populated by lesser mortals.

The predominance these spatial constructs have for the ordinary constable is essential to an understanding of the police mind. Ideas of centrality and marginality of place link to the status of activities and tie in with perceptions of derogatory and despised areas of operation. As a result, actual and symbolic transitions across spatial boundaries continue to create a crucial means of analysing the way police reality deals with the changes in power politics at all levels within the institution, and of describing the way status can be won or lost.

The structural load which exists within seemingly minor career moves or internal transfers around the force is enormous. Everyone inside knows or speculates endlessly on the politics of power implicit in the most minute gradations of change. The weekly Force Orders which every force publishes for internal circulation have a section listing the latest transfers in departments, specialist units, and divisions. 'Out on the ground' these moves are seized on and discussed avidly. The internal phone system springs into life and the moves are analysed or colleagues contacted to speculate on who has 'blotted his copy book', or who seems to be on his

---

[4] The terms 'real polises' and 'real polising' relate to a self-identity taken on by the constables at street patrol level in Newcastle upon Tyne. This use is historic and the first syllable 'pol' rhymes with 'doll', while the 's' in the centre of the word 'polises' is stressed with a strong 'ess' sound, so the words could almost be written 'pollisses' and 'pollissing', and derive from the Scots 'polisman', where the first syllable is pronounced as 'pole' and not 'poll'. Around Newcastle the use of the terms is ubiquitous and immediately revealed the 'outsiderhood' of the assistant chief who had interviewed me about my 'escape' to university. His use of the term 'practical coppering' immediately set his marginality, and showed his origins were from somewhere down in the despised deep south of the country, way beyond Sunderland. To the men on the ground, he could never be a 'real polis' simply because he could never be one of us.

way up the hierarchical tree in the mad scramble for position and preference.

From 1958 to 1963 I went through various initiation rites, learned the values of the institution, and underwent the training all new constables were then required to follow. As a uniform constable, my boundaries were very clearly demarcated and my peers in the city centre division set out the parameters of my social reality. I quickly became aware of what a 'real polis' was and more importantly what boundaries one had to cross to cease being real and in effect become unreal, inauspicious, and inhuman. The derogatory phrase 'he's not a real polis; he'll never be a polis as long as he's got a hole in his arse' quickly set out markers to define who was one of us and who was not. We were thief takers, while others outside were excluded, perhaps to be dismissively described as 'mere uniform carriers'.

Douglas (1966: 1973) has described how the boundaries which lie between the structures of holiness and the anti-structure of pollution are potential power bases and always the source of emotive reaction. Such relative positions were clearly set out for me in chains of metaphoric relevance, with 'real polises' largely symbolized by the use of the body and its social and physical space. Each link in the chain expressed a perceived correct place and tied this into an all-encompassing behavioural ideology which in turn determined our action. In the symbolic construction of this community (Cohen 1985) boundary images of inside and outside were elaborated to an intensity, making us crucially aware and 'conscious . . . of dirt that has ambiguously got onto the wrong side of the frontier' (Leach 1976: 61). In the police this desire for a clearly defined world of order derives from an implicit understanding that control of social behaviour is always surrounded by the dirt of structural ambivalence. For 'real polises' there is a rarely articulated awareness that this ambiguity can always turn in on itself and be used for good or evil, or even as an instrument of oppression or release. For even the least reflexive or philosophical seem to be aware of the potential for reversal inherent in this system of power, where the sacred and the profane have the possibility of turning upon each other at every conjunction. During my early career, for instance, when one of the shift was caught and sentenced for a string of burglaries, the others skirted around their implicit knowledge that 'there but for the grace of God goes everyone', and comforted themselves by recalling (with the aid of the hindsight-ometer) that he had 'never been a real polis . . . always been a bit of a loner, something of an outsider . . .'

A knowledge of police systems therefore requires an analysis of both sides of the coin, to explore how anti-structure defines structure and in turn redefines and motivates other anti-structural elements in the system, for anti-structural activity has the potential to make bearable some of the constraints inherent in such a closed world as the police. However in such an institution, the elements of anti-structure are often suppressed, denied, or concealed in an attempt to maintain the idealogical purity of the group. Jung (1964) has described these hidden facets as being creatively generative, but possessed of danger in any confrontation and difficult if not impossible to harness; for they are in effect alternative domains of power.

In my early career, I set out to meet the demands of my peers and fulfil the necessary qualifications for assessment as a 'real polis'; although there were few opportunities to flirt with any real forms of marginality! I was in a numbered uniform of massive symbolic importance with nuances of style which clearly defined our social indentity. This uniform of dark serge symbolized our insider status and separated us completely from the 'civvies' out there in the rest of the world.

This use of uniform as a symbol of separation had not changed in 1977 on my return from university. I found the same classificatory system in use with the same unconscious linguistic divisions being applied as I had learned in the mid-1950s. Indeed, there was now more of an emphasis on the separation, with an enhanced denigration of civilians. This elaboration indicates the process of social change, for it reveals an increasing separation between 'real polises' and a public who are much less likely now to accept police versions of reality; while increasing 'civilianization' within the forces presents another perceived challenge to the defensive integrity and introspection of the institution. Chaos now seemed poised to threaten the system from inside and without, and it is almost inevitable that the term 'civvy' should have become a derogatory reference. As John Stalker (1988) pointed out when he retired from the service, he had made the transition and had joined that group of persons pejoratively known to the police as 'civilians'.

The structural invisibility enjoyed by the uniform wearer is a strange matter to experience. You become a symbol with no personal identity beyond the small, specific numeral on the shoulder. 'Civilians' you know well can walk past in the street without recognition, for although the uniform itself is apparent it is a forceful barrier, expressing a demonstrative separation between the culture of control and the individuality of the controlled.

Like other symbolic non-verbal devices, the multi-vocal nuances of our uniform were used in a variety of other ways as boundary markers to maintain our cultural identity and define our institutional specificities. Just as the white-coated doctors in hospitals symbolize the clean and purifying nature of the healer, so the dark uniform of the police symbolizes not just the force identity, but also the presence of the avenger, who purifies through retribution rather than by cure. It is the marker of 'force' and hence continues to sustain the continuing paradox of 'police force ~ police service' which remains unresolved, on which I will say more later in relation to the role of women police officers.

The dark uniform we wore had a military cap with polished brim, and in our fashioned tunics of soft serge and shiny boots we presented an avenging image, clothed in the symbolic colour of death and darkness. Black is a light absorbent, non-reflective colour and most suitable for controllers who operate with a degree of social anonymity, upholding the rule of law and the abstractions of the legal system. In such a world, individuality is never a prized characteristic, and an attempt in the early 1980s to remove the one remaining individualizing feature—the shoulder numeral or 'collar number'—was correctly rejected by civilians as a structural move towards an even greater anonymity. As Reiner (1980) suggested, the riot gear in which the police are increasingly seen, with shields, visored helmets, knee-length boots, and flame-proof overalls, enhances their avenging appearance.[5] I suspect it is no

---

[5] Morris (1985) argued this avenging figure of retribution in riot gear was damaging the police image and might best be separated from the traditional police role. He thought the time was ripe for a separate public order unit (dressed in black?). Perhaps, one might speculate, this would then allow the 'service' unit to adopt a more approachable colour!

accident the politics of the times seems to parallel the growing toughness of the police image, or that the police have taken on an increasing resemblance to the black-clothed enemies of goodness who sprinkle the popular science fantasy films such as *Star Wars*, *Superman*, and the like. In these mass cultural replays of the eternal dichotomy between good and evil, the use of highly symbolic black uniforms as an indicator of anonymous evil predominates.[6]

Within the separate police forces, the nuances of uniform difference were always embroidered by 'real polises' to produce symbolic boundaries from which to assess other uniform wearers. Thus our contacts with firemen, St John Ambulance men, special constables, and the like were all used to define them as being somewhat 'unreal' and therefore slightly less than human. Such groups were said to be like the foreigners in the adjacent forces, for it was constantly repeated that many wanted to join us but failed because of some inadequacy. This was especially true of the Fire Service, our immediate neighbours,[7] and it applied equally to those in the adjacent Gateshead Borough Police and Northumberland Constabulary, who were always talked of as being a lesser breed of mortals.

This characteristic supports Peter Evans (1977), then *The Times*'s Home Affairs correspondent, who described the police as being 'peculiarly tribal by nature'. In the small forces of the late 1950s these separations were made much of, with those in the adjacent forces essentially seen as belonging to another tribe. Even today, in the amalgamated forces, this structuring principle holds good; and many old hands still refer to the 'real police forces' as those small units they joined in the late 1960s and early 1970s. Quite often the divisional boundaries in the amalgamated force mirror the old, small force boundaries and men define themselves

---

[6] In 1987 at the Police Staff College I was involved in many emotive discussions on the growing use of the military style 'Nato' sweater. Many were adamantly against their use, arguing in terms of pragmatism rather than symbolic or semantic content of the paramilitary connotation. A lively correspondence on the place of the 'woolly pullie' has also been carried out in the columns of the *Police Review*.

[7] In 1958 the memory of an era when the police and the fire brigade had been run as the Joint Newcastle Police and Fire Service was still alive for many of the older officers. In 1977–8 the use of the yard between the fire station and the bridewell was still a source of continual bickering and skirmishing between the two units, who always lived in an uneasy state of truce, verging on open warfare.

in relation to their early experience with perhaps an inner city ethic, a large-town police style, or in the framework of a more rural situation. In each case they inevitably begin to denigrate their opposite numbers for not doing 'real police work'.

Tribalism in the pre-amalgamated forces produced a very constricted vision of the world, so that spatial concepts and a narrow geographical containment held a paramount place in determining police reality. Today these are still of immense import, with men deriding those in another division or section, bragging that their villains are the toughest or their section tasks more numerous and arduous. An expressed desire for rigidly determined geographical units separated from a despised neighbour occurs again and again in my fieldnotes, and is clearly illustrated in a note made in 1981, when a superintendent in a somewhat remote subdivision laughingly told me:

one of my sections in the subdivision is thinking of declaring UDI [unilateral declaration of independence] from the Divisional Headquarters ... as for Headquarters and the Force organizational structure, well that's just a joke as far as these men are concerned.

This rejection of a distant headquarters and enhancement of their own special identity occurred some seven years after the last amalgamation. In that same year I was posted to South Shields on the south bank of the River Tyne and quickly became aware that I had an enormous burden to carry, simply because I had spent all of my previous service on 'the other side of the river'. At one point a uniform sergeant listening to me discuss some tactic, gloomily pointed out that my style was not theirs; but then, he rationalized, 'how could it be, you're from the *north* side of the river'. The emphatic denigration contained in this locational insult had to be heard to be understood, and in many ways it paralleled the dismissive tone used to deride the 'civvy', for nuances of speech and tone have immense meaning to insiders.

Figure 1 shows the existing Northumbria Police area where most of the ethnographic data was collected. This force is an amalgam of nine smaller units (Figure 2), some of which went into the melting pot in 1969. The remainder were taken up in the amalgamations of 1974, which coincided with the creation of the Metropolitan Councils, and today's amalgamated forces often seem to owe as much to local and national political opportunity

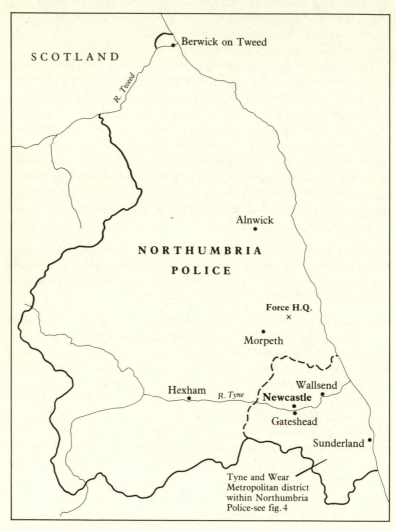

FIG. 1 Map of Northumbria Police area, following the 1974
amalgamations

Fɪɢ. 2 Map showing the constituent forces which made up Northumbria
Police prior to the amalgamations of 1967, 1969, and 1974

than to any operational logic; and even two decades after the first melding together of the small forces, attempts to standardize uniform and systems of operation has consistently failed to dislodge many localized, small-scale beliefs and practices.

In 1958 then, I was a member of what we knew was *the* premier force in the area with the external boundaries of the adjacent forces as our immediate threshold to what Douglas (1966: 137) had called 'new status'. Minor nuances of detail in our respective uniforms were built upon to form a taxonomy of meaning and used to maintain our in-group (or tribal) knowledge of ourselves. Not unnaturally a police world values uniformity, for as the language infers it embodies the essentials of a system obsessed with physical and ideological concepts of order and discipline. Massively symbolized by the uniform itself, as Douglas (1973: 16) indicates, this obsession tends to focus on the body, for 'the more value people set on social constraints, the more value they set on symbols of bodily control'. Helmets exemplified this 'new status' for 'real polises', for they were *not* worn in the city force, but *were* part of the apparel of the surrounding Northumberland County force, whose immediate boundary was only some three miles north of our divisional centre. They policed Northumberland with its rural areas, small towns, country villages, and tracts of moorland and hills. It was an alien place to us city-dwellers, and both their uniform style and their culture was despised. 'County' men were transferred around at short intervals, while we were static in the city, never moving more than a mile or so between the three divisions to undertake *real* 'city work'. We had to be 5' 10" at least and most were 6' 0" or over. They were 'dwarfs' at 5' 8" and were disparagingly said to 'need a helmet to help them appear big enough'.

Other differences of practice were exaggerated to suggest they were 'the foreigners' and we were 'real'. We could purchase our own houses while they lived in police colonies, denied the privilege of house purchase until they had fifteen years' service; this classified them as 'peasants, serfs, living in the feudal world of tithed cottages'. After an eight-hour shift we went home—off duty—free men, while they in contrast went to their police houses and were available for 'discretional duty', at the call of the system twenty-four hours a day; proving we were independent free men and they were slaves! All of these social differences were embodied in the symbol of uniform. Our expensive, good-quality tunics were well cut and belted, while our 'guard' style cap, set up at the front to emulate the officer class, made us different. Helmets and unbelted tunics were for the despised 'county men', 'those sheep-dippers up the road in the sticks' whom we continually used to reassert our own status by looking on them as 'hicksville country cousins' and definitely not 'real polises'.

To the south across the Rive Tyne lay Gateshead Borough Police, a small force with less manpower and fewer resources than our unit in the city. They also wore the helmet, like the similarly attired British Transport Police at the main railway station (who are also despised as police marginals).[8] Like the county 'sheepdippers' and the borough men, both the specials and the British Transport Police were used to sustain a view of our own preeminence.

To my contemporaries then at this time, a helmet was possessed of immense symbolic importance. We saw this one item almost as a totemic object, tabooed for our clan, and filled with a spirit of otherness.[9] Later, when I was a city detective in the early 1960s, we again used clothing to mark off our separation and dirty, ragged tramps shuffling off to shelter in rubble-filled dens under the Tyne Bridge would become a referent to our despised neighbours: 'look [we would point] there's a Gateshead detective hurrying off on the scent . . .'. Again Douglas (1966: 138) has suggested there is a liaison which exists between the physical body and its use as an expression of the social, so that one becomes a paradigm for the other: 'the [human] body is a model which can stand for any bounded system . . .'. It should come as no surprise, therefore, to find that a well-disciplined human body with clearly defined parameters of correctness will provide a symbolic mirror of the

---

[8] Publicly the official voice will always deny that special constables or the British Transport Police are denigrated or are attributed with lesser status by those in the 'real police'. However in the columns of *Police Review* over the years there have been series of letters where the validity of such groups has been challenged, denied, or defended and where scathing castigation of specials or the BTP, which is the norm of the canteen culture, is often only tempered by the need to maintain public decorum.

[9] When I transferred to West Mercia in 1983 I found the constituent units of the force (Hereford Police, Worcester County and Worcester City, and Shropshire Police) still defending individual identities which had been officially welded together some seventeen years before. One great regret of the Worcester City men was the loss of their fabulously decorative helmet.

preferred police social formation in which the human condition can be enacted. We can also expect to find that any discrepancy in this preferred social formation will be reflected and transferred to the physical body as a metaphor of chaos.

These adjacent police forces were physically aberrant in nuance of bodily style and were therefore deemed to be socially incorrect. In their metaphorical indiscipline they had gained 'new status' and slipped across a boundary into marginality, for as Foucault (1977: 25) has suggested, the idea of discipline revolves around control of the physical body and 'proceeds from the distribution of individuals in space . . . it is always the body that is at issue— the body and its forces, their utility and their docility, their distribution and their punishment'. This disposition of the body reflects an institutional ideal of the social distribution of individuals in spatial purity, and is a major structuring principle for police organization; examples of this will emerge throughout the ethnography.

As 'real polises' we were correctly distributed in space and our bodies were properly turned out with the symbols of order. These modes of thought are so deeply embedded in the collective conscious that ten years after the amalgamations, when the chief constable (from the south) replaced the flat cap with helmets, a number of ex-city men could not discuss the impending change without exhibiting distress and described this event as being something of an Armageddon, even though the expensive guard-style cap of the pre-amalgamation days had long since given way to what was always derided as 'a cheap and nasty alternative'. Some continued to make a stance and in 1982 I worked with a sergeant who lovingly took out his old city cap each nightshift and wore it as a symbol of everything which had been lost in 1969, when, as the station graffiti had then affirmed, 'T.J.F.'[10] and a fall from Eden had occurred.

---

[10] In 1969 on the first amalgamation, graffiti announcing 'T.J.F.' (The Job's Fucked) appeared everywhere around police stations in Newcastle. It peppered the staircases and lifts; it appeared on ceilings and noticeboards; it was scratched into desks and door frames. The hierarchy carried out a dedicated campaign to eliminate it, but years later the totemic sign 'T.J.F.' was still apparent everywhere, for its power lay in its ability to articulate the fear that this was the end of an era; a time when identity was being subsumed in a joining together with second-class neighbours. The grief and antagonism to this situation was never really made public, but the loss of a carefully constructed identity was acute.

Conversely, many of those in the amalgamated force who had previously worn helmets in their earlier life and had been moved into flat caps in 1969 welcomed the return to 'natural' apparel and their own version of a correct bodily disposition which had been prescribed in a 1958 edition of the Northumberland County Police Standing Orders. This was set out in a section headed 'Dress and Deportment', and illustrates Foucault's point (ibid.) that in such situations the body is 'docile' to authoritative orders from above. Nothing is left to chance. Even the angle of the helmet is defined; and the order ends with the instruction: 'the strap will be worn under the point of the chin, but during the summer months the strap maybe tucked inside the helmet'. I recall summer commenced on 1 May in Newcastle for our 'shirt sleeve order'; meanwhile at the other end of the Northumbrian body, para. 32 of the order commands that 'trousers will be worn with the bottoms of the trouser legs, at the front, just touching the instep'. Twenty-five years later in West Mercia, as a newly promoted superintendent, I listened at my first conference as my peers discussed a chief constable's agreement which allowed officers to discard ties in hot weather and wear open-necked shirts. For over an hour the meeting wrestled with an undefined problem in the order. No one had thought to specify how many shirt buttons could be undone and fear was now patently manifest that some uncontrollable disorder would be let loose should more than one button be opened to reveal 'chest hair, or even a medallion'. Underlying the disquiet was a strong current of belief that the act of going tieless was tantamount to social chaos! Four years later, as I mentioned above, I was party to the same fear at Bramshill, in relation to the use of the Nato sweater. One of my colleagues, no doubt swayed by the heat of the discussion, turned on me sitting in my short-sleeved uniform shirt, and rebuked me with the warning that 'in my force, you'd be disciplined for mutilating police property...'. Initially I was puzzled, until I realized he thought I had cut off my shirt sleeves, for in his force (noted for its disciplined enforcement of a correct uniform presentation), all uniform shirts had long sleeves.

These few examples show the constancy of a principle which defines police reality across time and space. Ideas of identity and insider integrity in the late 1980s are sustained by the same symbols of status and denigration which have existed since at least the mid-1950s. And of course, all of the 'stories of the great days of policing', told 'at the charge room desk' were passed on to me by a series of venerable 'real polises', who, in turn, had learned these structures of significance in their own formative years, often before the Second World War.

The rigidity of such concepts and their retention in the institutional psyche enables the organization to deflect the aberrant ideas of any new social order, simply because of the strength of these dispositions. Such generative practices structured my early experience, and built a constructed hierarchy of 'us' and 'them' which was set up and passed on to all initiates. For analytic purposes, these can be cast into a binary model, suggesting positive and negative polarities of:

real, localized	ambiguous, distanced
properly uniformed	variously (un)dressed
socially centred	socially aberrant
tall, city polises	small, unreal policemen
(we, by analogy, were)	(they, by analogy, were)
purity, humanity	polluted, inhuman
centered, clean, us	marginal, disordered, them
positive	negative

Such spatial and temporal fixations are also deliberately elaborated in other institutions of control, such as the armed forces. There we find similar bodily constructs built up as series of organizing principles, so that the other regiment or unit is perceived to operate in some kind of polluted time and space, and its aberrant nuances of uniform styling used as a marker of significant difference.

The police also use concepts of a disciplined body in their dealings to effect the 'capture' of the local villains (or 'prigs'). In any public confrontation a quick assessment and early resolution is the order of the day, for on the streets pragmatism always rules and 'real polises' set out immediately to 'fix' their adversaries by using deeply imbued constructs relating to time and space. Always the disorderly acts of the 'prig' must be stopped, curtailed, arrested, disciplined, and contained; and in pursuit of a 'docile body' the law inevitably seeks to negate, constrain, prevent, and deny movement. For the legal process demands that incidents and occurrences be ideally fixed in time and space. Because the

'prig' has to be nailed, it comes as no surprise to find that electronic tagging seems set to join the introduction of ID cards as
a means of controlling the 'dangerous classes', for as many
anthropologists have shown, the concept of movement itself is
possessed of dangerous ambiguity and prevents easy classification.
It is essentially a nomadic principle, remaining deeply resented
and problematic to most dominant, sedentary political systems
and their law enforcers. Concepts of social movement are therefore synonymous with problems of social change, for they are antagonistic to conservative beliefs; and this gives a further insight
into why the idea of social research is antithetical to police
thought and has seditious connotations for an institution in which
metaphors of stasis are of paramount importance. It also reveals
why movement becomes problematic for 'real polises', for it
defeats a belief in a fixed and bounded world.

Yet movement is the very essence of being human and of the
human condition which policing sets out to nullify. It therefore
creates something of a paradox which ensures that those who make
a marginal move are inevitably referred back 'to the centre', as
being the realm of 'real policing'. I have many examples in my
fieldnotes which show this mode of thought to be so ingrained,
that even when the possibility of making such a journey 'back' to
basic police work has long since evaporated, the supremacy of the
belief still remains:

I am in Corporate Planning at HQ, as part of a department which
incorporates Research, Computer Development and Communications.
The Chief Superintendent is being posted to division after heading the
department for some 2 years. He has a 'track record' in uniform, CID,
Fraud Squad, and Complaints and Discipline. He talks enthusiastically
about 'getting back to some real police work' in 'the real world', even
though his responsibilities as Divisional Commander will be mainly administrative and give him little or no contact with the 'dangerous classes'.
We take the piss out of him, because of this idea that he will be doing
'real police work', but we all know that divisional work has higher status
for a Chief Supt. than Research, and this is the cause for celebration.

Within 3 days of his successor's arrival, we have a Dept. meeting where
our new Chief Superintendent outlines his plans. In a run down on the
style of deference he anticipates (which I note will stifle any critical point
from 'below decks'), he talks about his length of tenure and how long
it will be before he can 'escape back into the real world'. The research

manager (a civvy) who is aware of my research interests grins across the room as this desire to 'escape' back into 'real work' is reinforced by yet another Chief Supt. (From fieldnotes, 1988)

The inherent dilemma caused by movement is encapsulated in this fieldnote. Senior officers applaud a world of 'real work' to which they can never return, and implicitly deny the world of managerial power to which they now belong. Their proclaimed wish to 'return to real work' is a contradiction, for it denies their own political scramblings to move out of the grinding realities of shift work. No wonder the 'troops on the ground' are cynical, for they know 'real work' is for young officers and is something to leave behind at the first opportunity!

RIGHTS OF SEPARATION:
THE MARGINS OF THE CID

Van Gennep's ideas on 'rites of separation' (1960) are a useful means of interpreting the social and spatial movements undertaken by the ethnographer as policeman, as he moves out from the early uniformed position of centrality described above. Each separation contains symbolic significance, incorporating transitional stages of liminality. At times it is even possible to lay out for examination the intense post-liminal rites and ceremonies of reincorporation required by the police institution as it seeks to draw the marginal mover back into the fold.

Usually, however, the social move is merely in the form of a transfer within well-developed sections of police society where the new experience is structured by the same ideology and beliefs which have gone before. Occasionally, however, the insider is moved across a new boundary severe enough to create a rite of separation and provide the scope for an introspective analysis to generate something akin to a new vision.

In this situation, the marginal mover acquires the power to reinterpret the way his institutional structure governs a desire for a rigidified world of immobility, and to understand why, for example, those few policemen who move into other areas, such as probation work or the legal profession, become totally suspect. Transition to the outside destroys the manufactured reality of one 'real world' and two ex-police probation officers I knew became

the equivalent of potential 'prigs'. Again it is this incompre-
hension of social mobility which seems to have caused my ACC to
describe an officer who took a degree and then left to become a
solicitor as 'a bad experience for the force' (and not a gain for
society). And it is the same logic which attributes those few out of
the 120,000 officers who pursue schemes designed to accelerate
promotion with the derisory and metaphorically ephemeral classification of 'high-flyers' or 'butterfly boys'.

I now see that between 1958 and 1977 I was involved in what
might well be described as a social drama of movement, often
crossing boundaries into very marginal areas of policing, where
the institutional ideal of ordered definition fails simply because
the 'use of power and exercise of authority are based in ambiguity
and particular interpretations of [what is often] poorly framed
legislation' (Burton 1980). In 1963 I became a CID aide or trainee
detective, engaged in run-of-the-mill work dealing with a flow of
petty crime. My only training and instruction for the job was
given by a detective chief inspector, who told us to 'get out there
and lock up thieves'. I was relatively successful and after three or
four months moved into the Criminal Investigation Department,
as a detective constable, pursuing local villains for the thefts,
shopbreakings, burglaries, and petty frauds which were our bread
and butter. I had joined a group who are still fixated on a classification of 'disorder' which homes in on those who attack property;
and since the amassing of property has been a primary aim of
capitalist society, it should come as no surprise to find that to prevent the dispossessed from simply taking from the élite has been
the primary structuring principle of policing. Once again, however, the declared aim and the reality are not actually cotermin-
ous, and prevention as such has always had lower status than the
task of catching those who do the taking. Crime prevention is despised work for detectives for it holds no place for the drama of
the chase and no opportunity for the symbolic warfare which
exists in the battles between 'polises' and 'prigs'. The result is
that the 'war against crime' fought by detectives becomes a symbolic re-enactment of conflicts in the economic world at large,
between those who have material property and power and those
who labour and are dispossessed.

Whether there is any social morality or justice in such a system
is not a matter which the detectives are given to question; nor do

they spend much time in reflecting on why some dubious property acquisition is outside their terms of reference, or what the relationship is of such practices to the maintenance of position and power. In the main, they are instilled with the pragmatic games of pursuit they play with the local petty thief; and if asked to consider the wider nature of their role, they tend to fall back on protestations of political neutrality. This is another skewed reality, of course, for in their pursuit of the 'prig' they are merely following a version of justice which depends on blind acquiescence to establishment values of honesty.

Leach (1977) has shown the ephemerality which lies in any attempt to classify deviance on a global scale; for what is criminal in one society or at one point in time is relative to that time and place and to who holds the discourse on power. The private delicts of one group may well be public crimes in another society, or acceptable social behaviour in a third, especially when the abhorrence of certain social behaviour wanes over time. In such inversions of social regard we can again see how movement will tend to confound the police preference for and reliance on a rigidly maintained classificatory world. The changing values attributed to our own private delicts such as divorce, slander, adultery, debt, libel, blasphemy, obedience to church, and the like, have turned some earlier 'crimes' into matters now governed by other social mores. With the public appropriation of certain categories of property, however, the police have been on more certain ground, for the status attributed to the 'capture of the thief' has remained fairly constant, at least since the police were created as a public body. The detective therefore has a legitimate target in the thief (again the metaphor is based in militarism); and this is currently reinforced by the politics of materialism.

The statistical expansion of recorded crimes and a success largely determined by detection rates support the inevitable institutional contention that more control is a necessity, and has been a corner-stone in police ideology for the whole of my service. Always the quantitative element is emphasized by the CID at the expense of any qualitative aspect of social order or harmony. I will expand further on this dichotomy between quality and quantity of 'crime' in Chapter 5, but would argue that the chase for numerical detections in which detectives everywhere are immersed moves them across another conceptual boundary and takes them into a statistical world away from their previous world as 'real polises' where the central classifier of conflict with the 'prig' remains, as ever, in a power struggle over the body (Foucault 1977).

There is no doubt the uniform policemen see their one-time associates in the CID as having crossed a divide, while the detectives know they have joined a closed and somewhat élite family group, whose strengths include the inside support of other members of that society. In many cases becoming a detective relies on a quiet system of patronage; of being invited in by those already inside with power. Having watched and assessed the track record of some young officer, the middle-ranking detectives will perhaps put him forward as a candidate, and I have watched as potential members were admitted only after a series of phone calls had ensured their acceptability to the department. I have also seen written applications for the CID ridiculed by those inside, and listened to the expressions of disbelief that these naïve applicants were 'so short of shillings that they didn't realise that admission was by invitation only'. I have also had to tell others they are unlikely to get in and then try to explain the politics of the department to them and watch their dismay when they realize that, perhaps regardless of merit, they do not fit in.

Once inside, the new detective will quickly meld into the department's style, pursuing its rituals to form a new link in the tradition of the CID. In my own case I was given a section—a small area in the central division—with just over 300 crimes per year. Most of these were undetectable in that there were few enquiries I could pursue after the event; for example, the purse stolen by an unknown thief an hour or two prior to the report and perhaps with the exact time and location of the theft unknown left little chance for skilled investigation. We were well aware of our limitations long before David Steer (1980) pointed out that 'the great majority of crime detections involve little of what the public would perceive as real detective ability'. In a number of ways, both vocal and non-vocal, the uniform branch disparagingly refer to this separation which occurs between themselves and their detective colleagues. They home in on what they see as the uncontrolled nature of CID work, and sneer and begrudge the detective his apparent freedom of movement. They are also well aware of the limited ability of detectives simply to go out and detect crime and know but cannot easily articulate that the symbolic import of the detection rate is a manipulation (see Chapter 5). All of this creates the fractured rivalry which has existed during the whole of my service and which has survived attempts by management to 'weld the uniform and C.I.D. into a more cohesive unit on Division' (taken from a Divisional Order). Inevitably such attempts are going to fail, simply because the two units have different perceptions of police reality and their own structures of significance to maintain.

As a result of the primacy of the statistical world we now inhabit, the quantity of detections obtained by each detective through the 'write-off', 'the NFA detection', or 'the TIC'[11] becomes all important. The quality of 'capture' which is often said to be the major aim of the department becomes another 'lip service' to the outside world, although once again the symbolic content of this truth is multi-vocal. A better version of reality is that although the quality of 'capture' has tremendous semantic significance for both uniform policeman and detective, it rarely leads to large numbers of detections for the monthly, quarterly, or annual reports. Indeed the quality 'capture' often means a lot of work with perhaps only one detection—if that—at the end of the day.

During my relatively short period as a city detective, I was implicitly aware that quality had to be sacrificed to quantity, for the 'arrest list' was checked monthly and the numerical totals counted. However this did not stop us making lists of those quality 'prigs' we would have liked to eliminate. In a game similar to that devised for the radio show *Desert Island Discs*, we listed those who would get one bullet from a six-gun, and placed them in order of preference, much in the way the FBI listed the top wanted men in the USA. Our lists contained the names of the family 'prigs' we knew were professional thieves and burglars; and of whom I was advised on my arrival in the department by an old detective: 'you only get one chance a year to nail these bastards if you are lucky, so when you do, its got to be watertight'. Again the élitism in the department is largely symbolic, for although

---

[11] These terms all refer to ways of recording detections, while not necessarily taking the offender before a court, and they are detailed in Chapter 5. 'Write-offs' are crimes admitted by convicted 'prigs' already serving a custodial sentence; 'NFA detections' are crimes cleared even though No Further Action is taken against the offender; TICs are extra crimes 'taken into consideration' by a court, before sentence.

detectives talk continuously of their special knowledge of the world of 'prigs', and despise the uniform branch as 'wollies',[12] often it is the uniform 'polis' who responds to a call and effects the 'capture', after which the detective moves in to 'squeeze him dry'. The detective has therefore moved away from the centrally important activity of seizing the villains into a manipulated world where the paper exercise of statistical detections is used to assuage politicians, the media, and a public obsessed with the moral panic of increasing crime rates.

Furthermore, the detectives are no longer in that basic symbol of police identity—the uniform. They are less constrained and have more individuality in their 'civvy' clothes, although there are strict, but unwritten rules about what is acceptable dress (sombre suits and ties) and what is disordered and undisciplined (jeans, T-shirts, training shoes, and the like). In the late 1950s this order of dress was even more carefully observed and I saw a detective sergeant ordered home to change from Harris tweed jacket and flannels into 'proper clothing'. By 1965 things had eased, but my detective inspector still railed against my three-quarter length corduroy car-coat with its red lining. He moaned about 'declining standards' and fondly recalled his own early days when each detective had to wear a dark striped, three-piece suit, an Anthony Eden homburg, and a watch chain at the correct angle.

Today, the detectives on the shoplifting squads, the burglary teams, and the crime squads are casual, but are still clean and orderly ('prigs' assert they can still spot 'a horney'[12a] because of his tidy style and his shoes). However, it is at the CID social functions which are sprinkled throughout the year (especially at Christmas and any departmental promotion) that you can clearly observe the CID style. To walk into a pub function room as I have often done during the ten years I was collecting fieldnotes and see two or three hundred detectives in their 'uniform' of modern suit and tie, neat haircut, and the fashionable moustache of the times, is to be visibly reminded that there is a narrow symbolic range of bodily correctness within which all policemen can properly operate. And even in this conformity the detectives are moving away from the uniform policeman's concept of correct

---

[12] 'Wollies' comes from woolly backs = sheep dippers = country hicks. Pronounced 'woll' as in 'doll'.

[12a] 'Horney' is 'prig' slang for a detective.

dress, for they are wearing 'civvy' clothing like those despised outsiders they have learned to keep at a distance. Furthermore they can move without the constraining presence of the very noticeable uniform and its 'big hat'.

Inflation of the theatricality of the social drama leads detectives to lay emphasis on 'the big job' and the arrest of the professional 'prig' who commits the big burglary or pulls off a daring robbery. The cold truth is that such captures are all too rare and it is a daily influx of petty offenders and successfully detected trivia that makes up the major part of the detective's world. The uniform 'polis', by contrast, feels that regardless of the offence or its value, he is primarily dealing 'at first hand'[13] with 'prigs' and is thus fulfilling another metaphorically prized position as 'a good collar feeler'. His 'real work' always lies in the bodily activity of physically capturing the 'prig', often to have this dangerous business transformed by a detective who then negotiates justice with the adversary, in the essential CID cause of returning a good detection rate. As a result, the uniform 'polises' often complain that 'the quality of prig has been forsaken to be replaced by quantity'.

This qualitative/quantitative dilemma produces a further schism between uniformed policeman and detectives, for CID systems of maximizing and negotiating both the crimes recorded and their eventual classification can drive a wedge between the two units. Once again the result is disjunction, for it is quality and not quantitative measures in the work experience which produce self-esteem for the individual. As Pirsig (1979: 277) correctly observes, qualitative value

is the predecessor of structure. It is the pre-intellectual awareness that gives rise to it. Our structural reality is pre-selected on the basis of value and really to understand structured reality requires an understanding of the value source from which it is derived.

One further consequence of attributing pre-eminence to quantity in relation to detection rates means that the 'prig' who 'clears his slate' (admits to lots of crimes, no matter how trivial) becomes a prized catch, simply because he helps the figures. His arrest, as I have suggested, will often be made by a uniform 'polis' whose

---

[13] Terms like 'dealing with prigs at first hand' are in common use and reflect the sheer physicality of 'real police work' and the importance of bodily contact with the 'dangerous classes'. Like 'collar feeling', it is a graphic metaphor of activity which has high status and meaning.

physical handling of 'the body' (the person apprehended) will be tempered by an acute awareness of the need to maintain physical domination. The immediacy of this world of conflict demands that regardless of his proximity to the metaphorical dirt he is controlling, he needs to erect and maintain social and psychological barriers and separate himself conceptually from the 'prig'. The detective on the other hand, immediately sets out to reduce these culturally created separations, for he needs to negotiate a statistical reality with the 'dirty prig opposition'. The 'real polis' is programmed to maintain a conceptual purity by maintaining structural distance, while the detective, of necessity, is forced to reduce this to carry out his deal with 'the dirt'.[14] By reducing the social space between the dichotomies of ordered law enforcers and uncontrolled 'prigs', the detective necessarily returns a degree of humanity to the 'prig' which the uniform 'collar feeler' is always structured to deny. The lowly 'polis', with little or no power in the system, deplores this situation and complains of its escalation, while the detectives moan about the incompetence of the uniform 'wollies' who never get close enough to their prisoners to extract their own 'coughs' or admissions and who fail to understand that the system largely depends on the ability of the department to manipulate a statistical norm in detected crimes.

Stead (1980: 305), like Mervyn Jones (1980), has also pointed out how police organization attributes low status to beat work, and asks the service to reconsider the value of the patrol officer:

I would enter a plea that I have often made that the street officer's authority . . . and discretion should be given better recognition. It has always seemed to me rather sad that almost any move from beat duty is regarded as a promotion.

Such a plea, although laudable, has little chance of becoming reality in the present organizational set-up, for it ignores the semantic difference in the uniformed 'polis's' role and that of the 10–15 per cent of the institution who form the élite in the CID. For the uniformed 'wollies' at the bottom of the hierarchical pile, any move

---

[14] There is an obsession with actual and symbolic dirt of the 'prig' which is used as a binary marker by the 'clean' ordered 'polises' to hold him at bay. It is also significant that the 'prigs' use the slang term 'the filth' to define the police. Both sides in the drama can therefore be said to maintain their semantic values by use of linguistic polarities of purity and danger. The structural content of such language and its symbolic import is essential to any understanding of these social formations of 'prig', 'real uniform polises', and detectives.

into detective work can have parallels with a marginal movement. It becomes a rite of separation into an area where the detective's need to 'juggle with statistics and detection rates' is diametrically opposed to the constantly voiced uniform preference for action which is simply programmed to 'nail the prig down'.

Once again the language is vital to the analysis, for the term 'juggling' is widely used in relation to detection rates and carries with it an understanding that what is happening belongs to a world where movement conceals as often as it reveals. In contrast 'nailing the prig down' is a quintessential statement about the value to uniform 'polises' of stasis, containment, and spatial control. Such vivid, metaphoric language epitomizes and illustrates the ultimate truths and values of the police world. In effect, even those who move across the margins into CID work have produced the first structural crack in the preferred coherent model of uniformed and unitary policing.

FURTHER INTO LIMBO

In 1966 I moved from the world of 'real polising' into areas of operational marginality which were further to confound the preference for the clearly delineated police world I had been brought up in. Although still nominally under the CID organizational structure, and still holding the title of detective, I was detailed to deal with the new and very ambiguous 'prig'—the drug user. As half of the first full-time two man drug squad in the North-East of England, I was tasked with defining and dealing with the new social aberration of 'flower power', 'the counter culture', and the 'psychedelic trip'. This was an era when phrases such as 'turning on', 'dropping out', and 'scoring shit' moved into the language; and when our newly discovered deviants caused an incredible moral panic as wreathed in clouds of incense or cannabis smoke and symbolically clutching well thumbed copies of iconic tomes such as the *I Ching*, they joined the 'hippie trail to Katmandu'.[15]

---

[15] I have written elsewhere on the creation of this new category of disorder and the reaction of the public, the media, the politicians, and the police to it. I believe certain senior policemen made specific use of the resulting moral panic and fear of the 'drug fiend' which was rampant at the time to expand police establishments, for they saw in the creation of such squads one means of enhancing their own prestige and power in the impending amalgamations which were then in the early stages of planning. The ninefold growth of this squad over a 6-year period is outlined in an unpublished BA thesis (Young 1977).

Victor Turner (1969, 1974) has explored facets of the anti-structure, liminality, and *communitas* which are contained in such periods, developing these from Van Gennep's earlier work on *rites de passage* (1960). However, he also suggested he would prefer to restrict the use of the concept of 'liminality' to those ritual periods in small-scale societies which *all* must pass through, and use the term 'liminoid' for those anti-structural periods personified by the 'counter-culture' of the 1960s (1978: 287). Whether you prefer to follow Turner, and use the idea of a 'liminoid' period for those times and situations when only *some* members of a society pass through the rite of separation, is a matter of personal choice. However, I find Turner's work on the results of such movement into the liminal state to be a very useful way of interpreting what an insider experiences when he moves to the margins of his own domain, and I suspect that many such transformations across fiercely defended boundaries of cultural experience lend the individual the chance to stand aside and reflect on his subjective place in the order of things. Whether or not the opportunity is taken up is another matter!

In many ways these reflexive moments are invaluable in helping to explain the specificities of what Evans-Pritchard (1951) suggested we might consider as an 'anthropological history', especially as these alternative periods and the movement through the liminal phase create points in a social process when aspects of structure seem to be made more clearly apparent to the analyst. Turner has also stressed the subversive character of the betwixt and between state of liminality which helps to explain the drives, inversions, and paradigms of the counter-cultural form, and which enhances the potential for the liminal journey to illuminate the postures and pedantic reactions of the dominant ideology to such periods of social upheaval.

In this instance, established authority and its police were set to oppose the threat posed by this new anti-structure, for the counter-culture renounced power and society feared their challenge, as it has feared the unworldly in every age. In this liminoid phase, which extended almost across a decade, as Turner (1969: 155–6) points out,

one often finds a simplification, even elimination of social structure in the British sense, and an amplification of structure in Lévi-Strauss' sense.

We find social relationships simplified, while myth and ritual are elaborated . . . if liminality is regarded as a time and place of withdrawal from normal modes of social action, it can be seen as potentially a period of scrutinization of the central values and axioms of the culture in which it occurs.

Movement from the centralities of 'real polising' in uniform, via the CID, into the marginal fringes of an extended period of drug squad work, had a profound influence on the absolute tenets of policing I had absorbed over the previous decade. In effect this was a period of withdrawal from a rigidly structured police world to a world turned upside down; where, in a 'counter-cultural' way, we were to find that the strict terms of reference we had carefully built up over the years no longer seemed to have relevance.

My own 'anthropological history' in this liminoid phase became extended over eight years, until 1974, and not only gave me time to reflect on many of the controls we were required to impose, but also to consider the nature of the social harm these unworldly folk devils and 'drug fiends' were actually causing; for established society has never really known how to handle the unworldly easily. My own marginality with its reflexive potential in some ways mirrored their experience, for some members of the counter-culture stood apart, in a position which allowed them to renounce, ridicule, or reject society's cherished structures of significance. As Turner (ibid. 99–100) records, this is a time in social history, when

the values of communitas are strikingly present in the literature and behaviour of what came to be known as the 'beat generation', who were succeeded by the 'hippies' . . . [and who] opt out of the status-bound social order and acquire the stigmata of the lowly . . . An emphasis on spontaneity, immediacy and the 'existence' throws into relief one of the senses in which communitas contrasts with structure. Communitas is of the now; structure is rooted in the past and extends into the future through language, law and custom.

Another binary is created here, for we became separated in our *communitas* of spontaneity from the rigid belief systems and certainties of a police structure rooted in language, law, and custom. Indeed there were many policemen who were totally unable to comprehend, never mind live in the haphazard world of marginality which we now inhabited. Yet there were those who moved easily around the margins, and I am certain the profound effects of this liminal time extended to more than a few of us who made this transition into structural limbo.

We had moved to the edges of our previously closed system of thought and action, both physically and philosophically, and almost implicitly came to recognize that the 'foundation metaphors' which Turner identifies as being crucial to transformational experience of liminality were making paradigmatic statements about our own cultural format; although I know we would have been unable to articulate this. In effect, the alternatives presented to the 'counter-culture' by the liminal experience were also available to some of us in our marginal police world, and we were forced to see that those concepts of order and disorder we had once taken almost as the natural way of things were in fact only one model for society; a single framework for social action! Social organization, we learned, was conventional and man-made and there were often realistic alternatives.

In our marginal universe, we pursued offences which were then not even classified as crimes in the Home Office Standard list, and were pitched into a new philosophical world structured by a number of alternative social constructs. These were amplified by a variety of non-verbal sign-systems such as gesture, posture, music, clothing, gender relationships, as well as other aspects of the hippie life related to an alternative political and social belief which were alien to our experience. These inevitably came to influence our own structures of significance and were made apparent by changes in our own subculture of style. Our modes of dress and consequent loss of deference to the rigidities of rank and other previously respected apparatus of the hierarchical system were all influenced. Deference to concepts of order based on such signifiers as exact time keeping, definitive shift systems, spatial purity, clearly demarcated terms of address, and other measures designed to maintain the systems of control were irrevocably loosened. In addition, we became experts in a new and complex world where everything from the intricacies of a changing semantic of underground language to the knowledge that tetrahydrocannabinol (THC) was the active ingredient of cannabis separated us from our previous associations and took us into a world where few in the organization could begin to operate with comfort. Inevitably, over such a long period, I became less institutionalized, more able to function as an individual in relation to belief and action and not merely accept the organization's definition of things; and this is a profoundly un-police like state of affairs!

There was no predetermined police model to follow in dealing with our 'counter-cultural' clients, no previous police experience to allow us easily to slot hippie behaviour into any comfortable niche. Unlike the skin-heads and punks of a later generation, or the teddy boys who preceded this era, many 'flower children' were non-violent and in their *communitas* even exhibited something of a constructive element. The philosophy which they never tired of expounding to us included visions of a new world, which although sketchy and inevitably idealistic often showed an artistic and positively creative side to their existence. It was often difficult to dislike the gentle, painted hippies, even though they subscribed to a strange new communal, non-hierarchic lifestyle incorporating the unlawful use of 'dope'. This undermined any pre-ordained police logic we might have employed to define them, so that pressures to produce a unidimensional model of 'polis ~ prig' were simply unable to be maintained, although we did home in on such facets as their long hair and frequently unwashed state to polarize them as binary 'animals', in contrast to our human status. And so although they were still the opposition, they could rarely be classified as 'real prigs'.

We therefore became aberrant policemen simply because what we were now living was not programmed by previous organizational knowledge and habit. The squad I ran became what can only be described as more 'disordered' and 'polluted' than had been the accepted norm, and we exhibited many verbal and non-verbal signals of this divergent nature. Our clothing became less sombre and much more casual and varied. Our hair became longer and—in police terms—almost verged on the wild, confirming Hallpike, (1969: 260), who argued: 'the hypothesis I wish to advance in this article [is] that long hair is associated with being outside society and that the cutting of hair symbolizes re-entering society, or living under a particularly disciplinary regime within society.... I would formulate the theory as "cutting the hair equals social control" ...'. The police obsession with hair returns again and again in my fieldnotes. Its use as a means of defining order or to set against those outside creates a subcultural style, which is reinforced continually. In a 1978 fieldnote I recorded:

a young probationary constable is recommended to shave off his fashion-able mandarin moustache before his first appraisal with the Divisional commander (who himself has a 1940s style bush under his nose). There is no reason, and he declines the verbal advice he has been given by his Inspector, so this has now become an 'order'. It is a disciplinary offence to defy an order from a senior officer, so he can only carry on if he is pre-pared to take on his immediate boss.

In a similar vein, a cartoon in *Police* magazine (January 1981) repeats an old joke but puts it into the mouth of a totally bald senior officer. He pulls the hair of a young uniformed constable, shouting at him, 'If God had intended policemen to have hair he wouldn't have created barbers'. This use of hair as a symbol of social disorder reflects Benthall's contention (1976) that an obsessive interest in the body was a result of people turning to its use as a medium of expression, because of their individual inability to shape modern technological and bureaucratic society. He argues that the body is an ideal vehicle for representing and symbolizing coherent models of experience and, at times, presents an intense framework for cultural expression. And at this point when a range of established values were under scrutiny, the body was made to carry a new symbolic load which reflected the change from the social conformity of the previous decades.

Anthropology has played a significant part in illustrating ways in which symbolic use is made of the body to make statements about the condition of society itself (Mauss 1935, Douglas 1973, Blacking 1977, etc.), and hair became an apposite symbolic indic-ator of the problems the forces of control were faced with at this time. Disordered hair is constantly used to reflect social chaos by the police and is a prime signifier of everything that is offensive to the world of 'real polising'. Its role in defining the structural marginality of 'Community Policing' departments, for example, can be illustrated by another item taken from *Police Review* (11 July 1980: 1449). There, an Inspector Fusco pleads for men to be returned to beat patrol from community projects, for these he realizes are 'an admirable aspiration, until one starts to notice that community involvement officers come to work to spend much of their time in track suits or jeans and tee shirts, and some grow longer hair and beards and mix with the locals'. There is no irony in this; indeed this is firmly in line with many similar statements collected in fieldnotes, which consider it to be totally inappropriate for policemen to mirror the style of the locals if they wear track suits or jeans or sport longer hair and beards. For although it is constantly argued that the police represent and are drawn from the community they serve, the cultural style required in the body of the police officer inevitably sets him slightly apart from the 'civvies' outside the institution, especially where such symbolic use of clothing and beards or hair is the province of the youthful innovator. Always the police prefer to exhibit bodily constraint in their styles, for restraint and decorum have a symbolic history as an indication of subcultural insider purity, a comfort with a vanishing status quo, and a rejection of the changing outside world.

This restraint expected in police hair was clearly illustrated in a large poster exhibited in the Northumbria police training department in the early 1980s, which ordered: 'male hair will be clear of the collar . . . [and] sideburns will not extend below the centre of the ear . . .'.

Faris (1968), exploring the way such symbols come to represent complex conceptual domains, coined the phrase 'symbols of high meaning capacity', which exactly fits the structural significance hair has for police ideology. In effect it becomes a reflection of an almost puritanical social containment of the individual, with metaphoric import as a statement of correctness for the society outside. Furthermore, it is also used to denote a belief in the uncontrollable and wildly sensual nature of women.[16]

Joseph Wambaugh (1976: 6–7), in his picaresque novel *The Choirboys*, uses the symbolic load contained in the control of hair to illustrate the dysfunction between 'real' Los Angeles cops and their incompetent, corrupt, and inept hierarchies. Wambaugh, himself an ex-cop, describes the ways in which wildly autocratic and psychotic bosses set out to undermine their own 'front line troops on the streets' and describes a manual which mirrors the poster in the Northumbria police training department described above:

[16] Female hair is the subject of great police concern. In Chapter 4 I discuss concepts of purity and the control of a perceived inherent sensuality of policewomen which the hair symbolizes.

Lieutenant Treadwell a figure of fun and contempt to the real cops[17] after his hair started falling out in tufts, earned his way back into Commander Moss' good graces by authoring that portion of the Los Angeles Police Department manual which reads

Sideburns

Sideburns shall not extend below the bottom of the outer ear opening (the top of the earlobe) and shall end in a clean-shaven horizontal line. The flare (terminal portion of the sideburn) shall not exceed the width of the main portion of the sideburn by more than one-fourth on the unflared width.

Moustaches

A short neatly trimmed moustache of natural color may be worn. Moustaches shall not extend below the vermilion border of the upper lip or the corners of the mouth and may not extend to the side more than one-quarter inch beyond the corners of the mouth . . .

This symbolic import of bodily hair in a novel about Los Angeles policemen is mirrored in the Force Orders of most British police forces and is part of an overarching use of bodily order and control as a marker of police purity. I will expand on this dichotomy between the clean and the polluted in the next chapter when I detail the ethnography of being a 'real polis'; however, these few examples indicate the cultural preference and the conceptual challenge which our appearance must have presented as we embraced aspects of the bodily style of our 'counter-cultural' antagonists.

Our lengthening hair and use of vibrant colour contrasted markedly with the accepted plain-clothes form of the detectives, so that the drug-squad style became a marker of cultural anomaly. Photographs of the squad taken in the early 1970s still evoke surprise in police circles, simply because they display such strong imagery of an unacceptable style, and at the time were made much of in the media, who saw the newsworthy potential of policemen in a disorderly form.

In effect we were becoming structurally and visibly undisciplined, in a world where discipline has its import spelled out

---

[17] Treadwell had previously been described by the men as 'a spineless jellyfish'. This metaphor again helps build up a vision of 'real tough hard policemen' set against 'soft, effete adminstrators', which will be explored in more detail in the next chapter.

on every occasion. For example, Section 5, para. 14 of the West Mercia Force Standing Orders is entitled the 'Maintenance of Discipline', and contends:

Discipline is the foundation of the Force and means not only the performance of specific orders but implies a willing and prompt obedience, proper respect to senior officers and loyalty to the service.

Over the years I watched as senior officers struggled to come to terms with our bizarre presence, which overcame any respect they might have had for our practical mastery of dealing with a world they were wary of. Of course, our bodily forms and somewhat disorganized working systems were in contradiction to their understanding of the correct codes of policing. We must have often seemed to deny them the obedience and 'proper respect' demanded by the institution, for we obviously did not emulate their style and in effect were a vision of impurity existing right inside the body of the organization.

On more than one occasion I caught senior management using our symbolic disorder to *dress down* young constables. One superintendent, keen to control the length of hair of his men, used to shout angrily at his probationers and young officers: 'are you trying to get a bloody transfer to join those long-haired yobs in the drug squad?' On another occasion when I was involved in the tense process of bringing prisoners into the charge room in the central bridewell in Newcastle, a very precise ex-detective colleague (by then a neat, uniformed chief inspector) stopped me to exclaim on my appearance. I had been up most of the night on surveillance and, dressed in 'raggies' in a seedy dockside pub outside my own police area, had posed as a 'driver' for a drug-dealer. I was somewhat dishevelled and unshaven: 'Look at the state of you [he exclaimed]. What a mess! I never thought I'd live to see the day when a detective inspector would look like this.' I was too involved in the capture and too tired to do other than make light of his comment. In the same way I was unable to do much else but grin and bear it when my then assistant chief constable (crime), Ken Oxford (later to be the chief constable of Merseyside) implicitly restated police concepts of correct bodily order, when he jokingly told a group of visiting journalists who had come to do a story on this wayward group of detectives, 'we pay him a plain clothes allowance you know'. There were few terms of reference for our operations and no previous squad activity to base our actions on. In effect we defined our own 'real work' and those activities we felt should have credence were given priority, so the role we pursued simply evolved. Initially we had to start from scratch to find out about drug use and drug users, for we were not even one-eyed kings in this land of the blind; and we quickly found we were delving into a new and complex social world. Many of our clients were from sections of society which had few previous dealings or contacts with the police. Some were embarrassingly naïve about the rules of engagement and readily admitted their drug use even when we had little or no evidence to prove the point; a most 'un-prig' like quality!

A good proportion of our work concerned our availability to act as an unacknowledged arm of the social welfare service to drug users in crisis situations, providing a front-line service for the 'speed freaks who's OD'd on the results of a bent script', or the 'acid heads having a bad trip', for we were in the streets, the pubs, the clubs, the crash pads, and communal houses frequented by the new 'alternative society'. Much of our daily work was ten years in advance of the official police community involvement programmes and yet our actions were only an extension of those social welfare activities the police have been heavily involved in for generations, but which are never given status as 'real police work' simply because of the institutional emphasis placed upon summons lists, numbers of arrests, crime detections, and other statistical returns.

Many of our new 'counter-cultural' deviants were articulate and presented very cogent arguments relating to their allegedly victimless 'crimes'. For example, they would link their cannabis use and an alternative ideology or religious vision to challenge our somewhat static version of social reality. Many of the 'underground' at this period in social history were consciously making a journey towards a new spiritual growth; and this, as Furlong (1973: 106) suggests,

resulted in the controllers making . . . a puritan attack directed at the drug taking of the (underground) movement; and since the drug-scene is complex and confused, and we have little time in which to develop a reliable folk-lore about drugs and how to take them (as we have long ago done about alcohol), they have been particularly successful in fostering anxiety among teachers, parents and establishment figures.

Our part in this 'controlling puritan attack' consisted of making the occasional arrest, while pursuing the unquantifiable social role which filled most of our time. Furlong is correct, however, in suggesting that anxiety was rife, and because of this and establishment obsessions with a belief in a statistical truth we were constantly being asked to give numerical estimates of how many there were 'out there' who were 'fixing', 'using the weed', or 'dropping acid'.[18]

During the first three years of full-time drug squad work (1966–8) arrests totalled some sixty-four persons—or less than two per month. In this same period I saw many hundreds of users who never featured in the arrest tables and took many to hospital. I acted as unofficial welfare officer for others and spent untold hours merely listening as the unworldly struggled to achieve the alternative vision of a new heaven on earth.

Our sixty-four arrests included a few for the traditional crimes of burglary (but now at chemist's shops), forgery (but of NHS prescriptions, not bank notes), as well as the new offences of unlawful possession of amphetamine or LSD. Court cases and the resulting media responses given to these new 'drug fiends' (to use the phrase coined by Stanley Cohen (1973)) verged almost on the hysterical (see Young 1977), and moral entrepreneurs began to press for more controls and increased action. Questions were raised in the House of Commons about a group of local hippies arrested early in 1967, and local MPs vied with each other to be in the vanguard of efforts to control the 'army of secret drug takers in the area ... (who need to be) brought back from the brink of madness' (*Newcastle Evening Chronicle*: 27 February 1967). Much of this fervour, as Furlong suggests (1973), occurred because of social confusion about this new activity. There was no existing model to use as a comparison of events and so the moral majority focused on clearly visible symbols such as disordered hair, clothing, and lifestyle, to articulate their fear of the 'alternative society' and its drug fiends.

---

[18] It seems almost unnecessary to translate these terms now when they have become part of the language. However, fixing = injecting; the weed = cannabis; dropping acid = swallowing LSD; while the 'speed freaks' mentioned earlier were amphetamine users who had OD'd (overdosed) on the products of a 'bent script' (forged prescription).

One result of this moral panic was that, even as the anxiety mentioned by Furlong (ibid.) forced us to react to these public demands with some arrests, we insiders with 'special knowledge', who were working face to face with the counter-culture, knew there was a different social reality abroad which we could never adequately explain to the entrepreneur or encapsulate for the media headline.

In effect this was a time when new worlds and new social structures were being forged; and in many ways we were closer to the world of the underground than that of the moral majority, for we were walking the same ground and like many in the alternative society were (somewhat unsystematically) following an essential and perennial theme of history—that of man's journey as 'hero'. In this search for a new spiritual awareness, they—like us—were finding new possibilities to achieve a revived sense of what it is to be truly human in the transformational experience.

This is basically the same anthropological journey pursued by Lévi-Strauss (1973) in *Tristes Tropiques*, which remains a suitable precursor for most of the current reflexive ethnography. In this account, Lévi-Strauss uses the 'hero's journey' to self-analysis in the field as a means of achieving or engendering knowledge (see also Caplan 1988); emphasizing that it is the journey to self-awareness itself, and not the arrival, which is the most important aspect of the *rite de passage*.

The forces produced in the individual on such occasions, in what Jung (1964) calls a 'journey to individuation',[19] manifest themselves in a number of very persuasive ways and in this case led to some radical reassessments of the existing moral, philosophic, political, and aesthetic order. These influences have also

---

[19] In *Memories, Dreams and Reflections* (1967) and in *The Integration of the Personality* (1940), Jung explores apsects of this journey by which man achieves a total potential for humanity. This parallels the experience of the anthropologist as meanings and structural forms unfold, and he sees the precepts on which a society is sustained laid bare. The ultimate participant experience occurs with this subjective self-identification and it is this fact which links the anthropological mode to the psychoanalytic approach in so many instances.

Lévi-Strauss's journey to individuation is rightly considered to be a hero's journey (see Hayes and Hayes 1970), for as Francis Huxley reminds us in his essay in that book, Lévi-Strauss was on a quest in his structural explorations for the ideal.

been likened to the forces effected by a millenarian journey to a new faith (Jacobi 1967), for they are compelled by an integration of the ego and the unconscious into a vision which demands more from society than the 'acceptable satisfactions'.

Indeed many of the counter-cultural ideas had troublesome millenarian or semi-religious elements which owed little to the existing moralities or acceptable satisfactions. One notable effect the alternative social format contained lay in the assault upon the senses which occurred at a pragmatic level. No one who was around in the late 1960s can have avoided the flood of changes which swept through the dress, sexual codes, language, food styles, cinema, literature, music, and other generative aspects of the new counter-culture. Many of these have since been taken on by the wider society and are to be found in all its corners influencing even those who would now deny them any real significance and tend to look back on the decade as only times of silliness and self-indulgence.

At the heart of the counter-culture there also lay a vision that was politically troublesome. As Turner (1974: 245) has shown in his essay *Passages, Margins and Poverty*, this philosophy epitomized the concept of movement as a rite of passage into liminality. It possessed a sense of *communitas* that was essentially perceived as being dangerous to structure:

> there is no doubt that from the perspective of incumbents in positions of command or maintenance in structure, communitas—even when it becomes normative—represents a real danger, and indeed for all those, including even political leaders who spend much of their lives in structural role playing, it represents a temptation.

Of course not all policemen are in absolute positions of command even though they represent the maintenance of structure in more than a symbolic way; and few can move into *communitas* to experience the temptations described above. Once again Turner (ibid. 241) outlines the constraints of structure and the potentiality of standing outside:

> men who are heavily involved in jural-political, overt and conscious structure are not free to meditate and speculate on the combinations and oppositions of thought; they are themselves too crucially involved in the combinations and oppositions of social and political structure and

stratification. They are in the heat of battle, in the 'arena', competing for office, participating in feuds, factions and coalitions. This involvement entails such affects as anxiety, aggression, envy, fear, exultation, an emotional flooding which does not encourage either rational or wise reflection. But in ritual liminality they are placed, so to speak outside the total system . . . transiently, they become men apart.

Like Furlong (1973) Turner defines the effects of the juro-political role as being possessed of anxiety and denying the reflexive possibility. While for those thrust into a position of 'ritual liminality' there is the possibility of becoming 'men apart', of standing aside and though not necessarily following political alternatives posed by any counter-culture, undertaking the hero's journey merely by seeking to comment on the social condition they now see with new eyes.

The resulting path to individuation means the conscious and the unconscious polarities within the individual become joined, so that the anthropological journeyman hero experiences a kind of crisis; for as Jacobi (1967: 22) points out:

to look such truths in the eye is a test of courage. It demands insight into the necessity of growing old, and the courage to renounce what is no longer compatible with it. For only when one is able to discriminate between what must be discarded and what still remains as valuable for the future will one also be able to decide whether one is ready to strike out in the new direction consciously and positively.

With benefit of the 'hindsight-ometer', it can be argued that my own movement into a structural limbo contained aspects of the unconscious journey towards a new self-knowledge, when the old values were able to be adjusted if not discarded; so that it was possible to break through the constraints imposed by the inculcated patterns of police culture, albeit in something of an unprogrammatic and fragmented manner. Through the daily use of our special knowledge of the counter-culture, we were forced to acknowledge and come to grips with many of the complex social factors surrounding some drug use, which a legal framework could never adequately encompass. We now had to grapple with problems of ethics, with questions of morality and of personal philosophy, as we tried to draw a simple police code of practice together to frame those new deviancies created in the 1960s by the Acts of Parliament relating to drug use. [20]

Furthermore, the reading I did for the lectures I was called to give as a 'drugs expert' generated queries about such ambiguous areas as victimless crimes and interference in private acts, and altogether raised more questions than were solved. This acquisition of special knowledge meant that when I was called to give evidence to the Advisory Council on Drug Abuse (chaired by Baroness Wooton) on the use of cannabis, I was perhaps more inclined to dwell on the symbolic dangers attributed to its use than on any alleged physical harm, simply because I was now aware that any reality in relation to cannabis use was more complex than could be contained in some easy binary of social value ~ medical debilitation. [21] Such awareness provided another means for the obsessive anxieties of the establishment to be counterbalanced from within, and as Jacobi (1967: 22) suggests, created the potential ability to look truths in the eye and 'the courage to renounce what is no longer compatible'. This, however, produces a further paradox, for this reflexive style, welding the practical mastery and special knowledge of the subjective insider to an objective interpretation of events is not one the institution of policing is

---

[20] The fear and anxiety generated by this new world of counter-cultural drug use is perhaps best reflected in the plethora of drugs legislation enacted during the 'swinging sixties'. Dangerous Drugs Acts had been passed in 1920 and 1950 (following two minor moral panics engendered by the social changes following two world wars). Between 1964 and 1971 they were joined by a flood of legislation. The 'pep pill panic' was legislated for by the Drugs (Prevention of Misuse) Act 1964 to control amphetamines, while amendments to control hallucinogenics and some soporifics (e.g. Mandrax tablets) were rushed through in 1966. Updated Dangerous Drugs Acts were passed in 1965 and 1967, with new Dangerous Drugs Regulations in 1964. Supplies to addicts and notification of addicts were controlled by Regulations in 1968, and in 1971 the Misuse of Drugs Act pulled much of this legislation together into one consolidating piece of legislation.

[21] For example the First Report of the National Commission on Marihuana and Drug Abuse, *Marihuana: A Signal of Misunderstanding* (1972), produced by a Presidential Commission and published by the US Dept. of Justice, tried to 'demythologize and de-symbolize it'. In a final comment (p. 167), the report concludes: 'considering the range of social concerns in contemporary America, marihuana does not, in our considered judgment, rank very high. We would de-emphasize marihuana as a problem . . .' The Commission recognized the high symbolic import that cannabis (marijuana) held on the public mind and attempted to diffuse it. It failed, however, even to be accepted by the Congress of the day, as did the Wooton report in Parliament. For both were dealing with a subject from the counter-culture and no government was willing to deal rationally with a root-metaphor of the 'alternative society'.

geared up to handle. We were now floating between a world of the street-wise, the gentle hippie, the communal 'crash pad', the lecture hall, the courts, the addiction unit or hospital casualty department, and the front page. Our peers included our recent colleagues of yesterday in uniform and in the CID, but also took in the professor of psychiatry, the Home Office Drugs Branch official, the NHS executive, the sociologist, and the media hack. Ours was now a multiple reality and our structural ambivalence can be illustrated by one example when one of the squad created a blazer badge in heraldic style (although we could never have been seen in a blazer at this time when faded denim was the order of the day). This badge had crossed hypodermic syringes and a Latin motto which when translated, read: 'Bodies in the cells, names in the papers'.

The blazer badge reinforced the 'capture of bodies' philosophy which had sustained our earlier lives, but was created at the same time that I was compiling a paper for presentation at the national BMA police surgeons' conference. I believe they came to hear jolly conference stories about 'drug fiends' and 'acid heads', but the paper concluded:

it would seem that the economics of the socially approved tobacco and alcohol industries means that we have to accept 42,000 deaths annually from cigarettes, and the cost to society of 50,000 alcoholics. These drug casualties are the price of minimal control and an accepted licence to use some drugs. It seems that we must similarly accept the quoted 3,000 poisoning deaths and 100,000 hospitalizations per year from barbiturate overdose, because the industry contributes £168 million each year in exports ... Meanwhile, we the wise, to quote Erving Goffman (1963) are allowed increasing manpower to pursue the cannabis/hallucinogenic using folk devil and to present the incompetent and the inept from the hippie element to the courts and the public for their solace; and to assure them that drug taking is being stamped out.

Such material clearly illustrates the new modes of thought we were developing. Our new semantic understanding was therefore linked to the changing epiphenomena of dress, hair, clothing, and the other symbols of the body I have mentioned; but it was also manifest in an irrepressible need to reinterpret and question the social condition, for I had journeyed beyond the norms of the police system, where action to control is preferably a simple matter of enforcing the rules and regulations as they stand. Yet this move into anti-structure was merely beginning.

The unconventional, questioning form I had begun to pursue was rewarded by an invitation in 1972 to attend United Nations European Social Affairs Division in Geneva. 'Experts' from a variety of European agencies were brought together to discuss and report on the various cross-cultural attitudes to drug-taking among young people. In this setting the qualitative was constantly under evaluation at the expense of the quantitative measure, for the 'wise' amongst us who were present knew that the statistical return often gives a skewed version of complex social events, although it speaks volumes about the way our systems of control are generated and maintained.

In this even more marginal world of cross-cultural perception and social contrast, the statistical truths I was consistently having to produce for local politicians, senior officers, the press, and the public in Newcastle were of little value, especially when discussion on the structures surrounding approval or illegality of some drug use was a matter which might encompass problems of economic, geographical, cultural, or even religious boundaries, or more likely the changing political whim or opportunity of the moment.

FROM LIMBO TO THE OUTSIDE WORLD

Shortly after the United Nations experience, I attended a middle management course at the national Police Staff College at Bramshill in Hampshire. This was known as 'the Inspectors' Course' and is now referred to as the 'Junior Command Course'. Of the 500-plus inspectors who attended the college each year on the course, a handful were awarded what is known as a Home Office Bramshill Scholarship. This took the form of a recommendation to a university willing to take on an inspector, who often had none of the usual qualifications. Two weeks after my course finished and I was back in the 'real world' on a murder enquiry, I received notification I had been awarded the second scholarship in the force. My predecessor had read law and obtained a first, but I chose to read social anthropology simply because of a pleasure in the subject.

As I have shown above, there is a strong tendency in the

organization to dismiss the social sciences, and it therefore seems
fair to suggest that any police officer who elects to read for a degree in that discipline is knowingly placing himself into a position
of outsider. My inclination to reject law as a possible course was
incomprehensible to many, and while I was waiting to go to university I was constantly challenged about this. If I had failed to
get a place in a law school and had been forced to take something
else as a second choice then this would have been acceptable. But
to avoid law and list anthropology as a first choice was inexplicable:

... why study—what's it called—anthropology? What's wrong with
law? Surely as a policeman it would be more useful for you to take a law
degree ... I would have thought it was your *duty* to take law ... (From
fieldnotes: detective sgt., 10 years' service)

Thus the move into academia and the world of the social sciences
was a move across a further conceptual boundary, another movement across time and space, encompassing another *rite de passage*. It can be likened to becoming 'them' or no longer being 'us',
for I had further increased my distance from the working lives
of the 'real polises' and had moved out of their known world to
become an outsider, a liminal mover.

At university I chanced to meet a detective sergeant who had
been in the Durham drug squad outside the Sociology building
in New Elvet, Durham city. He was now in the CID in the city
and somewhat tentatively asked what subject I was reading. He
seemed relieved when I told him I was reading anthropology and,
looking somewhat apprehensively over his shoulder at the sociology building, he muttered 'well thank goodness you're not
taking bloody sociology, with all those left wing bastards who hate
the polis'.[22]

An inspector who came to Durham at the same time as myself
to read Law and the Sociology of Law, found the latter course

---

[22] I find it significant that at Durham and other universities I have since
visited, the anti-police graffiti in the toilets of some departments of sociology
seems to illustrate that students need the police as binary antagonists, just as much
as some policemen need them. There must be many greater social problems which
do not feature in the graffiti, but as Leach (1976) has argued, 'a symbol only
acquires meaning when it is discriminated from some other contrary sign or symbol' and in this case the two institutions seem set against each other as contrary
units.

required a move to concepts outside normal police experience. Coming from a police family and married to a police officer, her inculcated beliefs were such that the alternative concepts which the sociology of law posed were beyond acceptability. From a perspective in anthropology where social systems were all equally valid, I teased her about cultural police rigidities which caused this rejection of the alternative views she was being asked to examine, to the point where she refused to lunch with me in the Students' Union, because, 'you're one of those bloody communists I have to listen to'.

Few former colleagues had much idea of what anthropology was and many seemed never to even have heard the word. For they live in a world of practice, where the idea of the rule of law forms an ideology or religion, replacing the waning moral power of the church (Hughes 1987: 29). Its practitioners operate in a world constrained by a belief in the immediate implementation of the legal precept, in which it becomes axiomatic that even the academic/criminologist will remain outside the world of praxis. For criminologists surely 'can never be successfully involved at the sharp end, or pointy end, dealing with angry men on the cold, hard streets' (from fieldnotes). Typically stereotyped as being 'absent-minded' cartoon types, intellectuals and academics are considered to inhabit ivory towers and need protection in their naïvety. Mythological stories about them suggest they are necessarily seen in this simplistic way to reaffirm to 'real polises' that it is they who are the true inhabitants of the pragmatic world of conflict and action. One story of how a local university academic had come into the police station to report his car missing, because he had forgotten where he had parked it, was repeated with relish; while another which I told on my return from university satisfied these deeply held views of the 'intellectual's' practical ineptitude:

I tell a small group about a noted professor who was spotted at a tutorial wearing one red and one green sock. He was described by one of his students as being 'a brilliant man but so practically inept that he needed help to cross the road safely'. A detective listening to this story nodded gravely, for it confirmed his beliefs, and as he said, 'these academics cannot operate in the cut and thrust of the real world, can they?'

When policemen label one of their colleagues with the term 'academic' it is always a derogatory term of reference, while 'college

man' is another derisory phrase used to define that tiny percentage who gain accelerated promotion through one of the special
course or graduate entry schemes generated through the police
staff college. Whitaker (1979: 229) records how these 'college
men' are described sardonically at police station level, as 'plastic
men—who know all about how to hold a knife and fork, but
nothing about how to catch villains'. During a sojourn in Northumbria one of these 'academic high-flyers' remained implacably
'not one of us', and I heard him summed up in the following
terms:

> . . . bloody man is in the fast-lane; comes off at junction 7 for a year or so
> here, and then he'll be off and away at junction 8, on to his chief's job
> somewhere else . . . and look at him! He's one of them educated bastards
> who wouldn't know his arse from his elbow on a Friday night in the Bigg
> Market . . . (From fieldnotes)

This 'high-flyer' was then in his early thirties. When he did leave
for his next promotion, the 'real polises' reading his c.v. in the
local press joked that if he had done all the write-up said then he
must have joined the police when he was about 7! One officer who
had worked with him during his short stay in the force laughingly
told colleagues that this 'college man' definitely had one arrest—
because he would willingly recall details of his big moment for
anyone who was prepared to listen.

'College men' or 'academics' are considered to be potentially
dangerous and polluting because of their limited understanding of
the 'polis's' real world; for they never stay long enough to experience the depth and complexities of the activities which lend him
his 'special knowledge'. Consequently they are said to be only
suitable for the rarified world of HQ where men with no 'bottle'
and the non-combatants have fled. This retreat into the safety of
headquarters with its separation from reality is the route for these
'bastards with no teeth'; it is the rightful place for those 'nine-til-
five administrators who turn up when real polises have been up
and at it for hours, and then ask their daft questions because of
their lack of practical experience'. It is the world of 'ESSO' men
(Every Saturday and Sunday Off), and the 'real polis's' scorn
is reflected in some of the language of definition which I have
outlined here.

Now, as a consequence of my eight marginal years on a drug

squad, visits to the United Nations, and the three years at university reading a subject which few knew anything about, but would be willing to dismiss along with all of the social sciences, I was in danger of being irrevocably cast into the mould of being a 'college man' or academic. I was close to being 'one of them' and definitely 'not one of us' because of an acquired list of significant differences.

Given that the police are essentially an organization constrained by an ingrained respect for the pragmatism of action—regardless of the lip-service paid to the police college, the 'special course', or the university scholarship—it was inevitable that the hierarchy would follow the dictates of institutional philosophy and pull the marginal mover in from the periphery; for there is a boundary beyond which the pilgrim cannot be allowed to stray.

In all the legends or tales of the journey to individuation and knowledge, the liminal mover always returns to the centre and is reconstituted into structure. With hindsight, it was inevitable my application to continue full-time study would be refused, for in their eyes I had wandered long enough in the margins and so my hierarchy now ordered that I return to the basics of uniform police duties.

REINCORPORATION: THE RETURN OF THE PILGRIM

In a Turnerian sense, the final part of a *rite de passage* is the act of reincorporation, when the liminal journeyman returns to structure. My police hierarchy decided, quite logically, that I should be re-inducted into those basic areas of policing which best represent the essentials of police thinking. I was to be re-centred and the pilgrimage in liminality was to be concluded by a posting to my first uniform job in almost fourteen years.

I was sent a short memo telling me to report to the central bridewell or prisoner lock-up, to commence duty at 2 p.m. one Wednesday afternoon. The process of reincorporation had begun and is outlined in this short section where I explore some of the modes of thought and attitudes of my new colleagues, who most assuredly saw themselves as 'working in the real world'; here I was constantly reminded of the cohesive nature of the police collectivity which determines most operational practice.

A carefully constructed world of order/disorder, crime/non-crime and 'polises'/'prigs' which was apparently sustained by the application of a well-defined system of extreme metaphors was immediately thrust before me. I had long been familiar with this, yet at another level I had never before noticed it! This articulation of a strongly metaphorical world provides a way of coping with the various tensions and ambiguities encountered in the daily round of law enforcement, and constantly reaffirms a deeply im-bued police ideology. My interpretation of this conceptual system started on my reincorporation and all the indications clearly suggested the institution saw itself to be in the centre of a world wrought by crisis and conflict, in which it maintained its cultural strength by enacting a savagely dualistic system. Polarities and oppositions, it seemed, were continually over-simplified. Ex-ploration of the symbolism and metaphor used in the everyday language revealed the strengths and the imposed logic of this bin-ary reality, which ensured a separation could always be main-tained between the 'polises' and those who were to be policed. The fieldnotes I began to record reflect an emphasis on the mean-ing which lurks in the everyday language as a way of revealing the processes I was now having to relive.

Some of the perceptions of status or revulsion contained in the language of the 'real polises' has already been outlined, giving vital clues to the semantics of the institution. Essential phrases used in connection with my *rite-de-passage*, such as 'getting your feet on the ground again' or 'getting back to basic coppering', are metaphors of socially auspicious categories of action for 'real polises'. They identify pure areas of activity and reinforce opposition to the potentially polluting activity of 'academic high flying'. The phrase 'basic coppering' which, as I have earlier suggested, should have been 'real polising' further reveals aspects of structural contamination and an alternative spatial reality: for the Assistant Chief Constable who used it had transferred in as an 'intruder',[23] and of course was one of the despised ESSO men.

His geographical separateness added another dimension to his inauspicious identification, for those originating outside the genus

[23] In 1983 on my transfer to West Mercia, I found a similar emphasis on this idea of correct location and inauspicious social space. Local differences between those who had served in the counties of Hereford, Worcester, or Shropshire were suppressed in a cohesive antagonism to those who transferred in from 'outside' (usually on promotion) and who were negatively labelled with the pejorative term 'imports'.

of 'real polis' always hold the potential of becoming tinged with aspects of the binary opposite—the 'real prig'.

Police reality can therefore be seen to be insistently concerned with social place, with physical location, with categories of time, and with forms of action. In this situation the body is constantly used to define and illuminate, so that the order to ground the liminal or marginal mover is merely a linguistic transformation of a belief that some social movement is an aberration. In effect the idea of grounding the academic flyer or the antagonistic 'prig' makes good sense, for it literally fixes the unclassifiable and the unacceptable in time and space. Always the same institutional perceptions were in evidence, as the 'polises' set out to simplify and reduce the complexities of dealing with the activities of both the 'dangerous classes' and their own administrators. Inevitably the ideal polarities they sought are unsustainable and eventually I found I had to introduce categories of what I chose to define as 'ambiguous or marginal prigs', for the perfect binary world of 'real polises' versus 'real prigs' cannot exist, except in theory.

On the ground and wearing my first police uniform in years, I was reintroduced to the preoccupying activity of identifying who should be 'fixed', and how they could best be 'nailed down'. Such definition was dependent on the most minute of distinctions. Long years of practical mastery in the ways of policing the policed has enabled easy classification of the 'prig' to be made with a minimum of analysis or reflexivity. And it is at this point of 'doing the business' that the polis's special knowledge is used to define and set apart the 'academic' or 'high-flyer'; for it is here at the point of praxis that he invariably reveals his separation from the conceptual world of 'real polising' by failing to speak the language or understand its semantic nuance. This use of quick and incisive classification as a method of imposing control is a police art, for classification is the basis of all legal systems (Maguire 1974) To understand the way this is achieved and to grasp the depth of meaning it has for the 'polises', it is necessary to feel the language; for as Crick (1976: 122) proposes, 'in any analysis of the semantics of such legal areas . . . the exploration of the rich structures of ordinary language [requires] detailed conceptual enquiry'. Maguire (1974) further suggests that all too often, modern criminology lacks this linguistic perspective, while Needham (1963) stresses the value of analysis of the structures of ordinary language. In his incisive introduction to Durkheim and Mauss, *Primitive Classi-*

fication (1963: viii) he refers to Evans-Pritchard's point that 'the investigation of classification [is the] prime and fundamental concern of social anthropology'. Evans-Pritchard himself (1951: 79) linked this classificatory task to the interpretation of language and the symbols it generates. He argued:

the anthropologist must learn the language ... for to understand a people's thought one has to think in their symbols ... in learning the language one learns the culture and the social systems which are conceptualized in the language ...

In consequence, much of my interpretation of the culture of policing and explanation of the structures of control was set for me during this period of reintegration by an awareness that I needed to explain the meaning and semantics of the ordinary language I was hearing all around me; for in its rich metaphoric content, it revealed exactly what it was to be a 'real polis'.

The derivation of the colloquial term 'polis' is apparent and I have described its origins above. However, to the 'prigs', the 'polis' is also known as 'the filth', so that the clean becomes inverted into their dirt and disorder. This phrase was supplemented by other descriptive nouns, and 'polises' were also referred to as 'horny' or 'the hornies', a 'finger', and the common term of the period—'pigs'—which was a revival in the 1960s of older conflicts which long predate its recent American use by their 'alternative society' in clashes with the police in anti-Vietnam War demonstrations.

In a way, 'prig' logic mirrors that which governs police culture. Often it seems to reflect their simplified dualisms and transforms the same animal classifications or makes use of the same bodily symbols of purity which programme police thought. It seems almost as if the 'prig' needs the 'real polises' as much as they need him to give meaning to his experience, for he uses the same reductive hierarchies of real and ambiguous crimes, criminals, and police officers and dramatizes his dealings in the same way.[24]

---

[24] When a well-known 'real prig' assaulted a British Transport policeman in the cafeteria at the Central Railway Station, Newcastle upon Tyne, it caused considerable satisfaction in the bridewell when he agreed to settle the matter only with the 'real polises' and refused to speak to 'these toy-town polises' (the Transport police officers). Even the 'prigs' separate out their 'real polises' from the ambiguous, and I have many examples from my life in the CID when 'prigs' refused to speak to 'county men', or senior officers and would only deal with 'real city polises'.

Thus when we see that the term 'horny' is defined as 'stiff, un-bending, hard, rigid, or firm' in the dictionary—all qualities the 'real polises' readily identify with—we can see a 'prig' world built on the same paradigms of meaning. For the 'prigs' then, the police are also symbols of inhumanity; they are unbending, animalistic hornies or pigs, constrained in uniform and rigidly fixed in time and space, who in this constraint are exhibiting their oppositions to the freedom from the normal disciplines and social controls which the 'prig' will (somewhat naïvely) assert is his privilege.

Such despised qualities of rigid inflexibility are reversed by the 'polises' to become their ideal indications of an undoubted superi-ority and a symbol of their humanity; for firmness, and a smart, disciplined hardness are categories epitomizing the 'real polises'. Their self-esteem also requires a proven ability to 'finger' a thief (and so earn the status which underlies the 'prig' use of the term). To 'finger' is significantly defined as 'touch, handle, thumb, paw, fumble, or grope', and soon after my re-induction I noted an occasion when a young 'prig' expressed some disgust at his own stupidity at failing to spot a 'finger' (a young detective in casual clothing on the shoplifting squad): 'I wondered for a minute if he was a finger and then I thought to myself . . . nah, he's just a nor-mal feller . . . He doesn't look like a finger does he? But I'll not forget his face now . . .' (from fieldnotes). This ability to 'finger' is allied to a belief that 'real polises' are renowned thief-takers or 'collar feelers' who finger lots of 'bodies'. Polises necessarily have to touch, handle, grope, or finger these 'bodies', which are then best classified as 'inhuman'. For in the street contests, where con-tact is always charged with tension or involves the use of actual force, it is easier and more suitable if your culture has set up a semantic view of these antagonists which allows you to deal with them as 'meat' or 'animals' and to avoid attributing them with human qualities.

The fact that 'polises' are metaphorically defined as 'hornies' and are therefore 'stiff, erect, and unbending', brings in a sexual analogy, and it is hardly surprising that policewomen can never really be considered to be 'real polises'; for in this carefully de-fined world, where images of masculinity predominate, they can never be stiff, hard, or erect! In the male/female binary which the police pursue with gusto, there are transformations of the same dualities they favour in their dialogues with the prig, and a tough, war-like male imagery is contrasted and set against a perception of women which mirrors that of the larger society. In this world view, men are hard, tough, rigid, and logical, while women are soft, emotional, and irrational. In effect, they become Mary Douglas's 'matter out of place' in the 'polis's' world. [25]

Today the term 'prig' is somewhat outmoded, and generally refers to someone who affects foppery or is disdainful and perhaps a bit of a charlatan. The older use of the word to mean 'thief' is almost extinct. In the North-East of England, however, there is a linguistic hangover and in and around the environs of Newcastle the police have hung on to an archaic meaning of 'prig' to refer to local villains. The old use of the phrase apparently derives from Old English as in the verb 'to prigg = to steal', or in the noun 'prig or prigg = petty thief' (Partridge 1972).

In the 'real polis's' world this use has been extended, so there are 'real prigs', 'prig vehicles' (typically overpowered, highly stylized cars), 'prig solicitors' (lawyers who seem to specialize in representing well-known 'prigs'), 'prigs-ville' (areas of the city said to be full of 'prig' families), and other manipulations of the adjective to describe some object or activity associated with known thieves.

As I have already suggested, a dual system of symbolic classification is eminently suited for most dealings with the 'dangerous classes' where conflict has to be urgently resolved. Hertz (1973: xxii) considered such oppositional classifications to be 'inherent in primitive thought', but pointed out that although they may have universal properties, 'each symbolic contrast has to be established by the ethnographic record . . . oppositions must be demonstrated . . .'. Throughout the ethnography of these 'pigs and prigs', I will delineate these binary schemes of symbolically created categories in a two-column form, so the various contextual polarities in metaphor and symbol can be illustrated to reveal the structural and ideological whole. The terms in either column, Needham (1973: xxv) reminds us, are not actual categories that exist *per se*, rather they

stand for collective representations, i.e., conventional modes of speech and action, and unless there is a specific ethnography evident to such effect it cannot be assumed that the participants themselves think of their

---

[25] I will expand on this classification of women police in Chapter 4, when I take them as a representation of all that is ambiguous to police culture.

symbolism at all, let alone that they think of the matters denoted by the terms in any unifying order.

In the ethnography such an order may become 'self-evident' (Douglas 1972), although I would not claim that the 'polises' were in any way conscious of the homologous nature of the dualities they use to structure their lives. However, when I pointed them out, they readily confirmed their existence by identifying other activities and examples of the same polarities I had detected.[26]

Such an inculcated and unconscious use of a mode of thought seems to reflect a process which may even be universal. As Lévi-Strauss (1966) argues, man sets out unconsciously to put order and pattern into his world by taking his cultural phenomena and then setting them against an opposition of natural categories and the cultural facets of those he takes on as his antagonists. With these he forges a semantic algebra of his social reality. The cultural phenomena of the 'polis's' world (Lévi-Strauss's *bricolage*)[27] is then laid out as a set of symbols, metaphors, and totems which support this perception of himself as fully human, different from others, and antagonist to the 'prig' and some of those within (such as the high-flyer, the academic, and the ESSO man).

A binary scheme therefore gives a set of cultural categories, one of which is the transformation of the next. Some of these dualities have already been clearly demonstrated, while others hold an integral place in the *bricolage* and are used by the 'polises' to contrast themselves with the 'prigs':

---

[26] Once these structuring principles were outlined to the officers in the bridewell, many joined in the interpretation of the patterning of their culture and easily built up systems of transformational binaries. However, one of the constables warned me 'not to let anyone outside get to know about this'. I was able to build on this and he quickly saw he was operating a further linked set of polarities of :

the powerful	the powerless
insiders, us	outsiders, the enemy
secret knowledge	ignorance

From this start (during a quiet night shift) he went on to develop a list of 'marginals' which confirmed my own fieldnote collection and which mirrored 'distances' from 'real polising' I had sketched at this time.

[27] Roger Poole in the introduction to *Totemism* (1969: 50–2) considers the meaning of the terms bricolage and bricoleur at length, and suggests: 'In a way, bricolage is society thinking itself. The bricoleur's job is simply to provoke a confrontation of the familiar and the accepted with itself. This confrontation is so jarring that a new form of thought, of classification, is released into the world.'

Real Polises	*The 'others'*
Uniformed, stiff, rigid, firm, straight, hard	disarrayed, slack, limp, weak, bent, soft
stasis of the body, control, centred, fixed, regulated, on the ground	loose, social and physical uncontrolled movement, dissolute, 'flying'
uniformed neatness, clean, smart, polished, short-haired, disciplined, order	slovenly, dirty, unkempt, undisciplined, long-haired, sloppy, disordered.
us, humans, real polises	others, animals, meat, bodies, real prigs.

As Lévi-Strauss (ibid. 55) tells us, in these symbolic codes, the binary terms or categories themselves 'never have any intrinsic significance. Their meaning is one of "position", a function of the history and cultural context on the one hand and of the structural system in which they are called to appear on the other'. Roger Poole (1969: 54) emphasizes this point in his introduction to Lévi-Strauss's *Totemism*. He contends there is

literally no end to the changes which might have been rung in the various systems. Lévi-Strauss gives many examples, but one of the most striking is the use of opposed colours . . . [to create] the diversity of 'semantic loads' which can be achieved by the classificatory function of opposition. Red, white, black, these do not mean anything in themselves. It is only as members of pairs of significant oppositions that they take on meaning.

These arbitrary but highly developed oppositions form the basis of police classification; they make bold statements about the police world and the individual place within that world. Each is a coherent system, the value of which, as Lévi-Strauss (1966: 75) asserts relates to its formal character as a code 'suitable for conveying messages which can be transposed into other codes'; and thus reaffirm Hertz's contention discussed above, that the actions generated by these modes of thought can only be demonstrated through an intensive ethnographic investigation. The differences which exist between men of different cultures and those between men and animals, which man extracts from nature and transfers into culture, are used to create classificatory differences between the self and other men. This predilection, Lévi-Strauss (ibid. 108) tells us, is because 'man does not want to imply recognition of a

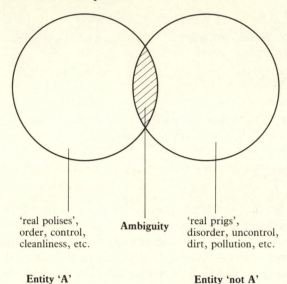

'real polises',   **Ambiguity**   'real prigs',
order, control,   disorder, uncontrol,
cleanliness, etc.   dirt, pollution, etc.

Entity 'A'   **Entity 'not A'**

FIG. 3 Euler model of social organization, from Leach (1977: 17)

"common nature" with other men'. Differences created by the use of such symbolic opposition are therefore an attempt to deny a unity which exists within mankind, and which Lévi-Strauss conceptualizes as 'l'esprit humain'. By decoding the symbolic pairs which make up the identity and patterns of 'pigs and prigs', the anthropologist is looking at the apparatus of conceptual sets, for these, as Lévi-Strauss (ibid. 153) indicates, '[filter] unity through multiplicity, multiplicity through unity, diversity through identity, and identity through diversity'. This diversity in which man denies his own animal nature as well as his brotherhood with other men is parodied in the final lines of Orwell's *Animal Farm* (1951). Here, 'the creatures outside looked from pig to man and from man to pig; but already it was impossible to say which was which.' So, although the tertiary precept is the preferred model for a police world where man, animals, and other men are used to create a system of order and pattern, the Euler model of social organization taken from Leach (1977: 17; see Fig. 3), produces a more realistic model of the marginal interfaces of ambiguous police thought and practice. Such anomaly helps break down the dualistic rigidities reproduced above, and allows the analysis to incorporate those interstitial categories of persons who fall outside each polarity and who therefore represent ambiguous categories of 'polis' or 'prig'.

In this overlapping area, the anomalous and ambiguous belong to neither 'real' category and immediately become set apart. No absolute classification exists here so there is neither the 'real prig' nor the 'real polis'. This becomes the true area of liminality in the model for those who have slipped across a border into marginality. It is the structural place of those insiders who pollute from within and turn the 'real world' into an impure complex of disorder, for here we find the administrators, the hierarchy, the ESSO men, the academics, the NCOs (non-combatant officers) and the 'men with no bottle'. Furthermore, the vision of ambiguity can be extended to include those such as the social worker, who is part of the criminal justice system, but who is invariably fixed with a negative perception as a 'soft do-gooder' by 'real polises'. Social workers, probation officers, magistrates, and the like should logically be in Entity 'A' in the Euler model, but are inexorably seen by 'polises' to be partially 'not A', and therefore destroy the unity of the idea of control. Inevitably the ambiguous 'prig' also intrudes, for he does not quite fit into Entity 'not A', and thus introduces structural conflict which ensures any preferred polarities are inoperable.

Yet in all situations the law always seeks to eliminate such ambiguity; in effect it sets out to define who must submit to whom in each case, and as representatives of this rule of law 'real polises' readily submit to this ideology, but then have to contend with the structural dilemma produced by these marginals within the system of power and control. Again these nuances of anti-structure and the anomalies and conflict produced by this failure to pull everything into the preferred duality of 'good and evil' were immediately apparent to me on my reincorporation, for I was acutely aware that I was on trial, with my own definition still very much in doubt.

Some of my bridewell colleagues had been companions in uniform a dozen years previous. They welcomed me back, but let me know in a number of ways that I was something of an anomaly. I was crucially aware that I was to be assessed to see if I was still one of them, or was 'someone who had sold out to the opposition' (whatever that section of the opposition might be!); and I could feel their caution.

However, although I was something of an outsider and an academic to boot, I was still an 'ex-real polis', and known to have something of a history as a 'collar feeler'. I therefore felt I had some advantages over the anthropologist who moves off to carry out fieldwork in the other society which he or she may only have read about. I did not feel I had to undertake the concentrated immersion into the culture in order to 'feel it in one's bones' (Powdermaker 1967: 172–3), for I was already aware of the strengths of the boundaries which separate 'real polises' from outsiders excluded from the innermost activities of police society; and I knew that suspicion would be aroused if I even hinted I might be carrying out any analysis of the practices I was now part of. On one occasion shortly after my reintegration, when I was scribbling a short note to record the exact language used, an inspector colleague looked hard at me and said, 'you're not writing all of this down for some bloody academic essay are you? I wouldn't like to see what goes on in here becoming available in paperback . . .'. Because academic research within such a power system is equivalent to the 'prig' getting inside and having access to information on how he is controlled, I was aware that any academic intrusion was likely to be viewed almost as a structural pollution. So I was very interested to record the reactions when a sociologist from the local university was allowed inside shortly after my return. I noted that he only had limited access, and was given the charge sheets for prisoners who had been charged with offences and crimes in the previous twelve months, and allowed to record the sex and age of accused, the classification of crime or offence listed against the 3,500 who had been charged, but little else. He left after two weeks delighted with the information he had been allowed to record,[28] while the officers were happy that the despised sociologist had 'got nowhere near the truth, or the real meat of what goes on'. He had been given a room adjacent to the charge room and there we fed him a diet of charge sheets from

[28] I noted that this researcher was uncertain whether he might call his activity 'warm research' (= subjective participant observation), for he distrusted the scientific relevance of 'warm, soft research techniques', preferring data obtained by 'cold, hard, scientific methodology'.

which he took his numerical data on males, females, ages, and numbers of charges for theft, burglary, drunkenness, and the like, which would 'tell him nowt about what really happens'. He knew nothing of the negotiations before the charge, nor of the activities with the 8,000–9,000 who were bailed, summonsed, or merely released without any further action. He had nothing on the culture of dealing with the streams of remand prisoners, for any true revelation of bridewell culture had been thwarted and the academic, or 'sociologist prig', had been defeated while believing that he had won. In effect, the 'real polises' felt that they had maintained the purity of their adversarial world of 'doing the business on the job'.

His visit was also useful to me, for it further revealed the mythology of seeking any objective statistical truth in this world of negotiation and wheeler-dealing. It emphasized the uselessness of attempting to maintain the false dichotomy between a world of objective data and subjective material, for as Crick (1976) and Ardener (1975a) have both argued, the misconception that 'soft data' is unscientific and the tendency to turn conceptual systems into statistical units destroy the very nature of the facts that should be investigated. Because of this I chose to make use of a 'thick description' (Geertz 1975), piling up statistically undeniable amounts of 'soft data' to prove the cultural patterns and structures of significance I found. This seemed to be the only way to reveal the true nature of the police world, and I began to follow Powdermaker (1967) and record most of my 'warm' data away from the direct scrutiny of my 'natives', for I knew they would fear the written account. As I have already suggested, these practitioners have an almost implicit understanding that to reveal the means by which power is implemented and sustained is to give an opportunity for others to undermine its base; and who inside such an organization needs to have revealed what is already well established and known through inculcated practice? My reincorporation therefore left me with a further unresolvable dilemma, as I now knew that in pursuing the academic mode I would always be placing myself in a marginal position. As Diamond (1964: 133) had suggested, 'in a spiritual sense, anthropologists are double agents. Anthropology is a scholarly discipline, but is also a kind of secretly structured revolt, a search for human possibilities'. This spiritual sense of doing fieldwork therefore returns us to the Turnerian analogy with the pilgrimage to truth through liminality, which I have used earlier. This search by an observing participant is not only one across the face of the crucial dynamics of a control system and its cultural preferences or obsessions; it is also an account of a journey to self-definition by the pilgrim who is made to face the structural anomalies and arbitrary constructs of his world. Hopefully this contains potential for the deconstruction of many well-established mythologies, and at the same time lends a further possibility for a reappraisal of the means of imposing controls over some decidedly unacceptable social behaviour.

3

The Ethnographic Record

IN THE FIELD: THE EARLY BRIDEWELL EXPERIENCE

By 1977 when my reincorporation commenced and my fieldwork proper began, the nine small forces I have previously described as 'tribal' units had been amalgamated for some three years. They were now one large force—Northumbria Police. This giant unit stretches from the Scottish border north of Berwick on Tweed, to Sunderland and Wearside in the south (see Fig. 1). The population is given in the chief constable's 1977 Annual Report as 1,471,000, while the police establishment is recorded as 3,248 officers, although this has increased since.

The map at Figure 4 shows the divisions and subdivisions surrounding Newcastle upon Tyne, where I was posted to the bridewell as a uniform inspector. The bridewell in the city centre is the main locus for the reception, control, care, and classification of the 12,000 prisoners who are brought in each year for a variety of alleged offences, crimes, and breaches of the legal code. In addition, it processes remand prisoners from HM prisons and remand centres who are brought in to appear at the courts situated above the bridewell complex. Up to seven courts operated on most days and so the field situation also contains a stream of solicitors, probation officers, social workers, relatives, and friends of the accused; as well as interpreters, children's officers, magistrates' clerks and their staff, and of course the police witnesses, store-detectives, CID officers, and those other sections of the criminal justice system who had an interest in the prisoners we logged and controlled.

The constant flow of those who make up the criminal justice system provided the human spectrum to the ethnography, and it was suggested—though we had no means of knowing how true it was—that some 20,000 persons pass through the bridewell each year, in addition to the prisoners. This is a remarkable figure

F IG. 4 Map showing Tyne and Wear Metropolitan county boundary 1974, showing location of bridewell and surrounding subdivisions

when you consider the physical restrictions and difficulties which the limitations in the building place upon those who work there.

I was one of five inspectors posted to the bridewell on a shift rota. We were accompanied by a team of 'gaolers' all of whom were long-service police constables. Each inspector had his own gaoler who worked with him on the changing early, late, and night shifts. A further eight regular gaolers worked day-shift and ferried prisoners up and down to the courts, or escorted them back to prison or remand centres. They supervised the security of visits by relatives and logged property belonging to the prisoners. The place was an insistent bustle of men in uniform, while keys for cells and detention rooms constantly jangled. The noise of human conflict was interminable and prisoners shouted, swore, and argued. At the same time visitors from the various arms of the criminal justice system could hear laughter ringing out, as the inhumanity of the place was made bearable for those of us forced to spend at least eight hours per day inside its confines. In retrospect, it is easy to define the bridewell simply as a grim, inhospitable place, yet my memories and fieldnotes are filled with a record of laughter and with the droll and sardonic humour which permeated our lives, as we sought to make the place more bearable.

Every force has its 'punishment posting'. Northumbria was no exception and over the years different locations and divisions have filled the role. In 1982, my chief superintendent reminisced about 'when you were sent to Wallsend for punishment ...'. In 1977 it was generally acknowledged that the bridewell in Newcastle was a 'punishment posting' and most of my contemporaries were said to be there because of their transgressions. One inspector had twice been breathalysed and after being fined at court was reduced in rank and sent to the bridewell. Another was nick-named 'the Thief' by everyone. He was reputed to have committed some excellent shoplifting and 'got away with it'. When the Director of Public Prosecutions finally returned the file of evidence and recommended no charges should be brought, 'the Thief' was sent to the bridewell as the only punishment the system still retained. He never talked about his arrest or suspension from duty, and the exact details of an agreement to resign—on which he was said to have reneged—existed only in the stories which were continually told by the incumbents and visitors.

It was ironic to watch well-known store detectives bring in thieves and be asked by 'the Thief' to describe what had happened. One never failed to express her disgust at this, for she openly talked of how she had stalked 'the Thief' for weeks to effect his capture and complained bitterly to me on one occasion that she wanted to reply to his question: 'they did just what you did; they came in weighed everything up, walked around the store, took what they were after, and then slipped out with the stuff well hidden'. Yet another of my associates was reputed to be in disgrace with the hierarchy because of his domestic and marital troubles. He had been a potential high-flyer, but had caused something of an embarrassment to the administration and a consensus of opinion held that he was reaping his reward by serving one of the longest 'sentences to the bridewell in recent years'.

The logic is clear! Those who transgress have to be reminded of the basic tenets of police ideology and have to relearn the ground rules of the institution in a place where these are most apparent. A superintendent, writing in 1982 about the system, concluded:

Inspectors posted to the Bridewell generally accept the posting with reluctance. Reasons put forward are the type and place of work. I am of the opinion that the main reason is that this posting has been used as a 'punishment' station, and as a result the job has lost status. (Report on prisoner escape, 1982)

A punishment posting in the bridewell was therefore prescribed for those who had to learn from their mistakes, as well as for those who returned from the outside world to be reincorporated. During my sojourn I was joined by an inspector who had been disciplined for assaulting prisoners, which the gaolers pointed out, 'was like sending a drunk to a brewery to cure his addiction'. However, it started to be used to train the newly promoted inspectors who, until then, might not have experienced the full hurly-burly of 'life on the ground'.

This training for life in 'the real world' was accomplished by taking the novice inspector, who had perhaps spent all of his previous service 'out in the sticks', and throwing him in at the deep end. As the superintendent's report (ibid.) pointed out: 'Inspectors are merely moved in and start a shift which might bring a range of problems, yet have no training of any kind for what is to come'. In my first hour on my first afternoon, I was told that a 'breathalyser was on the way in . . .'. I had last dealt with traffic matters over a decade previously, when the law in relation to drink/driving had been completely different and before the breath test system had been in existence. My gaoler saw me through the procedures, however, and I took my first step to reintegration by coping; or as he put it, 'by not totally fucking it up . . .'.

The bridewell is in the centre of Newcastle. It has been in its present position and more or less in its 1977 lay-out since it was built in 1931. A hard, uncomfortable feeling pervades the place, but staff quickly acclimatize and come to accept their rough, spartan surroundings as normal. It is enclosed within a larger police and courts complex, set apart and deliberately built as a 'prisoner area' to exclude easy access for the outsider. Most prisoners arrive via a narrow arched entrance tunnel into an enclosed yard, from which a set of stone steps leads up to a heavy locked door with spy hole. A further locked door gives way to the charge room itself, which is the scene of furious activity on most days. Policemen, gaolers, detectives, prisoners, lawyers, and others from the system mill around in what looks and sounds like chaos; great bunches of keys rattle while cell and grill gates clash as automatic locks snap into place. Yet these is always a pattern to the activity in this 20' square room.

The inspector sits on a high stool, a symbol of his power as the titular head, and works at an enormous brass edged desk over a dozen feet in length and 4' 6" in height. This is the 'charge desk' and it plays a central part in bridewell activity. It is scarred and marked from its fifty years of continuous use. Charge sheets, records of bail, and a record book with particulars of every detainee cover its surfaces. The desk is the prime symbol of the power of the charge room and with its two sloping surfaces and central flattened top for pens, rulers, and books it forms a most suitable place to lean on and discuss recent arrests and the latest transfers or promotions and re-embroider the endless 'stories from the great days of policing'.[1]

Two other desks and a table of doubtful age (at the time they were twenty-two years old to my knowledge—and the worse for wear) make up the other main furniture in the room. A further ancient table, scarred and battered, is propped against one end of

---

[1] In 1981, when the whole complex was enlarged, with new detention rooms, juvenile holding areas, interview rooms, and the like, the old desk was simply refurbished, repaired, and polished up before being reinstated. Its significance to the area was such that a modern replacement was unthinkable.

the charge desk. This is the 'property table' on which all of the possessions of the client are placed for recording. The floor is a dull grey vinyl, while a wooden bench fastened along one wall forms seating for the clients. Alongside this a dozen old green institutional lockers are provided for the gaolers' personal possessions. Many of these were *in situ* when I first saw the place in 1955 as a 16-year-old cadet.

In one corner a cooker is squeezed next to a broken sink unit and a kettle heats water for the endless tea drunk from white pint mugs. The cooker and the sink unit have been changed since my cadet days; then the cooker was an old pre-war model, while the kettle I had to fill to make the continuous brew-ups was a huge, black cast-iron beast. Now I see we have graduated to an aluminium monster, capable of holding several pints of water.

There are two rooms off the charge room. One is known as the 'Doctor's Room', while the other is designated 'the Detention Room'. The former, supposedly used for medical examinations, is rarely used by the police surgeon for anything other than the most minor medical matter; for it is totally unsuitable. It has poor lighting and a complete lack of hygiene, yet it has a medical couch, a desk, and other equipment indicating its supposed connections with a surgery. Because of the chronic lack of space it is used continually to store the less difficult prisoners or to interview juveniles with their parents.

The detention room has a loose table and chairs which makes it less 'hard' than a cell; however, it has barred windows and a lockable door. It is used to house the slightly more contentious juvenile, who remains marginal because of his non-adult status. The juvenile is always classifiably ambiguous, and because of this his place of detention is hardly ever within the depths of the cell complex; for this remains the province of the 'real' or 'ambiguous prig'. The detention room is never identified as being as 'hard' as a cell, for the door is 'softer' than a cell door and therefore gives the place a different status. [2]

Occasionally the detention room is used to house the adult

---

[2] In 1981 I was heavily involved in the extensions and refurbishment of the bridewell. One of the major features of the new cell complexes, which we installed in stations around Tyneside, was an all-purpose detention room/juvenile holding room/interview room which was 'soft' in appearance, but was actually as 'hard' as a cell. The built-in furniture in these interview rooms was tested by having a 14-stone joiner jump on it, and was finally accepted only after the first three versions had been shown to be 'too soft'.

prisoner who is not easily defined as a 'real prig' and perhaps has never been in an arrest situation before. These marginals are therefore treated like juveniles, as outside the cultural pattern which always sets out to determine a binary of 'prigs' and 'polises', as if it were a perfectable reality.

Essentially the bridewell is the central point in a large city where the conflict over street-level social disorder and power is resolved. It is the locus of the conflict between 'prig' and 'polis' and the immediate follow-up to the street occurrence where the arrest is defined. It is an area where spatial confinement is used to make non-verbal statements about the severity of the offender's actions and about his or her place in the world of 'cops and robbers'. It is here that the ability quickly to define and place the individual and his action becomes crucially important, and is made almost within seconds of the offender's arrival. As we shall see, this is rarely misjudged and says much for the officers' implicit knowledge and practical mastery.

The 'real prig' or 'body' is always controlled by a series of measures designed to deny him freedom of movement. As his identification and definition as a 'real prig' becomes absolute and any possible ambiguity is removed, he is subjected to the deepest spatial containment the complex has, in the cell block; and control over his movement, visits by friends, easy access to legal assistance and his personal belongings is intensified.

On one side of the charge room a barred gate gives access to a stone staircase and white glazed brick walled area. The staircase leads to the courts above and the cell block below, in a basement devoid of any natural light. The upward flight is broken by another system of barred gates, with a stone floored landing where prisoners sit waiting their call to the courts above. Often in the late afternoons and evenings, when the other areas available for ambiguous clients are filled to capacity, these stone stairs and the tiled landing above are used to house the overspill of these arrested persons, most of whom are short-stay prisoners. Prior to their bail, such clients might be contained on the stairs behind the locked and barred gate, still within sight of the charge room inspector and gaolers so their actions can be monitored. They may perhaps spend an hour or two with us but never see the inside of a cell, for they are not perceived by the staff to be subject to or need what I have chosen to call 'hard confinement'.

On Saturday afternoons when the flood of juvenile shoplifters is such that the detention room can no longer comfortably house those waiting the arrival of parents, guardians, or the social services, then accommodation to the rules is necessary. Often the variability in the juveniles is such that it becomes impossible to keep them in adjacent confinement. Sex and age differences, as well as demeanour and their assessment as 'potential prig' or 'silly kid' will intervene. All of the areas described can then become the temporary home for the juvenile offenders, as we strive to maintain the spatial separations which systematize our lives.

Halfway between the stone landing on the staircase and the door leading into the court dock is an area of bars and white brick tiles known as 'the cage'. This is set off from the staircase and is the most austere holding area within the complex, consisting of white glazed brick, metal bars, and a barred gate. The 'cage' is the last resort, and is kept for the 'animal' who cannot be constrained by the normality of being placed in a cell.

During my fifteen months in the bridewell, the cage was used more as a threat than as an actual lodging, but one berserk, drunken young man who smashed up an accident ward at the local general hospital then tore his clothes to ribbons and started to wreck a cell, was placed in the cage. He was a problem for us on that nightshift, for he shook the bars of the cage and screamed and slobbered continually. Yet he was not a 'real prig', for our practical knowledge told us that when he sobered up from his severe drunken binge he would probably be apologetic. Because of his demeanour and his physical wildness (which meant he would probably end the night with many self-inflicted bruises and lacerations) it was to our benefit to have him in the cage rather than in a cell. His noisy proximity to the charge room meant that we were constantly aware just what stage his drunkenness had reached and, more importantly, that he was still alive! (The hospital had declined to handle him, though he was as much a sick person as he was criminal.) The cage, then, was the ultimate sanction we had for the absolutely 'wild animal'; usually a cell sufficed.

Cells are identical for males and females, with terrazzo marble-chip floors, walls, and ceilings, hard wood slab beds, and wooden fixed pillows. Each cell has its own toilet basin bolted to floors and wall, with a press-button flush system. Corridors to both male and female cell blocks are bar-gated, and between the two areas lies a small room occupied by the female matron, who maintains the security of the female prisoners. Often a civilian matron would be unavailable and the position would then be filled by a uniform policewoman.

Male prisoners kept for any length of time and not dealt with in one of the 'softer' options such as the doctor's room, the detention room, the landing, or stairs, are all afforded the same 'hard enforcement' of the cell block. What I have also chosen to define as 'softer enforcement' might be given to certain female prisoners detained overnight, and sometimes the matron will leave a cell door open and allow a single female detainee to come out of her cell and walk the length of the 30′ corridor, or sit on a loose seat behind the grill gate. From there she can talk to the matron through the gate, or exchange banter with the gaolers going to the male cell corridor opposite. Such a relaxation of the norms of 'hard enforcement' would depend on how many others were being dealt with, for if the bridewell is busy such small gestures become impractical. Furthermore, this privilege can only be given to a female who is not a 'prigess'. Such a prisoner might be given more than one blanket, or be given tea by the matron as she brews up for the inspector and the gaolers above.

None of these small indicators of different status—or 'soft enforcement'—is ever made to male adult prisoners. All are locked in a cell, and always in odd numbers of 1, 3, 5, or more to a unit. [3] No one is ever allowed to wander the cell corridor unescorted—because of the design of the male cell block, which has created a corridor on three sides where loose prisoners could be out of sight and up to mischief. As the female corridor is a cul-de-sac only some 30′ long, they can always be observed through the grill gate and allowed some freedom without compromise. However, this asymmetry in the containment of males and females is not just because of the geography of the bridewell, it also reinforces the masculine domination of all aspects of the criminal justice system, which invariably attributes to women a different perspective.

In addition to being where the 'bodies' are brought subsequent to their arrest, the bridewell is the transit point for 'bodies' arrested and detained for court in the surrounding subdivisions to the west and east of the city centre (see Fig. 4). It is also a central

---

[3] 'Never two to a cell, always one, three or five.' Two prisoners in a cell means no independent witnesses to any fracas, and also has potential for homosexual activities.

collection point for those convicted and sentenced by northern courts, such as Berwick and Morpeth (see Fig. 1), for onward transmission to Durham prison some twenty miles to the south.

Linguistically these prisoners are always referred to as 'bodies'. These is a 'body count' sheet kept on the charge desk to ensure the numbers are correct and that none have escaped; there are 'Body Receipt Books' which are filled in each day by the gaolers for those in transit to prison. These are no longer human beings, rather they are animals or cattle, or even just meat! As I have already suggested, the body is a symbolic means of representing the social condition; and Foucault (1977: 24–31) has shown that those involved in systems of discipline and punishment have always understood that it is the body which is to be controlled, utilized, and manipulated. In the bridewell the correct distribution of the bodies is essential, but such obsessions are not confined to the police, for hospital patients also become bodies. In a *Times* report (20 June 1980), the legal director of MIND is reported as saying of a mental hospital situation: 'there was a monstrous body-swapping exercise which resulted in patients not needing secure conditions being sent to special hospitals'. As Goffman (1961) shows mental hospitals and other 'total institutions' contain a range of mortifyingly symbolic ways of dealing with the control of people. To translate them into non-human terms allows those in control to short-circuit the rules of interaction pertaining in normal society and ensures any conflict created between humans in such situations becomes more easily resolved. This reduction of prisoners to 'bodies' is linguistically set by the initial action of the 'capture of the prig', which transforms the humanity of the opposition into the animal. The hunt for 'the prig' is carried out in language redolent of the capture of wild beasts; for example: 'we've captured three bodies, but one got away—got free; he'll have gone to earth, but we'll soon ferret him out . . .' (from fieldnotes). Any marginal actor stumbling into this social drama can easily reveal his lack of insider's knowledge, simply by failing to understand these uses of the body as metaphor. A story of how an ex-county man (a sheep-dipper from the sticks) revealed his true colours as a 'bloody 9 til 5 administrator' was repeated on more than one occasion during the time I was in the bridewell. On the amalgamation this man had been moved to the city to head a group of 'collar feelers' and 'fingerers of bodies'.

One of his subordinates, aware that his new boss had an obsession with administrative niceties, phoned to tell him of an arrest but used the language of the city: 'I'll be a while boss; I'm at the West End with a body.' There was a gasp and a short silence before the 'sheep-dipper' retorted, with horror in his voice: 'A body! What did it die of?' Seven years after the event the roars of laughter this story always produced reinforced the dual classification of 'us' and 'them' which permeated the organizational thinking. Knowledge of the harsh realities of how 'prigs' or 'bodies' are handled or lodged and a firm understanding or the nuances of how control is patterned suggests another binary refinement which sets out aspects of bridewell thinking:

real polises	ambiguous or marginal polises
collar feelers, fingers, body snatchers, capture machines	administrators, ESSO men, the hierarchy, men with no bottle, non-combatants who've 'never seen an angry man'.
Hard crime-fighting city men	soft country, sheep-dipping, village yokels

The creation of this cultural identity for 'real polises' is a psycho-social event occurring beyond the realm of consciousness, and in the theatrical world of the criminal justice system this complex series of logical oppositions is built up in a series of Lévi-Straussian transformations, to become part of the bridewell bricolage. Their subsequent use as metaphors of disorder and potential chaos is essential, for these bridewell bricoleurs are forced by the crucial dynamisms lurking within the world of human conflict to seek to be always in command.

This account of fieldwork then revolves around how these conflicts are resolved in respect of the 12,000 brought into the bridewell, who are logged, searched, questioned, haggled with, haggled over, harrassed, sympathized with, fought with, manipulated, negotiated with, transported, occasionally shackled, laughed with or laughed at, 'nailed down', fed and watered, charged, bailed, remanded, summonsed, reluctantly released or eagerly processed and 'got shot of'; but who, in the final count, are always to be controlled by us.

All of these clients are short-stay visitors and most are bailed. Only the weekend prisoners are in for two days until the Monday morning courts and we rarely have any prisoner for more than two days. A procession of bodies, arrested for everything from minor disorder to murder, are controlled by 'real' and 'ambiguous polises'; it is the 'customers' who form the basis of my first detailed fieldwork.

The term 'bridewell' is derived from a palace near St Bride's well in London, which was used as a house of correction and a gaol. Taking centre stage in the drama of correction, where a dynamic tension of order is laid down, the bridewell becomes a place of power. It is the point where a particular set of rules in relation to contact/separation is brought into play to create boundaries of action between 'polises' and their antagonists; and the charge room in the bridewell, as a result, is charged with special meanings for those involved in this game of power, discipline, and control. [4]

Although the struggle to control 'the dangerous classes' is ideally set out as a series of polarities, these never produce a stable duality of the 'police' and the 'policed'. For although the severe social and spatial aspects of bridewell policing enhance the dualities I have outlined, creating an imprisoned perception where all classification is necessarily collapsed into tightly confined categories, the result is not a symmetrical world of 'good ~ evil'. Always the rigidified practices are set up to maintain a sound defence of the 'real polis's' ideological boundaries and ensure that power runs in one direction. The bridewell is therefore an unbalanced, asymmetrical world.

The bodily contact in the charge room, between the institution of enforcement and the alleged offender, results in the inequalities

[4] I do not believe it is just chance that generates the specific language of 'charging' someone with a crime in the 'charged' and tense atmosphere of the 'charge room', for as Francis Huxley (1956 and 1976) shows these 'accidental parallels of language' clearly exist and can be made explicit. In effect such linguistic puns are always available for analysis, but are rarely articulated as being yet another part of the bridewell bricolage. Like the language of 'captures, bodies, meat' and other metaphors of 'prig' animality, they sit comfortably but unexplored with the users, simply because they add meaning to what it is to be a 'real polis'. In a similar vein, I can conjecture but cannot prove it was the same unconscious semantic that saw the telephone extensions in the 'charge room' given the number 252 by some long-forgotten engineer who saw the implicit irony in using the number of a 'charge' under Army discipline. Older gaolers with a history of army service often referred obliquely to this accidental parallel of significance when allowing a 'prig' the opportunity to use a telephone, by jokingly parodying a sergeant-major and ordering 'put him on a 252'.

Leach (1977) tells us will always exist between the categories 'entity A' and 'entity not A' in his Euler diagram (Fig. 3). As he reminds us, there is always a tendency for the dominance between the categories to run from the institution to the individual, with power exerted by the former over the latter. In the charge room, the ideology of the rule and institution of law is to take others and bend them to the will of those empowered with its implementation. Again this is expressed in metaphorical language, so that we constantly hear the desire expressed to 'straighten him out' or 'nail him down'. Such linguistic devices convert into action, so that the prized and most highly valued activity is that which takes 'the prig' and subverts him to the 'polis's' belief that order equates with stasis; for if disorder is equivalent to uncontrolled movement it is best countered by the bureaucratic devices of labelling, categorizing, imprisoning, or converting. All of these negating actions are expressions of dominance, energy, power, and control, running from the institution of law to the individual.

To have the dominance run in a counter direction, i.e. from the 'prig' to the 'polis' is inconceivable. It is tantamount to chaos and social disaster or energy without order, and hints at an unacceptable vision of a reversible world. Any attack on the 'polis', either verbal or physical, is a challenge to the symbols of legal discipline, for in an ideal world all the symbols of dominance should be sacrosanct. Any breach of the purity of law is an attack on the establishment concept of its own élite place at the head of society and inevitably results in furious defensiveness.

To be brought into the bridewell is therefore to be brought into the initial place of purification; to be taken through a subsequently complex set of symbolic procedures concerned with restructuring the social defaulter. It is a beginning of a conversion from crooked and bent to the straight and narrow, via punishment. It seems almost scandalous to question its right to exist as it does, for, as Mary Douglas (1966: 191) suggests, 'the yearning for rigidity is in us all. It is part of our human condition to long for hard lines and clear concepts.'

IN THE FIELD: FIRST IMPRESSIONS

The culture shock the anthropologist experiences when he returns to his own society after the experiences of fieldwork has been described graphically by Burridge (1969: 160). The shock I experienced on my return to work in the bridewell, was as great as if I had been away in some exotic field situation for years. It was as if I had never seen such a place before in my life, yet I had taken dozens of prisoners in during my previous police career and had worked in the place as a cadet in the mid-1950s and later as a constable; and physically the place had not changed. The specificity of the return to structure from the marginality in which I had been living is vividly displayed in my fieldnotes, on my first day, as I moved back across a boundary on the *rite de passage*, to be reinitiated into structure.

Case Study 1

Fieldnotes—Day 1—Wednesday 2 p.m. In the Bridewell—first impressions—how austere it all is. The surroundings have not changed in 22 years. Furniture—large, grim, battered and Victorian. The charge desk is enormous and is best written at standing up . . . there is a high stool provided. Sitting on the stool raises one above the client and so one maintains status. Fluorescent lights 24 hrs a day, for the windows are dull, opaque glass blocks and let in little light. The room is about 20' square. I have been allocated a slim, dull green locker. There is no key and it is locked, so I can't use it. These lockers have mostly been here since 1955 when I was first in this place. The sink unit and the cooker in the corner are changed, although not new. The grill gate at the top of the stairs to the cells has changed colour. The bars are a hideous shade of orange. They used to be dull green. Have the swinging '60s had an effect on 'institutional green paint'? The overall impression is of a grim, harsh, miserable, unlovely place; dirty and seedy.

The place is bustling with the gaolers, i.e. the resident 'polises' who work in the Bridewell; and with the prisoners and the visiting polises and detectives from the courts and adjacent divisions. The half dozen regular gaolers run the place and transit the 'prigs' to and from the cells to the six courts which are sitting upstairs above us. The gaolers log the movements of the prigs—e.g. 'to court—2.15 p.m.; from court to cell 6— 3 p.m.' They list prigs' property onto records called 'body receipts', to be returned with the 'body' to prison, when the courts have finished. They also mark up all the decisions of the Court on the charge sheets piled on the charge desk and show the movement and decisions made for each body, e.g. remanded in custody; bailed by the court to (date); sentenced to 3 months, etc. They ferry the bodies (as they are always called) up from the cells, back to the cells, out to the prison van—'two by two, like the animals in the ark'; and the grill gates slam and the automatic deadlocks clash as they smack into place. There are several sets of master keys. I am given mine; we all have one and guard them at all times.

As it is Wednesday, it is a 'crime' day in the courts. The half dozen courts have been dealing with some 200 cases during the day, all thefts and criminal damage, assaults, and robbery. Traffic cases, I am reminded, are on Tuesdays and Friday. Over 20 prigs have been brought in from prison or remand centre this morning. Most of them will be further remanded during the day until the case is eventually heard. The odd one will be sentenced, but most will return to prison, joined by the odd extra one or two who are newly remanded or sentenced to imprisonment during the day. They will go off about 4 p.m., and we spend much of the time logging and preparing the 'body receipts' and 'property lists' for these 20. The progress of the process of law is inexorably slow, and always there are records and signatures for each prisoner, over and over again. Each prig requires entries in a maze of books and always there are signatures to show the regulations and petty rules of the place have been followed. As the prigs are ferried to and fro, they are handcuffed, because the corridors to some of the courts are not secure. The gaolers treat me like a novice and gently instruct me in the correct practices, which I should know, because I am nominally in charge here. They warn me to 'watch the young 'uns, because they tend to be the runners'. The regular prigs, some of whom have been on remand for weeks and have made regular Wednesday visits, spar with the staff and try to get little favours, such as cigarettes out of their property or visits from friends and relatives. The regular staff deflect these requests with ease, because practice and the chronically overcrowded space says that is how it should be. . . .

From this first case study, which illustrates only a tiny fraction of the fieldnote I wrote up at the end of the first day, we can see how the place and its activities determine the modes of thought and practice. I recorded that 'it is as if they were not human at all. We see them as bodies, to be ferried about and "vanned up", like animals in Noah's ark'. The premises are harsh and have nothing at all in the way of comfort. The noise in the place is indescribable, with names being shouted, people and bodies constantly coming and going, and the clashing of the doors and gates almost continual. As soon as one door is clashed and the deadlock bangs into place, someone else opens it to take another 'body' in the other direction. I draw the analogy with a market place, but this is a meat market where the produce is not for sale; it is merely moved around continually and logged.

The stark inhumanity of the place shocks me, especially when I consider that it handles thousands of human transactions each day. Of course, the initial refusal to acknowledge any humanity in the 'prig' customers, I reflect, means that any need for human surroundings ceases. Furthermore, I note that all the inspectors are themselves in this 'prison' for punishment, while the gaolers are all long-service constables with no political power at all and rarely any hope for promotion or any other perk from the system, other than their 'day-shift' job in the bridewell, which keeps them out of the rain and snow and off night-shift. I note that 'I am seeing the world with new eyes, and I am numbed at that which had been so familiar.'

Measures designed to enforce the social 'death' of the 'prig' are perpetually in hand, and his inhumanity is constantly re-emphasized in the wheelings and dealings following his arrest. There is a progressive depersonalization designed to remove the 'prig's' power for pollution. He possesses this quality as a result of his position as a prime symbol of anti-structure, for he personifies the main target of the rule of law, which as Thorpe *et al.* (1980: 42) remind us,

is still . . . as it was more explicitly in the nineteenth century, the 'dangerous classes'—unorganised labour or the unemployed, marginal, transient and easily stigmatised groups, the non-respectable workers and the undeserving poor.

Almost at once I note how scornful the gaolers are to those who reply 'unemployed' when asked for their details for the charge sheet or record book. Likewise, a rejoinder of 'no fixed abode' to a request for an address is met with ill-concealed shrugs of dismissal and immediate loss of status for the client, for unemployment and a transient nature are not welcome in this world. Redemption of the 'prig' requires fixed status and a settled future; and in consequence, an institutionalized depersonalization of the 'prig' is set in motion to reduce the power of this potentially chaotic symbol of disorder and danger and to commence his or her purification.

The bridewell client is stripped of personal identity to start this process. The name is taken and is written down. It is fixed to a plethora of records which are always indexed. All of the arrivals are numbered and given a year prefix to allow for annual statistics, while a date of birth and an address is assiduously sought. These, along with the physical description (height, colour, weight, eye shade, hair shade, scars, tattoos, etc.) are removed, taken possession of, and recorded over and over again, for above all, the rule of law esteems the written record as a main plank in the continuity of the theatricality of the legal process.

The outer surface of the 'body' is transformed. In some instances the clothes of the 'prig' are removed altogether. Always the tie and belt are taken in case the client decides to commit suicide and thus take his destiny into his own hands again. For the same reasons shoes are left outside the cell doors, for shoe laces are seen as dangerous objects. Cigarettes are also denied, theoretically to prevent self-immolation and arson, but in reality because they are a major commodity to trade and negotiate with. Primarily they are used for the benefit of the institution to maintain power over the 'dangerous classes' who are said to be 'unable to last an hour or more in a cell without tobacco'.

Items which would help to maintain self-identification such as watches, rings, charms, medallions, jewellery, and the like are removed, if at all possible. These are counted, listed, signed, and countersigned, then locked away. Explanations for this practice always relate to an expressed concern for the safety of the 'prig' and the protection of the 'polises'. He is thought likely to use them either to injure himself by slashing his wrists or carry out some other act of self-defacement, or use them on others. Another fear is that he will set out to dispose of them (say by flushing them away) and then allege theft against a gaoler or other police officer. All of these are possibilities and instances do occur, although they are not excessive considering the numbers of prisoners the police handle and the amount of property they list, record, and return. However, the system demands that all clients be treated as if this were the norm, for in such cases, control has been wrested back from the institution and repossession of the self has been gained by the individual.

Inevitably the facilities and the numbers of clients means such practices are only paid lip-service, and the prisoner who is going to be with us for a very limited period, such as the middle-class motorist who has been breathalysed and is from the 'almost human/non-prig' section of society, will not have his watch taken or his tie removed. These clients rarely go into a cell to be left alone. Usually they are dealt with, charged, and released without experiencing what I have defined as 'hard enforcement' (although what they think of the experience is not necessarily coloured by the same perception!).

In contrast, the 'real prig' will be inevitably stripped of all of these small signifiers of individuality. Some clients are also washed or deloused because of their actual dirt, which has the potential for immediate, physical pollution. On my first day in the bridewell I noted just how often we washed our hands after dealing with the 'prig' and his belongings to maintain our separation from his potential impurity.

Once stripped of personal possessions, cleaned up, and fully recorded, the prisoner is moving to a preferred institutional uniformity. Just occasionally this need to depersonalize him reaches excessive limits and fights arise as the client tries to maintain control over some item. I was usually willing to back down over items fastened to the skin and saw little point in having a tussle over such items as the increasingly prevalent nose studs which the young punks were wearing at that time. I suspect my reluctance to force the issue and remind the 'prig' just who was in control was looked on by the gaolers as a weakness. No doubt they believed this stemmed from my long absence from the 'front line'.

Occasionally the need to remove all the potential weapons which might be used against us (or the self) produces hilarity. One young punk, arrested for one of the 'hooligan offences'[5] had a coat and trousers which were built up from separate pieces of denim, each carefully safety-pinned together. To have stripped him would have meant unpinning him because he was literally fastened into his clothing, and we would have been left with some fifty or sixty safety-pins and perhaps a dozen and a half pieces of denim, He pleaded with us to leave him as he was, quite rightly concluding that if he was undone he would be unlikely to get the pieces together in order to leave the bridewell as he arrived.

Other instances of the removal of items are not so funny and they reinforce my observation that the whole system is a symbolic action of stripping in order to deny identity. *Justice of the Peace*

[5] Thorpe *et al.* (ibid. 44) describe 'hooligan offences', as those which in practice are only offences if the police define them as such. They are offences without victims, such as breach of the peace, insulting behaviour or words, disorderly conduct, obstructing the police, etc., where everything may depend on subjective judgement by the police, on context, on mood, on stereotypes, and gut reaction.

magazine (20 May 1978: 303), under the heading 'Undignified and Unnecessary', reported:

I was astonished and repelled to read of the goings-on at a West Yorkshire police station recently when three policemen were used to restrain a 19 year old married woman while a fourth used soap and water to remove her wedding ring. The Bradford magistrates' court was told that it was standard police practice to remove all the property which could be taken for safe keeping ... [the report continues that the police have said wedding rings will no longer be forced from hands and the Clerk to the Bradford Court was] ... pleased to hear that the rule has been changed ... In future, rings will only be removed if they are sharp or ornate or if there are indications that they would be used to cause injury or damage ... Are there any other police areas where this archaic and humiliating practice still goes on?

The answer to this final question must be in the affirmative, for even the 'new rules' outlined here are so vague as to make any differentiation in action impossible, for all rings might scratch and cause damage; and police general orders written to cater for any eventuality can rarely cope with exceptions of this nature.

Furthermore, the point about 'humiliation' is well made and supports the idea that the system is essentially about the maintenance of control. It mirrors the obsession of some local commanders with the problem of the graffiti which the 'prigs' still manage to impose on their cell doors, even without their rings or other belongings. This is not inconsiderable in some instances but in the bridewell it was tolerated, for the down-market state of the decoration was difficult to reduce further. Regular graffiti includes incised names, nicknames, dates of visits and remands, particulars of sentences, names of loved ones, sexual abilities, and a hatred of the 'polises' or particular officers who have effected an arrest. I have known superintendents convulsed with anger at this denial of the normal flow of power from institution to individual, although they always couch their annoyance in terms of 'destruction of police property' (even though the impact of a scratch to the paint on a steel door is minimal!). Invariably the 'prig' can then find himself facing another charge of 'criminal damage to police property' in relation to the graffiti. Needless to say it is not too difficult to find the culprit who writes out his nickname and his remand date, e.g. 'Tozza was here. Remanded to Durham 6.11.77'.

There seems to be something of a compulsive aspect to this

activity as confined 'prigs' seek to reassert their identity. Occasionally grudging admiration is expressed for the often astounding ingenuity used, when all personal items appear to have been removed. One prisoner removing his sole item of clothing—a pair of trousers—used the metal zip-pull to scratch his own personal message on the newly painted door of his cell. He then fastened up his trousers and waited to see the incredulous face of the station sergeant in charge of the subdivision, who was said to be 'under pain of death from his boss, if the newly painted cell doors were ever defaced again'. He had diligently searched his prisoners to deny such activity but was now confounded.

Items from my first day fieldnotes illustrate all of the institutional stereotypes I have touched on above, and graphically demonstrate the norms of police culture:

Case Study 2
Day 1 I look at the list of 20 or so who are in custody and find that three now being escorted up to court are known to me; not that I recall the individuals, rather I see they are from a family of prigs who have been going through this process for what must be 3 generations now. Three brothers from the family are going up for robbery—a classifiably serious offence. They are aged 18–21 years. This is a statistical 'mugging', but I note the charge concerns the robbery of £5 and a jacket worth another fiver from a man. I talk with them and discover that an elder brother I arrested 15 years previous for warehousebreaking is now 31. The detective in the case growls and snarls pure hatred for the family and mutters about the 'prig solicitor' who is representing them. I then discover that the robbery is essentially an inter-familial dispute between half-cousins, and that the injured person is an equally well-known prig from another family of prigs. None of this will be revealed by this statistic. I scan the charge sheets for those in custody, most of whom are already due to return to prison on remand. All are charged with offences which, in any reality, are 'small beans'. The largest (in quantifiable terms) concerns criminal damage and burglary totalling just over £200. I am brought up short at how much passion is present in the face of so much trivia, but I recall that as a detective, these families of prigs were my major targets. The gaolers once again relate to my three years at University and eight years on the drug squad, when they instruct me in the realities of this world, and they point out which of the 20 on remand are 'real prigs'. All are from 'famous families'. I note that one rather pathetic and seedy looking man who is going back to prison on remand is set apart by the gaolers and is shunned by the other prisoners. He is, I'm told, 'a "consenting gross indecency in public"—a wanker or gobbler from one of "the

cottages" (public toilets) . . .'. He stands apart from the burglars and thieves as the prison van is loaded. There is a hierarchy of prisoners and all of the 'real prigs' know their place in the age, family, and status groups.

Two detectives from another division visit the Bridewell to see one of the prisoners. They look through the court lists for the day. One has been in the East End division for a number of years and reminisces over the 'family names'. He recognizes one and asks, 'is old H— still coming in then, I remember locking him up years ago?' Then he realizes from the dates of birth on the charge sheet, that the particulars of the 'prig' are for old H—'s son.

Of the 200 cases at court on any day, it is these regulars who are of prime concern and interest. It is these 'real prigs' from the 'prig families', their fate at court, their relationships, their capture, and their defeats which are discussed and mulled over, when other prisoners and incidents are long forgotten.

Case Study 3

Day 1. 5 p.m. Of the 21 who are returned to prison at 5 p.m., all but the odd one have famous family names. All are young men between 18 yrs and 22 yrs. They are all familiar with the procedures; much more so than I am! They line up in twos behind the grill gate that leads down to the cells, sorting out their own relationships and creating their own order. The gaoler who goes down to bring them from the cells, mentions lining them up for the ark in twos. I note the constant reference to animal metaphor when dealing with prigs. There are enquiries about property left by families and good-humoured jousting with the gaolers about the chances of getting cigarettes, which are all deflected. I am struck forcibly by the numbers of lurid and colourful tattoos and mutilations I see. Most of the 'prigs' have arm tattoos, some have face and forehead illustrations which set them off most effectively from the clean and shiny polises. Bodily symbolism is rife! I had forgotten about the tattoos in this area of police work. University students don't go in for them much, and neither did the drug clients I had for eight years—although they were concerned with bodily symbolism in relation to hair and clothing in a big way. But these young 'prigs' are covered in lurid designs; I am very aware of them and must start to record them, to look to the semantics of this very identifiable and specific social form.

Just before the prison van leaves, a sentenced man comes from Court with a gaoler. There is a flurry of recording in the books and body receipts, but he knows the ropes. Before anyone says anything to him, he turns out all of his property onto the table next to the charge desk for listing. He automatically asks to keep his cigarettes and this is automatically refused and he automatically accepts it without question, obviously through familiarity. It is fascinating to watch these 'prigs' co-operating in their own containment. They almost do it for us.

The removal of personal possessions; the signatures required from the 'prig' to attest to the charge or the removal of his belongings; the denial of the visit from friends; the identification of the 'prig' as a 'body' over which power to dictate movement is maintained, are all signifiers. The dominion maintained by the 'polises', even to the point of 'loading the animals two by two', are actions which as Goffman (1961: 47) contends, are intended to 'disrupt precisely those actions that in civil society have the role of attesting to the actor and those in his presence that he has some command over his world—that he is a person with . . . self determination, autonomy and freedom of action'. These processes which are clearly evident in bridewell culture, are described by Goffman (ibid. 50) as 'mortifying'. They are, as he contends, essentially generated by 'efforts to manage the daily activity of a large number of persons in a restricted space, with a small expenditure of resources'.

In such an encapsulated world, where definition is all things to the identification of a correct social order, 'dirt' is an essential metaphor of disorder. Often the exploration of systems of taboo and conceptual dirt in anthropology can only be shown by analogy or probed with difficulty, but in the bridewell this means of defining the opposition is ubiquitous, and dirt abounds in both its literal and metaphorical sense. Yet actual dirt is no indication that we have a 'real prig', as the following cases from the first day of fieldnotes illustrate.

Case Study 4

Day 1. 3 p.m. An elderly drunk is brought in. I think I recognize him from years back. Everyone knows him and greets him with cries of 'Not again Willie'. But the admonition is accompanied by smiles and rueful shakes of the head. There is no aggression, or the overt hatred the prig receives. Through a haze of meths and cheap wine or cider, the old drunk grumbles about the inconvenience of the searching and logging procedures and tells us to 'give is a lie doon'. The search is carried out somewhat tentatively because old Willie smells abominably. Warrant officers go to check for outstanding fine warrants. A gaoler instructs me that old Willie likes to spend the cold weather inside, so that the outstanding warrants are usually put into effect only after the summer has gone. Willie's arrival sparks off stories about famous winos and dossers. 'OMO' and 'DAZ', two famous tramps of the late 1950s are recalled, and I am told there are current dossers called by the same names, even though 'OMO' washing powder, after which one was named, vanished from the store shelves some years ago. One gaoler recalls being sent to a burglary where 2 dossers grumbled they'd had to wait for an hour and a half at the scene of their half-hearted burglary on a freezing winter's night before anyone had called the police. They'd had to ensure they would be inside for their Christmas dinner!

None of these clients are 'prigs'. They are almost affectionately discussed and the general consensus is that they 'shouldn't be in prison'. Most of the staff accept there is a section of dosser society for whom we in the Bridewell become almost friend and family. Indeed we have to fight off the institutionalized dosser over the winter months I recall, or be swamped by those who come in to be arrested, seeking the warmth of the cell for a night.

A young man is arrested for theft from a shop. He is quiet and undemonstrative, articulate and unlike the 'prigs' who have just left for Durham in the van. But it is his body that causes comment, for he is slim and beautifully dressed and in complete contrast to the dossers. He is clean and perfumed with very aromatic deodorants; and has stolen more perfumes. The gaolers and passing constables extract enormous fun from the situation using typically exaggerated stereotypes. The detective assigned to the case goes to interview him in the detention room and jokes, 'if I'm not out in half an hour come in armed with a corkscrew.' There are a lot of jokes and limp-wristed pantomiming. The prisoner's overt homosexuality is used to define 'our' necessary masculinity and purity.

Although this man was absolutely clean in a literal sense, like 'Willie the drunken dosser' he is impure and polluting. These 'polises' dealing with such real and classificatory dirt are, in effect, the scavengers of society, and I often hear it said we are 'refuse collectors, sweeping up the human dross'.[6]

---

[6] It is interesting to speculate that the use of the metaphorical term 'pig' in relation to the police is structurally correct, for the pig is an interstitial animal (Leach 1964), perfectly situated between the domestic world and the wild. The 'house-pig' was a common part of the Victorian domestic world even in the towns, and was used to clear up the dross and refuse. It became a family animal, treated almost as a pet, yet was always destined to be killed and eaten by those who had given it such a peculiar structural place in domestic society (see Harrison 1982). In many ways, the 'police-pig' is similarly placed betwixt and between ordered domestic society and the wild criminal; needed yet denied, necessary but often unloved and unwanted.

Because 'real polises' must be hard, tough, and masculine in the extreme to maintain their culture and its symbolic purity, the risk in sweeping up such human dross is constant. [7] The homosexual is therefore a creature to be ridiculed, for virile heterosexuality must be defended and any possibility of a bisexual nature for man has to be denied; for if this macho image is threatened and ambiguity becomes acceptable, then the system itself must be at risk.

During my drug squad days it had become apparent that the police preference for rigidly separate gender roles was not something we could now rely upon. For our counter-cultural clients not only challenged the belief that alcohol was the only substance to be used as a mind-altering drug, but included many who denied any absolute or exclusive sexual classification. On one occasion in a dingy club, a homosexual who used the name Fiona and had a penchant for amphetamines casually told me that 'he'd had three policemen' and asked if I was surprised. I was not, but the superintendent to whom I related the story—in passing—was appalled and set up an immediate investigation. We had no names, no proof, and no evidence. However I knew of two or three policemen who seemed to have homosexual leanings and said as much. My chance remark was now becoming as problematic as if we had found policemen in the very act in the High Street! For even the possibility of such a deviance was a potential threat to the absolute ideals of the institution.

In the Bridewell, as we have seen, 'dirt' itself does not necessarily define the prisoner as a 'prig', though all 'prigs' are said to be 'dirty animals'. Even the alleged contaminatory potential of the homosexual does not automatically make him 'a prig' and indeed few of the obvious homosexual prisoners we came across were ever defined in this way. Finally on my first day back, I was once again forcibly struck by a long and quarrelsome incident, encompassing all of the ideas on dirt and the body that I have outlined:

---

[7] The police were in the forefront of those expressing fear of contamination by AIDS from prisoner contacts. This fear of 'dirt' was more than a functional response to reality and the haste to issue protective clothing to all prisoner-handling areas in some forces was undertaken without any planning or research as to the need, the cost, the practicalities of storage, and the like, as the omnipotent fear of conceptual 'dirt' took another hold on police society.

Case Study 5

Day 1—It is early evening on the first day. Another 'simple drunk' is brought in. She is 54 years old, rough, very dirty and smelly; stinking of wine and cider. She has an incomprehensible Scots accent and swears prolifically at everyone, leaping to her feet constantly and threatening violence to anyone near at hand, while invoking the name of Celtic football club as she does so. Her property is removed with difficulty and is listed. She fights over a tightly knotted scarf around her neck, as a policewoman tries to remove it. The woman snarls and threatens violence to her. She tells the policewoman 'it's me tinkers scarf' and tells us her mother was a gypsy.

Lots of fun is had in relation to her smell, and lots of bad jokes are cracked. She peers rheumally at us, asking 'warra ya laughing at?' Much amusement follows when the contents of her old, scruffy pink plastic handbag are tipped out. Inside is an ornate box with a tablet of expensive, perfumed soap, as well as a large bottle of Fabergé perfume for men. The price tags are still in place. This is a regular and obvious sign of shoplifting but no one really pursues this; yet many of the 'prigs' who went to prison on remand just two hours ago are in for property theft which is equal to the value of these two items. The staff discuss the possibility of her pleading guilty to theft of these items or telling where she got them from. There is little likelihood of her telling us anything except to swear at us, and it is doubtful she even remembers where she stole them from. We would have to charge on circumstantial evidence and perhaps invent an 'injured person'. It is quickly decided that it is more trouble than it is worth and the property is listed and returned to the handbag amidst laughter at the idea that this extremely dirty and grubby dosser should steal these items. Both drunks today have been arrested in response to calls from the public, who have phoned in to report alarm at the state of first Willie and now this woman.

The fact that the public have reported these drunks causes the staff to grumble that we have to deal with such 'dossers'. I note that we are the 'experts' who know what is good for society, while the public we serve are considered to be too naïve and merely intrude on this binary:

if the bloody silly public who have no real idea of how the world operates would only mind their own business, then we wouldn't have to deal with half of this rubbish . . . D'you know Inspector, the silly old bag who rang in to say Willie was in danger, was quite surprised when he suddenly got to his feet as the panda arrived. He'd climbed into the car almost before I'd got it stopped. (From fieldnotes; day 1—arresting officer)

The misdemeanours of these dossers are something to fill in time between the real work relating to 'prigs'. The arrest of a dosser during a busy period when the place is filled with 'prigs' is often the signal for admonition of an arresting officer who has caused such inconvenience; but even with the stolen soap and perfume, the female dosser (Case Study 5) was never perceived as being a 'real prig'.

We can see from these few case studies recorded in the first few hours of the first day, how simplified and over-determined categories of social interaction are preferred by the 'polises'. There is a constant shorthand of logic used to maintain their stereotypical world in this real-life conflict situation. They allocate and make use of actual and conceptual space to set out what Shirley Ardener (1981: 14) has called 'ground rules and social maps' and link this to a conceptual use of impurity, although without ever referring to such abstractions by name. Rather they operate through an instilled inculcation which allows them quickly to pursue even the most unexpected and bizarre occurrence, as if all events were the result of self-evident concepts inherited at birth:

> in short, the habitus, the product of history, produces individual and collective practices, and hence history, in accordance with the schemes engendered by history. The system of dispositions ... is the principle of continuity and regularity which objectivism discerns in the rational world without being able to give them a rational basis. (Bourdieu 1977: 82)

The consequence is that just as initial training in the Army is programmed to remove a personal perception from the individual soldier and cause him to function without recourse to self-analysis, so the 'polises' are similarly constrained. As Bourdieu also points out, 'the reason is that, treating the body as a memory they entrust to it, in abbreviated and practical (i.e. mnemonic) form, the fundamental principles of the arbitrary content of culture' (ibid. 94). In this cultural imprisonment, the constructs of body and space link together to form an indivisible structural bond. Again Bourdieu (ibid. 89) describes the process:

> it is in the dialectical relationship between the body and a space structured according to the mythico-ritual oppositions that one finds the form par excellence ... which leads to the embodying of the structures of the world ... Inhabited space is the principal locus for the objectification

of generative schemes; and, through the intermediary of the divisions and hierarchies it sets up between things, persons and practices, this tangible classifying system continuously inculcates and reinforces the taxonomic principles underlying all the arbitrary provisions of culture.

Even on this first day in the field, however, it is apparent there is a problem in maintaining the mythico-ritualistic oppositions of 'prig and polis', for the ambiguous starts to erode this classifying process and the basic dichotomy begins to fall apart. Always the introduction of the anomalous category produces the tension which would be missing if the ideal duality did in fact exist; and it is the resolution of this tension which introduces dynamism to the social process.

In effect this fieldwork sheds some light on the semantic perceptions shared by the largest but generally most unreported and silent section of police society. Rarely are the preferences of the powerless given a voice, nor do they tend to find a public stage on which to exhibit their cultural forms. The position of spokesman is usually reserved for the privileged and is not easily handed over to the likes of the inspectors, gaolers, or 'collar feelers' at this basic point in policing. Always the systems of policing are set out and justified by the senior officers who ultimately control the fortunes of such as the bridewell staff. Those senior officers in these seats and echelons of power can never view the bridewell life and work as being centrally important, for it is their own administrative world and their own climb to power through the ranks which must colour their own objective view of police *habitus* and history (to invoke Bourdieu once again). They must view these subordinates negatively in the light of their own perception of police reality; yet, at the same time as Jones (1980) indicated, they must publicly proclaim that such men are 'the backbone of the service'.

In the case studies presented here, we are observing structure from the point of view of the bridewell staff and the 'real polises' on the ground. In their eyes the chief constable, his assistants and deputy at headquarters, as well as all the other ESSO men constitute an intrusion, for they are extremely marginal to this world of practice. Continually I recorded a total distrust of anything said by such men, while their written orders and instructions were always seen as action destined to hinder practice, and only rarely as attempts to help the situation of those at the bottom of the pile. In effect these 'admin. men' are therefore the structural equivalent of the 'ambiguous prig', for both exist between Entity 'A' and Entity 'not A' in the model proposed by Leach (Fig. 3 above).

The beliefs and actions in relation to bridewell clients displayed for my benefit on this first day were therefore equivalent to the processes I had undergone as a novice some years previous. They were a first corrective lesson given to me in the house of correction, necessary for my gaining acceptance by my peers and even more necessary if the marginal mover was ever to gain acceptance into the institutional hierarchy.

In such a situation the act of recording the fieldnotes and the practice of subjectively living the fieldwork takes on a continually reflexive quality. The insider/anthropologist uses this total history and theory of practice to complete what Ricoeur (1981: 23) has called 'the hermeneutical circle', where explanation and understanding creates interpretation, and where 'understanding and self-understanding of comprehension and commitment [become] an ineliminable aspect of social scientific knowledge'. Such involvement is uncomfortable, not least because of the impossibility of leaving the field, but also because it means that the analysis goes beyond the experience Douglas (1975) envisaged when she pleaded for anthropology to be relevant in every daily discourse. In taking on this hermeneutic knowledge, the subject and object are incorporated to form an awareness of the unconscious process and create a never-ending theory of practice in the analyst, for 'human action ... displays a sense as well as a reference; it possesses an internal structure as well as projecting a possible world, a potential mode of human existence which can be unfolded through the process of interpretation' (Thompson 1981: 16). These initial attempts at an interpretation of life in the bridewell are therefore concerned with comprehension, commitment, and understanding; but above all they are an attempt to map the semantics of thought, action, and human experience which police social practice embodies at this base of the pyramid of power and control.

CLASSIFYING THE 'REAL PRIG'

There is a constant effort to pull all bridewell clients into a black and white binary. The urge to fit and classify everyone is all pervading and a desire for systematic and clear-cut categories is uppermost:

for penal semiotics to cover the whole field of illegalities that one wishes to eliminate, all offences must be defined . . . they must be classified and collected into species from which none can escape . . . and this code must be sufficiently precise for each type of offence to be clearly presented . . . defining crimes and fixing penalties . . . (Foucault 1977: 99)

This, of course, is hopelessly idealistic, for in reality the field of illegalities slips and slides continually and the myth of a clearly definable order of disorder is only poorly maintained at the best of times.

However, it is not just the aberrant social behaviour which needs to be defined; for the same precise criteria are choreographed to classify 'the prig'. The overriding need to codify every offence precisely is extended to those who commit them. 'Prigs', like their illegalities, should ideally be eliminated; so the need to define extends to encompass the sinner as well as the sin!

What then is a 'real prig'? How is he classified? What acts and semiotic indicators are associated with the 'real prig' to set him off from any 'ambiguous' classification. What relationships are embodied in police culture to set up such a tangible, taxonomic logic of who is a 'real prig' and who is not? It is never just the nature of the offence that causes the label to be attached; always there are other factors at work. Some are obvious, others are less apparent and yet are loaded with significance.

Usually the illegality or offence would include some public category crime, such as theft, burglary, or assault, although the value of the property stolen can often be quite trivial. As Case Study 2 shows, the three young men remanded for robbery of £5 and a jacket, were 'real prigs'; yet within a few days I noted that a rapist 'is considered a despicable animal . . . but is not a "real prig".' Similarly, an awkward breathalyser client who fought the system and the staff during the whole of his stay in the early hours of one morning, because of a surfeit of drink, was hated and grumbled over by the 'polises', but he was never spoken of or dealt with as 'a real prig'.

Leach (1970: 40) describes some of the homologies which British society uses to distinguish men from creatures, and our bridewell categorization follows these constructs. 'Prigs' are feared and are hated, for in effect they are 'vermin'—the 'scum of the earth'—the epitomy of enemies. Delight is shown on his arrival in the bridewell, when he is likely to be taunted and denigrated verbally, and great pleasure is expressed should he get 'sent down' by the court. In effect he is always someone who is known, for he or his kin have 'been in before'. His classificatory assessment as a 'real prig' is swift—usually within the first twenty seconds of his arrival—and this almost unconscious process is decided by a number of semiotic indicators.

If the client arrives in the bridewell and goes straight to the side of the charge desk and starts to tip his property on to the old battered table beside it, he is well on the way to being 'a real prig'; for knowledge of the rules classifies him as such. If this understanding is then compounded by any other action attributed to 'real prigs', then the signs are quickly interpreted and he can be 'fixed' and 'nailed down' firmly according to well-attested precedents for dealing with the traditional enemy.

If he is a 'regular' from one of the famous 'prig families' then he is 'a real prig'. If he comes through the door shouting, 'Aa'mm sayin' nowt, until me dog gets here . . . ' and then makes a request for one of a small group of well-known 'prig solicitors', then he declares himself to be a 'real prig'—'a real animal'. This category of despised individuals—'the prig solicitors'—are a few well-known local lawyers who specialize in representing 'prigs', 'and fighting tooth and claw for him . . . right through to the crown court, even when it is obvious from day one that the bastard is as guilty as hell' (from fieldnotes). 'Prig solicitors' are seen as the local version of that small group of 'bent lawyers' the Metropolitan Commissioner, Sir Robert Mark (1977) complained of; and tales of the slippery practices of our own regular 'prig solicitors' are a constant feature of charge desk mythology. Any request for these men immediately supports the perception that an accused is a 'real prig', for such a demand declares knowledge of the system.

If the client is aggressive this enhances the speed of the classification, but fighting or aggression in itself does *not* define the 'real prig'. The difficult, drunken youth on a Friday night, fresh from the late night licensed disco, will probably just be assessed as a 'daft lad with fighting man's beer on board', and is forgotten once he is bailed. Such clients do not exhibit the other signifiers which would put them into the 'prig' category, where the main taxonomic classifier is genealogy, allied to regularity. The following case study, from many similar in my fieldnotes, shows how these two themes come together. The incident concerns two sons of a famous 'prig' father of the 1950s, who are also the brothers of a famous city prostitute: 'a cow of some accomplishment, Inspector . . . she can perform more tricks in a night than the rest of her team put together . . .' (conversation with the plain-clothes vice squad). This family qualify both from genealogical and the frequency criteria and in addition they live in what are derogatorily known as 'the African villages'. These metaphorical wild places lie in specific parts of the suburbs, where the residents are all said to be bridewell regulars and therefore classify immediately as 'real prigs'. (I will say more on this 'African village' classification later.)

Case Study 6

Fieldnotes—Day 123—During the morning, the CID come in with M— (yet again!). I check the books and sheets—this is 13 times in the past 5 months, so he is not very successful. Yet this is the top class, A.1 prig opposition. He has been brought in with O—, who is known and has been in before. He is also a 'real prig' but cannot contend with M—'s status. They have been brought in for screwing shops in the City centre two nights previous, when goods valued at £1500 were stolen. Part has been recovered, but most are still missing. It is predicted by the polises and detectives that within 5 minutes of their arrival, *** (a famous prig solicitor), will be on the phone. Sure enough, the prediction is right and it is just over 4 minutes after their arrival that, as the detectives say, 'the jungle drums have called the beast from his lair'. At M's house, his mother has called him 'Colin' and his brother and sister have joined in the deception. This almost worked, because the detectives who had gone to the house did not know M— by sight. However a uniform officer who had gone as 'back up' had come in to the house as the sparring had gone on and identified M— to the CID men.

M— is surly, verbally abusive and disagreeable during the whole of his stay, but the polises are just as vitriolic in return. However, his threats to invoke some 'complaint against the police' in relation to the search and the mode of his arrest, further reinforces his classification as a real prig. Then surprisingly he tells one of the detectives that the stolen goods have gone to a Pakistani shopkeeper. A warrant to search is hurriedly sworn out, but too late, the premises are empty. 'But it doesn't matter, we've got two in the bag (again I note the hunting metaphor!), part property has been recovered so the crime is statistically detected . . .' and as the detective in the case reminds me (for my fieldnote!) 'now we know that black git is taking stuff, he'll come into the frame eventually.'

The two will be charged with burglary and the injured persons will have no difficulty in claiming on the insurance. M—'s appearance in the Bridewell has been greeted with delight by the gaolers and passing polises. He is already on bail to the Crown Court for 4 or 5 different burglaries and thefts and is considered to be merely spinning out the time to put off the inevitable day of sentencing when everyone is certain he will get some 'well deserved porridge'. One of the polises watching the negotiations and manipulations in the case grumbles and growls about M— and he says, 'we should just exterminate these bloody animals when we get them.' There is grim satisfaction that M— 'the real prig', has been 'captured dead to rights this time'.

The polarities and oppositions revealed in this case study exemplify the logic of basic police modes of thought, echoing the Lévi-Straussian contention that a universalistic metaphoric concern in man is to use his own cultural identity and set it auspiciously against the others, who are to be despised and cast with inhuman or animal qualities. By perceiving 'prigs' negatively as wild animals, the 'polises' metaphorically transform a variety of animal categories from thought into speech and then on into action. These are repeated and lived so continuously that they quickly objectify the structures of policing, and are then 'reproduced consistently in the form of durable dispositions, which are unitary and systematic' (Bourdieu 1977: 85).

This intensive use of animal metaphor supports Lévi-Strauss's assertion that 'animals are goods to think with',[8] for they serve a substantial symbolic purpose for the 'polises' by promoting further instances of Bourdieu's durable dispositions. Leach (1970: 36–7), reflects on these symbolic divisions which men use to separate out, so that 'my family, my community, my tribe, my class ... are altogether special, they are superior, they are civilised, cultured; the others are just savages, like wild beasts'. Lévi-Strauss, he concludes, comes back continuously to this conundrum of where does culture divide off from nature, and from his

---

[8] Leach (1970: 34 and 121 n. 7) reflects on Lévi-Strauss's verbal games, arguing that the idea of 'goods' should be treated in a totemic sense, where animals are items or categories for use in symbol and metaphor—i.e. 'goods to think' (*bonnes à penser*)—which is literally translated as good to think, but which is not English; and not as has been suggested elsewhere as 'good to eat', which would necessarily be 'bonnes à manger'.

volume *Mythologiques III* (1968: 422), Leach quotes him as saying:

We (Europeans) . . . have been taught from infancy to be self centred and individualistic 'to fear the impurity of foreign things', a doctrine which we embody in the formula 'Hell is the others' (l'enfer, c'est [les] autres)' [while] primitive myth has the opposite moral implication 'Hell is ourselves' (l'enfer, c'est nous-mêmes).

This fear of the hell existing in the 'other' is dramatized for the police and stereotypically symbolized by this insistent classification of the 'real prig' as being of untamed nature and resistant to culture. By extension we find that if the polis = humanity therefore prig = animal, there are whole chains of homologies in everyday police language which build on this use of symbol and metaphor. When it is said that M— and his family (in Case Study 6) live in one of the 'African villages', we can see how a further self-confirming binary system is constructed to extend on those already in play:

Polises	Prigs
Humanity	Animality
Free	Captured
Cultured	Wild
Suburban residence	African village squalor

As we have seen the 'prig' is 'captured' or is 'in the bag'. Like the wild animals he is said to live in 'the jungle' in and around the 'African villages' which house families of 'prigs' and are therefore a further metaphorical homology to the wild, non-European world. In reality, these 'villages' are merely locations of low quality housing in the suburbs to the east and west of the city centre, where 'prig' families live and 'spawn further generations of dirty little prigs'. Once again 'dirt' is used in its symbolic and actual sense to stereotype the enemy in the 'African villages', as the following case studies show:

Case Study 7

Fieldnotes—Day 121 From S**** Grove in one of the 'African villages', we have Rosemary T—. During the past few months, we have had many of the occupants of this street, and like M***** Avenue in the East End of the city, the polises reckon we could go through the books in the Bridewell and find that we'd had the greater part of the street in at one time or another in a year. Given as an address by the new arrival, this signifier immediately classifies a real prig.

Rosemary has been bailed on 3 charges of petty theft and fraud—she has failed to appear at Court and has 'gone to earth'. She is brought in snarling and sneering, and is greeted by the gaolers: 'hello Rosemary, nice to see you, hope you are prepared for a bed in Durham [prison] to-night . . .' Rosemary is not yet 20 and is described by all as being 'as hard as the hobs of hell'. All of the visiting detectives and polises remark on R's 'enormous tits'; but are certain that no one in his right mind would get sexually involved with her, because 'what state will her knickers be in when she's from the "sticky mat" houses in the African village, yaagh! . . .' Officers from 'summons and warrants' tell me her mother and father might try to get a visit to her and as she is a prig from 'prigland' I ask the usual: 'are we too busy to allow time for a visit?' 'No', the summons officer replies with a huge grin on his face, 'let them in, both of them are wanted as well.' It is accepted that because they are also prigs, they will have shielded Rosemary during the 3 months she has been 'off the side'. Mother arrives, is ushered in and presented with a warrant for £50 fine or 21 days which is outstanding. She has no money and has to take the 21 days. (Within 2 days the fine is paid off and she is out—the gaolers are dismissive and say the fine could have been paid off at once, but the 'bastard prigs never pay 'til the last moment if they can help it'. I tell them I know of businessmen who do the same, but they don't want to hear this!)

Fieldnotes—Day 128 Rosemary (see Day 121) appears on remand and applies for bail. Her mother goes before the court and offers to stand as a suitable surety. She is believed, by the polises, to have hidden Rosemary during the 3 months she was 'off the side' and now tells the court that she has never been in trouble for years, inferring that she is a suitable surety as a result. The prosecuting solicitor asks her, 'isn't it true you were convicted here in December for theft, failed to pay the fine and have just spent time in prison, in the last few days, as an alternative?' Mrs T— agrees that this is the case, but that she had forgotten about it. She is rejected as a suitable surety but her sister is accepted. It is said 'to be one big farce'. Obviously any sister of Mrs T— must also be a 'prigess' and have helped in Rosemary's avoidance of the law. She should never be acceptable, 'because they have no respect for the law, they're just bloody animals . . . the whole family are right bloody prigs and should never get bail.' The father failed to come in to visit Rosemary, but has been arrested during the week and so all 3 have been inside within a week.

I check the sheets. Rosemary's fiddles total less than £50. 'Prigs' are therefore not defined by the amount of goods obtained, although it is always said that they steal far more than they are caught for. Rather it is who they are, who their family is, where they live, how often they are brought in, what their attitude is, and how many brothers, sisters, parents—step or real—uncles, aunts, common-law spouses, wives, or husbands they have who are also known and similarly identified.

Fieldnotes—Day 110—2 p.m. A boy of about 13 is brought in for shoplifting. One of the gaolers says, 'I can almost smell the African village on him . . .' All his actions are of one who is already very conversant with the system and its rules. As he comes through the door he is taking his property out for listing, and he tells me immediately that he is not giving his name or address or saying anything, but that he will give a telephone number for his mother and 'fuck all else'.

The store detective pantomimes behind his back that she would like to give him a good kick, and the staff smile. They classify him as a real prig and treat him in a curt and brusque manner. The telephone number is an East End one, and odds are laid that it will be in a certain area of the 'African villages'. The juvenile prig is given a seat in the detention room and directory enquiries come up with the subscriber as T— of No. 2 Y*** Court. There are roars of delight when the name and address is read out. This is 'the younger brother of X and the son of old Z, the bastard!' The boy is brought from detention and is told his name and address. The particulars of his last arrest and court appearance (which have been obtained) are read out to him. He merely says, 'I'm saying fuck all 'til me mother arrives' and turns and walks away to the detention room. Another juvenile shoplifter is brought in, but this one is female and is weeping and contrite. We cannot lodge our 'prig' with a 'non-prig', so we take him downstairs to harsher confinement. Mrs T— arrives and tells us that her son has been advised never to give his name and address to the police, as he's had hard times in the past. The detective who has now been assigned to the case, and who has worked in the East End for some years and knows the family well, snaps back that the police have had some 'bad times with her family' and that 'if her son didn't go stealing so consistently then he wouldn't know the police at all'. The detective questions young T— in the presence of his mother. He denies the theft and alleges the two store detectives have 'fitted him up' and gives a story about the shoe polish found up his jacket sleeves which the detective later says, would have taxed the imagination of Hans Christian Andersen'.

The staff hate him and his family. He is the 'juvenile prig par excellence' who will be the adult prig of tomorrow. This is the prime opposition, 'the bastard T—s, who cannot even tell the truth when they are caught' and whose mother says, 'if that's what my lad says happened then that's what happened, because my lad doesn't tell lies.'

Later the detective sits and drinks a coffee after they have gone. He grumbles to me, 'if only all the prisoners were the T—s and their cousins from the other criminal families, and we could exclude the social workers, the solicitors and the other do-gooders, we could really nail the bastards down.'

As 'real prigs' are 'animals' and are therefore non-human, they are subject to what I have called 'hard' as opposed to 'soft' enforcement; and to hard physical confinement in relation to their place of lodging. In addition, the 'prig' is regularly subject to aggressive verbal directives to enforce this control. Once captured the prig is 'caged or bedded down for the night' just like any other animal, and is unwillingly given blankets for his sojourn. There is a grumbling dissent from the gaolers about this prescribed facility which is seen to emanate from the machinations of the 'soft do-gooders' in society. The cells are centrally heated, they argue, so why give them blankets as well? During my own sojourn in the bridewell the blankets were only rarely cleaned and were jokingly said to be 'full of animals [fleas] which will provide company for the animals we bring in'. The logic of the system is apparent. The inhuman 'prig' is never really perceived to need a blanket simply because he is 'an animal' and in the wild, animals seldom use blankets! His classifiable dirt further makes it suitable that he should receive a dirty blanket (if such a system must be condoned), for clean blankets rarely feature in the houses in the 'African villages', where he lives when not in captivity. Scathing comment is made by 'polises' who have to go to these houses about the lack of blankets on beds or of their substitution by old coats or dirty rags. I myself have been in dozens of these 'sticky mat houses' during my days as a 'collar feeler', where a 'polis' sits down with reluctant trepidation, and often lands on sticky furniture in surroundings where the stench of ingrained dirt is achieved only after some considerable time. In 1983, the *Guardian* (28 June 1983) reported a visit by an NSPCC inspector to a typical 'claggy mat house'[9] which any detective or 'real polis' would immediately recognize:

My feet were sticking to the carpet as I made my way through the litter of derelict furniture I realised that the floor was covered with dog and cat excreta . . . the kitchen floor was strewn with dirty smelling clothing and

---

[9] Another phrase used in the North-East is 'claggy mat houses'. 'claggy = clarts = muddy clay = sticky dirt'.

empty tins, there was no food in the house ... The bathroom was unusable ... everywhere the smell was overpowering ...

Defined as 'dirt', the 'prig' must be purified to effect an ordered society, but 'You only search his socks and underclothing for stolen property at your peril' was a reminder I was given by the gaolers on my return, for his power to pollute is enormous!

At meal times in the Bridewell, the food is brought by the gaolers from a café where we have a contract. It is too far away for easy delivery and we use a van to collect it. We have a system of metal carrier containers, but eventually it is served on cardboard plates with plastic spoons and almost inevitably by the time they have got through the traffic and brought it back to the Bridewell, the food is cold. (From fieldnotes)

The gaolers always 'go down to feed and water them' and lin-guistically create another link in the negative perception of 'the prig' as an animal in a zoo. During my time in the bridewell the quality of food was so poor that we even changed the contract to another café although the gaolers deplored this move and the slight improvement in the quality, equating it to 'soft enforce-ment' and the influence of 'do-gooders'. Even when breakfast is a rubbery lukewarm fried egg and a slice of white 'plastic' bread and marge, it is still said to be 'much too good for them'.[10]

The 'prig', as we have seen, is often represented by a 'prig solicitor' or 'a dog who barks for him'. He is often informed of his arrest within minutes of the 'prig's' arrival in the bridewell by the 'jungle telegraph'. When the 'prig' is wanted for some offence he is said to be 'on the run', or has 'gone to earth'. Alternatively he is 'off the side' as opposed to being straight-in-line, like the un-bending, rigid 'polis'. The female 'prig' is always said to be 'a right hard little bitch (or cow)'. This use of animal metaphor

---

[10] In 1980/1 I was involved in a piece of research to install microwave cookers and pre-packed frozen meals for prisoners, with a choice of five main courses and breakfasts. A 6-month trial in the bridewell coincided with the extensions to prisoner facilities mentioned above. The gaolers were dismissive of such generous facilities to 'prigs' and when I moved to South Shields division in 1981 and the 'Prisoners' meals project' followed, I noted the station sergeants were outraged at such generous and humane treatment of their adversaries, and were especially con-temptuous of the 5-choice main meal system. 'I put me hand in the bloody freezer for six dinners for six prigs and they get whatever I take out ... and they should think themselves bloody lucky they get anything at all ...' (sergeant: South Shields).

reverses the symbolism which defines the 'polis's' ideal woman in society at large. Here the female is a 'hard' bitch and not the soft creature to be found in the metaphorically pliable 'bunny girls or turtle doves'. In effect we are witnessing another inversion to maintain the logic of police practice and belief and to ensure the integrity of a negative 'prig' identity.

The 'prig' is also 'crooked'. He *is* a 'right crook', which is defined in the dictionary as a bent or twisted thing (as opposed to something straight), or even as illness and death (as opposed to health and life). The 'crooked prig' is therefore bent or of death, as opposed to being straight or of life.[11] In effect he is physically and socially deformed and has to be straightened out in a purifying process.

As I have indicated, the 'prig' is to be 'nailed down' and 'fixed' both in time and space. He is perceived as disorderly movement across the face of society and his fixture is therefore analogous to the imposition of social control. This stasis Purce (1974: 21) contends equates with death: '[and anything] which prevents and obstructs [movement] by imposing rest and immobility, is the death principle'. Foucault (1977: 218), writing of this predisposition in the control agencies for the prevention of uncontrolled movement, argues convincingly that 'one of the primary objects of discipline is to fix; it is an anti-nomadic technique'. Once 'nailed down', the 'prig' becomes disciplined and his pollution becomes somewhat neutralized. This belief in the control of movement is a primary means of containing ambivalence and can be found in many other guises across society. Okely (1975*b* and 1983), for example, has shown that movement and stasis are primary structuring binaries for gypsy society in the United Kingdom, and how any control of the gypsy's ability to travel is often equated with social death; for the ability of the dominant non-gypsy society to impose such controls over the traveller renders the gypsy visible to the power of that larger society. It is not surprising, therefore, to find that the 'prig' is often said by the 'polises' to be descended from gypsies, or that some of the most

[11] It is interesting to note that in the counter-culture's alternative language of the late 1960s, 'straights' were tobacco cigarettes and therefore of straight or legalized culture, while 'joints' ('bents' or 'crookeds' I might suggest) were made from cannabis and were in counter-cultural opposition to structure.

famous 'prig' families on Tyneside are said to be 'second generation gypsy horse thieves'.

Another linguistic aspect which may have significance is that
the 'prig' is always said to be a 'right b*a*stard', with the flattened
northern 'a' of 'b*a*stard' vehemently emphasized. This may be
just a useful expletive, but its insistent repetition seems to reveal a
possible metaphoric role of semiotic import for the idea of being
born out of wedlock. The 'real polises' who use this phrase
ad infinitum, are from an institutionally ordered world where
regulations demand every facet of social life be declared for approval. A discipline code controls vast areas of private activity
which most other citizens would feel was their own concern. For
example, written permission to live where one does is still necessary and an ordered, respectable address is required (an 'African
village' address would fail to win approval). Furthermore it is
only twenty years since a potential spouse had to be offered up to
the hierarchy for examination of social acceptability (see Young
1984, *re acceptable* wives). I suspect then that a 'real b*a*stard' to
these policemen is more than just an expletive. As the animal
'prig' is the primary classificatory disorder in the real polis's'
world, he is 'matter out of place' in any conventional marriage—
for in the animal world, the cultural trappings of marriage are
unknown. Inevitably the offspring of these non-cultural animal
liaisons will therefore produce further aspects of the body-
unsocial in the 'right b*a*stard'. Like the term 'prig', I suspect the
phrase and its use might be steeped in linguistic conservatism,
denoting more than it might initially suggest.

The hated 'prig' is also called the 'scum', 'the dross', or the
'dregs of society'. Such straightforward real 'dirt' ideally needs
to be removed to deny the disorder which dirt produces. Total
power over the body is the primary objective, for the control of
the 'prig' and his social death by confinement (or literally by his
physical demise) is an ultimate achievement. 'If only we could use
the humane killer on them,' I hear on more than one occasion.
The humane killer, used to dispose of problems such as a dog
seriously injured in a road accident, is a gun which fires a bolt
into the brain. Again it seems entirely fitting that this means of
disposing of useless animals should be seen as the ideal way of
dealing with that other useless animal, the 'real prig'.

The actual demise of 'prig' is an occasion for some celebration. The death of a 'real prig' in a road accident was noted with some satisfaction, and when a burglar fell from the top of a building he was attacking it created great happiness in the bridewell among the officers. The short visit by another well-known family 'prig' brought recollections that his younger brother had died early from cancer and had 'saved the country a good deal of time and money keeping him in custody'; while the early demise of C—, noted in the deaths column of the local paper, set off reminiscence about the fortuitous deaths of a number of 'real prigs'. Of course, in death, the 'prig' is finally straightened out, totally controlled, and literally 'nailed down'.

However, since the death penalty is no longer in use, and incineration—which is the best way to purify dirt—is socially unacceptable, incarceration is seen as the method by which 'prig' extermination can now best be achieved. Minimum mobility results in the social death of such 'dirt' and thus all the bridewell measures used to purify and depersonalize the body of the 'prig' are methods for achieving this slow, social death in the 'cooler' and create modern day transformations of the fast, hot, physical death sought in purification by incineration. Like the linguistic hangovers, these attitudes are a continuity of deeply held views about the need for pain in punishment and a rejection of ideas about rehabilitation.

TATTOOS AND THE 'REAL PRIG'

The 'real prig' in his 'African village' is not as free and unrestrained as the 'polis' believes. He is perhaps even more constrained in thought and action than the 'polis'. Ill educated, socially deprived, and often in custody or prison for long periods, especially during his adolescence, he inevitably belongs to the lower socio-economic classes. Poorly educated, physically and mentally undernourished, and often living in squalid and undistinguished surroundings, he has a narrow social existence, living on what is said to be his 'regular diet of brown ale and chips'. Contrary to the movement and freedom of a wild animal, the 'prig' is always oppressed and not infrequently physically constrained. His apparently wild and undisciplined natural life is therefore illusory; indeed it might more easily be seen to be a dull, sombre world of control and limitation.

To offset this reality I believe the 'prig' uses alternative conceptual systems which metaphorically express his own inner freedom and humanity and deny those negative perceptions of inhumanity presented continually to him by society and his captors. By adorning and illustrating his body with tattoos, the 'prig' symbolically uses his body to make a statement about his own perception of social value and status. In an unwitting support of Lévi-Strauss's (1969) belief that animals can be considered as categories or goods to think with, the 'prig' uses their totemic potential by drawing certain kinds of allegedly free species all over his body. This use of animal metaphor and symbol makes a positive value statement for 'prig' culture, and transforms the negative use of animality by the 'polises'.

In his own war against the 'polises', the 'prig' uses the tattoo as a structuring system which no institutional ordering can remove. Even with his name and address taken, his clothing and personal property removed, his human identity stripped and depersonalized inside the 'total institution' of the bridewell, he can still maintain his identity. He has his freedom, his movement, his life and humanity, and therefore his individuality illustrated all over his body. Furthermore he uses the tattoo to deny the normal direction of power, which, as I have said, flows from the legal institution to obtain control over the individual. When a 'prig' clenches his fist and presents the initials A.C.A.B. tattooed on his knuckles, he is making a symbolic assault on the institution of law by proclaiming '*A*ll *C*oppers *A*re *B*astards'.

The semiotic nature of tattoos has occasionally been denied or their designs merely written off as being of a decorative nature. Yet Lévi-Strauss (1973: 239–56) recognized that body painting often contains unconscious social meanings. Geertz (1975: 351), describing Lévi-Strauss's interpretation of Caduveo body tattoo and elaborate designs, suggested he 'thought he could see a formal representation of their aboriginal social organization'. I would not suggest the tattoos on the 'prig' reveal his whole social organization, however they seem to contain more than even he himself attributes to them. When I asked about them, I inevitably got the usual reply: '... well everybody has them ... it's the thing to do ... all me mates have got them ...' (from fieldnotes). However, in 'prig' tattoos there appears to be a whole unspoken language. They seem to be a perfect indicator of the 'prig's' own semantic and structural identity, defining for him who and what it is to be 'one of us'. It can hardly be accidental that the chosen forms of the tattoos with their wealth of animal symbolism seem to express an inner freedom which can never be totally controlled even when the wearer is in prison and denied normal human identity. For not only do they invariably symbolize the wild, free, untamed animals of the world, they also restate the 'prig's' name, his identity, his girl-friend, his wife, his mother and father, and his own allegiances.

The 'polis', of course, recognizes this structural indicator and further uses the 'prig tattoo' to define who the 'real prig' is.[12] In the police world where short hair and scrubbed body are equated with cleanliness, culture, and correctness, the animals on the 'prig tattoo' support the contention that he is dirt, polluted, bodily impure, wild, and uncultured. Consequently, to effect his control, in a further mortifying process, the tattoo is taken and used to identify; and although it cannot be removed it is recorded and collated on the charge sheet and the criminal indices. For 'real polises' then, the very idea of 'tattoo' equals 'prig', while to 'the prig' the tattoo equals identity, humanity, and a corresponding individuality made manifest on the body.

Case Study 8

Fieldnotes—Day 88. . . . the first 13 are brought in from prison on remand. I log them in and record their property. Of the 13, eight have extensive tattoos: David D— has an eagle's head on his left thigh. Frank E—has a girl, flowers, red indians, daggers, scrolls, his parents' and girlfriend's names. He has hearts and initials on his hands, arms and chest. H— has a splendid technicolour scorpion seated in the joint between thumb and forefinger of his right hand, with claws extended across the back of the hand.

[12] D. R. Smith (1981), a Merseyside policeman, in an unpublished thesis, considered the various non-verbal cues policemen considered to be indicators of criminality. Tattoos were 'rated highly amongst the single cue, static factors' (p. 84). On the incidence of tattoos, Smith quotes data in respect of Borstal trainees for 1976, which showed 64.4% of 6,796 subjects to be tattooed. Unfortunately in the pages of analysis (pp. 84–94) priority is largely given over to the statistical incidence of tattoos and only slight attention is paid to the meaning or content, which is broken down somewhat bizarrely into categories of non-obscene and non-facial; non-obscene and facial; obscene and facial; obscene and non-facial; but without any comment on the semantics of this classification.

J— has multiple tattoos on the face, arms and body. On his face and earlobes he has stars. He has the common 'borstal spot'—a blue dot—on his cheek (which also appears as a series of spots on the knuckles). On each hand between thumb and forefinger he has large, deadly looking blue/black spiders. When I show an interest in them, he tells me, 'a lorra people divvent like them . . .'

Day 127 Fieldnotes—2 young men are brought in for committing criminal damage. They are both covered in 'prig tattoos'. I ask about them. They have had them done professionally, although many of those I see are self-inflicted. They can give no reasons for having them, other than the regular, inarticulate, grunted replies of 'me mates have gorrem . . . we've aall gorrem; its what yi do roond here.'

B— O— has a peacock, a shark and a butterfly in glorious colour—reds, greens, yellow and blue. He also has his nickname initialled onto his arm and on his left arm he has a lightly clad cowgirl with bare bum, stetson and six guns, which stretches from elbow to wrist. He also has a bulldog with a fierce face and boxing gloves on, and a dagger with a hideous snake coiled around it. On his arm he has N.K.A.B., indicating his connection with the North Kenton Aggro Boys. His associate has Jesus on the cross, on his chest in full colour, along with the initials INRI, which he understands to mean 'Jesus King of the Jews'. I ask why he chose this design (I've seen it four or five times recently) and he tells me he had it done because he 'is a bit religious'. He also has scrolls and flowers, daggers and snakes; but the one we like the best is the wriggling pink worm he has coming out of his navel, with a passing swallow catching it in its beak.

Day 82 Fieldnotes R— R— comes in (again). He has a panther tattooed on his forehead, in red, green, blue and black. He has the professionally created Red Indians, naked women, hearts with scrolls, and Mam and Dad on his arms. He also has some self-inflicted ones and on each finger he has the letters l.o.v.e. and h.a.t.e. Above each knuckle he has a small matchstick man with a halo, like the Saint emblem in the Leslie Charteris novels. One of these little matchstick men has been given an enormous penis and has the word 'sexy' tattooed below. On his right thigh, he has a tattooed Christ on a cross, while on the other (the left and symbolically inauspicious), he has the devil.

James M— is in for robbery. He has tattooed flames coming from his anus—and on the left buttock he has the devil stoking the flames, while on the right, he has an angel blowing out the flames. Again the left and right symbolism is manifest. He tells us of his cell mate in prison who has a full hunting scene tattooed over his body. The huntsmen on horses gallop up his front and over his shoulder, following the hounds which stream down his back. But too late, the fox disappears up his arse hole, and only the tattooed brush sticks out.

Fieldnotes—Day 129—one of the 3 who has been hit by the pick-axe handles has some splendid tattoos drawn by the professional—Ossie, who has a studio in the East End. He has the cowgirl with the bare bum and stetson, who looks coyly over one shoulder—this is a regular in the Bridewell and I have seen it four or five times now. He also has the cartoon logo from the McEwans beer advert of the little old, bearded man, and the words 'I'm a geordie' on his other arm. He has 2 colourful swallows and hearts on his chest, with his own and his girl's name in each heart. He is examined by the doctor in relation to his injuries and we find that he has an eye tattooed on each cheek of his arse. I've seen them on each shoulder blade, but this is the first time on the buttocks. He tells us 'aah just got the idea in me mind and so aah went to Ossie and had it done. Me lass just laughed when aah told her aa'd had it done.' The two widely spaced eyes stare out at us as he bends down for the doctor; they cost £4 each.

Fieldnotes—Day 109—N— F— (known as Benny) is in with his new wife. He is a fat, unshaven, rough looking 26, while she is a thin, pale 17-year-old. They have been stopped in a stolen car which he has borrowed from 'a friend'. (It later turns out it has been dumped in the 'African village' every night since it was stolen and if it is still there on the following day is used by anyone who wants a car.) They have been married only a few days and while 'Benny' is interviewed we talk to her. 'Benny' writes her out of the incident in his statement and takes all the blame. No one believes in her innocence, but it is convenient to accept it. He has dozens of tattoos, with swallows, hearts, daggers, scrolls, 'death before dishonour', l.o.v.e. and h.a.t.e., and ACAB (All Coppers Are Bastards). He has professionally done red indians, birds and women. On his chest he has a mountain with a snow capped peak and a large eagle's head above it, with curved beak and sharp eye. On his back he has the two eyes, one on each shoulder blade; in between he has an eagle with curved beak and talons extended. I ask about these widely spread eyes and he tells me, 'they're so I can see anyone coming up from behind me, and then the bird will scratch their eyes oot.' She tells us they've been to Hexham for the day (about 20 miles west) on honeymoon. We are incredulous that they would go to this small country town, but it turns out that they *had* to go, because they were on bail to appear for shoplifting!

Fieldnotes—Day 140—M— has tattoos all over his arms, his hands, his chest and his stomach. He has lots of birds, red indians, animals, eagles. Around his neck he has a carefully drawn linked chain around which swallows are flitting.

Fieldnotes—Day 75—'Spider' H— has been caught climbing into a house through a first floor window. But his name is not only derived from his ability to scuttle up drainpipes. He has a huge triangular spider's web tattooed on his neck, exactly covering the V shape where any open-necked shirt would fall. Sitting in the centre of the web is a huge, fat, dark blue/black spider.

Many of these tattoos are superbly illustrated in *Skin Deep: The Mystery of Tattooing* (Scutt and Gotch 1974). Benthall and Polhemus (1975: 32) have also suggested that the body is a premier medium of expression and that 'scarification and tattooing—the permanent body arts—are aggressively conservative and unfashionable, for typically they are the bodily expression of small, social enclaves which are being swallowed up in the overall wave of social change'. In a footnote, Polhemus (ibid. 32) tells us:

tattooing and scarification . . . are interesting because they are extremely social and extremely antisocial at one and the same time . . . Tattoos and scarification are a kind of declaration of belief in the permanence of a particular small social group, be it of a group of prisoners, soldiers or the members of an isolated indian village. [13]

Burma (1965: 274), while arguing for a relationship between concepts related to delinquency and those related to self-tattooing, felt the delinquent subjects studied were 'usually unconcerned with the symbolism of their tattoos'. The bridewell clients could rarely pursue a symbolic assessment of their decoration, and it seems foolish to expect they should. However, Ross and McKay (1980), taking a more semantic approach to the self-mutilation and scarification carried out by adolescent girls in Borstal in Canada, argue that by carving the body, the girls were expressing independence, autonomy, and personal freedom. In effect, like the 'prig', they were declaring, 'it's my body and I can do anything I want with it. It's mine—it's the only thing I control completely. I'm its boss. The staff, the kids, or you and your rules can't stop me from doing anything I want to do to it. If I want to carve, I can—you can't stop me . . .'

For the same reason that graffiti on cell complexes is a restatement by the incumbent of his own personality and thus enrages the officers, so the tattoo fulfils a similar symbolic role by

[13] See also Hambly (1925), Schilder (1950), Speigal and Machotka (1974) for other accounts and illustrations of tattoos and body imagery.

making something of a psychological and social point to those in power. For the 'prig', it is a restatement of his individuality, where his progression from the amateur, self-inflicted tattoos of his juvenile life gives way to the more professional images he purchases during his adolescence, and mirrors the transition he also makes as his petty thieving becomes more adept and culturally structured.

Animal tattoos therefore seem to reflect the opinions, values, feelings, and meanings the 'prigs' attach to their lives. They provide clues to the underlying logic of 'prig' social structure and reveal much about his modes of thought and the nature of his valued categories of action. This whole area of animal symbolism and metaphor encompasses a maze of verbal and non-verbal referents, where one form of expression triggers off the next to build up into a total 'prig' logic which is as vital to the police as it is to the villains; for the 'polises' conceive of 'prigs' only as caged animals, moving to prison and back into the smelly squalor of their impoverished domestication. Metaphorically they are likened to domesticated birds who are collected, caged, and trained to 'be able to do their bird without complaint'. During their periods of release they become prized 'captures' for the hunter 'polises', especially if they can be 'netted and made to sing like canaries', or be made to 'squeal on their associates' (like pigs?).

The mediating role some ambiguous animals are made to play in the symbolic world of mankind is revealed by Leach (1964), while Tambiah (1969), Bulmer (1967), and Douglas (1957) have all shown how such animal categories as 'wild, domesticated or interstitial' can often relate to the conceptual understanding of social structure, or be linked to human social stratification and classification; and I suggest that animal tattoos play just such a role in this world of 'polises' and 'prigs'.

Inevitably the animal, insect, reptile, and bird tattoos symbolize independence and exemplify a common refusal to be controlled, tamed, domesticated, or caged. Consequently the primary mediators of 'prig' reality are the eagles, swallows, flies and spiders, scorpions, crabs, foxes, snakes, dragons, butterflies, tigers, peacocks, and other undomesticated animals or beasts, all of which are represented in the 'prig' tattoo!

Of course it follows that these tokens of prig' freedom are anathema to the 'polises', who use body cleanliness as a prime symbol of identity separating them from the 'prig'. As a result the 'polis' becomes keenly aware that he is precluded from using body mutilation or painting as a means of creating social identity. Nails must be cut, and as I have outlined above hair must be kept short and neat. Moustaches are clipped and have a military precision, while those who would stand aside to defy such conventions are rare; for they quickly learn to conform to the social norms or face the scorn and derision of their peers:

we are obsessed with the tiny nuances of order and style. 'Hair' really offends!! A constable on my shift has a full beard and moustache and this earns him constant derision and criticism. This is usually made in a jocular manner, but reflects the rejection of this physical form. One of his shift colleagues laughingly asks him: 'why grow all that fur around your face, when it grows wild around your arse?' The languages supports the ideology—and is significant! Hair equals fur i.e., it is animal, it is wild and should be hidden! 'Polises', are human not animal, and should ideally be smooth, clean and hairless. (Fieldnote: bridewell)

An increasing prevalence of pierced ears for men caused some problems in the 1980s, when police recruits appeared for interview sporting two or more gold earrings. Usually they were quickly dissuaded from continuing with their adornment, for tattoos and self-mutilation in the form of ear piercing are cultural devices primarily used by the opposed section of society. They are indicative of 'dirt' and obviously must be negatively attributed and consequently must be cleaned up and purified, as any such aberration must. We therefore find that when a 'polis' is tattooed it causes disquiet:

Case Study 9. Police Tattoos

Fieldnotes—Day 138—One of the PCs is very interested in my growing collection of 'prig tattoos'. He is an ex-submariner, about 30 years old; a cheerful man who is extremely neat, with a carefully cultivated moustache and clean military appearance. His uniform is immaculate. He has been in submarines for some years and tells stories of 'being locked away in the can', which seems to have close analogies to the life of the regular prig. He has been locked away for months at a time with an all male crew, then was released for short periods of leave before going 'back inside the can'. I note he has now joined another closed and disciplined male order.

He has animal tattoos on his legs and arms and tells me that he has a spider tattooed on his toes. He grins conspiratorially as he shows them to me and I note they are all homologous to those the prigs favour. They are the animals of the wild and uncontrolled kind. He talks about the pride in having them put on, and I again note that the perception of this cultural form as positive or negative symbol depends entirely on where one stands, and in which society.

Because 'polises' cannot wear tattoos and need to maximize their perception of animal tattoos as being negatively concomitant with the 'real prig', this relatively new 'polis' had felt it necessary to remove two swallows he'd had tattooed on the back of his hands. This operation had been done after he had joined the police, when the cultural barriers expressive of this separation between clean 'polises' and negative, dirty 'prigs' indicated an inversion of the status which tattoos had enjoyed in the navy. Such bodily anomaly in the police can never be auspicious, for the severe social constraints embodied in the semantics of law, order, rigidity, and control make for intolerance of ambiguity.

Across the various police forces this symbolic power of tattoos and other bodily scarification continues to be used to make statements about cultural value. Kent police put would-be recruits on notice that tattoos below the elbow are unacceptable (*Police Review*, 12 December 1986), while Suffolk police announced they would reject applicants if 'they are marked in a way that offends accepted standards of decency'.

A proclaimed common belief in a standard of bodily decency clears the way for prejudice to be exerted against those who offend and policemen with tattoos quickly learn that this prejudice can easily mar a career, for their decoration is a case of matter being very much out of place:

An ambitious sergeant who has the potential of reaching a relatively high rank in due course has a panther tattooed on his forearm. He is very conscious of it and constantly apologises for it. He tells me he had it done when he was only thirteen and lived in an area which, as he puts it, 'produced a high percentage of prigs, and where tattoos were the thing to have'. He now intends to have it removed by plastic surgery. (Fieldnote, HQ, 1980.)

AMBIGUOUS 'PRIGS', AMBIGUOUS 'POLISES'

In the charged situations of the bridewell the 'prigs' are controlled by an all-encompassing and somewhat tautological system of logic. By merely 'knowing the ropes' or because of genealogy and a residential qualification, these 'real prigs' reinforce self-confirming principles for the 'polises'. Such gross perceptions close the circle and ensure the system is seen to be correct; for always these 'polises' are consoled by the repetition of established classifications and are disturbed by the unknown and the ambiguous. The awkward category which fails to fit easily into a well-attested world will confound; and is said to be an unfortunate trend which is on the increase.

For 'real polises' and especially those with the status of 'collar feeler', 'body snatcher', or 'capture machine', there was allegedly an era which can be equated to something like an anthropological 'dream time'; a mythological golden age when the duality of 'prig' versus 'polis' is said to have been the only factor in the game. This was a time, it is proposed, when the two sides existed in something akin to splendid isolation 'and when the animals could be dealt with as animals'. Stories are continually told of this mythological epoch, when 'prigs' were allegedly 'nailed' without any interference from the now burgeoning social justice administration machine. I am reminded by 'the polises' of my own days as a cadet in this same place, when the 'prigs' were battered physically if they so much as lifted a finger to the officer. Now the police complaints system protects them, and the violence of two decades ago has simply vanished. I am reminded that few 'prigs' would have legal representation then, or that few seemed to have the temerity to plead 'not guilty' when they were caught dead to rights. This was a time without real interference from the police hierarchies, who have also burgeoned and moved out of the 'real world of policing' into a world of 'power politics and grappling for promotion'. This was an era, it is fondly said, when the media was pro-police, and the critical article was unheard of. At that time the dogooder, the social worker, the publicity-hungry MP, the hated sociologist, and the 'lefties' of organizations such as the National Council for Civil Liberties had little or no credibility, or simply did not exist. This was a time, the mythology repeats, when the 'prig' stole or burgled and the 'polis' locked him up by force to show who was boss.

Now, the 'polises' complain, the non-controller increasingly intrudes. This decidedly ambiguous 'polis' may not 'feel collars'. He may not even be clean, uniformed, and smart or wear a detective's suit and tie. He may deal with marginal crimes such as homosexuality, gaming, prostitution, drugs, fraud, political deviancy, or licensing offences; or he may not be dealing with crime in any form, however ambiguous. He may have 'spent a life-time avoiding "real work", moving from training department to community relations'. He may even be a juvenile liaison officer or in charge of the traffic wardens. He may be a boss—one of the despised nine til five administrators—or from what the 'real polises' describe as 'the dreaded British Transport Police'. He may be a Ministry of Defence policeman—who is definitely not 'us', even though a long correspondence in *Police Review* in the mid-1980s sought to claim his place as 'real polis'. He may even be a special constable, whose status throughout my 33-year police career has always been revealed simply by a disparaging and descending tone of voice used to intone, 'specials! . . .'

In a similar vein, the various 'private' police forces, such as the parks police and the docks police, constantly proclaim their validity in the columns of *Police Review*; and just as regularly, articles and letters appear to deny them any comparable status. Such marginality is almost to be expected in such a world, for any ambiguity destroys the idealistic duality of 'them ~ us', and so the perfect world of 'real polises' becomes set about with 'unreal polises' and 'unreal prigs'.

Who is in control now? Allegedly in the 'dream time' it was our war with the 'prigs', while everyone else from the uninformed outside was kept out. Today, however, the illegal act and the per-petrator may show aspects of marginality not easily categorized into black and white binaries; and even though the anomalous be-haviour may be illegal, this may be challenged. Often the new deviancies seem to defy easy classification and, though unlawful, may not easily be seen to threaten the body social or physical. Many of these ambiguous crimes do not lie easily within the prov-ince of the traditional enemy from the underprivileged 'prig' society; indeed they may well be carried out by the literate and powerful and be supported by individuals or groups from within the dominant society.

As I have suggested above, some drug-taking, though visibly harmful, is not only culturally respectable, but is assiduously advertised and promulgated; while other habits are harried and pursued relentlessly by the forces of control. Nor does it seem to the 'polises' that the courts can now be relied on to support or share their desire to 'nail' the 'prig'. No longer is it possible to put someone up before the court the next morning and see him 'weighed off', for now there is disclosure of prosecution evidence, legal representation for all defendants, and a battery of 'ambiguous controllers' to intrude on the game of 'cops and robbers'. As a result, the ritualistic war against crime is increasingly separated into different phases by the 'polises'. First there is the action on the streets, where the initial phase of justice is subject to the least interference by these new intruders in the drama of discipline and punishment. Subsequently there is the journey into the custodial situation in the police station or charge room. Here, in the back of a police car, deals can be initiated; and as the occasional disciplinary action shows, instant justice and punishment extraneous to any court proceedings will sometimes be imposed (although its prevalence is on another plane entirely to that of the 1950s when many hidings were meted out!). Later in the bridewell a further version of negotiated justice occurs, where bail and other small perks of the system can be used to maintain the dominance of the controllers. Subsequently there is the administrative file creation, when the officer in the case has to find enough evidence to make a charge fit and ensure he has at least a 51 per cent chance of winning. Here he has to satisfy a battery of file checkers and administrators, who seek potential flaws as he tries to reduce the complexities of social behaviour to a statement on paper.

Finally there is the court appearance which now only comes into effect long after real control has been applied at street level. The court hearing is always seen by 'the polises' to be a specifically legalistic ritual in the war between the two sides, where a peculiar institutionalized version of 'the truth' is sought, and which is beset by the adversarial format and a concern for rules of evidential practice. To the 'polises', the lawyers seem to be tied up in a system obsessed with legal precedent and the nuances of gamesmanship rather than with any search for the truth. Here again a system of judicial negotiation often removes (for the police) the last vestiges of practical reality, leaving a mere symbolic ritual to be played out and enacted largely for the benefit of the 'ambiguous controllers' in the legal drama.[14] In consequence, a credibility gap in the legal process occurs, and even 'prig' solicitors regard it as a game; while the 'polises' understand that:

what goes on in court hàs nowt to do with what happens out there in 'the real world' . . . By the time all the lawyers have done their deals and the social workers and probation officers have been led up the garden path by the 'prigs', they might as well give all the villains a pound out of the poor box, and let us all go home. (From fieldnotes: detective sgt)

As Reiner (1978*b*) indicates, cop films reflect a growing feeling that policemen no longer know where they are. Having created a self-confirming system, fiercely intolerant of ambiguity, they seem increasingly to be faced with new phenomena which cannot be fitted into the preferred polarities. As Reiner reflects:

the emergence of the cop as hero cannot simply be explained by a grow-ing fear of crime in the streets and a public preoccupation with law and order . . . I think the new blue-coated heroes signify a growing doubt about the meaning and possibility of law and order' . . . In the recent cop films [the] optimism has gone. But the reason is not just that the sheer volume of crime has increased. What actually prevents the crime being cleared up in the first reel are the own goals scored against the hero by people nominally on his own team . . . In the conservative kind of movie, like 'Dirty Harry', the people who shackle the cop are liberal do-gooders who are 'more for the criminal than the victim'. In the liberal variety like 'Serpico' . . . the problem is corruption within the police dept., or fatal flaws within the cop personality, as in 'Electra Glide in Blue'.[15]

For the bridewell 'polises' such ambiguities are believed to be the staff of life to a increasing range of 'anomalous prigs' who exist in-

---

[14] Baldwin and McConville (1977) earned the displeasure of the legal pro-fession by showing just how theatrical the world of negotiated justice has become. Plea bargaining, which is an integral part of the American system, was shown to be a norm in the British Crown Courts, but of course could not be admitted even though all the participants know it goes on. It is this sort of juggling with reality which confirms for me that the whole criminal justice system can best be under-stood as a ritualistic, social drama, where the exploration of metaphor and symbol can be allowed to reveal truths which cannot be spoken or admitted by the actors.
[15] The various police representative bodies have been very concerned with the portrayal of police culture in some TV drama series in the 1980s. Early editions of *The Bill*, and especially Roger Graef's *Closing Ranks* series, which expressed sim-ilar doubts to those identified by Reiner, earned vituperative comment in some quarters. The fact that these series were set in Britain is not insignificant, for no similar fear was expressed about the inevitable flaws in the individual police psyche which were contained in such series as *Hill Street Blues*, where ambiguity is just as prevalent, but is American.

side the control industry. These social workers, do-gooders, probation offices, investigative journalists, sociologists, academics,
left-wing councillors, and the like, although *within* the structure
of the criminal justice system or control-industry[16] rank alongside the criminal opposition, for they seem set to deny the 'polis'
his freedom to nail the 'prig' in ways which 'the ordinary man in
the street really wants' (from fieldnotes).

Of course the daily reading matter of many policemen extends
no further than the *Sun* or the *Daily Mail*, and so their views and
understanding of any liberal philosophy is somewhat coloured by
a jingoistic and simplistic right-wing view of the world, in which
such groups are arraigned with the villain as antagonists to 'law
and order'. This is especially true of the socialist politician and
the social worker, who are used continually by 'the polises' in
their defensiveness. Always they castigate the left and throughout
the 1980s have denigrated the Labour Party in the columns of the
Federation magazine *The Police*, with Gerald Kaufmann, 'Red'
Ken Livingstone, and Arthur Scargill perhaps holding key position as chief bogeymen.

Many of these caring sections of the 'control industry', and especially the social workers, are stereotyped to set them off against
the 'polises'. In 1987/8, I worked with a chief superintendent who
used laughingly to contrast political items from his copy of *The
Times* with those in the *Guardian*, which is not a paper to be seen
carrying![17] His somewhat jocular image of the social worker

---

[16] On visits to some universities and polytechnics to give papers, I noted with
some wry amusement that departments teaching the qualification in social work
(CQSW) reluctantly acknowledge they are part of 'the control industry', though of
course 'the prigs' have few illusions. Bridewell 'prigs', I recorded, even call their
social workers 'soft cops'. I particularly liked the fact that 'prigs' use their own
'hard' and 'soft' binary to define their opposition to all of these groups in the 'control industry'. As Hughes (1987: 174–5) also tells us, the nineteenth-century
criminal world despised authority and held 'do-gooders in contempt'. Little seems
to have changed.

[17] Ten years before this I used to buy the *Guardian* on the early shift in the
bridewell, earning all-round condemnation from my peers. In 1984, a uniform
Chief Inspector, seeing me with a copy at HQ, asked: 'do Special Branch know
you read that thing?' In 1988, when I deliberately carried a copy into the HQ's
canteen to see if there was any reaction, I had to wait no more than 10 seconds before two derogatory comments came my way, and a Superintendent told me 'ahh,
this explains everything!' As a survey (*Police Review*, 9 Oct. 1987) showed, the
Guardian is the least favoured daily paper amongst policemen, while the *Daily
Mail* and *Express* were read by over 50% of the lower ranks.

which we built up on a white board was a cartoon image of a bearded, bespectacled, unkempt sandal-wearing hippie and reader of the *Guardian*. To complete this paradigm of police stereotyping, he declared this 2CV Citroën owner to be a member of Green peace, Friends of the Earth, and animal rights groups, and he would inevitably sport an anti-nuclear badge on his car.

I was not surprised to find that in the bridewell the officers cut items from their daily papers and stuck them on the wall, to reinforce the view that 'hard enforcement' was their creed:

... Sick Society blamed on do-gooders ... (*Daily Mail*, 12 April 1977)

... How I'd wipe the smirk off the face off Juvenile Crime—William Whitelaw, M.P., the next Home Secretary ...[18] (*Daily Mail*, 18 July 1977)

... Misguided Judges—Lord Denning apart, so many have gone soft ... (*Daily Mail*, 14 October 1977)

All of these media declarations were much appreciated by the 'polises' for they help to redress a balance. They feel that radical responses to crime have gone too far and believe it is largely because of these 'ambiguous controllers' who have removed the temporal and spatial disciplines contained in their perfect world of crime and punishment. Reiner (1978*c*: 22– 3) describes a Police Federation Conference where such antipathies are clearly displayed:

[the police] doubt the commitment to 'law and order' of the government which is more interested in 'releasing from prison, pimps, perverts and bombers, than it is in the Police Force', in a phrase used by a loudly applauded speaker. Not that they place much trust in the Conservatives either ... although it seems that most policemen would have more faith in the Tories. In non-party political terms too, the Police remain profoundly conservative. Targets like homosexuals or race relations organisations are subject to ridicule and abuse ... Organisations for prisoners' rights and Radical Alternatives to Prison were condemned ... 'There's one alternative to prison—going straight.'

Such conservatism causes the 'polises' to reject anything other than a punishment model of penal discipline as being a well-

---

[18] In due course this Tory party 'promise' delivered 'the short, sharp, shock' as an extension of detention for young persons and allied it to a regime of physical discipline. Although no subsequent analysis suggests it had any real influence on crime, this measure met with great favour amongst the 'polises', for it was essentially about physical control, with restricted movement and enhanced discipline for 'prigs'.

meaning but futile attempt at social rehabilitation. They know and quote the old Jesuit maxim, 'give me the child and I will give you the man', and argue that as a 'prig' is created from birth, their ways are deeply ingrained 'in the blood' by the time we get them at the age of criminal responsibility, which is currently set at 10 years of age. As few juveniles under 15 years receive sentences which the 'polises' feel invoke 'real control', any redemption of the offender is considered a utopian dream, 'for we get them several years too late'. In the mid-1960s I worked with a detective sergeant who pre-empted James Anderton by two decades in firmly believing castration was the only means of ensuring that new generations of irredeemable 'prigs' would not be generated.

Indeed, because of long practical mastery in this melodramatic world of crime and conflict, the 'real polises' seem intrinsically to understand Foucault's argument that regardless of whether one is involved in treatment or punishment of the offender, the eventual objective is to obtain power over a fellow being. Conditioned by conservative beliefs in matters concerning crime and punishment they follow the style of the Tory party, which as James (1978: 144–5) observed, 'tends to take satisfaction in a brittle, punitive retributive stance . . . [where] law and order is essentially a means of enforcing conformity'. But the 'polises' deride Tory politicians who vote not to reintroduce the death penalty, for they believe softer options cannot work with an enemy whose criminal practice is engendered even before birth. And although they tacitly acknowledge the whole meritocratic social system is weighted against those born into the dispossessed sections of society, they nevertheless argue with passion that as social reclamation does not work, we should revert to punishment, if for no other reason than as a means of revenge: 'we should think of the injured persons, and lock these 'prig' bastards up and throw away the key . . . for if they are locked up, then at least they can't go out screwing, or committing more crime'.

Constantly, I recorded there was grumbling dissent, ridicule, and abuse of proposals for any attempt to humanize the penal system or to introduce better welfare measures for prisoners. Almost inevitably the 'polises' rejected these out of hand and argued for retribution and the imposition of pain and suffering!

What is the reaction when ambiguity is created and the anomalous crime or the undefinable 'polis' and the marginal controller splits open the binary of 'us' and 'them'? The answer is that the 'polis' defends his mythological 'real world' or invokes his 'dream time', and in his defensiveness lashes out (metaphorically) as he draws in on himself and his peers to deny anything that cannot be fitted into the preferred categories.

In this situation he blames the police organizational system and derides his hierarchy. He is scathing of politicians for their perceived weakness and echoes a widespread view that society had changed for the worse, as respect for authority has paralleled a declining moral standard. In a study on the Metropolitan Police (Olins 1988) a range of perceptions similar to those I had witnessed a decade earlier in the bridewell were reported, with the rank and file described as being 'wary at best' in their attitudes to the way the world works. Again, the study indicated yearning in the ranks for a 'golden age' and a feeling of being beleaguered by problems of assimilating all the rapid changes in organization, new legislation, and changing social values.

Of course, when men are happier with yesterday's ideas and practices, there is always the tendency to look backwards to a better time. In 1987, in West Merica, when it was pointed out to a chief inspector there was nothing to be gained by the arduous and time-consuming stripping down of excess staples and superfluous note sheets from court files after the case was completed and finalized but before filing them in the archives: he was almost shocked, and complained:, 'what's the world coming too? . . . It's the thin end of the wedge . . . it's the slippery slope to ruin . . .', (from fieldnotes). [19]

Such insecurity and defensiveness was most evident in the bridewell, becoming almost tangible as the equivocal nature of the behaviour or incident became more obvious. It is observable in the following case studies, the first of which outlines an ambiguous crime and the marginal 'prig':

Case Study 10

Fieldnotes—Day 66—We have an interesting client. . . . He is a quietly spoken young man who has never previously been arrested. He has been brought in after a woman has complained of an 'indecent exposure' in a

---

[19] This obsession with unnecessary but comforting rituals meant that in West Mercia a cumbersome system of hand-written Occurrence/Incident books was only laid to rest with difficulty in the mid-1980s, long after they had vanished elsewhere, and even though the books duplicated manual or computerized records of incidents, accidents, minor complaints, and the like.

park at 8 p.m. She has been walking past the park in the dusk, when the young man has appeared from the bushes proudly waving what she describes to us as 'his weapon'. The enormous size of 'his weapon' is remarked on in her statement to a policewoman. The penis protruding from the trousers, however, is a simulated one, about 12″ long and made very realistically from a piece of nylon stocking stuffed with cotton wool. Her complaint, cannot classifiably be fixed. 'Flashers' are required in law to have 'wilfully, openly, lewdly and obscenely exposed the person' and in so doing to have 'insulted a female'. 'We may have one insulted female, boss, but we haven't got a real prick, so what's the offence?' It is not a crime (in the Home Office list of classifiable crimes) and so has low status to start with, but now we have something very ambiguous! A sergeant, an Acting Inspector and other 'polises' search diligently through the reference books to fix the behaviour within the boundaries of disorder, but of course it is too bizarre to be anticipated by any specific act of parliament. 'Try looking up the Waggling of Wool Willies Act . . .', says one gaoler. We fall back on the tried and trusted 'insulting behaviour whereby a breach of the peace can be anticipated'. The client is not a 'real prig' but is a 'bit of a wierdo', and the 'whole incident is really outside of the central tenets of the system, but the men and women search to make it fit known patterns of disorder. A policewoman, half in jest and half seriously, says, 'do you think he would plead guilty to drunk and disorderly?'

This is behaviour which falls into a structural no man's land, or into a classifiable limbo outside experience; for as Leach (1977: 23) has shown, 'the law concerning offences against sexual morality . . . is always ambiguous. In most Western legal systems there are certain categories of sexual offences which rate as crimes, but the police are usually very reluctant to do anything about such matters'. Nevertheless, the sex offender or 'flasher' is always seen in a somewhat disparaging light, whereas other ambiguous crimes occur in which the offender becomes really anomalous. At such times paradox and social enigma generate real difficulties for the 'polises'; for ambiguity denies them the use of emotional hatred of the opposition which is an essential part of their traditional binary practice and ideology. It is fascinating to watch as they attempt to reduce aspects of such an incident into simplified and easy to handle categories. For example:

Case Study 11

Day 116—fieldnotes—Detectives from the Drug Squad bring in two 'old friends' from my drug squad days. It is 7.45 p.m. and the gaoler, the

matron and I are playing interminable card games of 'beanie' as we wait
for the next arrival in the Bridewell. I am greeted by name by the two
clients. It is nine or ten years since I first came across them in the early
days of the counter-culture. Now they are responding to bail and are to
be charged with the manufacture of a form of amphetamine. Almost original 'flower' children, they have been following the associated philosophies of the counter-culture since the mid-1960s. Both still exhibit the
styles of that era, with long flowing hair, full beards, fringed caftans,
sandals and hand-made felt purses covered in symbols of the '60s hanging around their necks. Both M— and H— might have been successful
chemists, but only work as lab. assistants because their researches have
inexorably taken them outside of the law as they have dabbled in the
manufacture of various hallucinogens and amphetamine by-products.
They enthusiastically tell me about their current research (offence),
which has explored some side chain in the molecular structure of
amphetamine like substances. I am told by the Squad that it has been
difficult for the Forensic scientists to unravel their 'work' and this pleases
them greatly. They are charged and the drugs officers, who seem perplexed by them both, leave the Bridewell. M— and H— talk about
cannabis and the beliefs and attitudes they have in relation to its use.
M— is certain that the control of cannabis remains a vast plot by the big
industrial drug and tobacco companies.

It is quiet in the Bridewell and after they sign their bail forms, they
drink mugs of tea and chat about mutual friends and hippie philosophy.
They urge me to call around sometime to have a chat and expand upon
the symbolic aspects of cannabis, on which I am writing a paper.[20] After
they leave, the gaoler discusses this invitation to me to call and points out
this is only possible in what he calls 'these bizarre areas of police work'.
He reflects that 'you could never do that with a prig, but really those two
aren't prigs. I suppose if drugs hadn't been illegal, then those two would
never have even come into the frame.' He fits them precisely into the
margins of ambiguity, when he says, 'they are very nearly the general
public, aren't they?'

Another constable, who has watched and said very little, and has a less
enquiring mind than the gaoler, remarks on their 'funny clothes and their
awful freaky hair . . . !' He wants no part in the discussion on the ambiguity of their 'crimes' and won't be drawn into any contemplation of
them other than to use their appearance to define them as 'not us'. He
denigrates their style and decides 'they're just a couple of scruffy junkies
who need a good haircut and a bath'. I chide him, enjoying his difficult
attempts to define the two in terms which allow him to retain his singular

---

[20] At the time I was writing a seminar paper, 'The symbolic language of
cannabis' (Young 1979).

conception of 'the enemy', by pointing out that in fact they are very clean, not dirty! He dismisses this and says as far as he is concerned 'they're just a couple of long haired yobs'.

This 'polis' uses all the rigidities engendered by the self-confirming system I have described. He has fixed on to the long hair and hippie appearance, which he equates with dirt and disorder. The gaoler, however, has clearly seen they are peripheral to our dualistic 'real world' and on the boundary of 'humanity', for they are 'almost of the general public'. Had the current classification of public offences not included the once private delict of drug taking, then these two, as he said, 'would never have come into the frame'. This language continues to make use of the images of an encapsulation of activity, for its purpose is to frame, surround or cage the 'prig' inside firm borders,[21] and in any murder enquiry it is common to hear talk of 'who is coming into the frame now (as a suspect)'.

In these ambiguous areas, definitive boundaries slip and slide around. Not only can the activity be almost indefinable, but those who should control and be on the side of order may well be seen to have crossed boundaries to become something akin to the 'ambiguous prig'. In such cases these ambivalent social controllers can easily become subject to the same terms of abuse and negative metaphors of animality usually reserved for the 'real prig'. As defensive devices of exclusion, their aim is to separate and place the recipient beyond the limits of acceptable humanity, so that when we hear the 'prig solicitor' scathingly referred to as 'the dog who barks for the prig' we are left in no doubt that this is a controller who has moved beyond acceptable limits. In this negative and inhuman classification he becomes almost less human than the 'prig', in that he is the 'prig's dog' or animal slave!

This same logic is applied to 'unreal polises', and in the next case study we find the British Transport Police defined as 'mad hatters'—another metaphor of ambiguity, while the client—a Scots 'prig'—is merely the 'animal' that all Scots or foreign criminals are said to be:

Case Study 12

Fieldnotes—Day 105—It is 2.10 a.m. when we have the next prisoner. The British Transport Sergeant who, last week, I noted had been

---

[21] See Goffman 1975: chap. 8, on the *anchoring* of activity by framing.

described as being as 'mad as a hatter' comes in from the Central Railway
Station with another of his 'typical loony prisoners'. This is a 4′ 10″ 'animal' who has been taken off an Aberdeen to London train. He is
travelling on a concessionary ticket obtained in London by presenting a
British Rail employee pass, entitling the holder to cheap fares. The
Scotsman tells us he found the pass in Clapham, bought the return ticket
to Dundee and is on his way back south after Christmas. Now some
astute ticket Inspector has spotted an alteration in the dates on the
concessionary rail card and the man is now in the Bridewell while the
'mad BT Police Sergeant' thinks up all sorts of rare offences contrary to
the British Rail Acts which are both unknown and of no interest to us.

We wearily set out to 'fix' the Scotsman into areas the Court will be
familiar with. The first consideration the BTP sergeant suggests is a possible theft in Clapham. But we cannot prove the card was stolen, so is
there a possible 'theft by finding'? But who cares? There are millions of
passes and a phone call to the south suggests that finding out if this was
lost is too much trouble, apart from which our Magistrates' Clerk will not
be much interested in hearing a 'theft by finding' which occurred some
300 miles away. We move onto the 'obtaining the ticket at Kings Cross
by deception'. This is easier—it is a fraud to pose as the person named on
the card and obtain the ticket at a reduced price, but again this occurred
elsewhere and is of no interest to the courts here (or to our nightshift detective who cannot easily get a detection out of it for our local crime
figures). So we settle for the offence of 'Railway Fraud' or travelling by
rail without paying the correct fare, which can be tried wherever the culprit is caught. I note, on the next night from the charge sheet, that the
man was fined £20 while his ticket had cost £9 and the full fare was £36.
Of course he is 'No Fixed Abode', and so even though he has been given
time to pay, no one expects to see him again or the fine to ever be paid.
But the activity and the incident has been fixed, dragged into some
classifiable shape and categorized sufficiently to have it taken before the
court, in spite of the difficulties.

The 'prig' here is anomalous! Although he is a 'a midget
Scotsman, of no fixed abode', he is not our local 'prig' from our
'African villages' committing our offences. His misdemeanours
are moving offences in time and space and cannot easily be
'nailed' or 'fixed', defined and classified. The Bridewell staff play
out the whole incident as something approaching a dramatic farce,
with two lots of non-human players. First there is the mad, fat
sergeant (who furthermore is said to be too small to be a 'real
polis') and then there is the 'animal Scotsman'. All in all, the logging, the phone calls to London, and the charging procedure takes

us through to 6 a.m., and everyone is unhappy about the incident except the 'mad sergeant'. He is said to have this problem all the time for his 'prigs' are always moving; and as the Bridewell staff say, 'only the mad hatters in the Transport Police would take on the job'. Such cases occur continually to afford the 'real polises' clear opportunities to redefine who are the family, residential, regular 'real prigs'. They also restate who are the 'collar feelers' and who are the anomalous law enforcers; and set out the boundaries of where our space and time begins and ends, and where *no* place and *nowhere* starts. Such shades of grey continually reinforce the black and white polarities to show us where our structural margins lie. One of the 'real polises' who has watched the difficulties experienced in defining this incident, seemed to speak for all and emphasize his dissatisfaction with the ambiguous event. Unwittingly he paralleled Foucault's (1977) idea that discipline is an anti-nomadic technique, when he said of the Scots traveller, 'If only we could nail these fucking nomads down with six inch nails through their feet.' As the perceived ambiguity of the 'prig' increases, so we eventually reach a category of bridewell prisoner who is merely described as a 'one-off client', and is forgotten almost as soon as he or she leaves the premises. These are the 'almost human' offenders who fail to exhibit any of the classifying distinctions of the 'prig' which would turn them into the inhuman animal. Often these non-prig clients who brush up against the law are assisted by 'controllers' who are considered to outclass the client totally in 'prigishness'. I have collected many examples of this ambivalence in the notes I wrote up during my Bridewell posting, and the following case study merely exemplifies a situation where the status of a prisoner fluctuates, until at times he almost qualifies as 'human'; while the 'do-gooders' who rally to his assistance become the 'animal prigs'. These 'bastard lawyers and politicians' who have crossed a boundary and chosen to move onto the wrong side in the drama become a real enemy to the 'polises', for they epitomize the ambiguity that lurks in this world of power and control:

Case Study 13

*Fieldnotes—Day 114—*we have 'Mustapha' with us on a deportation order. He has stayed beyond his permitted time and has been served with a notice to quit Britain, but has failed to do so and now has been detained prior to deportation on a warrant signed by the Home Office. 'Mustapha' is an illegal immigrant and is treated with 'soft confinement' during his stay. He has lots of visitors while he waits for the Immigration Department to arrange his removal from our shores. Meanwhile we have to lodge him on the authority of the warrant. We send out to an Indian restaurant for suitable food, although I note that when this is obtained it is still said to be 'much too good for him'. But he is a 'wog' and so will always be seen to be less than human, simply because of his foreignness and the racism which is inherent in a system built on such rigid binaries of 'us' versus all the rest. Then from his mass of property we find that he has a Doctorate and he immediately becomes an 'acceptable wog'. The men, who only minutes earlier had been describing him as less than human, now question the wisdom of deporting 'such a brain'. Then the story moves on, and we hear that he has been dealing cheap goods from a market stall and has not been working at engineering in which he has his degree. The fact that his illegal status probably prevented such a career move is ignored. He loses ground again and his 'human' rating slips back to that of 'illegal wog'. But during the few days he is with us, he is never a 'real prig'.

Although foreign and not 'us', 'Mustapha' is on the borders of perceived humanity—especially with his qualification in engineering. His treatment is always 'soft' as opposed to 'hard', though it is doubtful if he realizes this! Several gaolers say the same thing during the few days he is with us: 'poor sod, he shouldn't be in here at all'.

Then I note the focus moves away from the client and shifts squarely on to the

[*Day 114 continued*] ... army of 'do-gooders' who have taken up 'Mustapha's' case. They become the target for the spleen of the staff. We have constant phone calls from the press and interested groups who the staff growl hatred for. We have well-known names from local and national politics on, and the staff moan about these 'bastard do-gooders who feel they should be involved for their own ends and jump onto the bandwaggon'. The Home office are phoning continually and the detective who has merely collected 'M' on the warrant for his detention prior to deportation, sits by the phone while a half-day of calls between London and the Bridewell ensues. He snarls and growls about the 'do-gooders who want a slice of the action'. We are informed of several well-known liberals who are household names and who are said to be 'interested in the case'. The staff are enraged and growl hatred for their interference.

One constable complains, 'If we got into any sort of bother in Bangladesh, do you think any of these fucking do-gooding wankers would move a muscle to help us? Would they fuck . . .'

There is raging contempt for the MPs who have now become involved. The detective is tight lipped with anger as they 'play their socialist politics, while the polises get the brunt of having to enforce the bloody laws they pass and then don't agree with'.

We now have a local 'prig solicitor' in who has been acquired to assist 'M' and the media are on from all over the country asking 'what is M. charged with? . . .', 'when will he be charged and with what offence, and if he is not charged when will you be letting him go. . .'. Television news shows groups outside Durham Prison with placards denouncing the facist police for holding similar illegal immigrants, and local MPs are interviewed saying they are 'worried because they cannot find out how Q— (in prison) is being held without being charged with any offence.' MPs ring us and a multiplicity of organizations are asking, 'what are the police up to?' The men moan about the hierarchy who are silent and fail to redress the imbalance over what is a simple matter of law.

The discussion on the event goes on all day in the Bridewell, involving everyone who comes in. A detective growls, 'do the bastards want us to implement their laws or not?' A gaoler and a passing polis reflect on the case: 'if these bloody do-gooders and socialists look up the bloody laws that *they* have passed they will find that *their* Parliament has ordered a man can be detained until deported if he is found to be an illegal immigrant. Now these bastards cannot make up their minds. Either these bloody prigs want us to act on their detention orders, or they don't.' The lawyers and do-gooders, the MPs and the liberals have now become 'bloody prigs', a status which 'Mustapha' has never achieved.

Of course 'Mustapha' doesn't have to commit any offence or crime, he is simply in the wrong place, at the wrong time, at the wrong point in history!

PRIGS OR POLISES: THE BINARY EXPLODED

The nefarious controllers have now been equated to 'bloody prigs' and 'bastards'. They have been assessed as controllers who simply do not control, for they fail in a perceived duty to ensure that the process of law and order—however 'soft' this may be—is necessarily imposed by the institutions of control on to those individuals who need controlling.

These intruders into what should be a perfect system deny the bureaucratic devices which ideally support the cultural perception of who is 'us'—the good guys—and what is 'them'. The singularity of 'us' it seems, is being eroded and fast becoming 'them', for it is apparent to the 'polises' that these capricious controllers have not really understood their role in the processes of control. Early on in my fieldnotes, I recorded how the 'polises' felt attacked from all sides by these ambiguous elements in the system, who, it seemed, were expanding at an ever increasing rate.

Case Study 14

Day 19—fieldnotes—just over 2 weeks into my return to work and I am forcibly struck by the constant complaints and resigned exclamations of frustration of the polises with their impotency in dealing with crime and prigs. There is fury with the magistrates and the Crown Courts, who are seen to have gone over to being 'hopelessly soft'. This frustration doubles (or trebles) when there is mention of any social reclamation attempt by the Social or Probation Service. The men talk constantly of an era when prigs could be dealt with in the same style by which they live (i.e. by the devious use of hard force). They despair that the polis now has no one on his side and even has to fight his own hierarchy. Anger towards the senior administration has to be heard to be believed; the constant cry is, 'they should get off their arses, out of their comfortable offices and come down on a weekend to see how it really is now at ground level'. The despised 9 till 5 administrators are akin to the denigrated social worker, but contempt is enhanced, and if anything they are viewed in an even more dismissive light; for they are seen to be men who should know what it is like to be on the ground, but have opted out. Now they live in 'ivory towers', in a land inhabited by 'high-flyers' and academics who are especially hated, for they are believed to have got to the highest ranks 'without ever having had to face an angry man'.

Ten years later these feelings have not been assuaged. New intruders into the criminal justice system, such as the Crown Prosecuting Service, have joined the fray to remove further slices of police power! This hurtful loss is rarely addressed or acknowledged in the many accusations the police have flung at the alleged inefficiencies of this new and independent tier in the system. Nor has the loss of police power been directly admitted in many of the criticisms of constraints included in the Police and Criminal Evidence Act in its detailed code of practice in relation to the care and custody of prisoners. Not surprisingly, these extra controls imposed on the controllers were not popular! Nor have the academic 'high-flyers' ceased to be a bone of contention:

The Havoc Makers

On the eve of his retirement, Ken Brown, a Detective Chief Inspector in No. 4 Regional Crime Squad, hits out at the legion of 'academics' in 9 to 5 Monday to Friday jobs . . .

This headline and comment lies above an article in *Police* magazine, which again illustrates the points I have made about the mistrust of academics and non-combatant officers, whose:

education had not prepared them for the fact that all 24 hours of the day were our responsibility. The shock of three shifts in sometimes hostile circumstances was not at all appealing. A simple solution was found: re-design the police force, only the proles need suffer the inconvenience of police work, the educated elite could take refuge in specialist departments . . . It is frightening to see how many academics it takes to fill those departments [which] are not staffed by police officers. These people have no intention of serving the community . . . they create havoc, instigating idiotic and irrelevant . . . in-depth studies, all of which cost a fortune, but themselves remain in the veiled secret society of the nine to five Monday to Friday Support Service . . . (*Police*, Vol. 20, No. 12, August 1988)

Detective Chief Inspector Brown brings a fine range of negative imagery and metaphor to his descriptions of these occupants of 'the mothercare environment'. So many of them now exist inside the 'dream factories',[22] he tells us, 'that they just ignored the service outside and started promoting each other. They created a great cauldron into which they all jump, the Chief Constable stirs,

---

[22] These 'dream factories' and 'ivory-towered' HQ buildings in which the high-flyers in the senior hierarchy hide from ground-based realities are the subject of a range of pointedly metaphorical references across the country. These reflect the view that the bosses have retreated from the real world into a world of make-believe. In Northumbria in 1977 the HQ building was known as 'The Glass Palace' while a move to a new HQ complex in 1981 saw the name 'Fantasy Island' bestowed. Men going to HQ on a course would say they were 'off on holiday to Fantasy Island for a week' and the Chief Constable even went public to deny the name in the local press. This only served to confirm the view of the men who used the name that he had little or no connection with their world. Elsewhere in the country men refer to their HQ complexes as 'The Big House' (West Merica's imagery of the still feudal style of the shire counties), 'The Kremlin', 'The Palace of Varieties', and 'The Crystal Palace'. Always the nick-name inverts the 'polis's' image of the tough and practical real world, separating the HQ complex into a mythological binary of an almost fairy-tale life, far removed from the grim reality at the bottom end of the pile, at the 'sharp end' on 'the ground'.

and when a certain cooking time is reached, up a rank they go'. Not unnaturally, in such a world Brown believes disaster occurs when one of them has to leave the 'mothercare environment'; for theirs is not a world of practicality. In consequence the culture breeds 'academic' subdivisional commanders who are literally terrified of their responsibilities, but who fortunately are quickly rescued and 'repatriated to the cauldron'.

In the following issue of *Police* (September 1988), Brian Davies, a temporary detective sergeant in the Metropolitan Police, joined a subsequent stream of those congratulating Ken Brown on what 'has to be the truest article of the year'

coming from a Force re-organised almost to destruction by that doyen of the Bramshill academics, now retired, oh how so true it all was! Good luck to you on your retirement Mr. Brown, and what a major loss you must be to the real policemen of your force. [23]

It is significant that Davies awards Brown this accolade of being a loss to 'real policemen'; here we witness the personification of the macho police world view. Focusing on opposing elements set in competition with each other, and always expecting to have its specifically erected and exclusive boundaries attacked from within and without, it operates a rigidly defined set of superior/inferior categories in which it always casts itself in the superior mould; and in which self-justifying modes of thought are translated into containing action aimed to fend off any potential threat of social or physical pollution from 'prigs' and other oppositional forces.

Exacerbated by the influences of a growing army of ambiguous controllers who must logically be analogous to the 'prig', these condensed metaphors of reality build into a multiple, mutually reinforcing system concerned with the maintenance of hegemony in an essentially defensive strategy of practice.

---

[23] The unnamed 'doyen of Bramshill academics, now retired', who 're-organised the [Met.] almost to destruction', must of course refer to Sir Kenneth Newman who had been commandant at Bramshill before becoming commissioner of the Metropolitan Police. He had set out to amend the management structures of the Met. totally, and in 1985 introduced and circulated to all his officers a 60-page hardback book entitled *The Principles of Policing and Guidance for Professional Behaviour*. This was reviled and derisorily known as 'the little blue book of the thoughts of Chairman Ken', or 'Chairman Ken's little blue book'. As I mentioned above, in 1988 he agreed that his new management systems had been defeated by police culture.

In this ruthless superior/inferior system the oft-voiced opinion that do-gooders and all the ambivalent social administrators are not as competent as the 'real polis' becomes axiomatic, for the 'polises' will always see themselves as the only ones who really understand how to enforce power:

Case Study 15

Day 10—Fieldnotes—3 youths are brought in for theft of clothing from shops. They are aged 15 to 17 and are covered in tattoos. They are somewhat monosyllabic of speech and not too bright. The 17-year-old is searched and takes off his shoes and socks. The smell nearly bowls us over. His socks are wet with rot and he leaves sodden footprints everywhere he walks. We open the doors and windows and retch at the smell. He is urged by the gaolers to steal some soap if he must steal, and he grins sheepishly while the polises berate him for the state of his 'plates'. He tells us he last washed them about 3 weeks ago, and the gaolers laughingly tell him he can't count for he must mean 3 months. All 3 are under 'supervision' by the courts for previous crimes and this produces what I have already noted is the usual derision of the polises at the 'ineffectual waste of money' in having social workers and probation officers involved. The sharpest of the three is asked about his probation officer, and after considering for a moment tells us, 'He's all heart but he knows nowt!' The staff are delighted with this confirmatory information.

In effect the whole 'prigs ~ polises' duality is believed to be coming apart, simply because known boundaries have been eroded and 'dirt' has been allowed to infiltrate. In the ideal world, where 'real prigs' are animal dross or the scum and dregs of society, it is argued that society would unquestioningly support its police as it deals with this filth! 'Real prigs' are known and know the 'polises', they know the rules and how to break them and the 'polises' know the 'prigs', know the rules and how to bend them! This is a world which should remain the concern of the two sides, but increasing interference from the social worker, the politician, the do-gooder, the press, the 'prig' solicitor, the magistrate or judge, the television pundit, the police administrator, and the chief officer in his 'ivory tower' merely intrudes to destroy the exclusive and rigid arenas of action which are preferred.

Such groups or individuals, who only 'join the game after the event' throw the 'polis' further onto the defensive and fractures the polarities simply by constructing an interstitial concept of a 'potential prig', who scavenges a living from the two vital sides to

the conflict. Such intruders can only pollute the purity of a semantic ideal, for the 'polises' firmly believe themselves to be the
only ones to understand the practices of this warfare.

In this disintegrating world, the increasing influence of the
social worker is a particular bone of contention. It is the social
workers who really threaten the integrity of the 'polis's' universe,
for they are considered to be the ultimate in 'do-goodery' and
'would let every villain off if they could'. Any defeat they sustain
is a triumph for the 'polises':

Case Study 16

Day 68—fieldnotes—Early shift, 6 a.m. start. I arrive about ten minutes
early to find out what we have in. I am told there is a 'right bloody female
workie-ticket in' who has been a right handful all night. She is only in for
being drunk and incapable, but has been aggressive and awkward. She
has not been bailed earlier because she had been too drunk to let out.
After I take over, the gaoler goes down with the matron to get her up to
see if we can get rid of her. I find that the nightshift have asked for a relative to come and stand surety, which is unusual as the drunks usually
stand their own 'recognizance' to come to court. However this one has an
address in a better part of town in 'smartsville'. She is brought up and is
truculent and aggressive. She has urinated on her clothing, has been sick
and she smells strongly. On the charge sheet she has been recorded as a
'civil servant'. I go through the various logging procedures and check her
occupation. I can almost feel the tangible pleasure that reverberates
around the charge room amongst the gaolers and polises who are supping
the early morning mugs of tea when she tells me she's 'a social worker'.
Here we have the evidence; the ambiguous controller is 'dirt'. She has
been 'stupid drunk', peed herself and vomited all over her clothes . . . she
is an 'animal' and logically she is a 'prig'. After she leaves, other visiting
polises in the charge room are all told about this example of social worker
unreliability; great satisfaction is apparent!

By the same logic, a successful detective who left the police to take
a polytechnic course in Social Administration was said to be
almost 'insane' and immediately became a potential enemy. This
assessment was seen to be totally justified when he later took up a
post in the probation service on completion of his course, for he
had now crossed an unacceptable boundary to change status. This
is the same process that those few policemen who take law degrees
and then leave to join the legal profession experience. Those who
then join the ranks of the 'prig solicitors' are especially hated, for
they have transformed into doubly dangerous 'prigs' by simply

having moved from the inside, possessed of insider's knowledge, and with a power that other ex-policemen who move into general areas of civilian life never project. These ex-police 'prig solicitors' who were regularly requested by the clients in the bridewell were subject to a special kind of loathing, for they had moved to the other side of the coin and crossed an ideological boundary, symbolically allied to the forces of evil.

During my bridewell sojourn, I watched as the defensiveness of the 'polises' was increasingly attacked as the preferred binary principles failed to materialize. Constantly the ideal is thwarted and the classic simplicity of a black ∼ white duality explodes and is fragmented simply because of the pluralism of a world where multivocal behaviour and phenomena expand and cannot be ignored. Meanwhile, the 'polises' continue to savour those occasional instances when these ambiguous controllers are found also to need control, and the MP, social worker, or the police academic or administrator is shown to be a real or symbolic 'prig'.

When the politician T. Dan Smith (know colloquially as 'Mr Newcastle') and Councillor Andrew Cunningham (who held a position on the Durham Police Authority) were caught up in the disclosures of malpractice in the Poulson affair and went to prison, the 'polises' read the accounts and expressed quiet satisfaction.

When John Stonehouse, the socialist MP staged a suicide and was then found and imprisoned for fraud, the bridewell staff followed the events with knowing smiles. Whenever other administrators were arrested or fell from grace the 'polises' discussed the outcome with a kind of grim satisfaction. When a local senior social worker was convicted of fraud involving the misappropriation of funds allocated to help the underprivileged, this evoked something close to delirium in the bridewell. The newspaper accounts were relished, for here were the 'bastard social workers shown up to be the prigs they really are'. [24]

The line between good and evil, between 'pigs' and 'prigs' continues to be finely drawn, for widespread concern seems to

---

[24] The various unfortunate deaths of children under supervision or in care situations throughout the 1980s have shown that it is not just the police who use the 'social worker' as a symbolic and sometimes convenient whipping boy to excuse other faults manifest across society. Indeed the profession of social work has experienced something of a crisis of confidence as their inability to succeed always has become inevitably apparent.

indicate that too often the controllers also need control. Meanwhile the 'polises' know who has caused this concern and are clear in their own mind that the trouble always lies with the ambiguous 'prig' both inside and outside of 'the job'. Accounts of the Metropolitan Police corruption enquiries, which resulted in trials, early retirements, resignations and dismissals from the Force (see Cox, Shirley, and Short 1977) were also read with great satisfaction by the 'polises'. The imprisonment of a senior commander was particularly relished, for the Metropolitan police are consistently seen as 'bogeymen' by the provincial forces, and in this instance the 'highest flying' boss was shown to also be a 'prig'.

Further happy reading for the bridewell officers was provided at this time by the fall of Stanley Parr, then the chief constable of Lancashire. Media accounts of how he had apparently shown favour to friends under threat of prosecution and had misused police transport were devoured with delight. Here was the hierarchy fallen! The hated administrator, the non-combatant ESSO man, the administrative oppressor of the rank and file 'polises' was shown to be analagous to the 'prig'. None of these men knew Stanley Parr, of course, but the antagonism which existed in relation to their own hierarchy was easily transferred to this symbol of power. [25]

Ditton (1977), Mars (1983), Henry (1978), and others have shown that fiddling, pilfering, theft, and white-collar crime is the province of all; 'polises' are not exempt! It is not only the chief constable of Lancashire who misuses his power, for the criminal abuse of position is the province of the financier and stockbrokers in their insider dealings. It is to be found across the world of power and privilege, with the MP, the do-gooder, and also the

[25] This oppositional form has a long history. I recall a 'polis' from my early days in the 1950s collecting examples of similar 'fallen angels'. Accounts of senior officers who 'fell' (such as the chief constables of Brighton, Nottingham, and Worcester), which were a basis for the eventual 1962 Royal Commission into the police, were avidly poured over. Another favourite of the lower ranks was any account of the death of a very senior officer who had stayed on beyond the time he might have retired, and who then 'died in harness'. As a result of his perceived self-aggrandizement, and to the delight of the 'polises', the deceased lost his pension and his right to commute part in the form of a lump sum. I had wondered if this might be a northern trait, still linked to an industrial legacy based on the extreme working-class distrust of the managerial classes, but in the mid-1980s I found the same attitudes to exist in the shires of Worcester, Hereford, and Shropshire, where the alleged misuse of position and the 'fall' of Alf Parrish, the chief constable of Derbyshire, was also relished and discussed with great satisfaction by the rank and file.

real 'polis'. The 'prig' is also the 'polis' and the dualistic model of the world collapses as the binary ideal falls apart. The complementarity of 'polis ~ prig' cannot be sustained and the paradigm must of necessity include the anomalous and might be redrawn:

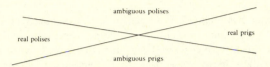

FIG. 5 Binary model of ambiguous and real categories of 'prigs' and 'polises'

But even this paradigm is too simplistic; the 'dream time' is over and the preferred dualism is defeated by the many practical transformations. These suggest the model of reality should be continually turning and spiralling, as law, order, controller, and controlled turn in on themselves. Figure 6 is therefore an attempt to show this inclusive world of criminal justice, in which the various actors in the drama move to or from their potential ideal place in an ideal world.

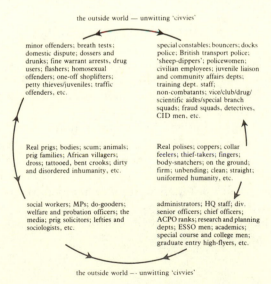

FIG. 6 Exploded model of the world of the criminal justice system

For the 'polises' in the bridewell who make up the 'thick description' of this section of the fieldwork, the 1979 Conservative election promise of a return to law and order invested the party leader Margaret Thatcher with the mantle of an earlier 'masculine' heroine, Joan of Arc. The new 'iron lady' was speaking their language:

Mrs. Thatcher has inclined more and more to combative imagery; the language of conflict and intolerance has come to prevail . . . [she] speaks of democracy itself as if it were a military authority; 'it is time for freedom to take the offensive' she told the Canadian parliament. 'There is a battle of ideas to be won. We are better equipped than our adversaries' . . . (Warner 1985: 42)

Her promise of enhanced law and order and straightforward methods of dealing with villainy and criminals was what the bridewell 'troops' wanted to hear. To continue the cinematic metaphor used by Reiner (1978*b*), she had arrived in the High Street at high noon, come to save the day in the last reel. It can surely be no accident that during her first decade of tenure as sheriff, the 'iron lady' was closely linked with that other cowboy of the Western world, Ronald Reagan! The imagery used to promote these two heroes of democracy cleverly used the hopes of a return to the values of the 'dream time', which continue to sustain the likes of the bridewell 'polises'. In a 1983 *Sun* cartoon celebrating Mrs Thatcher's re-election, a further cowboy image was used as an 'icon of [such] pioneer bravery' (Warner 1985: 39). This attributed Mrs Thatcher with phallic power yet retains many of the images of female sexuality which Warner (ibid. 38–60) penetratingly shows are interwoven with her masculine and 'iron' persona.

It is this image of her as a 'guardian of moral virtue' which has continued to earn her the unquestioning support of the great mass of policemen, who see in her unremitting and simplistic values a reflection of their own stance on such issues as 'crime and punishment'; and yet their willingness to have her as a leader is in direct contrast to the power and position they have been prepared to cede to women within their own institution, as we shall see in the following chapter.

4

Women in the Police: A Case of Structural Marginality

INTRODUCTION

The police organization I have described can be defined as forming a primarily masculine domain, where metaphors of hunting and warfare predominate. Categories of prestige, power, and status are allocated to tough, manful acts of crime-fighting and thief-taking. Tensions experienced in these battles and conflicts with antagonists both inside and external to the organization have created a rigidified and defensively aggressive world, with a cultural style in which superior male logic discards or denigrates factors identified as inferior or threatening to it.

The creation of oppositions by which the police lend meaning to these 'collective representations' (to use Durkheim's term for symbolic patterns of universal significance) reproduces an exaggerated duality at every turn, with categories of superior and inferior clearly delineated to all events. These asymmetric representations form part of what Edwin Ardener (1973, 1975) has conceptualized as 'world structures', elaborating slightly on what have been described as universal symbolic patterns (Hertz 1973). Inevitably in such an obsessional world, the opportunities for women are constrained by hierarchies of dominance in which the masculine view prioritizes and polarizes (Chaplin 1988) and the asymmetries created by the warrior life are taken on as a basic tool of the male 'prestige structures' (Ortner and Whitehead 1981: 13–21).

The ideology of status which exists within a 'prestige structure' is especially useful in an organization such as the police, for it has always given gender a specifically significant place within its cultural domain. 'Prestige Structures', as Ortner and Whitehead (ibid. 14) tell us, are always supported by ... direct expressions of definite beliefs and symbolic associations that make sensible and compelling the ordering of human relations into patterns of deference and condescension, respect and disregard, and in many cases command and obedience. These beliefs and symbolic associations may be looked on as a legitimating ideology.

The police world has always allocated priority and respect to male categories and symbols, finding it difficult to contend with the lurking problems of gender, simply because masculinity has historically held the prime position and is deferred to and understood. A perceived ambiguity in the homosexual 'prig' (outlined in Case Study 4 above), illustrates the anxiety generated by sexual ambivalence or when gender classification is confounded.[1] Such dogma makes police structures an effectively male cultural preserve, with values that Smith and Grey (1983: 91) found to be 'in many ways those of an all-male institution such as a rugby club or boys' school'. These values, they go on to tell us, create cultural attitudes amongst policemen which stress drinking as a test of manliness, lend importance to physical courage, and see glamour in violence. All these amount to a 'cult of masculinity' used as a 'prestige structure', in the course of which women are denigrated, given low status, condescended to, and denied social value:

I've come across sexism, racism, harrassment and violence, but the worst thing is sexism. (WPC Pamela Burrell, in *A Policewoman's Lot*, BBC 2, 10 November 1988)

Sarah [Barnes] [after 6 years in the police] is convinced that masculine hostility and prejudice is keeping valuable women out of the force ... Men who should be exploiting the special talents of women are instead wasting their time with sour-faced rivalry, sexist insults and schoolboy pranks. ('Third Person', *Guardian*, 7 October 1987)

As Figure 6 indicates, in this culture women can never be centrally located or seen as 'real polises'. Indeed the prime symbolic associations attributed to women in the police world mirror the ideology and social patterns found elsewhere in society, in which a masculine world view has predominated for decades (Chaplin 1988). Ortner (1972), although criticized for allocating women to 'nature' in an allegedly universal 'nature/culture' opposition, in which nature was equated with the weaker, dependent

---

[1] See Smith and Grey (1983: 92–3) for other examples of the anxiety that ambiguity in gender roles causes the police.

side of the binary largely because of women's physiology and partly because of reproduction,[2] had valuable points to make, even though she failed to show that this binary allocation was mainly concerned with the legitimation of pre-existing relationships of power. As she correctly points out, however, this asymmetrical bias in the male/female antagonism is primarily sustained where men control all the wider spheres of social co-ordination. Such polarities do not exist as complimentarities, for they are generated by social bias, with subunits of status invariably associated with females.

My own observations suggest that policemen are overtly and consistently hostile towards women in 'the job', and that the social control of these women is inevitably a burning issue. This supports Ortner and Whitehead (1981: 7), who argued that gender differentiation creates stereotyped oppositions, such as nature/culture, domestic/public, social good/self-interest, and consistently produces an undervalued place for women within 'prestige structures'. In such circumstances, it is not surprising to find only marginal value afforded to women in the police, or that factors associated with or commonly ascribed to be the rightful province of the female gender, such as softness, emotional vulnerability, and physical weakness, are negated and always given low status.

Because of the transformational nature of binary qualities, however, these same categories are sought in women *external* to the organization, which results in the ideal structural place for them to lie *outside* the service. Women who do breach the boundary to penetrate this masculine world can only ever be partially successful and will often have to subsume 'male characteristics' to achieve even a limited social acceptability. Ideally they are best returned to a place outside the system, married to policemen and reconstituted into the domestic sphere. Then, with knowledge and experience of 'the job's' specific peculiarities, they are able to provide an extremely important but relatively unacknowledged role as 'police wife' (see Young 1984).

In the following sections, I briefly explore the history of the subordination of women in this masculine world, and analyse various aspects of what can only be described as the social

---

[2] See for example, Diana L. Barker and Sheila Allen (1976: 10); and many of the essays in MacCormack and Strathern (1980), especially 'Nature, Culture and Gender: A Critique' (pp. 1–24).

pollution caused by the intrusion of women into the male police universe. Social command over the female body, perceived fears of their rampant sexuality, control over their limited access to rank, and the prevention of their involvement in some specialist areas of police practice are all the results of a subjection of the feminine side of life in much of the criminal justice system, and has led over the years to systematic suppression of female aspects of identity and modes of thought. The few women who make a career out of the police and even those who stay for only a short period are tolerated almost as honorary men, but still have low cultural status. This is primarily determined by the ferocity of the pre-existing structural oppositions between the male public sphere and an inferior female domestic sphere (Rosaldo and Lamphere 1974: 41), and which, in the police world, is enhanced almost to the point of dogma. Such a rigidly hierarchical system of thought inevitably creates an arena for social conflict and humiliation (Chaplin 1988).

This exaggerated asymmetry is supported by a fear of the anomalous public woman, so that the intruding female is considered not only to be dangerous, but weak; not only sexually provocative, but in need of protection. In this situation she can never be suited for physical work relating to the control of the street-visible 'dangerous classes' (who are also male dominated), for the ideology of police 'prestige structures' places the men in such roles and restricts women to an extended world of domesticity, to the extent that this role becomes almost self evident:

A young woman constable, with senior officer, suffering annual report review:

Senior officer: 'Well Miss, you've been married several years now, isn't it about time you started a family?' The young lady groans inwardly [at] the annual reference to her childlessness . . . (Sgt Karan McKerrow, *Police Review*, 1 April 1988)

. . . there is the traditional belief that you should be a housewife; one of my colleagues with young children has been told on several occasions that she shouldn't be working. (Sgt Jane Simmons, Northumbria police)[3]

---

[3] I am indebted to a number of policewomen in Northumbria police who read and commented on a seminar paper 'Ladies of the Blue Light: An Anthropology of Policewomen' (Young 1979c), which set out some early thoughts on the place of women in police society.

... before I was promoted, a senior officer told me that once I remembered I was a 'mere' woman and not a police officer, I would get on far better. (Sgt Sheena Thomas, *A Policewoman's Lot*, BBC 2, 10 November 1988')

I don't like women. I don't want women down here and when you came down here I was looking for faults in you to send you back to division. (Traffic sergeant to woman constable after three months' trial on the section (Jones 1987))

These few examples can be replicated dozens of times each day across the country, and it is the strength of this legitimating logic which has precluded anything other than a token gesture to the Sex Discrimination Act of 1975. It perhaps would be somewhat optimistic to expect one Act of Parliament to influence a whole range of deeply ingrained attitudes and amend a conservatively male culture which is never keen to pursue radical change. No new social formation has emerged, nor have the power relationships between men and women been subject to any radical change, although some organizational adjustments have been made. On the surface these might seem profound, for at a glance women appear to have been integrated into all aspects of what had been all-male areas of action. Any closer inspection, however, reveals nothing has altered. Semantic attitudes remain unchanged; sexism and inequality remain; bias in opportunity is prevalent; and this of course replicates the situation which exists across wider society.

Indeed, the police, who talk constantly about obedience to the rule of law, have even set out to reject the Act of Parliament. This in itself is a further indication of the ideological omnipotence of their 'prestige structures' in relation to any challenge to their practices. Many chief constables, the Superintendents' Association, and the Police Federation all immediately called for exemption from its provisions; and a dozen years after its introduction *Police Review* (17 June 1988) carried an article (mirroring others over the period), in which an Inspector James Blacker suggested that 'given the fact that 12 years have elapsed since the legislation was placed on the statute books it seems insufficient effort has been put into providing an ambience in which equal opportunities can flourish' ('Unequal in the Eyes of the Law'). It is these aspects of male power and hegemony which a burgeouing feminist

anthropology has tackled head on in the past two decades,[4] showing how dominant public models are consistently and perhaps
universally expressed in male terms; and this branch of the discipline has been particularly forceful in spreading an awareness
that modern society has a potential to afford women an equal status, no longer necessitating biological difference to be socially
translated into a perceived 'natural' lower status. But in police
circles a new semantic order has not been forged, for, having been
largely pursued by women and posing a threat to the entrenched
male structures of dominance, such ideas are readily symbolized
as only the aberrant considerations of those who are already
'known' to be disordered, emotional, vulnerable, and devalued.

If the police are 'of' society (as they always claim) and reflect
the male structural bias which reigns in most other Western
institutions and organizations, can we really expect them to promote and seek any new moral ambience? For when their present
defensive attitude makes them resistant to criticism, fearful of
change, and unwilling to reform (Adams 1988), any plea for a
revised system of policing with a more equitable human face
requires enormous structural and conceptual alterations in cultural and ideological attitudes.

In the following short history and ethnography of policewomen
the strength of the stereotypical belief that women should be
'caring, child-rearing creatures' is explored and linked to an examination of the restrictions on role and rank achievement for
women. Symbols and metaphors of the body are demonstrated to
be a tool of the masculine cult of superiority and are linked to an
overwhelming male perception that women are weak, yet sensu-
ally dangerous creatures. Consistently throughout my fieldnotes
this weakness of policewomen is referred to as an actual hindrance
to their ability to enforce the law, and their physical size and
strength is allied to an alleged or inferred mental weakness in
which women (in accord with beliefs prevalent across society at
large) are said to be 'illogical', 'emotional', or 'irrational'. In many
societies the idea of a deeply sensuous and dangerous nature to

---

[4] See for example, Rosaldo and Lamphere (1974); Reiter (1975); S. Ardener
(1975, 1978, 1981); Hutter and Williams (1981); Dube, Leacock, and Ardener
(1986); MacDonald, Holden, and Ardener (1987); MacCormack and Strathern
(1980); Holden (1983). Comprehensive bibliographies on the 'anthropology of
women' can be found in these volumes.

women is deeply ingrained, and starts in the West with the creation myth and Eve's original sin. In literature, mythology, and social practice, this belief has been replicated again and again across history, and policewomen have not escaped the effects of this classification. As we shall see, they are considered to be similarly afflicted by a rampant sensuality and an uncontrollable appetite for passion, which is again used by the male 'prestige structures' to exert further social control over the women. In effect this long history of the use of an allegedly male logic and objective nature in contrast to the negative imagery of women's 'nature' determines the roles and constraints on the woman's place, and in consequence women have tended to enter police society only as 'one of the boys'.[5]

THE ORIGINS OF THE WOMEN POLICE

The history of women in the police service has been described as a 'depressing one of apathy and prejudice' (Critchley 1967: 215), with only eventual 'grudging acceptance' (May 1979: 358). This grudging acceptance, I suggest, still only occurs when women accept a place of structural dependency and inferiority which assigns them to a suppressed or muted position in police society. Where integration appears to have been achieved it is often only skin deep, or is accompanied by a symbolic transference of gender which temporarily ascribes the female with male categories so that she can operate as 'one of the boys'.

In 1914 the National Union of Women Workers reached agreement with the Metropolitan Police Commissioner in London to set up women patrols in the Metropolitan area to carry out what was known as 'preventive work' among women and girls in the vicinity of military camps and munition factories and in the parks. The union trained over 4,000 women during the First World War for this work, which was primarily concerned with a fear for female morality. Dorothy Peto, who in 1922 became the first sworn

---

[5] Sgt Jane Simmons, in her comments on my seminar paper (1979c) wrote: 'if you can show you can deal with any job competently, you are accepted, but only as "one of the lads", having crossed the barrier of female :: incompetent to male :: competent, and so become a surrogate male'. See also 'One of the Boys', Bryant, Dunkerly, and Kelland in *Policing*, Autumn 1985; and 'Not Yet One Of The Boys', by Joan Lock in *Police Review*, 27 February 1987.

woman police staff officer in the Metropolitan force, recorded in her memoirs: 'as men left the police to join the Services the need for Women Police increased as problems of order and decency in public places cried out for urgent solutions' (quoted in May 1979). In Birmingham, where Peto had obtained her 'first real police post' as a lady inquiry officer without any police powers, much of the work of the unattested women patrols 'still entailed the rescue of fallen women' (Lock, *Police Review*, 5 December 1986: 2462). In Grantham, a call from the army to the self-styled Women Police Service to 'help control vice' had brought volunteer patrols and the first woman (Policewoman Smith) to be given a power of arrest (something not achieved in some areas for another twenty-five years) was sworn in as a police officer in 1915. As the Bishop of Grantham told a meeting later that year, Policewoman Smith's role was primarily to 'keep young girls from temptation and evil' (Lock 1986*a*). PW Smith's first report for 1916 set the model for women's work, with its record of)

10 prostitutes proceeded against and convicted, 2 disorderly houses, one fortune-teller and two landladies proceeded against under the Defence of the Realm Act regulations re lodger forms. In addition she reported 10 dirty houses to the sanitary authorities and dealt with 24 illegitimate baby cases. (ibid.)

In Bristol, where Peto also had patrolled as a member of the National Union of Women Workers, the 'quayside was colourful and afforded good opportunites to patrol among stranded girls, begging children and fighting women' (Lock 1986*b*). In all these early statements of a correct place for women and location for women's work, a narrow and constraining structure was subsumed and taken on by the women themselves as they struggled to infiltrate the male bastions. With no powers and facing male opposition, these unpaid patrolling women wore only an armband to indicate their inclusion into a controlling organization, as they set out to 'deal with the stray girls, begging children and . . . amorous couples incidental to an evening beat in wartime. . . .' (Peto, quoted in May 1979). In this way, the *care* for children, the maintenance of decency, and the protection of the morality of young girls became real work for women. Seventy years later these still remain ambiguous areas for police*men* and 'real polises'.

In 1914, a Mrs Nott-Bower, the sister-in-law of the City of

London Police Commissioner addressed a meeting of the British Women's Temperance Association on the need for legislation to suppress the white slave traffic. This seems to have produced great alarm at the time, and she advocated, 'it would be an enormous help to the moral purity of the community if there were women police officials' (quoted in May 1979). In 1917, Mrs Nott-Bower defined the correct role for the women police:

the first point is the necessity of having a woman to take statements from women and girls with reference to sexual offences ... There are other strong reasons for the appointment of women police in work outside the police court. Few people realise the scandalous indecency involved by sending young (male) officers to collect information in such cases as concealment of birth, or abortion, or cases that involve intimate personal investigation.

... the need for women to patrol streets, parks, open spaces and railway stations has been so long recognised by philanthropic societies that many have for years privately employed women workers for this purpose ... At the present time there are certainly special reasons for desiring the immediate employment of women in the police force, e.g. ... the great increase of women workers, many far away from their homes, often obliged to be out late in the evenings on account of their work or having no other possible time for fresh air, exercise or amusement. These often run into danger and not infrequently come to grief just for the want of the friendly help and counsel of a member of their own sex ... (quoted in May 1979: 359).

This threat to society from its uncontrolled women is a reflection of the place women held in a society where the system of polarities embedded in male 'prestige structures' generated distrust and contempt for anything tarnished with the inferior female attribution. An alleged female capacity for an uncontrollable sensuality leads to restrictions in their life chances, producing an almost unquestioned acceptance of their need for close control. This ideology generated practices designed to prevent social chaos by the act of constraining the female, which Sir Leonard Dunning the Inspector of Constabulary illustrated nicely in 1921, when he called for a 'definite place for women in the police force': 'a woman by advice and personal influence can do more than a man to protect a girl from the temptations of her own nature'. These 'temptations of feminine nature' were, of course, to be defined to fit the Inspector of Constabulary's own masculine template:

'principally owing to the decay of parental influence, the girl of today does not attach so much value to chastity, while modern knowledge has deprived the fear of natural consequences of its value as a protection' (quoted in May 1979: 261) The direction of women's work in the police was therefore logically tied into a continuity of the well-established male precepts of order and disorder. Women were only to be used in those dangerously ambiguous areas concerned with the control of their own disordered natures, or subsequently with the natural results of their disordered temptations—the illegitimate or undisciplined child!

The self-evident statement of structural order here seems to follow the maxim that 'it takes a thief to catch a thief'. It seems because of her sexuality and vulnerable nature, a patrolling woman could best spot the potential feminine 'fall from grace' occurring at the munition factory gate or in some park. But then came the dilemma, for this feminine weakness produced problems, and these patrolling policewomen then in turn had to be protected from their own hazardous susceptibilities. In 1919 the first women police patrols were closely followed through the streets by two attested male constables (i.e. sworn in with powers of arrest denied the women), who were directed to protect them and keep them in sight. This perceived inability of women to avoid the pitfalls of their own helplessness and their feminine animalism has consistently been used since to deny them access to certain areas of the male structures, and neither the constitution of the Metropolitan Police or the other county and borough forces provided for female detectives; for as a Scotland Yard spokesman explained in 1916:

Women are particularly adapted for work which comes outside the scope of the ordinary detective but unfortunately it is sometimes unsafe to trust a woman with an important investigation where young men are concerned. They are swayed by emotion. They can't help it: it is their nature, and they have been known to fall in love with the man they have been sent to watch. (Quoted in May 1979: 359)

We therefore had the situation where women were patrolling in London, Birmingham, and elsewhere yet had no power of arrest, nor the authority of their male counterparts. They had the 'restrictions of a constable, but not his privileges, Dorothy Peto told the Home Office in 1919' (Lock, *Police Review*, 5 December 1986:

2462). The Home Office had not been impressed by the swearing in of Policewoman Smith in Grantham in 1915, declaring that since 'the law does not admit of a woman holding the office of constable' (Lock, *Police Review*, 6 June 1986: 1193), it was illegal. This partial intrusion into male space had caused provocation and unease, and most of the men simply dismissed the idea that women could be employed as fully attested constables. In 1917 a Scotland Yard spokesman, when asked if such a situation could occur, replied, 'No, not even if the war lasts 50 years.' In a similar vein, a *Police Review* reader of the time defended the male preserve in a vigorous letter to the magazine:

To have women in the police offices where business and correspondence of a most private and confidential character is being carried out day and night; sending them out at night to tackle the burglar etc., lying out in the fences at night to catch the thief and the poacher; dealing with the thousands of soldiers and bad characters who will be roaming about after the war, many of them maddened by drink; and carrying out scores of complicated Acts of Parliament; if these are what the Women Police are agitating for, all I can say is 'lead us not into temptation, but deliver us from evil'. (quoted in May 1979: 359)

In 1920 the Baird Committee reviewed the question of the employment of policewomen and produced fairly revolutionary proposals for the time. The report suggested women should be highly trained and form an integral part of the police force, but as Critchley (1967: 216) recounts, 'these forward looking proposals had little effect'. Indeed, in 1922, in the face of calls for economic cut-backs, the number of women police in London was reduced from 112 to 24, and by 1924 there were just 110 women across the country. Most of the county and borough forces had none, and when the question of employment of women police was raised at a meeting of the Cardiff Watch Committee in 1935, for example, the chief constable said they had excellent women probation officers in Cardiff, and these could be called out in special circumstances. He told the committee that 'police work in uniform was not a woman's job. The idea of Women Police filled him with nausea' (Police Review, 22 November 1935). In a second inquiry, the Bridgeman Committee of 1924 reached similar conclusions to its predecessor, advocating for women police officers. But there remained a strong feeling in most of the constabularies that the work women were doing could be better done by the voluntary organizations. The Police Federation consistently opposed their introduction, expressing hostility to the idea of women in what was 'naturally' a male occupation. Lilian Wyles (1952: 12), one of the first of twenty-five women police on the London streets in 1919 complained how, at times, she faced 'the downright malice and vindictive spirit shown by some of the men'. A third inquiry, part of a 1929 Royal Commission on Police Powers and Procedure, again proclaimed the value of women police, although their potential intrusion into male space was again to be limited to a narrow range of options considered suitable for women. Their availability to take statements from young girls and children in sexual cases was deemed especially important! In 1930 the Home Office raised the matter of employment for policewomen with an apathetic Police Council and laid down regulations for women which standardized pay and conditions of service. In addition they proposed areas of action to include patrolling, and duties in connection with women or children reported missing, found ill, destitute or homeless, or in immoral surroundings. Other tasks were to include the taking of statements from women and children and dealing with women prisoners. Yet by 1939 only 45 out of 183 police forces in England and Wales were employing women.

One reason that these male institutions could resist the inclusion of women lies in the way women themselves have acquiesced with the male power game at times. As Chaplin (1988) has suggested, women have been complicit in and even embraced a distrust of the feminine world view, exhibiting contempt for their own feminine strengths which are seen as weaknesses. By pursuing this line, she contends women have downgraded their female potential, while striving to polish up masculine attributes, thus warping their true nature to fit the masculine model. From the beginning, attempts to emulate the men or deny women's abilities have been prevalent. In 1919 Dorothy Peto told the Baird Committee that women recruits needed to be over 27 years of age and should be of a higher social class than the men. They were preferably to be a minimum of 5′ 8″, but 'should not be asked to do a full day's patrolling since they were really not able to stay on their feet for eight hours'.

Until the 1970s, policewomen's work was dictated by such

restrictions and their marginality confirmed by their exclusion from mainstream areas of policing. Invariably they were in specialist 'women's' departments dealing with women and children, sexual offences, and missing persons. Always they worked shorter shifts than the men, were paid less, had their own establishments within each force, and their own rank structures. Occasionally the equivalent of the 'token black' managed to struggle to middle management rank or into an area not usually considered suitable or 'natural' for women; but the situation had changed little from the 1920s.

In 1955 when I joined Newcastle City Police as a cadet, there was one woman chief inspector in a force with an establishment of approximately 500 officers. Twenty-five years later, and even after the Sex Discrimination Act and Equal Opportunities Act, there was only one woman superintendent and two women chief inspectors among the 3,500 establishment of Northumbria Police. In 1983 on my transfer to West Mercia I found there was one woman superintendent who was about to retire, and one woman chief inspector in a force with an establishment of just under 2,000 officers. By 1988 the chief inspector had been promoted to superintendent, while the next senior post for women was at inspector level.

In 1984 a GLC Police Committee report on the Metropolitan Police pointed out that 'few women reach senior positions . . . Of 227 Superintendents only two are women; just four women are Chief Superintendents out of 211; and there is only 1 woman among the 57 commanders.' The resistance to change means that the integration of women into the police preserves challenges the status of male structures which are built on a belief in and the prestige of 'real polis's' work. Men who dominate the top stratas of police society and who exercise power in the realms of policy-making, have all come through and succeeded in this system, by subscribing to the traditional masculine imagery and adhering to the style of the organization. In such circumstances, the restricted arena for women and their direction into narrow channels of operational activity becomes almost given—a natural state of the institutional mind. These cultural assumptions of male supremacy and female 'place' are strategically reinforced at every turn, so that however women try to manœuvre to enhance their lot, they risk rejection:

Fieldnote: 1985—Bromsgrove Subdivision

A woman detective constable on the Subdivision has her annual career appraisal with me. She is a candidate for promotion and asks about her chances of becoming the first woman detective sergeant in the force. In Northumbria there have been women Det. Sgts for some years, but West Mercia is more traditional in many ways, and so I tell her I will make some enquiries. We discuss the paternalism of the CID and I use the metaphor of 'family' to describe how access is controlled, so that many posts are filled by invitation only. I make a tentative enquiry with a Detective Chief Inspector, who is centrally placed in the CID system of politics. He grins as he tells me that he thinks the Force might be ready for its first woman Det. Sgt in about 10 years! I know what he means by this, for he will be retiring about then. There are no women Detective Sergeants in the CID at this time, even though it has about 300 officers, or 15% of the Force establishment.

This use of an existing male/female asymmetry to justify the continued power relations between men and women in the police is such a cornerstone in the legitimating ideology that it may well be impossible to dislodge without major upheaval!

THE CONTAINED WOMAN

As Ardener (1978: 33) suggests, there are English parallels to the Islamic concept which requires women who move in the public sphere to be made structurally invisible, hidden behind real or metaphoric veils. Such containment is, of course, not confined to English or Islamic societies, for many cultures based on 'prestige structuring' consider the presence of the female in male social space to be provocative or offensive. Moves towards a degree of female liberation, which allows women unrestricted access to previously exclusive male arenas, present more than just a pragmatic difficulty with role identification. For the feminist movement has created a dilemma and something of a problem in autocratic and paternalistic organizations such as the police, whose very modes of thought and practice have been challenged and undermined. A few concessions have necessarily been made to these new ideas; however, the asymmetric model of police society remains largely undisturbed, in spite of Equal Opportunities legislation. At a superstructural level it is constantly argued that women now enjoy full and equal involvement in the social order, but on many more occasions the forcible denial of an equal place for women in police society has been unequivocal and restates their rejection as a contaminant of male police power.

Over the years the maintenance of the male prestige structures has been achieved in two primary ways. First, it has been pursued by controlling the physical body and appearance of the women; second, it has operated by controlling the social arena in which the women have been allowed to manœuvre; for an alleged sexual vulnerability of women and the weakness of their gender must be guarded and guarded against.

As a result, the perceptions of yester-year still prevail, and the women of today are still subject to the vindictive malice of the men. This disaffection is so deeply implanted as an organizational principle that it affects even those who appear to have surmounted it. The first woman assistant chief constable, Alison Halford, admitted her own problems of male malice when she deliberated on how long it would be before a woman chief constable was appointed ('Until the 12th of Never', *Police Review*, 9 October 1987):

the conditioning experienced by some men . . . seems to leave them with a jaundiced view of a senior woman's capabilities. The inability of some very senior men to cope with a woman of comparable rank is bewildering . . . In some ways the male seems threatened by the female of the species.

A year later the *Independent* (9 August 1988) suggested Miss Halford had paid the price for her intemperate remarks, for she now declines to talk to the media after 'a serious row with her boss, Kenneth Oxford, the hardline Chief Constable'.

Once again the emotional, irrational nature of woman is hinted at and is veiled by suppression, for in the police, both curtailment of the female voice and control of the physical body of police-women are linked by restrictions on social movement and the direction of women to certain traditional 'women's interest' areas (ibid.). These restrictions, in turn, are proscribed by an almost archetypal belief that women are possessed of a nature which produces the extremes of a rampant Medusa-like behaviour on the one hand, and a shy, defenceless, wilting, violet-like disposition on the other. This unresolvable paradox of virgin or virago thus leads to their control, repression, denial, or protection, and is

negotiated by men who are responsible for the bias in the classification in the first place, which remains a primary means of
legitimizing their pre-existing relationships of power.

The clothed woman and her physique

The control of the body of the policewoman is first obtained by
ordering its demeanour and its carriage. It is subject to verbal
abuse and is clothed into a state of subjugation; the body of the
women is discussed, measured, and laughed at. It is ogled and
lusted over, sneered at, ridiculed, drooled over, and constrained
into a repressed form. The sexism which marks out much of
British society is also clearly visible in police culture.

Mauss (1935) in his seminal essay on the psycho-social variations imposed as a control of bodily activity in different societies
shows these are invariably determined by a preconceived understanding of what a society considers to be biologically correct and
'natural'. In police society the symbolic form for this 'natural'
state insists that women are physically larger than is the norm for
the rest of society. The setting of a minimum height restriction
(although lower than that for men) means that a proportion of
women in the service are 'large' ladies,[6] and this immediately sets
them apart from the rest of society, as this fieldnote indicates:
'have you seen the latest batch of burglar's dogs; most of them are
built like brick shit houses! How do we pick them, with their upside down Queen Anne table legs and faces like a bag of spanners?'
Yet despite this alleged grossness, sexual dimorphism has been
consistently used in the controversy over the role of women which
has followed the Sex Discrimination Act of 1975. Their lack of
inches has been used as a primary male strategy to exclude them
from the main discourse and to deny them the equal opportunities. With monotonous regularity, the male voice in the police has
denied women an ability to deal with the violent public incident.
So that regardless of their alleged bulk, these 'burglar's dogs'[7] are

---

[6] In August 1979, West Yorkshire Constabulary raised the minimum height for
women recruits to 5′ 6″ because they now had to 'tackle the same jobs as the men'.
The Police Federation, however, were reported to 'still be against an equal role for
women' (*Daily Mirror*, 3 Aug. 1979)

[7] The derogatory term of reference that some policewoman is as 'ugly as a burglar's dog' occurs again and again in my fieldnotes, and has been in common use in
police circles in and around Newcastle since I was a cadet. Its derivation may well
relate to the bull terrier owned by the notorious burglar Bill Sykes in Charles

always alleged to present a problem because of a lack of physical strength. This presumed weakness is then further used as a major defensive strategy by the male culture in its solidarity against any call for further increases in the percentage of female recruits. Over and over again the two main police periodicals publish letters and articles from those within the institution which reiterate this belief.

In some instances the women themselves have fallen into this male trap, and use their body size and form to define their own social value to 'the job'. Inevitably the masculine service has used these constructs of the body to its own ends and has generated support for the low opinion that police culture and society in general has for feminine systems and modes of thought; so that when women use the same principles to define their own place in male society, they inevitably find that body size and physical strength become labels to illustrate the belief that they are too big (unfeminine) or are too small (too weak). In this double bind they can never come out on top, as Sergeant Janet Curtis vainly proclaimed in a letter to the predominantly male audience of *Police Review* (6 October 1972): 'I have had experience of all the arduous duties quoted as being the province of male officers alone and there is nothing unusual about me. I am but 5′ 6″ tall and weigh 9 stone.' At the 1978 Police Federation conference another policewoman defending her ability to do a man's work told the audience she was the tallest and heaviest constable on her shift! She was rewarded by the patriarchal daily newspapers who gleefully pictured this 'amazon' on street patrol. Of course, it is always the women and never the men who are discussed in this way, in relation to measurement and weight. This obsession with the bodies of the women is of immense significance, for even though there are some very small and scrawny or excessively fat male officers, the low status of the women always ensures it is their physique which is commented upon. The only time the police magazines comment on male size is when the perennial arguments about the ambiguity of the British Transport Police or the 'dwarfs' of the Special Constabulary are up for review. As Coward (1984) has shown, the men's bodies and their sexuality

Dickens's *Oliver Twist*. It use in the North-East may parallel the conservative use of the archaic term 'prig', which is another word commonly employed by Fagan's team of pickpockets in the Dickens novel.

are taken for granted, whereas women's bodies are extensively defined, so that sexual and social meanings are imposed upon them.

During the whole of my police service it seems as if little has changed in relation to the repetitive remarks about the larger ladies.[8] The men jest about their bulk or ugliness, joke about their unfeminine form, or marvel at the continuous stream of heavy-bodied female recruits who apply for the service.

Disparaging comments are couched in the same vein as in the traditional British jokes about that symbolic dragon, the 'mother-in-law'. Implicitly they repeat the belief that any female entering male police society will necessarily abandon the femininity which defines women in the rest of society; yet still be denied any full acceptance into this male world.

Even when the policewoman meets the normal definitions of femininity and is petite, slim, and shapely, she runs the risk of being defined as too small or too weak to be effective; while her perceived sensuality will almost certainly pose a challenge to the integrity of the masculine model of sexual order. By her very presence she risks being labelled as either an icy virgin or something akin to the scarlet woman or whore. She is in a double bind, a Catch 22 situation, and cannot win; for she is a woman who is loose inside an extreme male society. Her presence is the equivalent of a woman having joined the Freemasons or leading the singing of bawdy songs in the Rugby Club bar after the game— both of which are activities dear to many male police hearts!

Terms of reference used to describe the 'typical lumpen creatures' who join the police are traditional. Over thirty years I have heard men complain we always seem to recruit women 'built

[8] I am grateful to Sarah Ladbury, who, after reading my early paper on policewomen ('Ladies of the Blue Light' 1979c), drew my attention to 'Language and Woman's Place' (Robin Lakoff 1975: 19–42). In this he assesses derogatory linguistic euphemisms applied to women. The word 'lady', he points out, is very much alive and is used to trivialize women, suggesting they are not to be taken seriously. As has often been noted, he continues, such derogatory terms for women are very often overtly sexual; and I am now keenly aware that my own use of the terms 'ladies, women, or girls' has been somewhat indiscriminate. That this reveals aspects of my own cosmology, in which (as Bourdieu (1977: 94) points out) 'principles . . . are placed beyond the grasp of consciousness' seems indisputable. I have not attempted to amend them here, because I believe they indicate the strengths of the *habitus* of police thinking, though, again echoing Lakoff (1975) I am now aware that: 'unless we start feeling more respect for women and . . . less uncomfortable about them and their roles in society in relation to men, we cannot avoid "ladies" any more than we can avoid "broads".'

battleship style, or like the [Co-op] store-horse'. I have heard it said, 'you must know ****, she's the new one with the moustache', and have been asked, 'have you seen the new policewoman, she's got a face like a bag of chisels?'

One sergeant, who read a draft of my seminar paper (1979c), told me in all seriousness that when he joined the police all women had to be butch to be acceptable, and it is a generally expressed belief that the majority will defy the image of the stereotypical perfect cover-girl woman. Of course this ideal woman is also unacceptable inside the institution, and indeed the slim, petite woman within the domain is equally resented, for the hostility is to women 'in the job' in general. In effect male police culture prefers women to stay outside, so that it is only when the female invades police society that the hostile imagery really begins to develop. To this end, the police tend to exaggerate a view of women as being naturally passive, obedient, quiet non-achievers, and to repress any credibility for their instrinsic mental abilities (Greer 1971: 99–103).

This enhances a view of a differentiated ability in the sexes and results in the secondary status of women or caricatures them as being incurably possessed of the denigrated and illusive principles of 'feminine instinct, irrationality and emotional illogicality'.

Such attributes are rejected in police culture, where status is conferred on beliefs in 'hard/control', and is structured to deny value to 'soft/caring' feminine principles. It is the force of this dichotomy in police culture which creates problems with external demands for change, such as those made by Lord Scarman (1981). Once again the strengths of these various homologous binaries can be illustrated in tabular form to indicate the conflict which is semantically generated in any institutional structure defined by such rigid dualities:

masculinity	femininity
hard	soft
logical	emotional
rational	irrational
scientific	instinctive
force	service
centrality	marginality
defining	defined
revered	rejected
inside	outside

Even if the 'butch' lady contradicts the norms of femininity and discards a soft image by taking on a hard, masculine style, in which she achieves a metaphoric invisibility by 'drinking pints in the club like one of the boys', she can only ever be partially acceptable. She may be a 'seven-footer with a face like a cathedral gargoyle' (all phrases collected in fieldnotes), but she is still a woman and remains structurally marginal.

The uniform covering the powerful bodies of these 'butch' creatures often seems to have been designed to allow them more easily to become surrogate men, by denying their feminine form. Lilian Wyles (1952), describing her 1919 uniform, said:

the uniform was unspeakable . . . designed surely by men who had a spite against us . . . When at last I stood before the mirror clad from head to feet in police provided clothing I shuddered, and for the first time regretted my choice of career.

There has been relatively little change to the basic uniform design since that time. For the most part it has been designed by men and reflect what they consider suitable for the male officers. Usually there has been some form of tunic or jacket—which at one time was encircled by a large leather belt. The cap or hat as a focal point of the uniform has been subject to incessant changes (for the women) over the years. These seem to follow the fashions in women's clothing and the idea that these must change at frequent intervals. At the present time, a dark brimmed bowler seems to have superseded the white topped, air hostess cap which has reigned for about a decade. Interestingly, the male bowler is just about extinct elsewhere in society.[9]

The jacket inevitably seems to deny the bust, while the cap hides the hair, which always had to be worn less than collar length. Any longer and it must be pinned or rolled up to keep it above the collar, and detailed written orders always confirm this control. Many career women over the years have adopted a total masculine style and with cropped hair, their uniform, and stout

---

[9] There has never been any attempt to put women into a replica of the somewhat phallic and bizarre male helmet, which has remained relatively unchanged throughout police history in England and Wales. The Scots, meanwhile, have maintained their own identity by resisting the helmet and using the flat cap.

build they have earned themselves a partial right to manœuvre more easily in male social space.

In subtle ways, the various garments and fashions for women in the police match those constraining uniforms of the girls' boarding schools described by Okely (1978: 128–31). The parallels between these institutions and the police are considerable, for both create a universe for women where the body is 'subjugated and unsexed' and demands:

the opposite to the notion of sexuality in the world outside. Our appearance was neutered. Our hair could not touch the backs of our shirt collars; in effect we were given the male 'short back and sides'. . . . The girls' uniform also had strange male traits: lace-up shoes, striped shirts, blazers, ties and tie pins . . . and denied an identity which asserted the dangerous consciousness of sexuality . . .

In the closed environs of the police, this neutralization is similarly accomplished by ordering the hair. It also demands black flat-heeled laced shoes, ensures the female form lies concealed beneath the military style uniform and requires that it submit to the constraints of a collar and tie. All these demands of style, like the thick black stockings which enhance the 'upside-down legs' or the abhorrence of jewellery and make-up, are bodily controls which deny women the conception of the self which is available to their peers elsewhere in society.

C. S. S. Kerswell-Gooch (1980), then a sergeant in Cambridge, tackled what the *Police Review* (12 December 1980: 2500) described as 'the vexed question of the impracticality of many women police uniforms'. Her findings were that short, tight skirts, handbags, capes, and soft, unprotective hats were handicaps women police could do without. She claimed that to do a police officer's job effectively, trousers were essential and should be regular issue, not just optional as in some forces. They should be wearable at all times, she declared, and not just at the dictate of some senior (male) officers who would order skirts for some occasions and trousers for others; it is 'too bad if some women don't look good in trousers—fat policemen don't either!'

She also mentions the endless redesigning of the uniform and the resultant air-hostess-type gear. Again this symbolizes a male view of changing fashions, which rarely affect the men in the same manner; a North-East policewoman cosidered the uniform to be 'an absolute misery for wearing to work in a town centre beat in January . . . [it was] pitifully inadequate to ward off the cold even with three pairs of tights, boots and a concealed woollen pullover.' Two years prior to this, a policewoman in Devon and Cornwall wrote to the *Police Review* (6 January 1978):

it came to me in a blinding flash . . . cullotes! That's what we emancipated policewomen should be wearing in these modern times. They combine the smartness and femininity of a well-cut skirt with the practicality of slacks, in which, let's face it, the majority of female forms look less than elegant.

I have since worked with policewomen in culottes, which at a casual glance had this smartness of a well-cut skirt, but the writer of the letter cannot have anticipated the response of the *Police Review*. Two months later WPC Glover of Surrey became the cover girl in culottes. The illustration cannot be said to depict the anticipated femininity in the 'elegant smartness of the well-cut skirt'. Rather it produces an image which perfectly states the unspoken principles of a male police cosmology which demands theses ideas of order are 'placed beyond the grasp of consciousness, and hence cannot be touched by voluntary transformations' (Bourdieu 1977: 94). This culotted policewoman stands with her legs wide apart in her long-short trousers, indicating that any possible sexual or feminine exposure is non-existent in such a garment. In many ways these culottes compare with the school shorts described by Okely (1978: 130). These, she tells us, were garments which 'concealed the existence of a split between the thighs. Two deep pleats in front and back made them like a skirt, but one which did not lift to reveal the thighs or buttocks . . . the lower abdomen retained its mystery . . .'. In addition to the control exercised by the culottes, the legs of this policewoman are neutralized in black lisle. Her shoes are laced and flat, her tunic is buttoned in regulation style, and at her neck she has the male version of collar and tie with a large knot. Her hair is short and boyish, or is pinned up revealing both ears. In effect she displays a male body!

A decade later, in a BBC television documentary on policewomen, *A Policewoman's Lot* (10 November 1988), Sgt Sheena Thomas described her fears when a gang of louts threatened to push her over the balcony of a block of flats. Her main concern, she recalled, was not for her safety, but that her feminine modesty would be destroyed, for beneath her uniform skirt she was wearing orange knickers, which were about to be revealed. It is almost impossible to imagine a policeman admitting fear of exposure of underwear, or concern for his sexual modesty, but then that is not a male preserve.

The ex-Metropolitan Police Commissioner, Sir Robert Mark (1978) is interesting in his references to policewomen. Although praised for being the first to effect male and female integration, some three years before the Sex Discrimination Act came into force (Hilton, *Police Review*, 17 September 1976), he clearly demonstrates views which are lodged in a framework of the male ideology. In the 320 pages of his autobiography he has only two items on policewomen. One I will recount later in relation to the women's perceived sexual proclivities, while the other concerns their uniform, where Sir Robert seems unable to resist the temptation to trivialize women or make weak jokes about their biology (ibid. 90):

The last change I made as Assistant Commissioner 'D' branch, related to women. This does not imply any need for alarm. I had always recognised that women were biologically necessary for the continuance of the force and were better able than men to persuade the public of our virtues as a service. In Leicester I had boldly ignored all the various Home Office exhortations and equipped them with court shoes, short skirts, air hostess tunics and shoulder bags. The effect was electric ... our recruitment rocketed. So, alas, did our matrimonial rate of wastage. My predecessor in the Met had asked Norman Hartnell to do something similar for the women and we had a special Press showing of the result. It took time to bite, but gradually had an effect on recruitment.

Sir Robert may have 'ignored Home Office exhortations' in his pursuit of short skirts and air-hostess-type tunics, but seems to have also 'boldly ignored' the practical mastery of those female officers, like the North-East woman quoted above, who deplore the impracticabilities which result from male opinion and 'expertise'.

This Norman Hartnell' creation for the Met women was only one of many male attempts to deal with the integrated woman. In December 1977, a *Police Review* cover previewed a 'New Uniform for Met. Ladies', created by the design team of 'Mansfield Originals'. The hat is 'by Mme Simone Mirman, the Royal

Milliner' and the cover illustration shows this allegedly, 'New Uniform' replicated some seven times on the same woman creating an image of a cloned creature marching towards us. Inside the magazine it is reported there is to be an innovation to go with this new style, for

the women will be able to mix'n match their garments to suit themselves, their duties and the weather conditions. The jacket is designed to be worn with skirt or trousers and outer garments include a double-breasted coat, a straight cut raincoat and a three quarter length coat. Officers can choose between long or short sleeved white tailored shirts and a cravat replaces the tie. (*Police Review*: 9 December 1977)

This is palpable nonsense! Uniformity by its very nature abhors choice, and many forces maintain strict written orders dictating when trousers, skirts, or short-sleeved shirts may or may not be worn. I have worked with commanders who were uniform martinets, and issued their own divisional orders to further tighten the controls on when and where certain items of uniform could be used or were forbidden.[10]

Another aspect of the regulation of the body which reflects the social experience of being a policewoman in a man's world is revealed by the marching clones on this *Police Review* front cover. For in an institution where the principles of control always prevail to entwine the social, the cultural, and the biological, a preferred carriage of the body is prescribed by the male obsession with uniformity, discipline, and posture, and is enhanced by the use of drill. From the time of its reception into the male police world, the female body is made to regulate its deportment. Drill is mandatory at police training schools, with marching, saluting, parades, and inspections by the equivalent of the regimental sergeant-major. Wyles (1952: 20) tells how, in the early 1920s, 'I enjoyed immensely the First Aid and the drill . . . We went to Wellington Barracks where under the strict eye of our drill Sergeant, we were taught to march'. Sixty years later, the *Police* magazine cover (Vol. 10, No. 7 (March 1978)) showed the modern equivalent of Wyles's drill sergeant. This shaven headed

---

[10] I have known a commander ban the use of the Nato sweaters even though these had long been officially issued by the force as an alternative to the costly and less comfortable tunic.

'drill-pig',[11] with his row of medal ribbons and swagger stick,[12] mimics the military formulae. He leans forward to scrutinize a rigidly immobile female cadet, while another waits her turn. These girls have short hair, collar and tie (no cravat for them yet), tunic and epaulettes. It is noticeable that in an era when the youth culture of the time was obsessed with highly visual punk styles, these 18-year-old women stand in contradictive imagery to their peers in society, for they are totally without make-up.

Make-up was banned for years in many forces by written order. A touch of lipstick might have been acceptable, but even in the permissive 1960s when attitudes relaxed and symbols of control were diluted, a heavily made-up policewoman on my division was derogatively nicknamed 'the painted lady',[13] while another who wore a rather pervasive perfume and had visibly dyed hair was dismissed as 'the peroxide hooer [whore]'. In 1919, Wyles (1952: 44) found:

All make-up had been strictly forbidden, and the hair had to be severely dressed, in fact not an atom, not even a stray end showed itself from beneath the close-fitting helmet, which looked so much like an inverted soup plate upon the head.

[11] The term 'drill-pig' is another symbolic use of animal metaphor in language, used to make a statement about ideology. Traditionally the drill sergeant is caricatured as an unthinking brute, who dominates and controls not because of logic or reason, but because of power and threat or force. Ideally he has a red shiny visage like his animal counterpart and sports bristles instead of hair.

[12] Swagger sticks were unknown as a uniform accoutrement in Northumbria, but one of the first questions I was asked on my transfer to West Mercia was 'have you got your stick'? These were the prerogative of superintendents and above, in a force which has many close ties to the traditions of military style. In 1988, a young inspector bemoaning the traditionalism and pomposity of some aspects of the force, laughed as he told me of his subdivisional commander who 'likes nothing better than to be invited to some local function which he can go off to in full uniform with stick. It makes his day.'

[13] Allison James (1979) has considered the significance of nicknames at some length. In the police the use of nicknames is considerable; structurally they are used as part of the institutional desire to obscure and conceal. This is consistent with the idea of 'defensiveness' I have mentioned, and allows the lower ranks to talk about each other in an insider's code, with the nickname often forming a humorous term of address. In contrast, nicknames used only as a term of reference are almost always bestowed on the despised senior officers, and allow the lower ranks to 'slag off' the command with some impunity. The significance of the women's nicknames will be discussed in due course.

The 1960 Northumberland Constabulary Force Order, Section 6, detailed the 'Conditions of Service and Instructions for Police-women, Cadets, Police Reservists and Special Constables'. Linking women with such other marginals further reinforces my point that policewomen stand defined as outsiders, ambiguous to categories of 'real polises'. The tiny establishment of fifteen women (in a force of some 450–500) is reminded that:

... the following instructions regarding dress apply:

(a) black shoes and stockings must always be worn with uniform
(b) cosmetics must be used in moderation
(c) hair must be neatly arranged and must not show under the peak of the cap
(d) jewellery will not be worn with uniform except a plain wrist watch, metal identity wristlet, a plain gold ring or simple dress or engagement ring. If two rings are worn they must be both on the same finger ...

In 1980, the Orders of the amalgamated Northumbria Force were reappraised. Not a lot had changed in the subsequent two decades. The new Orders, Section 2, para. 27 set out the current thinking:

(a) Cosmetics may be used in moderation
(b) Hair must be neatly arranged and must not fall below the top of the collar of the jacket nor show under the front of the hat
(c) Jewellery will not be worn with uniform except a plain wristlet watch, wedding ring, engagement ring or simple dress ring. Earrings will not be worn ...

This fear of an indiscipline in uniform matters is a constant concern of all police units. In March 1987, the weekly Force Orders of West Mercia reminded officers that in relation to jewellery 'the Force Policy General Order 6, as reproduced below remains unchanged':

The wearing of jewellery by male and female officers whilst on duty will not be allowed, with the following exceptions:

Earrings will only be worn when specific permission has been granted by the Officer's Divisional or Departmental Commander. Officers may insert a small sleeper or stud during the immediate period after piercing to prevent natural healing (normally six weeks).

Necklaces, neck chains and pendants may be worn if completely obscured by being worn underneath clothing. Wedding rings, eternity rings, engagement rings and signet rings may be worn, but the wearing of dress rings or a multiplicity of rings is not permitted.

All officers must clearly understand that the wearing of jewellery whilst on duty in uniform for decorative purposes is totally unnecessary and contrary to the principles of a disciplined service.

I have described how, when I was in a drug squad, our aberrant hair was problematic for senior officers and difficult for the culture to incorporate, where the action of cutting the hair always equates to social control (Hallpike 1969). Its containment has the effect of allowing cropped women to operate more easily within male space, and contrasts forcibly with the imagery of female hair in the outside world, where long, flowing hair has been consistently used as a marker of women's sexuality, and also as an organizing principle to symbolize their potential for disorder and social chaos (Firth 1973: 262–98). As Leach (1958), Polhemus (1978), and Greer (1971: 37–8) have all shown, hair is often elaborately woven into cultural systems, with its style and form used to indicate social approval for beliefs and ideology, or as an extremely visible form of symbolic anti-structure. In modern Western society, such women with long, flowing hair have been extensively used in advertising to symbolize an idealized femininity, both sexually alluring and compliant; and of course to sell lots of conditioner, shampoo, and other commodities!

Finally in this consideration of the control of the female body, it seems necessary to make mention of the voice. Whoever defines the agenda in an institution inevitably controls access to the lines of communication and retains prior claim on the positions of power. After generations without any real say in the social discourse, women have only just begun to acquire a public voice; for in many areas such as the law, politics, religion, education, and the other power bases of society, women have always been without rights or regarded as 'male property' and denied the right to contribute.

Just like the hair, this controlled or silent voice speaks metaphorical volumes about the restrictive practices of a social order; for by controlling this access to the social discourse, the body of the woman is further subdued. This construct of the silent woman is deeply embedded in police ideology and is strongly resistant to change. Inevitably this silent presence is a further reason why women rarely reach the top echelons of police society, for having been symbolically struck silent in voice and rendered numerically absent, they remain doubly invisible. When men control the public discourse, vocal women tend to be dismissed simply as 'clucking old hens' and denied hierarchic place; so that many competent women leave simply because of the tremendous inhibitions they face in working such a system. Always the institutions of power demand the rational voice of logic, which as we have seen is considered the prerogative of the men. It is no surprise, therefore, to find that other male bastions reflect a similar female absence in their discourses. In 1978, for example, only 44 of 3,218 university professors in Britain were women, none of the 44 Vice-Chancellors was a woman, and out of 36,000 members of the Institute of Directors, only some 900 (or one-fortieth) were women. Ten years later the situation had changed little and figures for female achievement in the police indicate their public voice remains muted; for men still define the agenda and the female voice is all but non-existent in the hierarchies:

In an appendix to the chief Inspector of Constabulary's annual report (for 1984) one finds that there are 11,226 men of the rank of Inspector and above, and only 219 women. There are six paragraphs on police dogs, but nothing in the body of the report on women officers . . . (Letter from the Howard League to the *Guardian*)

It is 10 years since women were officially integrated and what have we got? Unofficial (illegal) entry quotas in many forces; . . . fewer women employed in some places . . . two commanders instead of one in the Met and one Assistant Chief Constable who is rumoured to have got the job because few men wanted it . . . (Lock 1987)

Further down the ranks the individual female voice remains firmly controlled and defined, as the following fieldnote indicates:

1978. 'B' Shift. City Centre Subdivision, Newcastle. I have a number of policewomen on the shift. One is young, well educated and articulate. She is bright and brash, with the self-confidence of youth, and is producing a range of conflicts in the men and in herself. Her University degree is the subject of the usual denigration and the men ask 'why has this bloody educated woman come into the police?' These grumbles indicate the emotive response female education still arouses in male society. She is dismissive of the many structural limitations and restrictions placed on women in police society and is becoming increasingly voluble and dismissive of the constraints placed upon females. The men, in turn, are increasingly dismissive of her loquaciousness and bestow on her the nick-name 'Gatling Gob'. In the symbolic content of this nickname the men are redressing what, to them, is a social malformation. This attempt to silence the provocation caused by the uncontrollable female and the nature of the nickname, restates the unspoken structural asymmetry of police society . . . the name is an attempt to redress the provocation caused by that uncontrollable social marginal—the vocal woman.

Other nicknames given to policewomen in the subdivision at this time further illustrate these modes of masculine thought and reinforce the message that in the police it is men who define the women. 'Giant Haystacks' (a tall and powerfully built blonde policewoman) was named after an all-in wrestler, repeating the belief that women should be petite and demure. 'Glenda Jackson', a look-alike who was as competent and outspoken as her namesake is in politics and the world of drama, was always treated warily by the men. As a result of her cool self-confidence and professional self-assurance she was rumoured to be lesbian, largely based on the fact that she failed to demonstrate any of the indicators of female dependence which the men expected of women. The 'Principal Boy's' name was taken from the English pantomime tradition of gender exchange. This ambiguous woman displayed ambivalent styles, some of which confused the male preference for a clear-cut female definition. 'The Melted Wellie', who answered to the name with no sign of distress, was literally said to have a face like a melted wellington boot (another version of 'the Burglar's Dog'), while the 'Beast from the East' and 'Dog Breath' were other ugly indicators. Like the 'six pinter', on the shift at the time, the 'double bagger' was a name defined by the sexist joke I heard again some seven or eight years later, told by a superintendent at the Police Staff College in 1987. This sets out the differences between a 'bagger', a 'double bagger', and a 'stumper':

The bagger is so ugly that you have to put a bag over her head. The double bagger is worse, so you put a bag over your head as well, in case hers bursts. With a stumper, you wake up in the morning after a night on the beer and she's lying cradled in your arm, sound asleep; and she's so bloody ugly that you cut off your arm at the elbow and leave it behind on the pillow rather than take the chance of waking her up.

The 'double bagger' is therefore another statement about women being used as the objects of male control, for they are to be gagged and used by men, and denied any say or any choice in their own destiny.

A woman's place

In sketching out a brief history of women in the police, I have outlined some of the arenas in which these marginalized and defeminized creatures were allowed to operate. Most of their duties were directed to areas considered suitable for women but unappetizing to men. Both Lilian Wyles (1952) and Dorothy Peto[14] describe the development of these specialist areas, which reflect a rigid belief in a correct situation for 'women's work'. Their memoirs are full of anecdotes about the anomalous and ambiguous areas of society, which are still not considered to be 'real work' for 'real polises'. Writing of that epitomy of social dirt, the prostitute, Wyles (1952: 31) denounces 'those most wretched of women, outcast from all decent society . . . accosting and suggesting, plying their abominable profession, to all appearances unashamedly and without restraint'. There is no consideration here of the part men play in the use of prostitutes and both authors follow the style of the times and display themselves as crusading women, opting to deal with these activities in a spirit of salvation, by using firm religious and moral discipline as a criteria for action. They engage us with a succession of anecdotes about the specificities of their work, dealing with fallen women, brothels, venereal diseases, and missing girls in grave sexual and moral danger. Wyles's (ibid. 240) shock at discovering the realities of 'incest' and its social invisibility, vividly shows the naïvety of the women recruited into the police in these early days:

Of all my duties . . . the most repugnant was dealing with cases of incest. This revolting crime, the intimacy between blood relations . . . has always been to me the one crime I could never understand. I must have dealt

---

[14] *Police Review* (9 March 1979. No. 4494: 358–65) has two photographs of Superintendent Dorothy Peto, whose memoirs cover the years 1922–30. Except for the name the image is that of a man, for the hair is close cropped and Supt Peto's uniform hat is the male version. A similar photograph (*Police Review*, 28 Aug. 1981) of four women officers arriving in Cologne in 1923, shows them in caps, greatcoats, and knee-length leather boots; all wear short back and sides revealing the ears. Only the names indicate these are women.

with as many cases of incest as any woman in this country ever has, but I have never reconciled myself to their cause or their effect. Leading psychiatrists and psychologists have held long discussions and conferences with me on this bestial, and to me inexplicable crime. I never felt impressed by any of the learned conclusions they arrived at which always appeared to me to be lacking in perspicuity . . . Incest is not a subject for polite society—the word is heard but rarely. Many people have never heard the word at all and would not understand the meaning if they did. Perhaps it is as well that they are ignorant of what is horrible in this world; as to the sensitive, the knowledge might bring with it depression and sorrow and most certainly disgust . . . I myself knew nothing of this particular crime when I joined the police. It came as a profound shock to me to know that a girl was going to have a baby by her own father. Quite a time elapsed before I really grasped what was going to happen.

Nowhere, of course, does Wyles pursue the point that incest is about the power men exercise over women's bodies, over property rights, and social place. It is a continuity of the same historic ideology that essentially defines women as the chattels of men, and paves the way for their continued marginalization. In effect, it is the same process which generates the concept of 'women's work' in the police and restricts this to the care and welfare of other women in trouble and children at risk. Always the emphasis is on 'care and welfare' rather than on the total arena of power and control, which remains the province of the men. Wyles (ibid. 18) unconsciously shows how this structural dichotomy was enhanced:

as the years passed I was to introduce into the machinery of the Metropolitan Police a system of welfare and after-care . . . Some high ranking [male] officers would remark caustically that it was police officers who were needed . . . not welfare workers.

So, even though women had been channelled away from the real work of 'thief-taking', and into the marginality of 'care' and 'welfare', their presence was still a structural thorn in the side of the male culture; and today there are still many who would like to set women aside in a separate organization, like the traffic wardens.

In the late 1950s when I was first in police society, all the various forces had specialist policewomen's departments. The occasional female equivalent of the 'token black' was to be found in the CID, but most were confined to their department, and called upon only when a woman or child was brought in. Invariably they dealt with shoplifting, which has long had a female identification (even though it is widely practised by young men). In addition they took statements from the victims of rape or indecent assault on females (it was not then legally possible to indecently assault a man!), while another of their main tasks concerned 'Missing Persons' enquiries. Again this activity has a police history which identifies it with women's work, and since the demise of the specialist women's units the Missing Persons' enquiry has remained in something of a structural limbo.[15]

One of their tasks allocated to women in Newcastle City Police again illustrates how they were set apart and given a separate location of action. Two policewomen commenced patrol at 6.30 a.m. in the city centre (while the early shift for men commenced at 6 a.m.) on what was affectionately known as 'netty patrol.[16] Female absconders from care hostels, approved schools, and the like were sought in the bus depots, railway stations, and parks where they might have found shelter. On 'netty patrol', these women were following a precedent laid down by the first voluntary patrols at the time of the First World War, although I doubt very much that they were aware of this.

On nightshift one policewoman was rostered to deal with any female prisoner who had to be searched, lodged, and interviewed. If there were no female prisoners, she typed, made tea, and answered the phones, but never officially went out on patrol for two unwritten reasons. The first was that it was too dangerous (for these weak creatures) to be out at night on patrol, while the second unspoken belief was that 'Eve' would prove to be a temptation to the men. Needless to say she still remained a sensual provocation inside the station, and no doubt there were occasional liaisons in the nether hours, when certain amorous pairings took the opportunity of a quiet lull in station activities.

In their specialist departments the women worked shorter hours than the men, were paid only seven-eighths of the male salary, and had their own rank structures. All forces had official

[15] In 1985/6, as a subdivisional superintendent, I was reminded how this area of police work has always been of limited symbolic import, and often has poor administrative systems for recording or following up enquiries. Nothing has occurred across thirty years to change its low status, and so the Missing from Home enquiry remains on the margins of 'real police work'.

[16] 'Netty' = toilet in North-Eastern slang.

limitations on the percentage of women allowed in the establishments. As Lewis (1976: 176) points out, this

meant that even in a large force women . . . had the limited promotion
possibilities of a small force; while in a small force they had few or none.
They took the same exams but had a set quota of ranks, and promotion
was by selection. The career girl was discouraged.

Indeed it was usually a case of 'dead woman's shoes' and even
then their selection was always defined by the fact that promotion
lay within the province of the senior men.

In the late 1960s in the Newcastle City Force, the women had
their department on the first floor of the main central police
station, with their own offices, rest rooms, and command, with a
top rank of chief inspector. I suspect it was an unconscious but
none the less illuminating structural decision that placed them on
the same floor as the other marginals, alongside the civilian typists
and female telephonists, the coroner's and aliens' officers, the drug
squad and the dog section.

Civilians, as I have indicated, are always reminded they are *not*
police officers and there is a constant tendency to use the word in
a pejorative or derogatory manner. The female telephonists and
typists were all civilians, while next door in the drug squad, as I
have described above, we were on the periphery of police society.
It was a matter of regular and jocular comment that my men
in the squad often had longer hair than the crop-headed women
across the corridor in the policewomen's department. The dogs
and the handlers are also on the margins of police society. The relationship of the dog with human society has been explored by
Leach (1964) and Kolig (1978) among others, who point out they
hold a peculiar interstitial place between human and animal
classification. In the UK, the dog has a special place in society. It
is an animal, but is not edible and is definitely not 'meat'. Kolig
(ibid. 109), quoting Eliade (1958, 1960) and Turner (1969), concludes dogs are often the equivalent of 'liminal personae', and this
I suggest holds good for the police dog and his handler; for a large
part of their specialist role relates to dealings in Community
Affairs, entertaining at carnivals and fetes and acting as a public
relations medium. Rarely, if ever, are they considered to be centrally situated in a structural binary of 'cops and robbers', and so
remain firmly on the periphery.

Next door to the policewomen's department, the coroner's officer's clients had all ceased to be human. The police officers given the task of supporting HM Coroner by sorting out the post-mortems and inquests of fatal accidents, suicides, and other sudden deaths, shared an office area with the Aliens Department, whose clients were foreign and definitely not 'us'. I suspect, therefore, that at the time the place for the women police was clearly demonstrated to be correctly situated with the civilians and the ambiguous, and well clear of those areas frequented by 'real polises'.

During the 1960s an emergent self-consciousness did begin to affect some women, and as they started to move slowly into the previously exclusively male domains, they began to write about the difficulties inherent in such an activity. Jennifer Hilton (1976), then a chief inspector in the Metropolitan Police, wrote:

> the danger is that because by custom certain tasks are almost invariably performed by women, they are likely to be identified with these tasks alone and so the role of women in the police service will continue to be seen as specialist rather than generic.

Hilton, it should be noted, refers to the police 'service' and not to a police 'force'. She seems somewhat ambivalent in her call for an undifferentiated place for women, however, and seems unsure how women will operate when they achieve a generic role (or she is playing the politics of compromise); for she concludes this essay (which won her the Queen's Police Gold Medal) with the suggestion that, although there should be more equal opportunities for women,

> the police service should probably continue to have a preponderance of men and not only for their strength and weight, but also for their 'hard' image . . . it is important that the police service does not drift into having a soft social therapy image, blurring 'right and wrong', as it might if women . . . came to equal policemen in numbers . . .

I am unsure where Hilton's sympathies lie, for this assertion repeats a belief in a dichotomized service, which will inevitably work against any generic role for women in police society; but in 1983 her unusual hierarchical place in the male world of policing caused some comment and her swift rejoinder when a newspaperman, working on the assumption that any senior voice in the institution must be male, attributed Jenny Hilton with male gender!

Malcolm Dean (*Guardian*, 28–9 December 1983), looking at male bias in the Metropolitan Police, and quoting from Hilton's paper (1976), tells the reader, '*He* concluded that . . .'. Hilton, at this time a chief superintendent in the Metropolitan Police, replied *she* was 'amused to discover, in an article on sex discrimination in the police service, the writer's assumption that I am a man'. The two articles followed a civil action taken against the Met. Police by a woman constable. Wendy de Launy had passed the necessary driving course with very high marks, but had then been refused permission to double-crew a traffic patrol with a married male colleague. Her chief superintendent believed this partnership between an attractive woman and a married male officer could create problems, but would not have imposed the ban if she had had 'a face like the back of a bus'. The Equal Opportunities commission said of the case: 'Her misfortune is to be both good looking and intelligent, a combination her employers don't seem to be able to contend with'.[17]

Although traffic patrol is not 'real polising' in that it deals with the 'ordinary public' and is only peripherally involved in the pursuit of thieves and 'prigs', it has always been a specialist area reserved for men, admitting only the occasional token woman. Many forces denied women access to traffic sections until the 1970s, some forty years after their inception. In West Mercia the 'first two women traffic officers' were celebrated in 1970, and their photograph was used again in 1988 in the 21st Anniversary edition of the force newspaper. W/Inspector Jan Field, recalls in an article 'Policewomen Take a Front Seat':

I was lucky enough to be chosen as one of the Force's first two women traffic officers . . . but the fact that we wore skirts caused problems—and a traffic hazard, as motorists were distracted by the sight of next week's washing as we carried out examinations underneath vehicles . . . (*West Mercian*, No. 16. October 1988)

Other specialisms still remain the province of the men. In an enquiry into the 'Suitable job for a Woman' (*Police Review*, 24 April 1987) Joan Lock asks 'women police dog handlers; why are they

---

[17] See also the *Guardian* 22 Dec. 1983; the *Sunday Times*, 18 Dec. 1983. WPC de Launy's 'married male colleague' was subsequently disciplined for giving evidence to the tribunal without formally seeking authority from the force. A *Guardian* leader (28 Dec. 1983) considered this situation to be 'unhealthy', especially when the Metropolitan Police claim the right to decide whether a key witness against themselves should have the right to appear with their authority.

such a rare breed?' Across the country she found only twenty-one women dog handlers, and the Metropolitan Police had only six women out of an establishment of 330 (1.8 per cent). Indeed, their first operational woman dog handler was only appointed in 1979. Inevitably the unacknowledged reason for this asymmetry again lies in the structural dominance of the male ideology. This leads to the self-fulfilling prophecy that women cannot do the job, and was a factor that the women dog-handlers who were questioned merely considered as 'inevitable'. Once again the primary reasons used to deny them access relate to a perceived physical weakness, and somewhat surprisingly, to the contention that their voices are not strong enough to command the dog! Having previously been castigated for being unfemininely loud and outspoken, we are now told (by a male chief inspector), that women 'don't seem to get the same passion [into their voices] as a man'.

Bloch and Anderson (1974), in an American study on the relative capabilities of male and female patrol officers, concluded women perform generally in a similar manner to men and could be used on patrol work on the same basis. Sherman (1975), from his own and other research, argued that the capabilities of policewomen could be taken as being equally comparable to those of policemen. However, such research findings fly in the face of the resistance to change and the durability of the masculine culture, where deeply forged principles merely reflect a continued rejection and long-held resistance to any belief in women's capabilities. In 1933, *The Times* commented on the first female appointment to the CID in the Metropolitan Police (Gornall 1975: 40):

the women who have now become detectives have proved that they can be employed with confidence in almost every type of crime detection. The contention that criminals would treat women detectives with scant respect has been found to be without foundation . . .

Yet across all police societies such a role for women was proscribed and it was not until 1963 that a woman was appointed to the New York equivalent of the CID. At the same time American policewomen won the right, at least in New York, to take the examination for sergeant for the first time; but only after a law suit forced the change through (Gornall 1975, Mishkin 1981).

In 1971 the Equal Pay Act decreed that in Britain there would be equal pay for women by 1974. It did not, however, direct that they would receive equal pay for equal work, but introduced ambiguities by stating women would be entitled to equal pay for work of equal value. The contentious argument over what is 'work of equal value' has allowed the general principles of asymmetry to continue, and many women today are still paid less for what might well be described as equal work—depending on who does the defining! In the police, Sir Robert Mark was quick to pioneer the integration of men and women. In his 1973 Annual Report, he said:

There is no longer a separate rank structure for women. They are able to compete for promotion by examination and before selection boards on equal terms with men and are being employed on any duty for which their individual qualities fit them.

Sir Robert's appreciation of political change was taken up by other chief officers and they belatedly followed suit, although some were less than happy with the idea of male and female integration. A letter (30 December 1975) from the Secretary of State to the chief constables then ordered that authorized police establishments of permitted police officers should cease to provide separately for men and women police officers. Women were to be fully integrated throughout the country as a result of the Sex Discrimination Act, although 'at least 16 Forces returned to or never dismantled their separate women's departments' (Sullivan 1979: 341). And as WPC de Launy's case showed, some ten years after Sir Robert's proclamation that women would be employed on any duty their qualities fitted them for, discrimination was still the norm. Again, in 1985, as I have recounted above, the potential for a woman to make the rank of detective sergeant in West Mercia was still subject to the whims of male definition and patronage.

Yet since the 1975 Act some highly reputable books on policing have suggested that a whole new social order has been founded by this one parliamentary measure. Lewis (1976: 176), for example, writes, somewhat naïvely, that women

now not only share promotion and career structures, but can and do command men ... the women's role has steadily evolved from specialising in women and children, sex offences, searches of females, domestic disputes, and a certain amount of quasi-routine, in R/T [radio/telecommunications] for example ... the general mood has increasingly enabled them to operate as all-round police officers, capable of any assignment.... They moved into the C.I.D. early on; now they not only excel in traffic work but form invaluable components in teams and task forces like the Special Patrol Groups, Regional Crime Squads and the like . . .

Yet within a year of the Sex Discrimination Act, chief officers and the Police Federation were proposing limitations on the numbers of women recruits, urging their restriction to certain activities, seeking to return them to their specialist departments, and even pursuing exemption from the requirements of the Act. The reasons put forward for these measures were always couched in terms which, I suggest, illustrates an inviolable belief in the sanctity of a prestigious male police ideology. An alleged feminine fragility and weakness which makes them totally unsuited to deal with the violent situation, has been the most frequently reiterated claim in articles and letters which have appeared regularly across the years in police journals and magazines. This of course led to a another structural paradox which Pat Sullivan (1979: 338), then a woman chief inspector, identified and described:

the men after clamouring for years for women to work nights if they were getting equal pay, suddenly decided that it was quite ridiculous for policewomen to be out on patrol at night and that women were going to be too much of a liability if involved in a fracas . . .

Other arguments against integration focused on the need to retain the specialisms which the women's departments had developed, for there is no doubt that many forces lost some expertise when the departments were dispersed. In many ways, I feel that in the circumstances the women lost out all round. First they lost much of their own self-esteem and the symbolic importance they had undoubtedly built up for themselves in dealing professionally with such emotive issues as rape victims, child offenders, missing persons, etc. But, then they also lost out when they failed to gain the generic place in police society which Hilton (1976), among others, had sought. In consequence they have been left in some sort of structural limbo and although a few have made a definite mark, mostly they are still defined by men, still discriminated against, still unable to have a central place in the social discourse on policing, and remain marginal to the central power bases of the institution.

In 1976 and 1977, an alleged increase in the numbers of women in the service was claimed by the Police Federation to be a cheap and unsatisfactory way of filling vacancies. Female officers, it was argued, were only partially acceptable because of the inadequacies of their sex, and a slight increase in the percentage of women officers (to 7 per cent of establishments) became a major factor in a federation campaign for a wage increase which they hoped would attract more *men*.[18] At their 1976 Annual Conference, arguments calling for a return to the pre-Sex Discrimination Act specialist departments for women were loaded with stereotypical views of the correct place for women, where their perceived fragility and emotive irrationality would not be subjected to the violent situation:

some girls have come to realise that working nights is not all it is cracked up to be . . . (Devon and Cornwall Federation Report)

. . . we do not think they are physically able to cope with violence . . . (attributed to Welsh delegate *Police* mag., June 1976).

The Superintendents' Association also came out against female integration at their 1977 Conference and were reportedly 'dismayed at the number of women entering the service' (*Police Review*, 7 October 1977). In Northumbria, the federation representative set out the official case for female separation:

we're not male chauvinist pigs—we're just trying to ensure the safety and protection of women . . . [the federation urged a] . . . return to the pre-Sex Act women police departments of two years ago, when the WPCs dealt mainly with women and children . . . (*Newcastle Journal*, 8 April 1978).

Such strident attempts to impose the continuation of a restricted role on women ignores the research evidence which has consistently shown that policewomen are equally adept as men at most police tasks. However, it is necessary to continue to deny this if the men are to support the deeply imbued ideology of gender hierarchy, which requires women to be persuaded into the traditional roles of wife and mother, caring for children, the elderly, and their own spouses. If they *are* to be allowed into the male world then it must be on male terms; and they must be only ever

---

[18] In 1960 women made up 3.16% of the total police establishment. By 1977 this had risen to 7.27%, although the figure reached 11% in some forces. By the 1980s the figure for women had stabilized at just below 10%, with variations between 4.7% (Norfolk) and 11.5% (Greater Manchester) (Southgate 1980).

allocated a tiny place on the periphery while undertaking a parallel role to their preferred domestic situation, and denied the right
to exhibit the accepted feminine traits while doing this.

This ideology is induced in the same way advertising quietly
but consistently impresses commodities and ideas upon the individual even without their conscious agreement (Packard 1960), for
in the immediate years following the Sex Discrimination Act the
police magazines and publications seemed consistently to promote
an image of women which tied them to their traditional role. In
the five years following the Act, innumerable illustrations in
Police Review and the *Police* magazine seemed designed quietly
to reiterate the message that policewomen should be properly
employed in dealing with children, with other women, with the
elderly, in the caring situation and in a range of symbolically
'softer' activities. At this time I was reading feminist anthropology and had begun to consider the imagery associated with
ideas of 'a woman's place' in the police and to collect examples of
these statements of structural order. The following are only a
sample (and are in no particular order).

1. *Police Review* cover 23 February 1979 shows a policewoman with a young female offender in a typical prisoner/inter-
view room situation. The caption: 'Dealing with Juvenile
Offenders' advertises an article inside on the 1969 Children and
Young Persons Act and the work of the Metropolitan Police
Juvenile Bureau. Nowhere in the article is it ever suggested that
women operate the bureau, yet the cover implies that policewomen and juveniles are synonymous.

2. *Police Review*, 8 December 1978. A cover illustration of an
article on 'Community Involvement in Dyfed Powys Police'
shows a young policewoman talking to a group of very old men on
a street corner. The nursing/caring/feminine role is clearly but
obliquely suggested.

3. The same nursing/caring role is again in evidence on the
cover of *Police* magazine (September 1979), where a policewoman
is photographed with an elderly Chelsea pensioner. There is no
inside story to accompany the photo-shot.

4. *Police Review*, 11 May 1979. The cover illustrates an article
entitled: 'A New Role for Women Police?' but shows the traditional tasks. A policewoman searches a young female (shoplifter?) in one photograph, while in another the same policewoman

holds a child who wears her hat and sucks a lollipop. The implication is, of course, that the child is lost and is being cared for by a
policewoman.

5.   *Police Review*, 30 September 1977 cover illustration of a
policewoman holding a child who is said to be, 'one of the Covent
Garden Festival's quota of lost children, who had chosen one of
the Met's better looking constables as a refuge'.

6.   On 3 March 1978, a *Police Review* photograph shows 2,000
found keys being handed into a television children's programme
(*Blue Peter*) appeal. The keys to be converted into cash had been
collected by the whole of Suffolk Constabulary, but it is a
policewoman and a female cadet who are shown as the two most
appropriate to hand over the keys to the children's programme.

7.   The *Police Review* cover (12 May 1978) previewed an
article by Doreen May entitled 'What Price Equality'. It shows a
smiling policewoman and child with ice cream, above another
photograph of a policewoman in a line of men at a public order
demonstration. This girl looks somewhat anxious—but then so do
the men! The inference is that equality is a bad business; policewomen should have stuck to children and ice cream!

8.   In yet another article headed 'What Price Equality' (*Police
Review*, 6 March 1981) Doreen May reconsiders the demise of the
policewomen's departments, quoting women who either support
or bemoan the loss of the specialist units. Under a photogaph of a
male police officer holding a small child and feeding bottle, the
caption asks: 'Who should be holding the baby?' We are left in no
doubt that this is not a role for a man. On the opposite page, beneath a photograph of a group of officers at some public demonstration, where the one female officer is shown with hat askew, the
caption asks: 'Playing their part in public order. But is this the
best way to use policewomen?'

The October 1977 issue of the *Police* magazine shows three
policewomen at 'band practice', which although a definite non-
combatant, community affairs activity and therefore one which
would seem ideally tailored for women, accompanies an article
headlined: 'Too Many Women Recruits!' A year later the *Daily
Mail* (7 November 1978) asked, 'Why are there so many women
in the front line?' Their photograph showed two armed policewomen at target practice, while the caption underneath asks: 'But
can girl recruits do a man's job?' The Scottish Police Federation

were certain they could not and the *Guardian* (27 April 1978)
reported their chairman's assertion that 'women have limitations',
under a headline which read, 'Police work hampered by sex
equality'. *The Times* reported the same item under the headline:
'Recruitment of women—no answer to fall in police manpower',
while the *Daily Express* (24 January 1978) suggested:

Petticoat police-power may be attractive to the men in the street, but it is
a distraction to the policeman on the beat, for while it is better for a
woman to interview sexual assault victims, they fall from grace on such
physical occasions as pub brawls . . . [and the men have to] spend more
time looking after them than arresting the criminals . . .

Almost inevitably the women are still being stereotypically
portrayed as 'falling from grace' and in need of masculine protection to avert this. Yet at the same time they are guilty of dis-
tracting the policemen by their 'petticoat' power and Medusan
charms, so that their presence in the wrong social space is indicated by a range of symbols of feminine weakness or subversion.

Gill Pyrah in the *Listener* (25 January 1979) commented on the
most regularly voiced objection to women in the police: 'they are
not as strong and do not look as intimidating as their male
colleagues'. In Northumbria at this time, a woman chief inspector
collected the views of the various divisional commanders on this
contentious issue, and reported '[the main theme] in the Divisional Commanders' reports is the natural lack of physical
strength of policewomen; and how policemen feel they have to
protect them . . .'. A large number of the covers of the police
magazines in my collection from this period reflect this message
that women are weak and need protecting by men. The visible
message contained in these images is that women should not be
involved in situations of physical confrontation, for they are best
suited to remain with the animals, the children, and the abandoned babies. Again and again they adorn the covers with seals,
pumas, dogs, and other animals, or can be found posing with the
flowers at the local shows or carnival. Sometimes they are simply
presented—in soft focus—in the police equivalent of the cheese-
cake shot, which inevitably draws the caption: 'She's a bobby
dazzler'.

The symbolic load asymmetrically attributed to the place of
women in police society is consistent with an imposition of the

concept of gender hierarchy (Cucchiara 1981). The examples above all suggest a cultural world where symbolic thought and language weld firmly into a reproductive system which takes an extreme view of women who breach the boundaries, and rejects any attempt they might make to subsume the male place or activity. Consistently an image is presented of feminine weakness and unsuitability for this world of public control, and this physical vulnerability, which also incorporates a sexual risk to both themselves and the men, is posited as a constant danger to the male structures. Any acknowledgement that an integrated or generic system of egalitarian policing might occur would require the existing male definition of self to be dismantled or amended, to allow the female to assert that 'male' characteristics such as social dominance, driving ambition, or hierarchical status were equally valid for women. This would require a total change in police modes of thought, so that women might be seen as rational rather than impetuous; as objective instead of emotional; and logically decisive rather than inept. And of course within this reversal, another alternative possibility exists, with those areas of 'male' status expanding to include some of these negative attributes currently apportioned to women. But, in effect, this would require a massive conceptual change to the whole cultural system (and not only the police model of social reality would need a rewrite), and such a revolutionary impetus seems unlikely to come from police society.

Indeed, the male prestige structures flow on unperturbed, and gender hierarchy and differentiation continue to indicate the incongruity of women in a male world. In the mid-1980s one of the most common images used to reinforce this point has been of policewomen in riot gear training at the Metropolitan centre at Hounslow, when questions about the appropriate nature of such a role for women is always placed on the agenda. Not unexpectedly women have largely been denied any access to these male areas of operation, just as the sight of a woman police motor cyclist in full leathers is a rare occurrence. Most forces have simply determined that women will be kept off 'the front line' in public order situations. As the police periodicals reported, 'although the [three policewomen photographed] have received public order training, women officers in riot gear still have a novelty value for the press' (Lock 1987). PW Fiona Roberts's 'novelty value' was apparent when she was widely photographed and 'made headlines as she lined up in riot gear with male colleagues at Fortress Wapping' (*Police*, March 1986). The magazine recognized the novelty value of riot training for Metropolitan policewomen at the Hounslow Training Centre, by showing 'Doreen', their regular cartoon 'burglar's dog' in riot gear. This gargantuan woman, perhaps eight foot tall, towers over a group of visiting senior officers who fall back in amazement at 'our Hounslow Boadicea'. Blonde curls bush out unacceptably from beneath her riot helmet, and though she carries a shield and baton there are no flame-proof overalls, for she is still in a skirt, while the protective boots are foresaken for slip-on shoes. To complete the picture a flounce of petticoat peeps from beneath her knee-length skirt. This petticoat has become her trade-mark, for it sneaks coyly into view on all her appearances in the magazine!

In 1987 Tracy Axten and Annie Fooks were pictured in *Police Review* (1 May 1987) as the 'first women instructors at the Met's public order training centre at Hounslow'. The rarity of such moves into male space becomes worthy of such comment, but there seems little likelihood that the 'natural' order of things will be reversed or that we will see the situation envisaged by Hilton (1976: 1167), who suggested that 'women may be better at disarming a violent situation and therefore there is nothing to prevent women increasing their numbers in the system to satisfactorily control any crowd'. This may well be the case, but seems to ignore the cultural values and institutionalized systems which ensure that female intrusion into the male domain of policing is unlikely to expand beyond the 10–11 per cent they now maintain.

When I suggested to a group of colleagues (at a time when I was sketching some early thoughts on this subject) that there was no logical reason why the existing male/female ratios could not be reversed (i.e. *c.*10,000 men and 111,000 women) this initially met with a blank response. About an hour later, however, a sergeant came into my office and in a worried voice queried: 'you know, what you're suggesting would mean changing not just the police, but the whole of the world . . .' (from fieldnotes). We later had a long discussion on what was 'natural' and what could be socially reconstructed, but I suspect that Hilton's plea 'that there is nothing to stop women increasing their numbers' still has substantial barriers to surmount!

In effect the structural modes of the pre-integration period have been maintained, even though a supposed equality has been legally introduced. The women now patrol with the men but are often protected on nightshift, or are used in the communications rooms and other non-combatant areas whenever possible. Most young women probationers find themselves on 'the front line' and on occasions seem forced to over-react to the 'real world' situations simply because of the cultural pressures on them to act as 'one of the boys'. As Heilbrun (1979) asserts, those women who refuse to stay out of the male public sphere and venture into the largely asymmetric world of male power do so only if they can function as pseudo-males, and I found that most of the young female probationers have neither the experience nor the strength of purpose to take on the rigours of dealing with the drunks and the disagreeable, except by following the well-established male precedents of confrontation.

Again, this principle was clearly revealed by the imagery in the police magazines, especially during the period when the structural place for women was being reappraised in the light of the change in the law. 'Doreen', and other pseudo-male 'burglar's dogs' featured heavily in cartoons which directly restated the ambivalent attitudes of police society to these large yet allegedly weak ladies. As Cathy Morrison (*Police Review*, 22 October 1982: 2034–7) in a review of 'Cartoon Coppers' asserts:

The role assigned to policewomen in cartoon humour is in the safe area of caring for women and children, away from 'real' police work . . . Policewomen are either young, shapely sex-bombs or singularly unattractive spinsters . . .

In 1979 the winning entry in the *Police Review* Christmas Card competition shows a huge policewoman waiting outside a building for a burglar who climbs out of the window with his bag of swag. She holds out a bunch of mistletoe while he looks suitably dismayed—and not just at his impending detention! (*Police Review*, 2 November 1979.)

In 1984 a similar gargantuan eight foot 'burglar's dog' towers over and brushes aside Arthur Scargill in a *Police* magazine cartoon. She is arm-linked to a line of men and because of her bulk lifts them completely off their feet, while two male officers illustrate the ambivalence by complaining that 'Riot training for policewomen is all very well, but we've enough on our hands without having to watch over the weaker sex.' In June 1987, in a response to a national newspaper observation that police officers should smile more often, the *police* magazine again used 'Doreen'. A tiny male officer looks up at the enormous figure of the grotesque policewoman and asks her, 'Do you smile to tempt a lover, Doreen?'

Hess and Marriner (1975) suggest the use of such cartoons may well be the most effective vehicle for expressing understanding and beliefs, for they use familiar symbols of cultural identity. I believe the cartoons in the police magazines provide clear insights into the structural form and social beliefs of the police. They are important indicators of institutional reality, for they display hierarchical principles and reveal the idiosyncracies which might otherwise remain unspoken or even go unnoticed in a society not noted for washing its dirty linen in public. And they speak volumes about the symbolic boundaries of male and female space!

In the early 1980s, following criticisms of police–community relations in the Scarman Report (1981), an increase in Community Affairs activities and community relations programmes became almost endemic in police organization. Specific departments were set up or expanded in almost every force, and in many of these the senior posts were held by women. Joan Lock, writing in *Police Review* (17 July 1981: 1399), said, 'I think it's a shame . . . but the highest female rank in Lancashire Constabulary is chief inspector and she, I believe, is chiefly concerned with *welfare* matters'. In 1980, the burgeoning Community Affairs Department in Northumbria was headed by a woman. Only one other woman was listed in the seventy-one senior ranked officers, and she was seconded on a Home Office Staff post concerned with the inspection and *welfare* of women officers. Of course 'Community Involvement' is not men's work, for it is consistently said to be 'only work fit for women' (from fieldnotes). On my transfer to West Mercia in 1983 I was therefore not surprised to find the only woman superintendent (out of twenty-nine on the establishment) was in Community Affairs. Hilton (1976: 1170) felt it will be another twenty-five years before we can expect to find a woman Chief Constable and I believe their confinement to non-operational posts in the lower ranks will be used to keep this situation as it stands. Because the women tend to get hived off into the feminine, caring posts or into the 'soft' areas of Community Involvement or Juvenile Liaison they subsequently fail to acquire the necessary career pattern of action-postings through to the 'tough' divisional command situations, which are considered the most suitable training for the highest ranks.

The expansion of these community programmes has seen a constant flow of complaints from 'real polises' at the 'sharp end' to the effect that too many men are being directed from operational duties into 'community affairs' without being replaced. Occasionally they will concede that this loss has been minimized, because those who are drafted out of the front line into such work are invariably 'men with no bottle' (i.e. frightened by the physical dangers of 'real work'). Such posts are for 'woolly-backs' (the sheep and the goats) who have 'never seen an angry man', or the individual who is 'soft' and therefore denigrated as being 'a bit of an old woman' (from fieldnotes). These classificatory 'old women' therefore work in departments run by the few senior policewomen who have been almost subconsciously but logically directed into this new work for women, which often mirrors and expands on the activities of the pre-Sex Discrimination Act specialist policewomen's departments.

The only female superintendent on my arrival in West Mercia was therefore in charge of teams of actual or classificatory women, who were perceived by the majority of male police society to be correctly in their place and doing women's work. In Northumbria, when I left, the situation was exactly the same. The woman superintendent in Community Affairs had collected a considerable amount of literature on the subject of women police and was somewhat traditionalist about a woman's place in police society. One item fronted the notes she used for lectures on policewomen's work and was taken from the New English Bible, 1 Corinthians, 14: 34–5. This text seemed to epitomize the view that social chaos is an inevitable result of women appearing in the wrong place, and seemed to sum up nicely the constraints that history, religion, and social ideology has imposed on policewomen:

As in all congregations of God's people, women shall not address the meeting. They have no licence to speak but should keep their place as the law directs. If there is something they want to know, they can ask their own husbands at home. It is a shocking thing that a woman should address the congregation . . .

These biblical edicts are so deeply entrenched in Western thought it becomes almost self-evident that women should occupy a separate place. But women do not naturally disappear from public social space, rather their absence is socially created and reaffirmed until it becomes the norm (Edholm, Harris, and Young 1977). An example of this occurred when I was subdivisional chief inspector and a policewoman complained of the continuing pressures her sergeant created because 'she should be at home with her children'. I spoke with him about his antagonisms but he merely grumbled that 'women should stay at home and men should work'.[19] He appealed to me, asking if I would let my wife come out to work while I sat at home, and assured me he could never tolerate such a situation. But this woman's husband was unemployed like thousands of others in this town, and she was now the breadwinner for the family. Four years later, in 1985–6, I had two policewomen on my subdivision in West Mercia who operated this role reversal for similar reasons. Again the men deplored the situation and also expressed disgust over the maternity leave that women were allowed. Over a two-and-a-half-year period, on a subdivision with an establishment of about a hundred officers we always had at least one policewoman off on maternity leave; and in one long period we lost four. These losses were a fierce bone of contention, for in a rural subdivision a shift of three on a section can easily be reduced to two officers for some weeks. In this situation the men argued that a simple alternative lay in the implementation of a 'men only' recruiting policy, for if the unemployment figures were up, then 'women could stay at home where they belonged' (from fieldnotes).

Six years before this, in 1980, the chief constable of Northumbria, who has been heavily involved in many innovations in policing, chaired sessions of the Association of Teachers' Management Conference at Lancaster University, on 'Social Trends in

[19] This sergeant has since been promoted to inspector and is no doubt still pursuing his views that women should not operate in the public sphere. Another PW told me he ordered her into the patrol car on nightshift and 'out of the cold'. She was convinced, however, that his concern was caused by his inability to come to terms with the idea of women on patrol at night, rather than with any consideration for her comfort on a cold winter's night.

the Next Decade'. His note on 'Female Role' is slight in the extreme, but gives a good indication of what a senior police officer[20] anticipated for the woman's presence in the public sphere during this period. The note, contained at the end of a series of sketches on policing possibilities for the subsequent ten years, was a mere three lines in length and observed that 'Women will join the dole queues in greater numbers and will revert to the traditional maternal role.'

THE SENSUOUS POLICEWOMAN

Justifying much of this social restriction of women is the underlying but rarely analysed idea that they are both sexually helpless to their own natures and sexually dangerous at one and the same time. A belief in their potential for creating social chaos because of what are seen as inherent characteristics is widely subscribed to in police society, although to some extent the potency of this aberrant sexuality is contained by controlling their bodies beneath the confines of the de-feminizing uniform and by restricting their access to areas of male space. As I have indicated above, these curtailments have been maintained to preserve essential aspects of the male gender hierarchy and to support the dogma which holds to the idea of 'women's vulnerability' to this insatiable sexuality.

Accordingly those women who defy the structural conventions and brave the ferocity of these male shibboleths often present a strong personal psychology, but even then can only really pierce the male preserves by operating as honorary men on male terms, or by openly defying tradition. Of course the ideal male image of these adventurers remains the sexless, butch 'burglar's dog' with cropped hair and masculine mannerisms, although such creatures are not nearly as prevalent as the cartoons or even the incessant banter of the men would have us believe. Indeed there are two other classifiable sets of women who venture into this fiercely male world.

First, there are a large number of women who slip in and out of police society, leaving after three or four years to pursue the more socially acceptable full-time role of home-maker, wife, and

---

[20] Stanley Bailey went on to become president of the Association of Chief Police Officers and was knighted in the mid-1980s.

mother. These short-term intruders are somewhat analogous to the mayfly, for they flit into and out of the system and scarcely disturb the surface.[21] Only rarely are they remembered in the 'tales from the great days of policing', and they may well be recalled after a year or so only if they marry into 'the job' and continue to hold a place in terms of their husband's rank and location in the police organization. One again the male prestige structures ensure that women are defined in relation to the men in the system, although as I have shown in an analysis of 'Police Wives' (Young 1984) there is often a huge and largely unacknowledged role for these women when they marry into 'the job'.

Second, there are that I choose to call the 'new policewoman'. These are the self-contained, self-consciously feminine women, unwilling to play the traditional role of home-maker, wife, and mother, or become the butch 'burglar's dog' taking the part of a surrogate male. Many of these 'new policewomen' remain overtly feminine, yet operate in the macho world of policing without inhibition. They are professional, competent, and attractive and in consequence are feared and revered, for they have upturned the prescribed homogeneity of the male ideology which assigns women a clearly defined place on the margins and which they are expected to fill gratefully. These women acquire status, are discussed by all, and avoided by the more faint-hearted of the men. They are a structural ambiguity simply because of their ability to be in control of their own bodies, their own space, and their own destiny. They are named and nicknamed to ensure that all are aware of their unusual status and are often grudgingly admired for their qualities of self-possession; while the men who share their social companionship (and perhaps their sexual favours) in turn become the subject of gossip, speculation, and envy.

These 'new policewomen' are often extremely capable and vocal, sensual and self-assured, beautiful and articulate. At the same time as they are attractively feminine, they are extremely professional and difficult to define in the traditional ways. They are definitely not willing to be considered as surrogate men and the male gossip (an endless feature of police society) always seems to refer to their sensual potential and sexual preferences, for their

---

[21] This is the average length of service for policewomen before resignation, which Sir Robert Mark (1978) was less than complimentary about.

non-butch appearance and competence is a structural problem. No longer is the female detective on the division a time-served veteran with the 'burglar's dog' appearance, indeed she may well be one of these tough, but feminine 'new policewomen' whose presence is difficult for men to accommodate, accustomed as they are to using sexual competition as a tool of the trade. In the extreme macho world of the detective offices this can easily create a challenge to entrenched stereotypes, which often cast the detective in the role of crusading knight-hero, at times combining aspects of 'Don Juan' and Clint Eastwood's 'Dirty Harry' in the same individual, and which tend to see intruding women in terms of sexual antagonism and conflict.

Yet many of the new policewomen who now live out this role seem possessed of a psychology peculiar to those who relish the specific tensions evident in the marginal life, and exult in the potential they possess for straddling the classificatory boundaries which exist on the peripheries of any such closed society. Today, these 'new policewomen' are present in the specialist squads and openly defy the traditional bodily strictures by rejecting the image of twin-set and pearls or costume and court shoes which were necessary for plain clothes work only two decades ago. Nor do they have their hair cropped today, but wear it with abandon. Working out of offices alongside the bridewell, the bra-less women detectives from the shop-lifting squads, in their jeans, cheese-cloth shirts, and training shoes (essential to catch the 'juvenile runners'), caused endless difficulties for traditionally minded male hierarchies. Their anarchic presence was clearly threatening to those socialized to expect unquestioning bodily conformity, but exhilarating for the insider anthropologist watching and recording events!

Slowly the numbers of these competent 'new policewomen' are increasing, although they still make up only a small portion of the 10 or 11 per cent of the total female establishment, and often make a token presence in the specialist squads. Yet even in small numbers the structural problems they present are formidable. For their underlying potential to bring about an acceleration to the rate of social change in the institution is perhaps only negated by the strength of the defensive ideology of the male domain, which has rigorously set out to restrict their numbers.

One of the ways a male status quo is maintained is by constantly invoking an alleged helplessness in the women and an insidious threat of physical danger, which requires their protection by the men. At another level, however, the danger seems to lie within the women themselves, for there is an underlying concern that women are not just physically helpless, but also sexually uncontrollable. Action is therefore directed to effect their containment and ensure they do not become analogously equated with the 'loose woman', for even in their limited duties they fall perilously close to becoming 'women of the streets', rather than remaining in the preferred domestic domain of wife and mother.[22]

While an allegedly unbridled sensual nature in women is seen as a positive danger, it also qualifies their desirability as potential wives (Young 1984); but only if they can be controlled by the men. As in many societies, a man must be able to control and command a wife if he is to maintain status.

Fear and obsession with female sexuality is also indicated in some of the nicknames given to policewomen, in which a wild promiscuity and passion is implied. In various forces at various times there always seems to have been women who were nicknamed 'the Station Bike' (because everyone rides them). An early 'bike' during my first few years in uniform chose to resign rather than be disciplined for 'discreditable conduct', following an accountancy exercise on her sexual appetites, which at other times and in other social situations might well have been considered normal. A dozen years later yet another 'bike' served alongside 'Miss Kronenbourg', who, as the TV advert for the product told us, 'has given more pleasure to more men across Europe than any other lager'. 'Miss Martini', as that advert tells us, was suitable (and available) 'any time, any place, anywhere', while 'G.T. Knickers' was 'extremely fast at the off'. In the 300 nicknames in my fieldnote collection, those relating to women almost always symbolize size and ugliness or fasten onto an allegedly sexual potency which draws on this fear and fascination with these

---

[22] The language of containment seems to reveal a wealth of terms aligning women with the two conceptual areas of inside (house, home, care, control, domestication, etc.), set against the outside (street, looseness, street-walkers, trade etc.). Bourdieu (1973) demonstrates the danger attributed to female public activity in Berber society, and such ideas linking space and sexuality seem to hold a firm conceptual place in many societies where a clear gender hierarchy operates; such as in the police.

intruders who carry the power of the virgin and virago at one and
the same time.[23]

In the early 1980s, while taking part in an internal inspection of
the force, I noted how this perceived uncontrollable nature of
women was used to deny them access to certain areas of work—a
situation which had been outlawed by the Sex Discrimination Act
some five years earlier and taken on as official force policy at that
time. During a six-week force inspection, for which I carried out
the initial spade work for an assistant chief constable, I found that
policewomen in some of the smaller towns in the rural division
were prevented from working nightshift and reverted to 'days'
when their normal shift rota would have brought them on night
duty. Although no written order on this was available (which in
itself was most unusual in a system where every such order is
written up), I was taken to one side and told that the divisional
commander had decreed that it was 'too dangerous for women to
work nightshift'. In these isolated areas, with few officers available on nightshift, it was argued that women created practical
difficulties concerning their need to be chaperoned.

It was convincingly argued that a situation might arise where
a lone woman in the station might have responsibility for the
security of a male prisoner, and this pragmatic difficulty was put
forward as the official reason for the shift pattern irregularities.
Suddenly, an inspector expanded on this, and I was told that
because of the limited supervision available on nightshift in this
remote section, there was a fear that the women would produce
some sort of sexual maelstrom. Apparently there had been an incident some years before, when men on night duty had been found
being 'entertained' by night nurses in the local hospital and it was
now suggested to me that a similar situation might occur with
policewomen. (I noted that the men were not spoken of as being
responsible for this incident; rather it was the nurses who were
seen to have created the mayhem!)

What would happen, I enquired, if, for some operational reason
(e.g. a female prisoner), a policewoman was needed during the

---

[23] Greer (1971: 263–6) quotes linguistic examples of this abuse which indicates
this fear of looseness and disorder. This derogatory name 'the Station Bike' is paralleled in the joke I was told about a young policewoman on my subdivision, in
1985: Q: What's the difference between X and the Blackpool Tower? A: Not
everyone's been up the Blackpool Tower!

night? The unwritten order was that a policewoman was to be called out, collected in a police vehicle, taken to the police station, then returned back home after the incident had been resolved. They were not to be allowed to drive themselves to the station for two reasons. The first was functional; it was said, 'had the PW used her own vehicle, she could have claimed travelling allowances and this might have alerted someone at HQ that the women in this Division were not integrated onto shifts, and the "wheel might have come off"...'. The second, and most revealing reason given to me was 'it is too dangerous for these young women to be driving through the night...' (shift inspector: from fieldnotes). Of course this situation produced all sorts of laughable dilemmas and hypocrisies. For example, one of two policewomen posted to one of the shifts (and for whom it was too dangerous to be out at night) lived in Single Quarters, a number of converted police houses some twenty miles away in the middle of Newcastle city. Ironically known to all as 'the Virgins' Retreat' this block of flats was the scene of many boisterous late-night parties at the time. One wonders how any young male constable delegated to drive a young policewoman back to the 'Retreat' in the early hours after she had been called out managed to avoid her unquenchable ardour during the journey? And what if she then invited him in for a coffee?

These hostels for single officers, although less numerous in some forces such as Northumbria, are also the subject of great concern to senior male officers and have stringent rules of conduct. Although their facilities can often be described as only just adequate, a primary concern of senior officers seems to lie in their opportunities for unbridled passion rather than in their suitability as a home for young officers. A chief officer writing about a proposed merger into one building of a male and female hostel, ordered: 'in this age of increasing promiscuity I would expect the Divisional Commander [in the area] to control the hostel tightly' (1979 Memorandum: assistant chief constable). In a similar manner, at the training schools for the probationary constables, which are often situated well away from the centres of population,[24] the accommodation for recruits is also subject to the same strict

---

[24] See Okely (1978: 114) *re* the secluded sites of girls' boarding schools, and the link with this isolation to control of gender and sexuality.

controls. To be found in a bedroom with someone of the opposite sex is a punishable offence requiring resignation or resulting in dismissal. The Discipline Regulations, with their 'catch-all' offence of 'discreditable conduct', are used to prevent such looseness and to govern all such uncontrolled situations. As Whitaker (1979: 221) contends:

the restrictions—petty or otherwise—imposed on the off-duty private lives of policemen and women are unknown in virtually any other occupation . . . Policemen are expected to continue to observe a 19th century moral code, while daily being vividly aware of its rejection by the rest of society . . . In Portsmouth, an unmarried policewoman was put on a charge for kissing a married colleague . . .

One unfortunate policewoman caught *in flagrante* with a male colleague was disciplined for having sex while she was on sick leave (with a broken bone). The fact that he was a married man led to a charge of 'discreditable conduct', while her 'late night sex on the sick' was classed as an offence of 'conduct detrimental to her recovery', though most of those on the subdivision I was working at the time felt that their real 'offence' lay in their 'stupidity at having been caught' (from fieldnotes). I am unaware if she was able to call any evidence to show sexual satisfaction might be beneficial to broken bones, but this incident gives some indication of the constraints imposed on the police and the fiercely conservative beliefs of some of its participants. Not surprisingly, I found the same underlying fear of the sexuality of women in West Mercia, as well as the same attempts to impose a morality on its members that at times borders on the farcical:

my interest in the controls and strictures of this rather feudal institution is well known now and I am gathering many examples of attitudes which I think reflect the somewhat Victorian nature of this rural police society. 'X', an Inspector I know well, is married to a policewoman. At a party, they tell me about their experiences in the early 1980s, when they had got together. At that time, he had been married to a 'civilian' who, in turn, had become involved with yet another policeman. Without any animosity and without children to create any problems over divorcing parents, the two groups had settled their lives, only for the three police officers to be called in and charged with discreditable conduct. They laughed as they recalled the outrage of the Chief Constable, and are certain he was only sorry he was unable to pursue a charge against the wife of 'X', who, as a 'civilian', was not amenable to police discipline procedures ... (from fieldnotes)

At a CID Conference in February 1980, I listened as the same senior officer who had urged tight control of the mixed hostel in 1979 reviewed a case of 'child abuse' where some administrative point had been missed by the officer in the case. He told the assembled audience: 'There are three areas where policemen have trouble. They've always existed and I suppose they always will. They are firstly, 'policewomen'; secondly, 'handling property'; and lastly, 'dealing with children' (from fieldnotes).

I noted that he placed policewomen at the forefront, and this fear of women is further illustrated in Sir Robert Mark's autobiography (1978: 219). Like his bizarre item on female uniform quoted above, this clearly indicates police attitudes towards women. Both are isolated items in Sir Robert's book; they do not fit into any unfolding theme. Indeed, I find it significant that this story about women's sexuality appears in a chapter entitled, 'Civil Liberty and Public Order'. He writes:

About this time also I had given way to the blandishments of Henry Hunt, Assistant Commissioner (Personnel and Training) who had long wanted to introduce girls into our (cadet) corps. I was not easily persuaded because recruitment of women police was going well. They are an expensive investment, because on average, they serve under four years before leaving, usually on marriage, and I was a bit worried at the prospect of 120 nubile young women at Hendon where the cadet school houses 500 young men, healthy, energetic and full of go. With a touch of the Valentines, I enquired acidly if Henry had provided for a professional abortionist to be assigned a police house at Hendon, or was it that recruiting was so bad that we now had to breed our own, as we had already attempted with dogs and horses? Henry bore all this with his usual good humour and was, of course, proved to be right. We had 40 applications for every place and were able to pick and choose. The amusing and encouraging effect, which we did not expect was the noticeable improvement in the behaviour and manners of the boys. Incidentally, the girls consistently took the major share of academic prizes.

Sir Robert, attempting a humorous vein, lumps women with the dogs and horses as potential breeding stock, whose offspring might only need to be aborted depending on the health of the current recruitment figures. As his afterthoughts show, any female academic ability is only to be regarded as incidental', for its very existence conflicts with the dominant male models of the culture, which deny the female such rationality.

Again this parallels the situation elsewhere in society where female education is still considered by many to be something of a luxury and somewhat unnecessary. This situation, in which low status is given to academic achievement for women (see Okely 1978), is another male police strategy, for any such acknowdledgement of female ability can only lead to the creation of a self-determined self-consciousness in women, which would be anti-thetical to the cultural style of unquestioning order and discipline required of the lower ranks in which the women mostly remain. The real trouble is that sexually dangerous and educated women are a double bind, for they logically will have twice the power and double the potential to disrupt the system. And so, the point is made, why train or educate them when they will inevitably marry and leave and thus fulfil the prophecies of the system which insists that women are expensively unsuited to police work and can only ever be a transitory factor in the institutional life?

Such ideas have been vociferously promoted since the Sex Discrimination Act, subconsciously linking this idea of the women's indiscriminate sensuality to their alleged weakness and risk of injury in the violent situation. Fed by the force press and public relations departments, the media have keenly reported that this 'soft femininity' makes women especially unsuited to the dangers of police work, until this eventually becomes a 'natural' phenomenon. By implication, these women would have been better off in the traditional role of wife and sweetheart, rather than be exposed and endangered by the conflicts occurring in the public male arena. In 1979, the *Newcastle Evening Chronicle* ran a series of major articles on local policewomen to show how their careers had been cut short by violence. Sexual stereotyping of the kind that reduces the objectivity of a great deal of reporting is apparent, and a policewoman is casually described as 'a bonny girl and full of life . . . it was incongruous to hear the smiling beauty talk of her injuries . . .' (*Newcastle Evening Chronicle*, 5 July 1979). Over two nights the paper ran front-page headlines and photo-features of policewomen who had been injured in the daily round of policework. Yet, as Southgate (1980: 24) points out from a collation of material, 'violent involvements are actually quite rare in police work for officers of either sex'. This is undoubtedly true, for across England and Wales there are tens of thousands of police/public interactions every day, if not every hour, which do not end in injury. Pat Sullivan (1979: 341) makes an even more important point, that women officers, in the main, are injured by women offenders whilst in custody, and cannot therefore be protected from contact with the violent or argumentative public:

The most important aspect of the figures for assaults, when relating them to the new role of women police since the Sex Discrimination Act 1975 is that over two-thirds of them have been committed by women prisoners and so would have occurred anyway even if the police force had been excluded from the Act.

The institutional process, however, prefers that aggression, violence, and injury should be male preserves, for they go with the masculine image and culture of 'warfare'; while beauty and femininity are binary opposites, to be separated and kept apart from the metaphorical world of conceptual 'warriors'. Women should therefore be excluded from the social interactions of the public arena, for although it is not easily admitted, they are primarily seen as sex objects. This is borne out by the embarrassment shown by John Stalker (1988: 68), who is somewhat apologetic in acknowledging what must have otherwise been a normal male conversation in his long career as a detective, but which looks somewhat more contemptuous when coldly translated into print. He tells us the Special Branch policewomen typists in the Royal Ulster Constabulary were 'unkindly referred to by the more macho officers as "the bitch squad" [working from temporary buildings] known as "the Henhouse" or "the Cowshed"'. Again and again the everyday language points to an ideology of sexual differentiation, in which women are held in derisory contempt by male cliques (Whitehead 1976: 200), and in which sexual relations are linguistically described by such terms as 'bird', 'screw', 'on the job', etc. As Whitehead points out, men do not expect women to shout to them in the street, 'Hallo sailor, I wouldn't mind half an hour with you' (ibid. 201), yet such a view of women means that any easy transference to a new regime where they could be treated in egalitarian and human terms is unlikely. Invariably the relations of power dictate that the men continue to control policewomen and treat them as sexual antagonists. As I have often heard said: 'the proper place for policewomen is on their backs with their legs open ...'. Jane Sewberry (1975), writing about American Police systems, suggested this type of perception of women has led to sexual harassment with rewards for those policewomen who submit to male officers; and she contends that this is more common than might at first be supposed.

During the time the media was pursuing the incidence of violence to policewomen mentioned above, the *Police Review* was running a competition to find 'The Prettiest Policewomen in the Land', and readers were invited to send in photographs of their favourite policewoman in uniform. Again the paradox between the world of 'new policewomen' and a caricatured world where 'burglar's dogs' like 'Doreen' predominate is apparent, and between April and September 1979 the weekly *Police Review* published many pages of pictures of attractive policewomen. On 14 September 1979 Lorraine Edser of Suffolk police became the 'cover girl', chosen as the most attractive woman in uniform. Her professional abilities may well have complemented her looks, but as in Sir Robert Mark's assessment of his woman cadets, these seem incidental to her face and figure. A half-page spread in the *Daily Mail* (14 September 1979) showed Miss Edser in a bikini on the beach and also in uniform, under a headline which inevitably proclaimed that she's a 'Bobby Dazzler'. The *Mail* tells how she beat more than a hundred contestants to win the title, and points out: 'Lorraine ... whose arresting figure is often seen on the beaches near her home in Essex, weighs $8\frac{1}{2}$ stone and stands 5' 6" high ...'. The *Police Review* (13 April 1979: 586) in announcing some early entries for the competition, claimed: 'what we hadn't realised was in what high regard policewomen are held by their male colleagues. Not a chauvinist in sight. For all the entries so far have come from men and most of them are working alongside their choices'. This 'high regard' for policewomen 'colleagues' was not shared by their wives, however, for during this same period a lively correspondence in the *Police Review* was taken up by the national press, under the heading 'Passionate Affairs in a Steamed-Up Cortina' (*Police Review*, 24 August 1979). Again the fear of an uncontrollable sensuality in women was indicated, when it was suggested that married constables, unable to resist the charms of their patrolling companion police-women, were succumbing in the rear of their patrol cars. An anonymous superintendent took the opportunity again to attack the Sex Discrimination Act, suggesting in a letter to *Review* that the influx of women would soon mean there were no men left for the women to have passionate affairs with; and in passing took a side-swipe at the 'Police College' and 'academics in the job' (*Police Review*, 12 October 1979). Anonymous letters from the 'wives' also appeared, as did a number of rejoinders from police women who firmly denied tempting their colleagues. The *Daily Mirror* (24 October 1979) summarized the wives' 'increasing fears':

they say married policemen get so suffused with lust when pressed in close proximity into a steamed-up Panda car on night patrol with a buxom police woman, they spend most of their duty having a cuddle on the back seat. Well I want any policeman patrolling the streets where I live to have a coldly alert, dispassionate mind. I want his attention totally dedicated to my property, not on the plunging regulation shirt on his lissom partner on patrol and I think we'd both be safer if he was on his own . . .

Once again the uniform of the women has been used to define their rampant sexuality, so that the uniform shirt contrives to 'plunge' on the 'buxom' or 'lissom' policewoman's body!

Such trivialization of women occurs continually in the culture. It is emphasized in the campaign to find the 'Prettiest Police-woman' and extends into the daily gossip about the possible sex-ual prowess of the latest female recruit. It can be found in every force, and is contained on the front cover of *Brief*, the magazine of the Greater Manchester Police (22 December 1977), where 'shapely policewoman Carole Mather' was chosen by the chief constable, James Anderton, the Christian moralist, to 'boost the morale of his men' (*Daily Mail*, 22 December 1977). Anderton, who had just been lauded in some quarters for his actions to cur-tail pornography and for raids against dealers in pornography, had chosen a cover photograph of policewoman Mather for the force magazine. She is shown in a desk-top pose, with her uni-form skirt pulled up to reveal the thigh, in a shot chosen by the chief constable from a selection of pictures taken by *Mail* pho-tographer, Barry Greenwood. Chief Constable Anderton's intention, the *Mail* tells us, was 'to cheer policemen who will be on the beat while the rest of us are tucking into turkey and plum pudding'. Revealing the legs and thighs to 'cheer up the men' also occurs in the pages of the *Police Review* (March 1979: 361). The account of the trials and difficulties of the first pioneering policewomen (outlined above) is broken by a full-page advert telling what has to be a largely masculine readership, that 'Pretty Polly supports lovely legs'.[25]

The illustration to this advert shows a full-page photograph of long, well-supported 'Pretty Polly' legs, a flounce of floral petticoat, and high-heeled peep-toed sandals that would have senior officers reaching for their copies of the discipline code should they ever be worn on duty.

In the task of controlling the street-visible activities of the predominantly male 'dangerous classes', the female has logically been excluded. And when she has breached the boundaries and intruded, she has been marginalized and attributed with dangerous qualities, for if she cannot be a 'real prig'—because the world of petty criminals is as male-biased as the world of 'real polises'— she can never become one of these 'real polises' for exactly the same reasons. In effect there is no real place for a woman in this world, and whenever possible it seeks to exclude this structural intruder by claiming she is a sensual, illogical creature, needing protection from her own aberrant nature and from the violence and malevolence of others.

And even when she is allowed across the boundary into the masculine world, it is under sufferance for she is always an irritant. Ideally she can only really be suitable when she has been domesticated and moved back out to get married, preferably to some policeman. Then all the tribal secrets she has learned about the mysteries of the police world, and which her dangerous emotionalism may still release, can be contained by the masculine

---

[25] One of the judges of the 'prettiest policewoman' competition some six months later, in Sept. 1979, was the London and SE sales manager of 'Pretty Polly' tights. I might add that the *Review* also carried a stereotypical cartoon of the event which showed the usual 'burglar's dog' holding the *Review* announcing the winner, and asking of her image: 'Mirror, Mirror on the Wall, who is the prettiest of us all?'

world she can be said to have come to acknowledge as being asymmetrically dominant, but correct.[26]

[26] If, as I have claimed earlier, the police are a secretive and defensive organization who seem at times to be primarily concerned to protect their own positions and place in the political structure of society, then it is logical that those possessed of irrationality (women) should be excluded or totally enfolded within. As an eventual wife to a policeman, the ex-policewoman is therefore structurally perfect, for she remains 'outside' yet within 'the job', as it strives always to provide a totally enclosing family situation for all its members, and to ensure that control of potential danger stays with the controllers.

5

'Crime' or 'Offence': A Structuring Principle

INTRODUCTION

In this section of the book I am concerned finally to pull the idea of 'crime' to centre stage, for it is *the* aspect of policing which most heavily structures the widest range of police activity and has a continuous influence on the semantics of most of the material I have described above. By putting some of the realities contained within the generic terms of 'crime' and 'offence' under a microscope of explanation and analysis, it should become apparent just how important and influential these concepts are to the police mind and how much impact they have on police culture.

Within society most individuals have a personal idea of what 'crime' means for them, for the human condition requires people to be able to sustain an ordered understanding of where they stand in relation to their neighbours and to their place in the social order as a whole. However, because of the ambiguities lying within an idea of 'crime' and 'criminals' any singular model becomes untenable and reality inevitably remains multidimensional as ambivalence and incongruity occur. A unidimensional model of 'crime' is therefore impossible, and yet, 'the police will act as if there were a single standard of community conduct—that which the law prescribes' (Manning and Butler 1982: 335). To explore this ideology in action, it is necessary, therefore, to understand how the police idea of crime changes and what it has meant at any one period in time. For the manner in which ideology, social history, and cultural change structures the interpretation of 'crime' reveals how useful this multidimensional aspect has been to police organization, as it sets out to sustain the institution by defensively concealing its practices. The very ambivalence of the construct has been used to manipulate and amend the categories of crime at certain times to suit an institutional reading of just what it is that society requires. Inevitably this view tends to fall in line with the police's own peculiar cultural view of social harmony and also with the needs of the organization.

A diachronic examination of the response to the idea of crime is central to any exploration of policing, simply because of the peculiar position which the construct holds in the police imagination. 'Crime' is *the* central tenet for action and administrative structures, for it pervades and sustains the ideology, defining police cosmology and marginalizing aspects, such as the attitudes to women and their place in police society which I have just outlined above. Indeed, as I have demonstrated, my own drug squad work was largely concerned with lower status 'offences' and not with those real 'crimes' which give recognition and centrality to certain police work while casting others to the boundaries of respectability.

Inherent in this classificatory system is a further example of the police preference for a binary world which has to be experienced to be understood. With the same intensity that any obsessive actor feels for his profession, the police imagination is beset by the knowledge of the primacy of 'crimes' over 'offences', lending an intensity to crime detection which only those who have spent time in 'the department' (as the CID is invariably known) can feel.

As John Stalker's book (1988) quietly demonstrates, the high esteem which the investigative detective takes upon himself permeates his thinking, so that those involved in the secondary or less highly rated tasks (and the tasks themselves) suffer the stigma of a lower symbolic importance. This status surrounding the idea of crime is what gives such special significance to 'the department', and those poor devils who lose the patronage of 'the department' for some reason, lose access to the inner sanctum; and I have seen many instances where those who have fallen from grace and been cast out of 'the department' have spent many anguished years over their fate.

At a divisional CID Christmas 'occasion' in 1986, I sat with detectives who exuded this inordinate pride in 'the department', and which my fieldnote only just catches:

We watch the various cliques as they drink, play cards, and spar with the new WDC [woman detective constable] . . . A detective sergeant looks around and says, 'it's a bit like a masonic club without the formality and the regalia. Everyone is a "brother" . . . we are all comfortable and familiar with each other . . . we spend considerable amounts of time together, and are always looking to spend more; work and leisure drift into each other. . . .' The detective inspector moves around the room having a word here and there with 'his boys'. The conversation is peppered with tales of 'captures', 'crimes' solved and success or failure in the 'detection rates'.[1]

In this world the detection rate is of vital concern, and a succession of poor returns in the monthly or quarterly detection figures can break the ambitious detective inspector. His 'boys' quickly understand that to ensure their own continuity in the department, they must be able to 'do the business'. As a result, those calls for a change of emphasis to such matters as 'crime prevention' have little or no chance of obtaining prominence when structural primacy is endlessly dramatized by the arrests and the detections they ultimately produce. The whole ambience of 'prevention' is nebulous to detectives, for it speaks of events that do not happen and cannot be identified or counted, while the 'detection rate' tells of 'captures' and the process of law and prosecution: of the creation of crime files and the punishment of offenders. It embodies a metaphorical routing of disorder, played out in a style that is recognized in the world of literature and drama as a symbolic rendition of the archetypal world of 'good and evil'. Turner (1982: 83), exploring the nature of such fiercely articulated social drama, quotes from Myerhoff and Moore's work on *Secular Ritual* (1977), suggesting, 'all collective ceremony can be interpreted as a cultural statement about cultural order as against a cultural void'. In the police, the drama of crime detection' is *the* cultural statement *par excellence* about an institution in pursuit of a perfect order as it sets out to repudiate the cultural void. All of the secular trappings of ritual and ceremony I have outlined are attempts by this semi-closed society to defend against and stave off ambiguity. For as Myerhoff and Moore (ibid.) point out, 'all ceremony is a declaration against indeterminacy'.

But as Turner (1982) reminds us, each ritually repeated expression of such a rigid social reality also contains elements of

[1] When I left the subdivision I was given a framed photograph of myself surrounded by the detectives, captioned 'Bromsgrove C.I.D. 25. 3. 87'. I had won the accolade of being classed as 'being one of the boys' and able to 'do the business' as a token member of 'the department'.

anti-structure, thus incorporating aspects of the archetypal struggle between order and the void, between continuity and chaos. So that for the police, the world of crime becomes the primary symbol and statement about form and formality, which as Turner (ibid. 83) affirms 'celebrates man-made meaning, the culturally determinate, the regulated, the named, and the explained. It banishes from consideration the basic question raised by the made-upness of culture, its malleability, its alternability'. In other words, the rituals must be endlessly repeated to deny any possibility that the system will be seen to be merely arbitrary. And so the fiercely macho images of waves of violence and wars with the criminally disordered masses are constantly promoted to ensure the system replicates its modes of thought and belief, while their dramatic content and the use of such archaic terms as 'prig' and 'vandal', 'hooligan' and 'villain' assures both the culture and the outside society that although the drama has a long and unsettled history, ultimately it is safely in the hands of the 'warriors' from 'the department', who are masters of the melodrama.

To further this end, a stream of 'hard facts' and objectified crime statistics are produced and artificially elevated in the public consciousness. Their function is to deny the social reality of a fluid and somewhat indeterminate social order, for the drama demands that the enemy is known and is about to be beaten or even exterminated. Always the implication has been that existing institutional knowledge and skill will stave off social disaster. And until the very recent past the police have been prodigious in convincing the public that only their mastery of the system could prevent the criminal ascendancy and the social void.

This potential threat has long been identified as lying with the 'dangerous classes' who have formed the basis of the 'cops and robbers' binary, and their activities have been used over and over again to create what Pearson (1983) calls 'a climate of respectable fears'. To assuage the 'moral panics' which continually erupt from within the hegemonies of property and land, and which are arcanely visible in the annual calls at the Tory Party in conference for more punishment and a return to hanging, a practical mastery of police control has been pursued by endlessly promulgating high status acts of crime fighting and creating satisfactory detection rates. 'Crime' is therefore constantly being dramatized by the police, to render support for their practices; for as Hulsman 1977) contends, 'Most people in our society participate most often in the criminal justice system in a way which we can compare best with the way we participate in a dramatic production.' Turner has again suggested that in such a system where endless rituals are inherently based on the Manichaean principles of 'good ~ evil', we will experience the construction of a sustained theatricality in which targets and classifications are nurtured by using classic symbols exemplifying the right hand of goodness or the left hand of darkness (Hertz 1973).

And, as Hulsman (1977) further points out,

The world [of the criminal justice system] is structured by a transformation of elements of the 'literal' world of another time (the Middle Ages) and relies heavily on myths which were in that time part of the indirect experience of most people . . . This situation is not immediately visible because some words belonging to the reality of the Middle Ages have been replaced by others belonging to our own time. Thus the word 'God' is replaced by the word 'Society' [but] these changes in words did not generally change the structure of the drama.

This view is supported by the ethnography I have outlined above, where archaic myths from the Middle Ages live on in the linguistic world of 'prigs' and 'felons', and the themes of good and evil are subject to wild exaggeration or gross simplification. In this dichotomous world, villainy and crime are measured on a unidimensional scale of seriousness and then set against an equivalent scale of punishment. And even though this aspect of the drama should rest with the courts and be outside police concern, it remains high on their agenda. Indeed sentencing is of insatiable interest and subject to a constant derisory comment, for heavy punishment finalizes the incident, becoming a symbolic essential in the whole theatrical performance.

This use of punishment as a coercive means of sustaining systems of power is eloquently described by Foucault (1977). Sheriden (1980: 135–63) teases out the ultimate strengths of Foucault's argument and shows how the overwhelming incorporation of the influence of punishment which occurs in a system of discipline would eventually allow for the policing and examination of the whole population. This notion of the surveillance and institutional expansiveness to meet it is one that is inherently understood 'on the job' and many policemen would be happy to see it occur in practice.

Meanwhile the negated feminine side of the coin incorporates concepts which the police find difficult to handle, for they contain aspects of the literary, the artistic, the musical, the sensual, and even the reflexive enquiry into systems of justice.

Such asymmetry, of course, contains the germ of further anti-structural possibilities and reveals why the feminine is so rigorously denied, while the idea of crime is adulated and endlessly pursued in the repetitive macho rituals. There are some who worry that such a direction of action and ideology seems destined to lead irrevocably to a nightmare scenario where a legalistic criminal justice system is pursued to its logical and ultimate conclusion. Germann (1977: 340–7) writing in *Police Journal*, envisaged such a world lying just over the horizon. In this coercive state the

police assume, unilaterally, all decision making authority for social control and apply immediate, massive force in any situation where police are not awarded instant defence and obedience ... the police continue their close affinity to conservative, ultra-conservative and very right-wing movements and philosophies. No radical changes are made in police organisations or in traditional police procedures. Sensitive and humanist members of the police establishments are even more ostracized; incoming recruits are more intensively screened to eliminate socially sensitive probationers and those who would question traditional procedures or postures ... Crime continues to increase in numbers ... citizens become ever more panicked and angry. The police, even more frustrated than ever, ask for more manpower, facilities and equipment, and suggest to the public that the 'war on crime' be intensified.

The preoccupation with crime is therefore a crucial subject for anthropological enquiry, if this fascist world envisaged by Germann (ibid.) is to be avoided.

That its practices and malpractices remain largely hidden and unreported is, I believe, a further result of the inability of the legalistic model of policing to contend with the fact that crime is not anything God-given, but is the product of man-made meanings. As we shall see, the world of 'crimes' and 'offences' seems, at times, to be a response as much to the problems of shoring up the police social formation as to actual social problems. In every case, powerful chief officers and others of the ACPO ranks at the pinnacle of police prestige have only succeeded by mastering the etiquette and norms of police practice. They have struggled to these positions by living out the prescriptions of form and formality, and by adhering to the rigid demands of known and regulated systems which do not easily take on board challenges to their ideological practices.[2] As John Stalker (1988) seems to have found out at rather a late stage, such a system of power and control demands obedience to the institutional truth and not to the actual truth, for the individual is expendable in order that the institution can prevail (even if it appears to be morally corrupt).

Crime, I suspect, will continue to sustain the modes of thought and language of senior police officers, for it has held the primary place throughout their history and dominates their structures of significance. Its precedence in the action world of 'cops and robbers' could, as Germann (1977) forecasts, see its extension to include other areas, simply because of a growing fear of sedition and social dispute, and we could easily find police hegemonies using their powers to generate even more disciplined structures than those which exist at the moment. For in an institution whose *raison d'être* is to exercise power and control, the only truth necessary to its own continuity lies in its chance to expand and demand even more control and more authority (Douglas 1987). If for no other reason than this, there is a definite need for the insider's hermeneutic analysis of what 'crime' means to the police, and the revelation of just what has been going on as they have used, ignored, developed, manipulated, directed, produced, and entrapped the idea of crime to support their preferred world of 'polises and prigs'.

In a world dominated by the ubiquitous need for 'clear-ups' and a good detection rate, any public demand for an enhanced 'community policing' model contains few of the symbols of status which would allow this to take up a central place in police thinking, for power and position still rests firmly with those who are

---

[2] This resistance supports my earlier contention that the police are an anti-academic institution of necessity! As Mary Douglas (1973: 102) notes: 'artists and academics are potentially professions of comment and criticisms on society'. Policemen cannot therefore be logically identified with the arts and if they *must* have academic qualifications then it is suitable for this to be in one of the non-reflexive disciplines. This polarity of a positively viewed objective world and a negated subjective once again forms part of police ideology and as Lakoff and Johnson (1980: 185–225) clearly indicate, is part of another deep mythology in Western philosophic thought.

best able dramatically to manipulate the rituals surrounding the idea of crime, and what has been described as 'the *ancien régime* of crime fighting' remains inviolate. As a consequence the criminal justice system continues to move nearer to the Orwellian vision described by Germann (1977: 340), who clearly foresaw 'there is one peril that requires more than science and technology and concern: [that is] the peril of excessive social control!' To prevent this insidious slide into a world where the idea of crime expands to incorporate even greater controls on social right and freedom of speech, we must re-think the goals and priorities of law enforcement, and we must re-direct our efforts in order to make it humane and effective' (ibid.) However, if the police are to emancipate themselves from their prison-like framework of cultural and ideological belief they will be required to acknowledge and reflect on how these structures of significance are created and maintained. Such a task is not seditious and need not be seen as such; indeed it is an essential social exercise if the police are to be accountable to the whole of the population and not just to a small minority of the powerful; and especially if the nightmare scenario of Germann's 'peril of increasing social control' is to be avoided.[3]

CRIME DEFINED: A NINETEENTH-CENTURY MODEL

'Crime' is a classification of behaviour defined for the police by the Home Office. Certain categories of what are described generically as offences are then subdivided and redefined as crimes. Standing apart in a hierarchy of importance, these classifiable crimes always have greater symbolic importance to the police than other villainies which are simply described and defined as offences.

---

[3] I am not hopeful this will occur. At the time of writing, a new Official Secrets Act is on the parliamentary agenda and seems to offer little hope of a more free and open society. The fact that it totally denies a 'public interest' defence to anyone who even reveals any criminal activity of those in certain areas of power and considers the 'public interest' and government policy to be the same thing, is consistent with a political style which has been increasingly authoritarian and economical with the truth over the past ten years. This has sought to destroy trade union representation, stifle media criticism, and is actively seeking to extend surveillance of the populous with a range of measures which encompass electronic tagging for ex-convicts through to computerized identity documents for all. Even Lord Hailsham, an ex-Lord Chancellor and not widely regarded as a man of liberal persuasion, has recognized the dangers of a benevolent dictatorship inherent in any government which continues to hold a large majority over such an extended period of time; and his fear seems well justified.

All of the classifiable crimes are now published on what is known as the Standard List. In police jargon these are invariably referred to as 'crimes as defined', meaning those defined on the Home Office Standard List of Offences. This list is not static, but is amended over time as some activities gain or lose symbolic prestige in the public imagination. However, the list has its continuing basis in the theft of property and assaults against the person.

Here we are plunged into a fluctuating world of semantics, for in this domain where acts of malicious behaviour may be defined as either crimes or offences, depending on whether or not they are on 'the list', it is perhaps only with an insider's awareness of the nuances of the game of statistical manipulation that we can gain an insight into what is actually going on at times. Indeed many policemen situated just beyond the immediate world of 'crime fighting' and 'detection rates' never understand their relevance to the institution.

Then again, many unsupportable acts of social behaviour which the public think of as crimes may not even be within the police purview or lie within their terms of reference, so that they hold no place within the idea of crime. Behaviour which *is* defined as crime reflects the values of the aristocratic and property-owning classes of the early nineteenth century and the definition was framed to defend their wealth and land from perceived dangers. This protection of the body physical and the body material was encapsulated for the new police forces of that era as their real work, by the phrase 'the protection of life and property'; and this dictum still forms a central tenet and theme for all initial police training.

The inception of the existing system of policing occurred at a point in history when society still suffered from an inordinate fear of revolution.[4] Any contentious act by the 'dangerous classes' was seen as a threat to the élite, and was dealt with by a harsh and

---

[4] There is a wealth of literature on the social changes of the times which helped determine the style of the new policing systems. See for example, *The Making of the English Working Class* by E. P. Thompson (1968), who details events leading up to the Industrial Revolution and beyond; and also Hughes (1987); Tobias (1967); Hay, Linebaugh, and Thompson (1975); Bailey (1981); Richter (1981) and Pearson (1983) for accounts of crime and social organization in the 19th century. Most have considerable bibliographies on factors surrounding the socio-political events leading to the tripartite system of the élite/the supervisors/and the operatives in this newly urbanized world, in which the new police acted for the élite as a symbol of supervision over the 'operatives'.

often barbaric system of punishment. Crimes against property or any signs of disaffection were pursued with a vigour which reflected the continued supremacy of an almost feudal landowning and powerful class, as well as the dispossession of a subservient peasantry and the new industrial working classes.

In the mid-nineteenth century a series of Acts of Parliament provided a framework on which the newly emergent police forces could build and operate. Pearson (1983: 126) describes this era as the 'culmination of the great modernising transformation of the criminal justice system', and three Acts of Parliament passed in 1861 effectively set the scene for a system of police action which still pervades police thinking as being the basis for 'real work'. A Larceny Act, the Malicious Damage Act, and the Offences Against the Persons Act were all passed in 1861, and together with a Licensing Act of 1872, encompassed perhaps 80–90 per cent of all police work. These Acts were so well framed and controlled the activities of the 'dangerous classes' so decisively that they were still in operation a century later, and beyond.

The Larceny Act of 1861 defended the power enjoyed by the property-owning classes, setting out primarily to secure their land, estates, buildings, and animals by listing many crimes of theft and protecting deer, rabbits, pheasants, crops, and stock. However, it also took into account the new property which was now manifest in the mills and businesses of the new industrial aristocrats, listing offences against those who attacked factories, shops, mines, docks, warehouses, offices, and stores. Today, in the late twentieth century, many senior police officers were initially trained to pursue the crimes listed within the provisions of this 1861 Act, for the Act continued to have effect until 1968 when the Theft Act replaced its sections and terminology, but retained both its philosophy and ideology.

At the same time as this system of policing was being established, the extensive Victorian system of prison building ensured that transportation to the colonies could end and the courts and prisons were soon filled with increasing numbers of what I heard described a century later in the bridewell as 'the several I's'. A somewhat laconic bridewell philosopher, looking through the interminable lists of prisoners we had logged on a particularly busy day, said to me: 'do you know, we deal with the idiotic, the insane, the inane, the inadequate, the inept, the incompetent, the incontinent, and the incomplete?' Almost inevitably, it seems the police are to continue to sweep up the trivial 'crimes' committed by this human dross of society, for as Germann (1977: 341) points out, 'I am inclined to believe that our police are really dealing with the unlucky, or inept or mentally retarded offender who represents that 10% (of those caught for committing crimes) and charged . . .'. Regardless of statistical accuracy, however, this 10 per cent were able to be counted and used as a major justification for further controlling practices, so that their threat came to be objectified in the hard data of the crime statistic and the court proceeding, both of which have been used by the police ever since to suggest that 'society is on the brink of chaos' (Holdaway 1983).

A main tenet for police action was therefore identified as 'the protection of property', and this has since become all important to police ideology. From the time of probationary training onwards, the young recruit has legal and practical aspects surrounding the appropriation of property instilled into his consciousness. Initially detailed by the 1861 Act, these thefts generally related to those small and easily transportable items which could be quickly sold or traded; and this 'real work' quickly became the cornerstone of a police construct of 'crime'. Today, the detection of these minor misappropriations still remains the mainstay of policework and a prime measurement of police effectiveness. And although the police are at last having to acknowledge limitations in their abilities to prevent or even contain crime, and chief officers increasingly emphasize a need for the multi-agency approach to crime prevention, the primacy of the idea of the war against crime and its ultimate detection remains basic to the ideology of the institution. Indeed, nothing suggests that its centrality as a construct for action has even been dented in the minds of the rank and file!

So although the police are beginning to seek new ground and moving to accommodate to the pressures of the financial initiatives required by the politics of the 1980s, they are, as Thorpe *et al.* (1980: 42) contend. still tightly constrained by the same systems of belief which determined their role from their origins in the nineteenth century:

the law is far from being an impartial mediator of social relations . . . instead it weighs most heavily upon the most defenceless and is hardly brought to bear against the illegalities of the powerful and well connected . . . The main target . . . as it was more explicitly in the nineteenth century [is] the dangerous classes—unorganised labour, or the unemployed, marginal, transient and easily stigmatised groups, the non-respectable workers and the undeserving poor . . .

In 1916 a new Larceny Act modernized and consolidated on its 1861 predecessor, although the 1861 Act still remained in force. This new act reigned supreme as the basic text for policing over the next fifty years until 1968. All the manuals on my initial police courses and at the detective training courses emphasized the importance of this Act. We learned definitions of larceny by heart, and, like children in the nursery, could chant the points to prove in order to make a case: 'a person steals, who, without the consent of the owner, takes and carries away anything capable of being stolen . . .' (etc.). We studied case law for definitive legal decisions on 'what the consent of the owner' might exclude and argued fiercely over the niceties of what 'anything capable of being stolen' might include. We were aware that our chance of dealing with the more esoteric crimes such as 'counterfeit currency' or 'concealment of birth' was somewhat limited. Nevertheless, we learned the points to prove for each of these in parrot fashion, but knew that larceny from gas meters, shopbreaking at the corner store, theft from the parked car and house breaking (or burglary) were to be our bread and butter.

We scorned the inability of the public to differentiate between housebreaking and robbery and derided the media's tendency to call every burglary a robbery, for we were the experts in the drama and its tiny nuances were our meat and drink.

Around this reverence for the idea of the inviolability of property the police have constructed a range of practices and a ritualized belief in the drama of crime which has taken on an almost fundamentally religious nature. Any increase in the detection rate becomes the absolute indicator of success. It speaks of the efficiency and value of police society in fiscal terms and hints at the health and morality of society. Its primacy also speaks volumes for the metaphorical value that even insignificant items of property hold for the police imagination. You merely have to consider the way in which the police treat what they call 'found and seized property' to observe the almost religious significance which has developed around the idea of stolen items. The amount of time and money the police expend in recording, logging, checking, and disposing of scrap or abandoned vehicles which come into their possession, for example, has to be seen to be believed. To outsiders and the new 'civvie' Organization and Methods researchers now tasked with making the police 'cost effective', the weeks of administration involved in disposing of abandoned scrap vehicles (often realizing only £5 or £6) is bizarre and breathtaking. In 1984, in West Mercia, after a committee had sat for months deliberating a two-year-old report proposing to simplify matters relating to the disposal of property (and already instituted in some forces) a newly recruited 'civvie' researcher suggested that the deliberations would be 'more useful as material for a TV comedy half-hour or one of your anthropological analyses on the symbolic aspects of totems'. And of course he was correct, for it is the symbolic import of minutely following the rituals for disposing of such property, however trivial and valueless, which is paramount. Always the defensiveness of the institution will find a champion to argue, 'Ah but, I remember when we had just sold a ring quite legitimately at auction after making enquiries for two years, when the owner turned up and made a claim against us . . . saying that it was worth much more than we had got for it' (chief inspector describing an event which had occurred some twenty-four years previous, in defending any need to streamline the seized property system, 1984). The illogicality of much of this defensiveness is lost on a service which thrives on ensuring there are double chains and locks on every stable door from which the horse has long since bolted; and always the cry is 'what if?' This phrase rings around police stations and headquarters' buildings across the country as policemen set out to prevent change by imagining often wildly implausible possibilities, or use one case in ten thousand across a period often spanning two or more decades to justify the retention of an enormously turgid and costly administrative process.[5] This dependency on absolutes of certainty and the need for a totally defined world means problems arise as soon

---

[5] Part of Geoffrey Dear's campaign to raise morale in West Midlands Police on his arrival in 1985 was to implement a review of administration. He quickly produced a book entitled *The War Against Bureaucracy*, which set out to sweep away these administrative nightmares. The ideas in the book were also considered in other forces, and although supported by some of the more dynamic members of ACPO, the changes they sought were often too radical for some commanders and others in the rank and file.

as the police are forced beyond the realms of handling 'bodies' for the theft of articles which can be logged, stored, recorded, and produced in court as 'real evidence' (another highly symbolic category in police status hierarchies). As Croft (1984: 531), echoing Leach (1977), points out:

historically, [the Criminal Law] is on less certain ground when it comes to forms of behaviour about which the social order is ambivalent or which are themselves subject to changes of attitude and indeed concept. Examples of the latter are sex, suicide, drink and acts such as pollution, where the victim and the perpetrator are less identifiable as private conflicts extinguishable or capable of solution by an objective criminal law . . .

However, these ambivalences have still to be dealt with, and the ambiguities even add meaning to the dramatic metaphors by which the criminal mode is enacted. The institutional obsession with correct definitions of physical property, actual space or place, and absolute time is illuminated in these struggles to define children, juveniles, adults, sexuality, and in the vagaries of such laws which attempt to define the correct place and times for drinking. Each has conceptual and spatial dimensions which are subject to social and temporal change and ensure that the world of policing remains a theatrical domain which is concerned as much about its own continuity as it is about any system designed to procure social justice for society. I find I am increasingly in agreement with Hulsman (1977), who argues that

A strong indication that the reality of the criminal justice system is for the most part a dramatic and not a literal one is found in the very unusual time dimensions which are applied in this criminal justic world. Those time dimensions are generally completely out of touch with normal time experience.

My experience in 1977 on returning to the bridewell, was that nothing had changed in police thinking or the institutional style since I had first seen the place some twenty years previously. Today in the early 1990s, I still see the same deep structures of thought and practice firmly directing the culture in its everyday routines. And even as challenges to the nineteenth-century models of crime and criminality have been taken up by some chief officers (especially John Alderson when he was chief constable of Devon and Cornwall), as they set out to redefine the police role and meet the valid criticisms of some social analysts,[6] so the institution seems, in general, to confound these attempts and reinforce existing structural forms without difficulty. In 1968 the new Theft Act re-emphasized the control of 'property' as being the primary module for police action, by recreating the Larceny Acts of 1861 and 1961 in principle, if not in actual clause and section. 'Counting Rules for Crimes' (of which I will say more later) were then issued by the Home Office, and these have been amended continually in the last decade, drawing detectives further into a melodramatic world in which there are rewards for the creation of a skewed but statistically suitable picture of social mayhem.

These counting rules have created a growth industry concerned with counting, measuring, and classifying relatively petty and minor criminal acts, and then presenting them in such a way as to create the best statistical impression of efficiency. And even though the newly emergent management orientated hierarchies in the forces have taken on board the demands for financial acountability on which their political lives depend (Reiner 1985) and seek to implement the new community-based programmes to help conserve social order, so they have found themselves hamstrung by the cultural strength of the numbers game and the significance of the detection rates. For this system of counting what policemen do has such a hold on the culture that it seems impossible to dislodge from its central place as *the* primary means of determining practical effectiveness. And of course the way the figures are created, manipulated, and presented means that what they represent in symbolic terms is never quantifiable; indeed the burgeoning new worlds of business management and the older symbolic world of 'crime fighting' are oppositional realities and cannot talk to each other, for they speak in different languages!

Strictures on the easy acceptance of social change ensure that this somewhat mythologized nineteenth-century model of social reality is maintained. A belief in a golden age or 'dream time' continues, so that any new or ambivalent activity which is indicative of change in social morality will often be assigned to

---

[6] See for example the work of McCabe and Sutcliffe (1978) and Bottomley and Coleman (1980), who question the ability of the police to have more than a minimal influence on the prevention and detection of crime. Reiner (1985: chap 4) summarizes and evaluates much of these recent research findings of police practice, effectiveness, and efficiency.

previously determined categories of disorder. For example, the student unrest in the 1960s, the activities of CND, the Peace Movements, the actions of Greenpeace or the Greenham Common women, or calls for Gay rights, are all indications of a search for a new political and social morality. Inevitably, given their cultural resistance to change, the 'polises' are scathing about such groups in the privacy of their stations and canteens, and could easily be persuaded that such activity might well be a source of further statistical material to justify their special place in the centre of the control industry and their own continued expansion.

In a similar manner, the dramatic inner city riots of the 1980s were multidimensional statements of discontent with government and local socio-economic or political policies, and have many parallels across British social history. The Scarman inquiry (1981) into the first of these current expressions of social despair argued that the police had some responsibility for the general dissatisfaction and suggested changes designed to enhance community and police contacts. Although the police have made some response to these criticisms, it would have been idealistic to expect any radical or deep structural changes to occur simply because of this one report and the surrounding events; and indeed the changes towards an integrated, multi-agency service style of policing or public control have largely been cosmetic.

Although local liaison and consultative committees have been set up, these have largely been controlled and directed by the police,[7] and while most forces have extended or set up Community Affairs departments and have made considerable public noise about changes in policing styles, they have also tested water-cannon, bought extensive amounts of riot gear, have operated as regional and nationally co-ordinated units to defeat the miners in what should essentially have remained a dispute over political

---

[7] Many of the papers at the 1988 Police Foundation Conference mentioned earlier (e.g. Morgan 1989, Bennett 1989, Fielding 1989) deliberate the results of police systems designed to show financial and social accountability to the community in such areas as neighbourhood watch, Consultative Committees, and Local Beat Officer systems. The conclusion was that many were political gestures designed to bolster the credibility of government in the debate on 'accountability' and the socio-legal nature of 'consent', which remains ambiguous in the extreme. Inevitably, it was agreed, that any assessment of 'success', efficiency, and effectiveness in these schemes lies in the problem of accounting, especially where measurable achievement has no firm historical basis and is of a subjective nature.

differences with government, and are increasingly well armed and can be seen to use their weapons. In addition, some offences have been upgraded and new crimes have been added to the Standard List. As the politics of control seems to intensify, so the police seem set to extend their perception of the 'dangerous classes' to include those who exhibit what Sir David McNee described over a decade ago in his 1977 Annual Report, as 'the increasing problem of political dissent'.

In 1984, the acts of assault and disorder in relation to the miners' strike were further visible manifestations of a changing political ideology which the police were ill equipped to handle other than by a system of control by confrontation.[8] Any attempt to pursue the much heralded alternative community liaison or consultation systems was never really on the agenda; for the problem was defined and dramatized by relying on the traditional conflict model of policing. And as a result we were left with the spectacle of mass arrests, mounted charges, roadblocks, and an array of uniformed technology and equipment, portraying the dramatic image of the battlefield rather than one of service to the community. At the time of the dispute, I found it somewhat ironic to watch my essentially working-class constables go off in convoy from the subdivision to 'do battle up North' with the working-class miners, and listen to their expressed hatred and loathing for Arthur Scargill, the miners' leader.[9] During the whole of the drama, while government sat back and denied the conflict was of their making, the police were left to apply their nineteenth-century legalistic model of 'crime' and criminality, while their newly proclaimed community service role all but disappeared. But, as I have argued above, this should not be surprising, for 'community service' is 'women's work'.

Indeed it has been accurately described as being a mere public

---

[8] At the Hillsborough football disaster in 1989, when 95 supporters were crushed to death, it seemed apparent that for a short but significant period at the start of the problem, the police were acting and perceiving the event as a public order situation to be confronted by force, and not as one which lay centrally within their mandate to 'preserve life'.

[9] I had fun asking these same men to mark lists of prominent men with positive or negative designations. Arthur Scargill was always a strongly minus figure, while Lech Wałęsa, his union counterpart in Poland, was always positively viewed—no doubt because of the way he was dramatized in the media as being antagonistic to the common Russian threat.

relations exercise, with no real commitment from within the force as a whole,[10] and Dr G. Cumberbach told the British Association in 1984 that

the greatest myth [is] community policing . . . it is not helpful for anyone to perpetuate this mythology by refusing to acknowledge that most experiments [in community policing] simply do not work in the sense of achieving anything other than a public relations exercise objective. Community policing projects had been stage-managed for the benefit of their architects and principal actors . . . (*Guardian*, 13 September 1984)

Again the metaphors are from the dramatic mode, with community policing projects being 'stage-managed' for the 'actors'. It is therefore not surprising to find that 'real work' for the rank and file is still concerned with crime as defined over a century ago, for this service work may be a temporary aberration, and all of the symbols of success are still linked to the dramatic presentation of this truth. Crime is still a matter of petty theft, burglary, and the appropriation of property by 'real prigs', so that regardless of the latest 'preventive' measure, the detectives are never happier than when a local villain is 'captured', and he is 'on a bender, but likely to clear his slate or take a few off the books when he goes down and gets settled'. Again the language in this fieldnote indicates the dramatic mode which both the 'polises' and the 'prigs' from the dangerous classes use as part of the consistent theatricality surrounding petty crime. In 1986, as subdivisional commander I had an 'injured person' (the aggrieved party in a crime) complain about what he saw as the complicity demonstrated by a detective in his case with a 'regular villain' who'd been 'captured' for the crime. As a somewhat puzzled member of the innocent public, he felt excluded and wondered if it was 'not just some genial game between the police and the criminals'. Both detectives in the case agreed this was the case, for the regular villain on a 'bender' (suspended sentence), who is willing to 'clear his slate' or 'take a few off the books' (admit outstanding, un-

[10] Superintendent David Webb, who set out to promote a style of community policing in Handsworth, Birmingham in the late 1970s, and vigorously sought public involvement and consent for police styles of action, announced his resignation from the force because of a lack of support for his work within the force, only a month before the Scarman report was published. Some three years later Handsworth went up in smoke during rioting sparked off by a police response to drug use in Afro-Carribean areas of the city.

detected crimes) when he 'gets settled' (is sentenced and is settled in prison after initial assessment by the prison authorities), takes a main part in the drama which he and the 'real polis' may have to re-enact again next year and the year after that. On the other hand the 'injured person' is an outsider who rarely understands the rules of the game, the dramatic mode, or the peculiar spatial and temporal aspects which are essential to the success of the production. No wonder he feels excluded, for this is an exclusive performance, designed primarily for the benefit of the actors and it needs no audience. Indeed it positively excludes them from the details of the script and only presents a statistical account of its success after the event!

This is how it has been since the start of organized policing 150 years ago, and the insularity of the institution ensures that even with the cosmetic changes created by such influences as the development of 'community affairs' or management by objectives, the central themes remain with crime and criminals, 'cops and robbers', or 'polises' and 'prigs'.

CRIME OR OFFENCE: SEMANTIC DIFFERENCES IN THE DEFINITION OF DISORDER

There are crucial differences between the categories of crime and offence within the police mind. 'Crime' is often set out in police instruction books in terms which mirror its legal definition as an all-encompassing concept to enfold 'any act forbidden or punishable by criminal law'. In effect this would include major and petty villainies, ranging from murder to drunkenness, as well as those matters such as the parking irregularity, which lies near to the bottom of a hierarchy of 'punishable acts forbidden by law'. However, there exists a whole range of socially harmful behaviour which is totally outside the police mandate yet is punishable by law, as well as many acts of disorder which the police never conceptualize as 'crimes', but which fall into the lower category of 'offences'.

The strength of this hierarchic belief in separate categories of crime and offence needs to be examined in detail to illustrate just how these modes of thought and ideology are then translated into action. The way that the Larceny Acts and Theft Act have come to define certain disorders which the police eagerly pursue while other socially untenable activities have been ignored or neglected needs to be understood. It is crucially important, as Chatterton (1976) argued, to understand why some laws are invoked on some occasions and not on others, and it is necessary to explore the semantics of why certain charges are used by policemen at certain times and places. As Chatterton (ibid.) emphasized, to fail to pursue the ideological factors on which these actions are based is to fall into the trap of making inferences about law enforcement from legislation or the legal books. In the same way, it is wrong to make any assumptions about reality from the 'detection rates' without understanding the practical relevance they have had over the years to the way control is directed and power is maintained.

What then is classificatory 'crime'? At what point in the history of the drama of disorder does an 'offence' get upgraded to become a 'crime'? What are the results of such changes? All of these questions require explanation, and the nuances of meaning incorporated within need diachronic interpretation.

Those deviant acts which *are* classified as crimes often seem identical to those which the lawyer might refer to as 'indictable', but again this is a phrase which has specific meanings for only certain groups in the legal drama, and is a generic term referring to certain villainies which, by law, have to be tried at High Court rather than the lower or Magistrates' Courts.

'Crimes' as defined for the police are now contained in a 'Standard List' made under Section 54 of the Police Act 1964, and published by the Home Office as *Criminal Statistics: Counting Rules for Serious Offences*. At the time of writing, the list contains over sixty categories of crime,[11] but as Chatterton (1976) correctly points out, it is essential to understand why some of these classificatory 'crimes' have symbolic import at specific times, while others are neglected and have fallen in status, and yet other 'offences' seem set for early elevation to join 'the list'.

To show the movements in this semantic perception, I have

---

[11] Again it depends how these are counted. Some categories are subdivided while the category numbers are not consecutive. The Home Office form on which the returns are sent to the Home Office (Crim. Sect. 1(*a*) 'Return of Notifiable Offences Recorded by the Police and Offences Recorded as Cleared up'), compounds the problems by referring to 'offences' but actually means 'crimes', and at Category 58*b* includes 'Criminal Damage under £20', which, as we shall see, is an offence and not a crime.

used a hypothetical incident at a number of seminars to link the idea of 'offences' and 'crimes' to a discussion on changes in the social milieux across my own thirty-year police experience. And although I still contend that police modes of thought are conservatively static, deeply structured, and resistant to change, it is possible to follow some adjustments to what I would call the 'police objectified reality' and show how concepts based on experience come to be seen as 'natural', so that 'new crimes' can be taken on and become actionable.

Nigel Walker (1971) has also presented social events as a methodology of asking how many crimes would have been recorded in certain situations, while the *Police Review* has a weekly 'Law Questions' column, where relevant charges have to be decided from a given set of circumstances. In my imaginary incident described below, a chain of social dramas is presented which relate to those street-visible activities the seminar audience might expect the police to have a hand in. I ask them to classify the drama and evaluate how many 'crimes' and how many 'offences' the police might have 'recorded and detected' in the 1950s, and then to consider what changes might have occurred in the statistical record in the 1980s:

In a street a man exposes his penis to a passing young woman and then pulls a large sheath knife from under his coat and waves it wildly around in her direction. She screams and runs off, whereupon he zips up his trousers, drops the knife and takes out a packet of cigarettes. He lights up and throws the empty packet and the box of matches on the ground, ignoring a litter bin only a few feet away. He then urinates in the road in front of passing women and children, before taking a nearby parked car which has had the ignition keys left in. He has no driving licence or insurance and is already a disqualified driver. He has been drinking previously and is well above the prescribed blood/alcohol level. As he gets into the car, he tears off the radio aerial out of malice; damage is later estimated at £19.99. He drives erratically and without lights for a mile, knocking over a small child aged 7, breaking her leg. Then, ignoring a 'Give Way' sign he drives into another vehicle on a Major Road, injuring all 4 occupants slightly. He abandons the damaged car and wanders into a nearby housing estate where a passing youth gives him a 'joint' of cannabis. Now slightly stoned, he wanders around the streets passing another 13-year-old youth who is busy taking the milk tokens left out by housewives on their doorsteps for their next morning's milk. In all, this youth takes tokens worth 28 pence each from 50 doorsteps, while his

9-year-old brother takes tokens from 25 doorsteps. The man is approached by a prostitute but he turns down her offer and throws a half brick through a house window, causing £21 worth of damage. The woman of the house comes out to remonstrate with him, but he forces her back into the house and rapes her. Her husband is in a nearby public house, where the manager waters the beer, fiddles his income tax and Value Added Tax returns. The woman's husband falls down a cellar hatch which the landlord has negligently left open and breaks his leg. At the time, the landlord was selling a bottle of whisky and ten cigars to a 15-year-old boy while his wife was having sex with his 16-year-old brother.

It may seem easy to classify the villainies in this mythology and to delineate their 'structures of significance' for subsequent police action. One might expect there would be a constant logic that would allow an assessment of which incidents were perceived to be 'criminal' acts, and as a result of which, society could display its defined order of disorder.

Deviance, however, is culture-specific and constrained by temporal influences. Furthermore, in a heterogeneous and secular society it is never easy to determine an absolute ordered hierarchy of unacceptable or offensive behaviour.[12] What *has* been classified as criminal and legally undesirable often derives from the broad spectrum of Judaeo-Christian morality and is deeply felt within the public conscience, but this is rarely immutable. As Leach (1977: 23) points out:

the prototypical public (that is criminal) offences in all the urbanised, police controlled civilisations of the West are homicide and theft. Every citizen who discovers evidence of murder or burglary has an automatic duty to 'call the police'. This duty flows from the doctrine that any threat to the lives and property of the individual citizens constitutes a threat to the very fabric of society. By contrast, the law concerning offences against sexual morality, especially those in which there is collusion between the parties concerned, is always ambiguous.

---

[12] For example, 'offences' under the Noise Abatement Regulations in relation to motor vehicles and more specifically to exhaustingly noisy motor cycles were more or less ignored at the time they entered the statute books. But then, noise 'offences' have never been on the 'list of crimes', and other forms of pollution remain outside the police purview. Only the current interest in environmental issues has dragged them into focus and instituted their partial move towards the centre stage of social control. Perhaps they are set to move even further towards vilification and may yet make the 'list'.

At a functional level, the police sometimes seem to operate as if they believed in a definitively ranked set of 'criminal' acts, and as if this ranking were inherently natural. Yet merely to ascribe all of the events in my hypothetical example to the 'criminal' sphere is to ignore the multiplicity of levels of meaning within the category of 'crime' and to misunderstand the variations and ambiguities that arise as social change presents new structures of meaning.

In reality, only a small number of the activities described in the 'incident' above are classified by the police as crimes or are recordable under the *Counting Rules for Serious Offences*. Some have recently changed status, moving hierarchically upwards from the more lowly status they held as offences, while others which the media and many other commentators on police life seem to assume are equally important to police systems as, say, burglary and robbery, are given little attention and minimum kudos in practice.

As Leach (ibid.) suggests, offences against sexual morality are ambiguous, so that the act of adultery by the pub manager's wife with the 16-year-old boy, for example, although originally proscribed by biblical commandment, is not a criminal offence in this society; although it remains firmly actionable under Islamic law and is still criminal behaviour in other societies. Indeed adultery might now be felt to be a normal pattern in the fabric of this society—if the novel or television drama is a reflection of beliefs and social ideology! Yet in the not too distant past, adultery, like witchcraft, was a burning issue embargoed by statute, and therefore ranked somewhere alongside robbery and burglary. In effect, this somewhat esoteric example shows how the idea of 'crime' reflects social values, and gives some indication as to how changes in the interpretation of social behaviour can even become inverted, so that concepts of purity and disorder can exchange places.

This movement or interchangeability in social belief and practice is at the root of all social change, and is strikingly illustrated by Foucault (1967) in his study of the ideology of madness. He asserts it is always possible for the saintly to become the reviled, while the denigrated stands to become the adulated; further suggesting that the concept of madness (and implicitly the concept of a criminal mind) is, in some cases, clearly an imposition by those who represent the idea of reason. This judgemental quality, he argues, has relegated the once acceptable idea of folly to the arena of denigration, exclusion, and purification, where images of evil and disorder abound and reverse imagery prevails. Such analysis suggests that it is as valid to see other aspects of 'crime and criminality' as being purely constructed categories, which at times might well have undue weight attached to them, and which can as easily have changing values thrust upon them.

In most police forces in Britain, the dastardly 'crimes' described in my hypothetical drama are the province of the detectives in the CID. And because crime holds an almost archetypal place in the dichotomy between the reviled and adulated, it is the detective who has come to hold the highly symbolic place in the public imagination, as he seeks out enemies and antagonists who would destroy the social fabric. Meanwhile the more lowly 'offences' have become the province of the uniformed officers, who are then often derogatorily nicknamed by the detectives to ensure they know their place in the order of things. Sarah McCabe (1980) describes the peculiar strength of this dichotomy and clearly shows how this perception can often elevate trivial crime work to an importance it might not deserve. I would also suggest that much of this social conjuring, where the trivial can become the adulated, is merely another indication of the truly melodramatic nature of this surreal and theatrical world.

Although holding less cognitive resonance than either adultery or witchcraft, two of the activities described in my hypothetical drama have altered their conceptual value within the past twenty years and have achieved a totally different response and an altogether new place within the police imagination. These two deviances have moved up the classificatory tree, acquiring the status of crime after spending long years designated in the lesser category of offence. Reclassification has meant that the offence of malicious damage was changed to become the new crime of criminal damage, while the offence of taking a car without consent became the crime of taking a conveyance. The wider implication of these two changes is detailed below, but one immediate effect of the change was to suggest that a crime wave had occurred, although the reality was much more complex (as we shall see). However, the reclassification of these two categories of villainy into fully fledged recordable crimes means that in Northumbria Police area alone there are now well over 20,000 crimes occurring each year which, until the recent past, would not have been shown in the crime returns.

Immediately this change in the designation of 'car theft' and 'damage' can be seen to influence the crime-count in my hypothetical incident and skew the statistical record; while other 'Counting Rule' anomalies make any statistical count somewhat tenuous and arbitrary. It might be that in the 1980s the police *could well* (the emphasis is on the uncertainty) record sixteen offences and five crimes in my example, yet had it occurred only twenty years ago when I was a detective sergeant, the totals would have certainly been different for a multiplicity of reasons. Although two of the 'crimes' were then only 'offences' and we might therefore expect the total 'crimes' to drop to three, my colleagues in the department in the 1960s could well have scooped over seventy detected 'crimes' for their monthly and annual returns. For as any detective knows, the statistical reality of the crime return is only as good as the actors who are playing the game.

I have tried out the hypothetical game on several of my colleagues. Each had his own assessment of what would happen in reality (i.e. his sectional or divisional version of police reality). Most were agreed they would ignore all but the most 'serious' of the offences and had little difficulty in deciding what this was, nominating the careless driving (controlled by the Road Traffic Acts) which caused injury. And although careless driving, reckless driving, and most traffic irregularities are defined as offences and are not crimes in the Standard List, the injuries meant they included them in their lists.

All the detectives considered the 'real crimes', before turning to the 'offences', and many dismissed the traffic aspects as not being worthy of their consideration. This denigration of traffic matters as being unworthy of the consideration of 'real polises' is further illustrated by the bridewell gaoler, who dismissively described to me these lesser beings: 'you know what the difference is between real polises boss and traffic men? No? Well, I'll tell you. Real polises have sandwiches for their bait [refreshment break], while traffic men drink blood.' The significance of this remark lies in the placing of traffic department officers into the areas of ambiguity and ambivalence I have discussed above. Traffic men, by and large, are not seen to deal with 'real crime' committed by 'real prigs', but are said to 'suck the blood' of the 'ordinary car-owning silent majority', who consider 'crime' to be committed against them rather than by them, and who would 'otherwise support the police in their wars against the prigs'.

As these and other accounts in my fieldnotes show, to be a traffic officer is to earn the derision of the detectives: 'if you look in the hair at the base of the neck, you'll see the scar where the traffic man's brain has been taken out'. They grudgingly admit, however, that 'when the traffic officer is transferred and leaves the department to return to the real world, he is given the reverse operation and his brain is replaced.' This leads to the situation where a careless driving or reckless driving offence causing serious injury can have lower value and significance attached to it than many 'crimes' of wounding, which might well result in lesser injuries:

the shift discuss the results of the horrendous car accident that has dominated the afternoon and evening's events. Two young women and a young child have been horribly injured by a car driven by an uninsured youth road-racing another car, who has ploughed into these pedestrians. By the late evening he is released and has not even been subject to a really 'hard time', even though the event has physically sickened some of the younger officers. I discuss this with an old colleague from Squad days who is now a tough Station Sergeant. He regrets this, but shrugs it off as 'no surprise'. Even though there has been gross negligence, he points out that there was 'no criminal intent to wound, and as we all know, it's being dealt with by the men who've had their brains removed, and its not a matter for real polises . . .' (From fieldnotes, 1982)

Structurally and symbolically this and other driving matters are always held in an inferior light to the 'crimes' of theft and burglary, although many policemen would publicly deny this by invoking their originally defined function of 'protecting life' to support their claim.

Other offences listed in my hypothetical incident mirror those marginal activities I have described above in outlining how the 'ambiguous prig' is defined. Lesser offences, such as indecent exposure, the soliciting for prostitution, the waving of the knife (an offensive weapon), the urinating in the street, the dropping of litter and the drunken driving, are *all* offences and *not* crimes. Usually these matters are the province of the uniformed branch, and some, such as the Litter Act offences (like the noise abatement legislation mentioned above) have been all but ignored by the police since they were placed on the statute books.

The sale of drink and tobacco to juveniles are offences the police have never really pursued with diligence, while the fraud in relation to income tax and VAT, the negligence causing the broken leg, as well as the watering down of the beer are all matters the police have no mandate to pursue. Few tax offences in Britain are police matters, which may account for the lack of any real fraud training for the police until the late 1960s. Fraud, of course, was never the province of the dispossessed 'dangerous classes' to any extent, rather it was the domain of the entrepreneur and businessman, and as a result was within the province of those whom the police were set up and developed to support. Not unnaturally, an immense amount of minor and even major fiddling is still of no concern to the police, nor is it revealed by official statistical records of 'crimes' committed. As the reports commissioned by the Home Office, and published as the British Crime Surveys (1983, 1985, and 1989), as well as a wealth of writings on criminology and the sociology of crime, such as the 'fiddling' and 'pilfering' analysed by Ditton (1977) have all revealed, large amounts of petty or minor crime remain unreported and unrecorded.[13]

Behaviour which *does* constitute high status crime in the police imagination follows those categories Leach (1977) mentions—i.e. homicide, theft, and burglary. In the Home Office Document *Criminal Statistics: Counting Rules for Serious Offences*, detailed rules are provided for 'aggregrating statistics on three categories of offences'. These are: 'VIOLENCE AGAINST THE PERSON; SEXUAL OFFENCES; and OTHER OFFENCES (including offences of burglary, robbery, theft and handling of stolen goods, fraud, forgery and

---

[13] Ditton and Williams in what I believe is an unpublished paper on the differences between research into that which is 'fundable' and to that which is 'doable', argue (p. 22) that such fiddling is 'theft defined as trivial'. Expanding on Becker's (1963) proposal that any deviance is a consequence of the application of rules and sanctions, they suggest that deviance is not just a matter of whether or not people react to it, but that triviality determines its classification as 'fiddling' or otherwise. I prefer to substitute the word 'meaningless' for 'trivial', to indicate a lack of relevance or import to those institutions tasked with defining just what does or does not constitute social chaos. The non-involvement of the police in many areas of tax-evasion follows their mandated pursuit of the visible, and their neglect of the invisible. Such frauds and fiddles do not occur in the public places frequented by the 'dangerous classes' and they are 'trivial' or 'meaningless' to the police precisely because they are *not* 'street visible'. In effect they are symbolic non-events and simply do not happen.

criminal damage) ...'. The Home Office still continues to generate conceptual difficulties by insisting on describing these 'crime' categories as 'offences', even though each requires the creation of a manual or computed 'crime report', the divisional and HQ's administrative record of 'a crime committed', and if possible a record of a 'crime detected'.

This official list of 'serious offences' (i.e. crimes) ensures the police response to burglary, theft, criminal damage, and the like enhances their import in the public imagination and diverts attention away from many areas of social harm which could be said to be equally damaging. This is not to suggest for a moment that murder, violent assault, and burglary are not socially harmful or should be condoned. Indeed in burglary, for example, the value of the property stolen may often be trivial, but the breach of personal space, the violation of the secure environment, and the resulting feeling of despoliation may well be so intense that they cause extreme distress.[14]

It is not easy to evaluate the social harm that a burglary can cause. As a result of the accountancy mentality adopted by many modern police managers, as they strive to meet the 'efficiency and effectiveness' criteria demanded of them by the Home Office in their circular 114/83,[15] abstract concepts such as social harm fail to achieve any real precedent for action. Harm, of course, does not readily lend itself to easy budget evaluation or statistical presentation, whereas property stolen, houses burgled, and time expended can be listed as values, percentage increases or decreases and cost of man-hours involved. All are quantifiable and allegedly capable of scientific or objective evaluation and because of recent demands for 'value for money policing', which are hugely reinforced by such coercive measures as this government circular, the energetic pursuit of ambiguous statistics for their own defens-

---

[14] Michael Maguire (1980 and 1982) has explored the effects of house burglary on the victims. Even when the victim's loss was negligible in financial terms (and therefore of less import to the police), the house owner often described the event in terms indicative of a symbolic rape, with concepts of violation, pollution, dirtiness, and shame being expressed. It is this symbolic weight which confounds the statistician, who cannot begin to measure its import, or send it on a return to the Home Office on a neat statistical chart.

[15] Home Office Circular 114/83 demanding 'Manpower, Effectiveness and Efficiency in the Police Service' has become an almost fundamental tract laying out the political expectations of police management. Its economic philosophy has been followed to the letter by many chief officers, not the least because their future advancement depends largely on eventual Home Office patronage.

ively structural purposes has maintained its pre-eminence in the police mind. As Bottomley and Coleman (1980) point out, this emphasis means that

a clear-up rate of crimes committed leads inevitably to a simplified, single-dimensional role for the police . . . based on a statistical measure of effectiveness that is totally flawed [and] leads to a conception of other aspects of police work as being regarded as 'not real police work'.

As I have discussed above (see also Jones 1979) the presentation of the uniformed beat man as being 'the backbone' of police society is a convenient myth for the watching world. Such metaphorical language is, in itself, a further guide to perceptual values and Joseph Wambaugh (1976) in his novel *The Choirboys* (based on his own experiences as a police officer) uses the same bodily metaphors of status and defines his 'real policemen' as having 'backbone', while they in turn refer to their leaders as being 'spineless jellyfish'.

Structurally the low value of uniformed police activity can be attributed to this unquantifiable nature of beat patrol work. Informal socio-welfare tasks make up the majority of the patrol officer's day and produce large amounts of somewhat invisible *soft* data. This is difficult to present to a public increasingly fed on media and televisual images of a crime-fighting style. Arrest statistics, crime detection figures, annual returns of crimes committed and of villains captured, convicted, fined, or imprisoned are presented quantatively as *hard* data, and surrounded by a metaphorical language which supports and reinforces this ascendancy. It is no accident that the police use of quantities of such *hard* data has increased dramatically in the recent past, and is now an essential element in support of their annual claims for more *hard* cash, more expensive *hard*ware, and more *man*power.

Again it is tempting to construct a binary to simplify the oppositional values placed on these concepts, and show how they are set against one another:

male	female
crimework	service or caring work
detectives	uniform wollies
hard data	soft data

This 'crime-ridden' perception results in uniformed beat establishments being constantly depleted by secondments to specialist departments and to short term initiatives such as 'anti-burglary patrols'. If career success is to be achieved, an early *rite de passage* must be made, for long periods of patrol work are seen to be synonymous with failure and lack of ambition. Both the media and police society contrast the lowly place of the 'beat man' by using the title 'detective' as a symbol of prestige, or as an equivalent to promotion. The press consistently talk about officers being 'promoted into the CID', even though the officer has merely been transferred from the uniform branch into the detective department at the same rank and pay structure. In 1980, Maureen Martin, a policewoman in Gateshead division, was shot shortly after she had been transferred from uniform work to the CID, and I noted:

the media have made much of the fact that she had recently been 'promoted' to be a 'detective'. Of course they are wrong and they are right! In one respect she is still a constable, but of course in metaphorical and symbolic terms she has moved *up* in the hierarchy of importance which the organization denotes by bestowing the prestigious title of 'detective' on the individual . . . ' (from fieldnotes)

Another uniform branch complaint which, in their powerlessness, is consistently ignored, is that they go short of established manpower, while the CID are always kept up to strength. Of course, any reduction in the strength of the 'detective' branch to enhance uniform patrols would need a change in the structures of significance, for any move in the opposite direction, from CID to uniform, is considered to be a demotion; as the following examples show:

If we are to believe what senior officers tell the public (through the media), then uniform or 'section officers' are the cream of the service and the foot patrol officer is the king. Who are they trying to fool? The uniform officer, far from being the cream is treated as the poor relation. What happens, for instance, to the detective constable who fails to make the grade, or the (specialist) officer who gets disciplined? Where are they transferred? Uniformed working sections [and] the public realise the situation. How often have we heard a civilian say: 'Oh, he/she's done well getting promoted to detective . . . (Letter to *Police Review*, 29 July 1983)

. . . in Liverpool instead of 'demoted' we say, 'It's the Big Hat for you!' This expression has made strong men tremble . . . I feel sure that if the 'demoted' detective is posted to a uniformed section (and wearing a 'big hat') like mine, he would enjoy the camaraderie and leg pulling that only the dreaded uniform men have. We are after all the very backbone of the police service . . . (Letter to *Police Review*, 12 February 1982)

These two letters again demonstrate all the metaphors of police reality I have demonstrated, with references to primacy of the backbone and to civilians as being structural outsiders. Always these metaphors are orientational (Lakoff and Johnson 1980), so that those who move out of the CID to uniform, move *back* (negatively), while those who move in, move *up* and *forwards* (positively).

Over the years, I have heard detectives talk with horror of the fear of a *return* to uniformed work, and have seen those promoted out, say from detective sergeant to uniform inspector, talk of their fall from grace. I have watched as ex-members of the department have grovelled and crawled to those in power in an attempt to be reinstated, and have myself felt the loss associated with my own remove from the department once I had gone off on the scholarship to university.

I have heard very senior CID officers tell middle managers to threaten those who were not pulling their weight with a 'blue suit', and at one CID conference in the early 1980s I listened as a detective chief inspector pointed out that 154 uniformed constables were now qualified as 'suitable for the CID', having successfully completed a period as CID aides. The assistant chief constable (crime) chairing the conference, told the inspectors, chief inspectors, and superintendents present to

have a look at men who are not contributing totally. The CID is not a sinecure—I would ask you to look to their performance and get rid of those who are not earning their corn. There has to be a certain competitiveness and the 'big heaveho' and a return to uniform for those who are not working. (From fieldnotes)

Again the metaphor is of a downward *return* to uniform for failure. This élitism of the CID is also imbued in the public mind, where the detective holds a special place in the collective imagination. In the late 1970s, Sir Robert Mark, then commissioner of the Metropolitan Police, attempted to make some impact on the apparent long-standing corruption in his detective branch by creating a system of constant transfers between CID and uniform branches.[16] In 1982, Stanley Bailey, the chief constable of Northumbria, officially scrapped the title 'detective' which had prefixed the CID rank of constable, sergeant, inspector, chief inspector, superintendent, and chief superintendent. Not unnaturally the media, the public, and the detectives resisted the move, still continuing to use the title in conversations, in telephone calls, and in newspaper reports. Like Robert Mark's attempt to diffuse the extraordinarily high esteem of the CID, this bid was also in vain, for their perceptual status was retained simply because all the other symbols and metaphors of the detectives status were still firmly in place.

Another example of these statements of metaphorical importance can be illustrated in the way that 'crime' is given highly symbolic ranking in the Annual Reports of the various police forces. 'Crime' and the work of the detectives is always described in detail near the front of these glossy and expensive productions, while traffic matters, general policing, and community affairs aspects are always relegated to the latter parts of the report. In Northumbria the 'Crime' section of the Annual Report follows on immediately after the structure of the force is described, and its importance in police ideology can be judged by its prime position, by the graphics, the photo-montages, by the statistical charts, and the accounts of the 'worst' crimes of the year. And although the incidence of murder is only around a dozen cases per year or less, each individual case is always fully described and written up in detail.

All forty-three forces trade their reports and watch their competitors to ensure they are not left behind in the constant attempt to be at the forefront of style and imagery, for there are awards for the best and worst reports and the results are published in *Police Review*. In 1983 I looked at my first West Mercia report to find the exact same structural logic in this report, where, in his introduction, the chief constable, Robert Cozens, got into all sorts

---

[16] In 1989, the élite Serious Crime Squad in Birmingham was broken up by the chief constable, Geoffrey Dear. Over fifty detectives were moved and two were suspended for alleged corrupt practices. The head of the CID—a det. chief supt—and his deputy 'have been *returned* to uniform duties in Research and Community Affairs respectively', according to news reports. Once again the true status apportioned to Research and Community Affairs in the police mind is clearly illustrated by this 'punishment'.

of ironic tangles concerning the traditional primacy of 'crime matters' (although I suspect this went largely unnoticed, except perhaps to the observing anthropologist!). He commences by complaining bitterly that lurid reporting of a few specific cases by the media contributes to the 'fear of crime', but follows this by going on to detail a number of cases of murder, manslaughter, armed robbery, woundings, and arson across five subsequent pages of the report, which the local press always report on at length. And although recognizing that the presentation of statistically rare events contributes to the 'fear of crime',[17] he is unable to break out of the cultural mould which necessitates that 'crime' comes first and is *the* dramatic event, while the sixty road traffic deaths in the first two quarters of the same year are only mentioned many pages later, lost among the statistics for fatal, injury, or damage-only accidents, and listed without any of the background details that the murders enjoy!

In Northumbria traffic fatalities of around 150 cases per year are twelve times more prevalent than murders, many of which have domestic connotation. A fatal road accident is just as devastating an event to the families of the deceased as any 'crime' can be, and although fatal accidents are investigated thoroughly with careful evaluation of the contributory causes, few traffic deaths are considered to be statistical crimes.

Only the offence of 'causing death by dangerous driving' is to be recorded as a crime, and is classified as a subsidiary to Category 4 (manslaughter) in the Counting Rules, along with infanticide (4A) and child destruction (4B). It is noteworthy that as far back now as 1968, the police reported only 500 'crimes' of 'causing death by dangerous driving', although some 7,000 deaths occurred on the roads in that year. Yet in that same year there were nearly 20,000 alleged cases of drunken driving and approximately 128,000 cases of alleged careless driving. Some of these were, no doubt as trivial as the minor crimes which make up the

---

[17] *The British Crime Survey, Home Office Research Study No. 76* showed just how rare crime is, in relative terms. The authors (Hough and Mayhew 1983) argued that statistically the average person could expect a robbery once every five centuries, an assault resulting in injury every century, and a burglary to the home once every forty years. In 1989 the third British Crime Survey again showed that the waves of crime intimated in the 'official' figures 'had been exaggerated because the proportion of crimes reported to the police has risen'.

majority of the statistics amassed under the Counting Rules for *Serious* Crime,[18] but many of these 150,000 incidents will have resulted in terrible injuries and mutilations, incurring considerable medical costs, social disruption, loss of earnings, and anguish for families and friends. Such statistics are not the bread and butter of most policemen, however, nor are they are day-to-day facts that even divisional senior officers will necessarily have at their fingertips; but this is unlikely to be the case with the crime figures. Most subdivisional superintendents are issued with weekly, monthly, quarterly, and half-yearly crime returns and will have daily meetings with their senior detective officers to ensure that the latest details can be fed to the press or other senior officers. Yet I suspect these same men would be hard pressed to say what the incidence of serious accidents was in their area, or how the patterns of such events had changed over the years.

Early in 1986, as a subdivisional commander, I was visited by my divisional commander (a chief superintendent) and his superintendent deputy on the day that the annual crime figures were due to be published. We were joined by the senior detectives on the division and when the telexed list of detection rates began to spill out of the machine, a bottle of whisky was broken open to celebrate our success in coming top of the divisional detection rates. We had beaten the adjacent division by less than 1 per cent, but this was enough, for we knew that following the publication of another aspect of this manipulated reality contained in 'the adjusted figures' (on which I will say more later), we would be well clear. In fact, we eventually beat our rivals by 4.4 per cent, but such was the exhilaration at this occasion, created by this narrow margin of less than 1 per cent, that their detective chief inspector was phoned up to rub salt in his wounds. The whole exercise confirms Radzinowicz and King (1977: 164), who point out:

---

[18] The emphasis on *serious* offences is mine, for they are often of a very trivial nature, and in any moral consideration of their social harm should perhaps be given much lower priority than that given to many aspects which are critical to the health of a society. In 1982, Vivien Stern, director of the National Association for the Care of Offenders and the Prevention of Crime reminded us (*Police Review*, 19 Nov. 1982) that 'publicity often obscures the reality that 95% of all "serious" offences (in the statistical record) are property offences and two-thirds of them involve less than £100'.

the élite in the eyes of both the police and public are the detective branches ... The police are to be seen as professional soldiers in a war against crime, to be organised and equipped as such. The crime detection role of the police gains further weight from the fact that it appears, at least superficially, the easiest to evaluate in objective terms. It is possible to compare crimes recorded and cleared up, the offenders brought to justice and convicted from one year to the next ... detection becomes a touchstone in judging police activity.

Of course this annual comparison remains just that! Little interest is really shown in assessing patterns over any length of time, for senior men who might be thought to need this information or be interested in such long-term analysis, are continually moved on.[19] In West Mercia much was made of reductions in some categories of crimes in 1986 over 1985, but ignored the fact that these statistical drops had merely returned some categories to where they had been in 1984.

If factors had influenced the 1985 increase these were largely unknown or were only to be guessed at. In June 1988, the in-house Force Strategy reports were returned to me in my position as head of Corporate Planning. All six divisions reported they had targeted house-burglary for reductions and then had to apologize in these half-year reports because figures had gone up in comparison with 1987. I subsequently had to cover these simplistic assessments by giving some reasons to the chief officers. In July 1988, I wrote a memo which included some simple points:

this police obsession with only 'this year v. last year' makes ... these analyses somewhat 'skin deep'. Why do we insist on only a 2-year comparison and then ... infer that significant trends can be assessed? In February 1987, this essentially rural force had a *very* low incidence of

---

[19] Early in 1987 I was called to HQ and asked to move from subdivision back to HQ into Corporate Planning. I demurred, for I had only been on the subdivision just over two years. But my doubts were overridden by the assistant chief constable who pointed out that of the thirteen subdivisional commanders in the force I was one of only two who had been in post for this length of time. Within twelve months a further three subdivisional superintendents had sat in the Bromsgrove chair and the subdivisional clerk was working with her tenth superintendent in eight years. In such a situation, which is not uncommon in many forces, any continuity or long-term efforts to plan to influence 'crime' matters is almost impossible; but the culture of hierarchical movement demands this style of personnel management.

house-burglary probably because of the weather. In Bromsgrove Sub-division, where I then was, we had no burglaries for a total of 27 days, no doubt because thieves from Birmingham who travel out to hit our properties were dissuaded by the snow and icy roads! The figures for 1987 were always going to be hard to match in 1988 simply because of this factor, which is outside of police control.... Any significance in house-burglary trends, for example over 6–7 years, tends to suggest we are on a downward path statistically—perhaps because of Neighbourhood watch, public awareness, crime prevention measures, targeted patrols or deflection into other crimes (e.g. thefts from vehicles) ... but seems to be outside the parameters of Force Strategy [or] divisional action plans and targets.

CRIME OR OFFENCE: WIDER ISSUES OF SOCIAL HARM

As my hypothetical example indicates, the police are geared to pursue only the most visible aspects of somewhat minor acts of disorder. This shades off as soon as the activity becomes less immediately apparent, and the social harm caused is more abstract or the responsibility for its occurrence lies elsewhere than with the 'dangerous classes'.

In effect the annual £4 billion police industry, with its 140,000 establishment, largely ignores issues of social harm and deprivation caused by what commentators have branded as the 'corporate crimes' of fraud, pollution, tax evasion, environmental hazard, health and safety omissions, and the like. Other bodies are tasked with monitoring such problems and many have recently experienced fiscal and manpower squeezes to meet a political philosophy which argues that private concerns are more than capable of imposing their own morality and possessed of enough public spirit to control any tendency to put profit before the well-being of society as a whole.

The criminal justice system has largely supported this structural invisibility, for its institutions are geared to conceal the crimes of powerful factions in society, while using highly symbolic strategies to spotlight and emphasize the 'crimes' of the powerless, thus ensuring they retain centre stage in the drama of good versus evil. As a result, the police are almost unable to perceive there is a problem of 'corporate crime', trapped as they are in their world of petty villainy and bridewell clients.

Furthermore it is only in the recent past that the vast literature on criminology and the sociology of crime has thrown off an almost positivistic belief in a knowable 'crime' rate and moved towards the more hermeneutic philosophical position Winch (1958) argued for some three decades ago. He suggested the deterministic, functional search for any 'true' statistical knowledge of crime then exercising so many minds should be abandoned. The issue which mattered, he argued, 'is not an empirical one at all; it is conceptual. It is not a question of what empirical research may show to be the case, but of what philosophical analysis reveals about what it makes sense to say'. Yet a dozen years after this, the criminologist Stephen Box (1971), who has since admittedly argued for a semantic approach to the analysis of 'crime' and social harm, was writing:

crimes officially known to the police must be an unknown and unknowable proportion of total numbers of crimes committed . . . since the 'real' volume of crime remains unmeasured, and given present research techniques and ethical limitations, unmeasurable, there is no possible method of estimating accurately the proportion that is officially recorded.

Even this stance, which argues that all statistical returns will be flawed, holds a positivistic assumption that a 'real' figure of crime is out there, but for the present time is unknowable. Like discussions which filled the criminological texts gave a clear objectivity to the idea of a 'dark figure' of unrecorded crime which may or may not exist and led a whole school of labelling theorists to research the way that 'crimes' are defined and counted. Only a decade ago Ditton (1979: 21) seemed radically innovative when he tried to move away from this formula, asking the rhetorical question: 'How many crimes are there? As many as you want [to react to] . . .'. I believe it is more useful to look at the way society gives meaning and symbolic import to events at different historical times, and to explore why some forms of behaviour are then defined as criminally harmful or socially unacceptable. To do this it is necessary to adopt a diachronic interpretation and help finally lay to rest the positivistic tendency which has bedevilled many of the deviancy theorists, who, as Ditton (ibid. 23) contends, have

an almost religious belief in the ability of official criminal statistics to reveal information about criminals . . . [There is] a tendency to pay introductory lip-service to the difficulties of bias, selectivity, and so on, but nevertheless blunder on to treat the figures 'as if' the difficulties were merely limiting rather than universal criticisms.

Ditton further suggests that much of the 'new criminology', or 'critical criminology' is still limited in that it starts off with the concept of 'crime' almost as a given,[20] and suggests an alternative science of 'controlology'. This, he indicates, will be concerned with an exploration of hegemonies in society and how these structure meanings to define 'crimes and criminality' at particular historical moments. Such a science already exists of course in anthropology, where hermeneutic and reflexive analysis of cultural forms have increasingly been used to explore the holistic nature of social constructs such as 'crime'.

There is need for a semantic enquiry into the meanings and ideology surrounding the idea of crime at various points in social history, for as Box (1983: 6) (now adopting a more hermeneutic approach) argues, ideas about crime still support the position of established society at every turn: 'the official portrait of crime and criminals is highly selective, serving to conceal crimes of the powerful and hence shore up their interests, particularly their need to be legitimated through maintaining the appearance of respectability'. Here we find the search for the semantics of meaning beginning to explore beyond and behind the concealments of the powerful, as they seek to legitimize such symbolic presentations as their 'respectable appearance'. Probings of this kind, which would seek to understand and reveal the culture of 'respectability', are far removed from the earlier struggles in which positivist criminologists attempted to make the statistical record give out some sort of absolute information about criminals, but they are the basic tools of anthropology, which has long set out to take a symbolic or metaphoric code and interpret structural meanings from it.

Box (ibid.) goes on to show how this skilful use of concealment adds to the melodrama of the criminal justice system:

At the same time, crimes of the powerless are revealed and exaggerated, and this serves the interests of the powerful because it legitimises their control agencies, such as the police ... [who are] being strengthened

[20] In this criticism, Ditton seems to be aiming his arrows at such works as *The New Criminology*, Taylor, Walton, and Young (1973); and *Critical Criminology*, Taylor, Walton, and Young (1975).

materially, technologically and legally, so that their ability to survey, harass, . . . [and] deter actual and potential resisters . . . is enhanced.

Once again, I think that this list of ways in which the police have been strengthened (i.e. materially, technologically, and legally) reflects a 'positivist' influence, for it ignores the 'symbolic strength' on which all three materialistic categories largely depend. However, the tenor of these charges by Box also helps to illuminate the illusory nature of the criminal justice system, for they show how the privileged and well-connected in society set out to manufacture and create a respectable role in what is always a dramatic scenario, in which sanctions are defined and imposed on others as a means of directing attention away from their own 'corporate crimes'.

Their misdemeanours largely go unrecognized, or become muted in the reporting, simply because of the control they exercise over those organs of publicity which might otherwise draw them into public view. Unannounced, these 'crimes' become structurally invisible to the extent that they cease to exist, although they remain like a hidden tumour, causing sickness in the social body. They are known and understood by the 'dangerous classes', however, for they have always been aware of the crimes of the powerful but have always lacked any public voice to air this knowledge. In the past, their recourse has lain in strategies of passive retaliation, through the use of drama, the literature of satire, the collective use of humour in which to deride their 'betters'; or, when the situation became truly intolerable, the pursuance of social revolution or acceptance of the inevitable by shrugging it off in such maxims as 'there's one law for the rich and another for the poor'. Occasionally the curtain is drawn back to reveal just how the powerful, while holding the centre stage of respectability, are totally involved in the commission of 'corporate crime'. In a graphic account, Box (ibid. 16–79) details the failure of corporations to maintain safety standards, causing injury and death. He shows how health hazards are caused by deliberate failures of government and industry to maintain standards and conduct adequate research;[21] we are made aware how known

---

[21] The various salmonella and listeria crises in the egg production and other chilled food industries in 1988–9 is a good example of this and may well have caused as many deaths as the 'crime' of murder. Yet the public debate about

design faults are ignored leading to death and injury; how the vast appropriation of money from small shareholders, from taxpayers, and the public is achieved during bribery activities, price fixing, fraudulent advertising, and excess charges; how economic deprivation is continually passed on to the powerless by the swindles and evasions of the rich and powerful. As he records, the social injury and bodily harm to the mass of society at large is endemic, but is kept carefully out of the public debate: 'corporate crime is rendered invisible by its complex and sophisticated planning . . . by non-existent social and legal sanctions, which fail to reaffirm or reinforce collective sentiments or moral boundaries' (ibid. 16). Although such issues are coming more to the fore (and Box quotes many research papers on the subject), 'corporate crime' is poorly represented in the mainstream of sociological and criminological research, because of its acceptance as a dominant form of social behaviour; and because much academic research funding comes from governments and the very institutions who would not want their unsavoury practices to be made public. The process of making this evil side invisible, Box contends, is a form of structural mystification,[22] which further strengthens my contention that the enactment of the whole of the criminal justice system can be perceived as a drama; for mystification and structural invisibility is a central device of theatre, comedy, and melodrama.

The cost of 'corporate crime' in comparison to conventional crime is enormous; which once again highlights the symbolic nature of conventional 'criminality' and its place in the public imagination. Quoting Reiman (1979: 75), Box tells us that estimates of the number of persons dying from occupational hazards, diseases, and accidents in the USA is seven times the level of conven-

---

standards of hygiene, inspection, research, and more healthy forms of production have continually been side-tracked by government and the well-connected, to the extent that at one point the egg contamination was being laid at the door of the individual housewife who was blamed for poor hygiene. At the same time a figure of 'only x eggs per million containing salmonella' was being touted, as if it were an acceptable proposition that only a few get poisoned, even though the causes can be eradicated but will no doubt cost the powerful some of their profits.

[22] Box entitles his volume *Power, Crime and Mystification*, and also explores 'police-crime' and 'crimes' committed by and against that muted section of society, women. In each case he clearly illustrates how reality is subjected to dramatic manipulation, so that processes of mystification and structural invisibility occur over an over again.

tional homicide victims. But of course, these 'industrial' deaths have little symbolic significance. Like the 'traffic accident' deaths which I have shown are less important than the smaller number of crimes of murder, the British pattern of deaths occurring from occupational accident and disease mirrors the sleight of hand of the American experience, so that deaths from such hazards are seven times more likely than by conventional homicide, and go similarly unregarded. Even this estimate errs on the side of caution and it seems reasonable to speculate that the financial controls on systems of inspection which have been generated in the current political climate will have exacerbated rather than ameliorated the situation. But then who knows what the reality is? For the ability to classify many deaths as being occupationally induced by deliberate neglect or risk is prevented by overt action on the part of the powerful corporate bodies who deter or deny any such inference. What then is a 'crime'?

Many accidents in the workplace are not pure accidents. Rather they are a consequence of conditions created by the corporate pursuit of maximum profit with the minimum of care for those workers who make the profit possible. These accidents are often avoidable and like work-induced illness and disease are known, understood, and documented. They continue to occur, however, and have a social acceptability that belies their terrible import. In 1976, for example, a letter was published in the *Sunday Times*, under the heading:

Asbestos: No prosecutions in 30 years
At Acre Mill, where at least 40 former employees have died of abestosis, and scores more . . . are suffering from the disease, no prosecution in connection with asbestos regulations was brought by the Factory Inspectorate during the 30 years the factory was processing asbestos . . . (30 May 1976)

The asbestos industry also falls under Box's scrutiny (1983: 27). He accuses it of deliberately pursuing profit in the face of known dangers, suggesting that by following such policies, the industry is guilty of what must surely be 'a criminal act'. His indictment derives in part from two damning reports. In one of these, Swartz (1975) describes the asbestos industry as *'silent killers at work'* (my emphasis). This ability of industry and its entrepreneurs for maintaining a silence and a blanket invisibility through the concealment of their harmful acts is formidable and pervasive, ranging from the quiet suppression of bad news on aspects of nuclear energy to economic truths on toxic dumping. However few of these acts are defined as crimes, or are pursued by the police.

During my posting to the bridewell, when I was processing the streams of 'conventional' criminals sent to prison for largely petty crimes which caused relatively minor social harm, I attended a short Management Study at which the Factories Inspectorate gave a talk on 'industrial accidents'. At the time I was recording fieldnotes and on this one-day course I became keenly aware of the statistics of harm and deprivation which these accidents created. I had become increasingly aware of my own difficulties in defining 'crime' or 'criminals' in any absolute way, and noted the cost of an industrial accident was estimated to be approximately £10,000, with many thousands of such accidents recorded each year in a variety of categories, such as 'Falls at Work'. I also noted that a 'classifiable accident' does not become such until the injured person has been off work for three days or more. A 'two-day accident' apparently could not happen and seemed to parallel other material I had on the classification of crime, for until 1968 (as I will detail below) a car was not stolen until it had been missing for 72 hours; so that a two-day car theft was statistically impossible. Again the Safety Inspectorate statistics seemed to be merely one version of reality, and without a semantic interpretation of what the rules were seeking to achieve for those in power, they simply added to the mystification of the drama.

The statistical report on industrial accidents made depressing reading, with accounts of innumerable 'accidental' amputations, lacerations, mutilations, poisonings, explosions, electrocutions, drownings, asphyxiations, burns, scalds, and the like. A picture was painted by the inspectorate which implied that the corporate urge for maximized profit would always offset any real desire to secure healthy or safe conditions for workers.

To my colleagues this course was an 'away day'! A day off, free from the tensions of work, with food provided, constant coffee on hand, and the only chore being the requirement to listen to one of the other agencies of control, with whom the police have somewhat tenuous links. At the time, however, it was another reflexive occasion for me to consider cultural norms and comparative social values.

The Inspectorate of Factories, Mines, and Quarries, like other regulatory inspectorates in Britain, has powers to institute prosecutions, but is primarily an administrative body. Contravention of safety regulations and failure to protect working people may, as the statistical record indicates, be endemic, but only 1,700–800 cases end up in court each year across the whole country.[23]

In effect these administrative bodies are set up by the powerful to make their occasional inspections and subsequent recommendations by what Box (1983) calls 'polite correspondence'. In the majority of cases this 'control by etiquette' ensures that breaches of safety remain invisible, for they fail to achieve any publicity through the process of legal enforcement. The perpetrators of unlawful or dangerous practices negotiated to resolution by polite correspondence suffer none of the moral stigma, retribution, or imprisonment which the 'dangerous classes' have experienced over the years for their conventional crimes; and in effect, the insubstantiality of corporate crime in the statistical record means they have no symbolic place in the public conscience.

Thorpe *et al.* (1980: 43) similarly points out:

there were only 17 prosecutions for false income tax returns (against some 80,000 cases settled without prosecution) [while] there were 12,000 prosecutions over the same period by the Dept. of Health and Social Security for fraudulent claims by its (largely working class) clients . . .

Income tax evasion and other corporate tax frauds injure the population and society at large. The ability properly to fund such basic social needs as education, pensions, a viable public transport system, or health and welfare services may well be considerably influenced by such 'crimes'. Yet it is indicative of the structural bias occurring, that the amount recovered in the 12,000 cases of social security fraud quoted by Thorpe (ibid.) was less than 15 per cent of the amount recovered from just 17 income tax prosecutions. In 1977–8, only 154 persons were prosecuted by the

[23] Carson (1970) shows how few prosecutions occur. Safety Inspectorate files for one district of SE England for the years 1961–6 show that of 3,800 offences committed, only 1.5% resulted in prosecutions and received an average fine of only £50. At the time of writing, the latest in a string of Transport incidents has meant another 50-plus deaths, this time on the River Thames, while at the same time the Safety Inspectorate has reported cuts of 20% in their staffing and funding since 1979.

Inland Revenue, yet in 1980 the government felt it suitable to employ 1,000 extra inspectors to control social security fraud. Always the attention is directed to the activities of the 'dangerous classes' and measures such as this, and those described below, continue to project the strategies of control away from the powerful and the well-connected.

Hugo Cornwall (1987), writing in *Police* magazine (October 1987: 34), tabulated many instances of this continuing bias:

In England & Wales there are 125,000 police officers spread over 43 forces. Of these, 588 belong to specific fraud squads, perhaps 5% of the total number of CID officers. Of the 588, 147 belong to the (London) Met (total strength 27,000) and 62 from the City of London Police . . . In 1984 they knew about frauds worth £867 million; if an insurance industry estimate that only 30% of employee fraud is reported is correct, the total amount of London-based fraud could be in excess of £2,000m. However, the total 'recorded' figure was 3 times the total cost of all other property crimes in London. In fact, looking at England and Wales as a whole, the combined cost of theft, burglary and robbery was only £1,015m.

If fraud is twice as extensive as all the burglaries, robberies, and the like put together, why is it so inadequately funded in relation to the manpower allocated to its pursuit? Why is this not high status police work where 'real polises' aspire to be posted? Its low symbolic status is further reflected in the ranks of the officers who are allocated to this minor aspect of the drama. For as Cornwall (ibid.) further tells us:

The Fraud Squad has a computer crime unit run by a detective inspector (the third lowest rank in the British police) . . . a recent achievement has been to set up a specialist training course at Bramshill Police College, lasting four weeks. By the beginning of 1987 a total of 18 officers, nationwide, had attended. Most regional fraud squads did not have a single officer trained even to a basic level in tackling computer related crime.

Meanwhile the pursuit of that scurrilous faction, 'the social security scroungers' continues unabated:

By the beginning of 1987 there were 1,000 Department of Employment fraud investigators operating, up from a figure of 350 in 1980. As a result of their activities savings in the year 1985–1986 were claimed to be £22m. . . . [while in the DHSS] there were just over 1,500 specialist fraud officers and 564 special investigators. (ibid.)

The comparison between 209 London detectives investigating corporate fraud estimated at £2,000 million and the 1,564 DHSS investigators pursuing a national saving of £22 million results in a situation where 'there were 30 to 40 times more prosecutions for social security offences than for defrauding the Inland Revenue ... and the Customs and Excise' (ibid.). Any attempt to estimate the harm caused by the cost of corporate crime has to face the inherently difficult task of knowing what is actually going on. Its invisibility ensures that the task remains speculative, but there seems little doubt that its cost to the social fabric of society is enormous and deprives those who are most at risk and under-privileged of more economic resources than all of the traditional crimes which the 'real polises' in my ethnography are trained to perceive as their prime operational target.

Moreover, we appear to be moving inexorably towards a further tendency to authoritarian 'control' over the activities of the dispossessed, for we are living through a political period insistently calling out for the increased imposition of order. Such demands, as Barthes (1983: 43) points out, always contain an indication of increased repression, inevitably to be directed by the well-connected and powerful and imposed on the powerless in a unilateral direction.

These continuous moves against the 'dispossessed', despite legislation to reduce prison populations, have seen even greater repression occur, so that in 1989 it was reported that the British prison population had, for the first time, grown larger (pro rata) than all other European countries and had just moved ahead of Turkey in the tables of incarceration. Almost a quarter of all receptions (some 20,000 per annum) are fine defaulters, and these, the 'inept' and 'inadequate' who commit conventional offences—not initially considered to merit imprisonment—eventually end up 'inside' for non-payment.

Prisons are bursting at the seams and are a social disgrace, but they are good enough for the 'dangerous classes', for they reflect the squalor, misery, and insanitary nature of their Victorian origins when they were largely created to confine this specific layer of society. As I have described above in the bridewell ethnography, streams of these inept and 'ambiguous prigs' are still sent off each day for fine default, along with a range of pathetic 'real prigs' for what seems to be essentially trivial conventional crime when set against the corporate crimes of the powerful.

Meanwhile, even as the 'law and order' campaigns of the 1980s have been played out for the political benefit and narrow self-interest of the few, the omissions and fraudulent activities of those committing 'corporate crime' seem even less likely to reach centre stage of the criminal justice system and appear publicly in court. Corporate criminals now have fewer chances of becoming a thorn in the social conscience, or of enhancing their symbolic import-ance as being a 'scourge' on the social framework, for they are now under less scrutiny than ever:

there are currently only 565 factory inspectors carrying out the enforce-ment function with responsibility for an estimated 750,000 workplaces with 17 million employees. This compares with 660 so employed in April 1980, representing a loss of 105 posts or 16 percent in under 3 years ... the current staffing levels represent a reduction of 24 percent below that considered necessary as late as July 1979 by Mr. P. Mayhew in Par-liament ... ('The Disappearing Inspectors', *Guardian*, 8 March 1983)

Estimates vary but according to figures for 1987, the combined fraud squads of the Met. and City of London Police had 462 cases of fraud in-volving £1,545m. on their books at the beginning of the year and took on another 590 investigations totalling £3,295 million. This compares with £125 million for theft totals, £70 million for burglary and £17 million for robbery ... ('White Collar Crime and Firms Who Keep it Secret', *Guardian*, 4 February 1989)

The first example merely shows how a very small part of the drama of the criminal justice system has been downgraded in the last decade, to become an even smaller side-show! The second needs to be considered in the light of the limited manpower which Cornwall (1987) shows is directed to what *Police* magazine (October 1987) headlined as 'The racket we all but ignore'. These 1,000 cases of fraud pursued by some 200 officers must be set against the 1,000,000 crimes reported across London which be-come the target of the combined establishment of some 27,000 officers. Although their combined value, as we have seen, is much less than the total for the frauds, it is their numerical superiority which is their main symbolic strength. Each has an injured person who has a vote and can add to the political call for more 'law and order'; each has a potential culprit and can become a detection to swell the impression of value for money. In total these 1,000,000 crimes are prime material to justify the annual police budgets of

£3.5 billion and bolster up and justify the images of 'real police activity', which then further guarantees them their own validity.[24]

Fraud investigation only began in a minor way after the last war, yet corporate or economic crime is estimated to have caused ten times the loss sustained through conventional crime (Conklin 1977: 4). Again it can only be assumed that the ultimate direction is in the hands of the well-connected and powerful, so that the melodrama continues to be focused on the insignificant of society and their minor misdemeanours.

Such an omission in the record means that any reflexive ethnography of policing cannot just be concerned with the exploration of crime as officially defined. If the objectified *habitus* of policing is to be made fully visible, then the deep structures of institutional ideology which ensure the subsequent direction of practice towards some crimes and some offences but not to others, must be explored and understood. That which has been veiled or concealed must be uncovered to show how police belief systems are laid down and reproduced over time. For I suspect that this narrowly conceived concept of 'crime' has played a major part in determining the way control has been exercised and manipulated over the years.

Control is largely concerned with the rituals of governing the classification and surveillance of categories of social space, action, movement and the definition of time, language, and political ideology. By exploring some examples of how the idea of crime has been used as a structuring principle during my own personal history it becomes possible to further weld the subjectivity of personal knowledge and practice with the objectivity of analytic debate, and to formulate a reflexive intepretation to create what Ricoeur (1981) has called the 'hermeneutical circle', in which 'understanding and self-understanding, of comprehension and commitment [become] an eliminable aspect of social scientific knowledge'. Any reflexive or hermeneutic interpretation of how crimes have been manipulated and presented for public consumption requires the insider/anthropologist to ignore possible charges of sedition and lay bare the system to reveal what I have come to

---

[24] This figure continues to defeat my attempts to include it in the book. On the first draft it stood around £2.8 billion then rose to £3.35 billion; and in 1990/1 exceeds £4.2 billion.

consider as a 'dramatic mythology of crime'. This ritualized 'mythology' is so all-encompassing in its support of police hegemonies,
that it has generated extreme defensiveness, secretism, and in-
group élitism, and uses structural forms which in turn have
engendered a xenophobic fear of any criticism of its philosophies
of control.

It is these in-bred conservatisms which, in turn, lead to the
negation of academic and social research, which I have described
above. It is also a primary reason for the increasing repression of
those who would set out to illuminate the immoral and criminal
practices of those in power.[25]

A diachronic exploration of the manipulation of classification
and action in relation to some crimes and some offences will help
to reveal the variations in belief and practice that I have witnessed
and employed during my own thirty years of subjective experience. The following sections describe changing semantic values
and some of the idiosyncratic practices considered 'normal' and
sometimes 'essential' to support the aims and objectives of the institution of policing. After a brief exploration of practice in the
1950s, and a look at aspects of the subsequent expansion in the
statistical record, the analysis concludes with a review of the ways
and means of bending and fiddling the account to meet the
demands of the organization.

CRIME AND OFFENCE IN THE 1950S AND 1960S: A DRAMA OF NON-EXISTENCE

In the late 1950s when I started my police career, Britain had
small, localized police forces. In 1960 there were 72,000 officers in

[25] The 1984 Official Secrets Act prosecutions of Sarah Tisdall and Clive
Ponting for leaking government memoranda on political misdeeds, as well as the
long-drawn-out saga of government attempts to suppress *Spycatcher*, largely on
account of its revelations of the machinations of those in power, are examples of
this repression. It is ironic and somehow very sad that the act of revelation itself
was considered to be the 'criminal' act, and not the political malpractice that was
revealed. Of course such diversion away from the 'economic truths' pursued by
institutions is another dramatic stock-in-trade of the well-connected, for an official
inquiry can often be used to diffuse the underlying misdeed, while focusing attention on other matters (*pace* the Stalker Inquiry, which quietly directed attention to
his non-existent crimes of criminal association and away from any open inquiry
into the real possibility of a government, MI5, or military 'shoot-to-kill' policy in
Northern Ireland).

125 different forces in England and Wales, each with its own chief constable, its own uniform styling, its own identity and localized idiosyncracies. I have described some of these above.

Many of these forces were poorly financed. None had the specialist departments or the varied civilian personnel that is the norm today. Some very small police units in the towns and boroughs operated on a shoestring and on the unquestioning acceptance of practices and systems imposed on an essentially immobile public.[26] A structurally optimistic view of the world was prevalent and was reflected in police society. This presented a vision of the world which still derived many of its values from ideas of respect and obedience to the social forms which had held sway before the Second World War.

Many small forces still followed the principles and styles of these pre-war times, with the manpower and equipment of the 1930s. In the Northumberland County Constabulary Centennial Handbook (1957), the establishment for this huge county area was 581 and the 'Crime Department' was celebrating only its twentieth year of operation. By 1965 in Newcastle City Police, the CID establishment was 84 and the recorded 'crimes' were 13,003. These had almost doubled in four years, as the style of the 1950s was swept away by the changes which heralded the 'swinging 60s'. The 84 detectives shared only seven motor vehicles and had few other technological aids. The chief constable in his Annual Report for 1965, regretted that 'a great disappointment has been the inability to equip each uniform officer with personal wireless ... Twenty Four sets have been acquired for use ... and experiments were being tried at the end of the year'. The existing Northumbria Force now covers some 1.3 million acres and has a population of some 1.5 million. I have described above how the small forces went into the melting pot of amalgamation to form the institutional, giant units of today, but in the late 1950s the small forces were still pursuing the 'dangerous classes' using techniques and systems that seemed to be unchanging. Men about to retire with thirty years' service operated in a style that had changed little since they had joined; as a new recruit I assimilated

---

[26] It is as well to remember that until the 19th century, 80% of the population travelled less than 5 miles from their place of birth, during their lifetime. Even in the 1950s easy access to a car in my city environment was still only for the privileged few; social immobility was the norm.

this unchanging framework, learning the values and practices of men who had joined in the 1920s. Systems were well established and the administrative procedures were known and understood, extreme change was unusual, and stasis was the norm.

Our limited geographical sense of place had an important and restraining influence on our style. The way the police are organized is hugely influenced by the classification of space, which is broken down into carefully delineated boundaries of force area, division, subdivision, section, and beats. 'My division' was considered by those of us in it to be the premier unit of three in the city (we did not have subdivisional units at that time) and we used this mode of thought to set ourselves off against our neighbours at every opportunity. We were the 'smart city-centre polises, in the public eye', while men of 'C' Division were derisorily referred to as 'the forgotten men of the East'. The chief constable and his senior officers were housed on our divisional site and it seemed logical to us that the city centre came first in the alphabetic ratings as 'A' Division, for we were 'real polises' dealing with 'real crime'. After this our sense of place tailed off. The men in 'B' Division (city west) were the thugs, and the men from 'C' Division 'were allowed to come to the city centre once a year on the Annual Inspection, to let them look at the big buildings'. Beyond this we only looked to our neighbouring forces to despise and denigrate them and their style; for they were beyond the pale, over the boundary, and stigmatized.[27]

This sense of place and personal space continues to be an essentially localized concept in the police mind, and has considerable import in the social definition of self. Even though the amalgamations have how reduced the numbers of forces dramatically,

---

[27] This idea of space is one that could be examined further, for it is a construct which has an influential effect on police action. Ardener (1981) has explored the idea of cognitive space and Ifeka (1983), in her review of Ardener's volume, pointed out: '"space" is one relatively unexplored topic . . . which many of us seem to assume is tucked away in some inaccessible nook in the anthropological mansion . . . Every now and then though, a distinguished luminary (Durkheim and Mauss; Evans-Pritchard; Leach) opens the door, gives "space" a quick dusting down and holds it up for a (too) rapid perusal. [The Ardener volume] indicates not merely a newly awakened interest in the perceptual, physical and cognitive parameters that bound social life, but also some hard thinking amongst anthropologists and others about the kind of directions our enquiries might follow . . .' (A. P. Cohens's volumes *Symbolising Boundaries* (1986) and *The Symbolic Construction of Community* (1985) explore the constraints of cognitive space in this manner.

it is still a commonly expressed view that every division and sub-division in each of the forty-three forces is still a separate force within a force, with its own identity, idiosyncratic practice, and style. This cognition has always had a specific influence on how crime is perceived, reported, and recorded as we shall see.

The most recent change in technology we had experienced related to an increasing use of the motor car, but the availability of vehicles was not widespread. In the main, the 'polises' and 'prigs' were immobile. Our division was considered to be well off in comparison to our neighbours, and yet we only had one divisional car and one divisional van. The unofficial post of driver was taken by a time-served senior constable, whose main function was to chauffeur the shift inspector (likened to God) and take out the van to pick up those who had been arrested by the foot patrols. The divisional superintendent and chief inspector were remote men who rarely, if ever, deigned to acknowledge the lowly constables and were not to be troubled with the incidentals of our daily round.[28]

Even in 1965, during the implementation of the Panda Car and Unit Beat system, our city centre division—heavy with traffic and divided by the main arterial A1 road to Scotland and the south—still only had two cars with wireless and one van. These three vehicles served an establishment of 152 constables, 19 sergeants, 4 inspectors, a superintendent, and a chief inspector. As I have mentioned above, the CID had a total of seven vehicles, but this was to cover the whole city, across the three divisions.[29] Our adversaries, the 'prigs' were similarly pedestrianized. Few had vehicles, and those who had were known and documented as they moved around our small world. One of my early instructions from

[28] I only once spoke to my superintendent in my first two years' service, and that was in the early hours when I was delegated to phone him at home and tell him of a large fire which had closed off several streets in the city centre. He listened to my account, and responded: 'The Fire Brigade's there! What do you want me to do; come down and piss on it?'

[29] Derogatory and apocryphal stories were told about the unavailability of vehicles in neighbouring forces to show again our superiority. However, I later worked with an inspector who had joined a small borough force at the same time I joined the city force. He laughingly remembered how their two patrol cars were locked away at midnight and were unavailable without a superintendent's authority. He, of course, was at home, and no one dared to ring him or disturb his sleep to ask for an authorization for their use, and so they remained locked away regardless of events.

a renowned 'thief-taker' was related to this belief in the prevention of 'prig' mobility: 'if it moves after 2 a.m. kid, its bent, so
stop it'.[30]

In 1983, in my much smaller subdivision of South Shields in
Northumbria, with an established manpower of just over 150, we
then had nineteen vehicles of various types. In addition, several of
the personnel had vehicle allowances and in consequence we had
some twenty-seven vehicles available, as well as access to squad
vehicles and other traffic cars.

In the 1950s the patrol officers walked the streets without radio
or other sophisticated equipment to link them to the station.
Their only contact was by hourly telephone call from one of the
'beat boxes' soon to be made famous in the Dr Who serial, which
were sprinkled at strategic places around the city. A system of
'ringing in' had been worked out so that someone phoned in from
one of the eighteen divisional beats every three or four minutes (in
theory) and everyone carried cards of 'ringing in times' for each
beat. In addition we were given a list which showed locations to
be attended on pain of discipline and punishment at the com-
mencement and conclusion of each eight-hour beat shift. These
included some points which had vanished thirty or more years
previous when new roads and redevelopment had swept old
landmarks away. But in the unchanging world of the 1950s this
was not a problem and things went on much as they had always
done. Many poorer forces avoided the expense involved in the
provision of these 'beat boxes', which required telephone lines
and maintenance, by using existing telephone boxes and a system
of patrol points. These required the constable to be at a certain
public phone box at an appointed time where he could be contacted if needed—but only if the phone box was not in use!

---

[30] Some twenty years after this, when I was writing early seminar papers and
exploring the idea of space, mobility, and control, an ITV programme (*In Evidence*) graphically illustrated the way that movement and stasis are crucially important to the police mind as it sets out to control public behaviour. The tried and
trusted resolution of getting people to vanish by simply ordering them to 'move
along there' was in evidence when a Metropolitan senior officer, a Commander
Mitchell, revealed his bafflement at the cultural phenomenon of high street-
visibility exhibited by a group of West Indian youths: 'we move them on and
break them up. Its inconvenient to have groups of youths blocking the footpath
. . . They should be at home at 11 or 12 o'clock at night. What are they planning?
A police officer needs to be suspicious' (*Daily Express*, 25 June 1980).

Scientific aids and specialist departments were in their infancy or were non-existent and patrolling policemen were expected to deal with and resolve or negotiate the trivial incidents and social conflicts making up much of the daily round. Many of these non-crime, petty incidents (which still make up the major part of all policing)[31] were resolved without any report to the divisional station or any record being made of the action taken.

The creation of statistics and 'hard data' was not a high priority in this world, and no waves of crime or disorder were reported or encouraged. A fully effective system was in place which was sustained by precedent stretching back over the decades, and which, in its style, mirrored the world of 'negotiated justice' which Baldwin and McConville (1977) described in the undeclared and unrecorded plea bargainings of the Crown Courts. The resolution of trivial incidents or minor conflicts on the street without any recourse to official documentation was a norm of policing that the recruit learned at an early stage, for it was a necessary survival technique in this world without technology.

Acquiring assistance to stamp down heavily on petty matters was just not possible and many situations which today would produce a heavy response in terms of manpower and technology, resulting in conflict between police and the street-visible public, generating fear of crime, court appearances, and the creation of waves of statistical mayhem, were then resolved without aid. On my first allocated beat on the quayside at Newcastle there was one specific public house where trouble could be anticipated at the end of the evening drinking session. I quickly learned to 'see the pub out' and the patrons off home by methods which avoided conflict or the need to make arrests, for my beat box was at the other end of the quayside and assistance could only arrive after I had run the half mile to telephone for help. This technological gap helped generate a self-reliance, producing a style of policing which required the foot patrols to calm and dispel disorderly tendencies in an 'opposition' who also were acutely aware that you stood alone and posed only a small threat. In any case, there was a certain reluctance in some of us to call for assistance, for this

---

[31] Radzinowicz and King (1977: 6) and Whitaker (1979) describe and list details of the vast amount of front-line social work which the police undertake and which is not 'crime' orientated. As I have said above, other estimates suggest such 'soft' work accounts for about 95% of all calls for police assistance.

would suggest we could not handle our beat on our own; and although the arrest of 'real prigs' was always justified, the gratuitous arrest of those who might have been 'talked into going home' was not always looked on favourably. Calls for the van for trivial matters on my shift could have seriously interfered with the inspector, the station sergeant, and the 'shift driver', who might well have had their game of dominoes interrupted at a crucial point!

In effect there was a style or image at large in the small forces which reflected the social etiquette of the times. This, I suggest, might be classed as being one of 'visible calm and containment'. Everything was geared to suggest all was well with society, that disorder and calamity were within acceptable levels, and the police were in command of the small amount of 'real crime' that was abroad. Nothing was seen to be happening and I clearly recall that an outburst of drunken violence in the 1950s was resolved by putting out the police rugby teams in two vans to give the culprits a chance to fight with 'real men'. Peace reigned within a week or two, but few arrests were made and no report or record of the events was published, even though some punishment was handed out. The Police Complaints system of course prevents such action now, and indeed it is hard to accept it happened so recently!

Regardless of such one-off events, there was usually little opportunity for the isolated, patrolling officer to present any tough, crime-busting image, although some men made their reputations as thief-takers. But there was little the individual officer could do to produce the hard data or statistical returns that such an image would have demanded. For there was no need to produce information for computers when the 'crime recording register' was a bound book with carbon paper for the copies and was locked away to prevent 'silly undetectable crimes being entered by the unwise'.

Furthermore, the patrolling officer was totally unskilled in the use of the media and excluded from access to the local reporters. The Press and Public Relations departments of today were unimaginable, and only one designated senior officer in the whole force was allowed to speak to the press. Local television was non-existent and there was little opportunity for the media to scrutinize police practices, except in the court proceeding where the 'disorder' and the record of 'crimes' became officially visible.

Of course by this time the actual street practice had become distilled, so the legal presentation formed a drama on an altogether different level from the original incident. It is often said that the court hearing is 'a game played out by the two sides and has little or no relevance to what went on in the street or in the police station'. I was reminded of this 'theatrical game' and some fine actors of my youth when the *Police Review* (21 September 1984) included a reminiscence by an ex-chief inspector which showed a fine use of practical mastery and knowledge of costume drama. Like the use of the rugby teams to calm periods of youthful disorder, these playlets were unseen and unrecorded, yet were not at all uncommon in the charge rooms as the 'inebriated prig' was being dealt with. This autobiographical note recalled how

as a detective constable in a small force adjacent to Manchester ... before 1960 I had never set much alight. That is until I teamed up with Walter Alcock, an ebullient figure of some 18 stones, with a voice to match ... A man of many parts, he could entertain as well as he could interview. Many's the time I've seen him *acting out the solicitor or playing the doctor* ... [my emphasis]

Those who have never seen a detective 'playing the part of a solicitor' or 'acting as a doctor' might be left to wonder what on earth this throw-away remark signifies. In fact, it was ancient practice in Newcastle (and also apparently in Lancashire) for the white coat used on the local traffic-point to be put to good effect as 'wardrobe' to convince the drunken 'prig' that he had seen a doctor; then again the detective in formal suit might take the part of the concerned 'defence' solicitor, soothing the inept and drunken burglar while urging him to tell the truth! This unseen and unrecorded theatre could never, of course, be acknowledged. Any subsequent court proceeding therefore became only one visible manifestation of the 'truth'—and was altogether different from that which had been enacted on the street or in the charge room.

Such practices were only possible while policing was largely contained and the media were kept away from the details of police practice. Structural invisibility was able to be maintained when activities went unreported behind closed boundaries. The current situation, where television teams and reporters are given access to police stations or patrol with officers was unthinkable; not the least because of their own inability to move out from their fixed studios. For this was prior to the advent of the outside broadcast and the use of taped or video material. However, a form of structural invisibility is still in vogue in dealings with the press, and I noted what happened when local reporters were given access and sat alongside us in the bridewell, recording the events of a busy Friday night. Our practical mastery, I noted, allowed us easily to amend our language and behaviour to suit the needs of the occasion and accommodate to what we knew was required; so that no visible deals were made during that visit!

In the late 1950s the media took what the police prepared for them, and to practically every call they made the response was 'all quiet, nothing's happening', even when newsworthy events were going on all around us. This reproduced an image of low-level disorder, while the manipulation of crime reports and detections reflected what the police considered to be socially acceptable for presentation to the public; and this image was faithfully re-created by the press who were (and still are) heavily dependent on the police for a great deal of local news material.

This low social visibility further engendered a 'durable disposition' in the organization, to use Bourdieu's idea again (1977: 82–3). This fostered a concept of well-being and security which mirrored other current social perceptions of optimism, growth, and stability. Such a *habitus* or acquired system of generative schemes (ibid. 95), allowed the young police officer the time and confidence to inculcate the rules and practical masteries of 'the job' over a longer period than is possible today.

There was no real need then for the probationer to pursue objectives which relied on a haul of detected crime statistics. Nor was it necessary for him to show prowess by producing lists of arrests or applications for summons during his first two years of service, for in the smaller forces of the era the young officer could easily be assessed. In the amalgamated giants, however, the computerized HQ personnel departments and divisional administrations need monthly, quarterly, and annual reports on the progress of every recruit. These usually include a pen-portrait completed by a senior police officer, who rarely has any training in personnel assessment. Inevitably some comment on 'work-rate' based on statistical records of arrests and summons reports submitted will be included. Nevertheless, it would be wrong to suggest that league tables did not exist in the 1950s, but today, with the greater need to justify higher budgets and continue the fights with Home Office and Police Authorities for increases in manpower levels, statistics have inevitably taken on greater significance.[32]

This historical recollection has a relevance beyond mere revelation of previously unrecorded events. It is the basis for what occurs today and sets a structural precedent for many of the modes of thought and practice which now occur. Indeed three or four of my senior officers in the CID of the 1960s spent most of the 1980s at the very pinnacle of power in various police forces, and learned their lessons in the same 'university of hard-knocks' which taught me such skills as those outlined here. Brian Johnson, my detective sergeant in city west in 1963 when I was an aide, spent the 1980s in charge of Lancashire Police. Ken Oxford headed the CID in Northumberland in the late 1960s/early 1970s and was the chief constable of Merseyside police during the 1980s. Hector Clarke, another powerful figure who moved through all the CID ranks in the North-East at this time, spent the 1980s near the head of Lothian and Borders police. There were others such as Gordon McMurchie, who joined the department in the early 1960s with me, and who now sits alongside other ACPO officers as one of the leaders of Northumbria Police. All of these men (and many others sitting at chief superintendent or other senior ranked positions) have experienced the hidden agenda I am describing, but few comment on it or are likely to acknowledge its influence. However, I feel it is necessary to unroll a few further aspects of this silent material, for its influence on modern police thinking and practice is still enormous.

Offences of drunkenness: structural negotiation

Even in those apparently placid times, there were certain incentives which helped to inflate the statistical record dramatically, and indicate a rate of 'disorder' which was not necessarily an ab-

---

[32] *Police Review* (6 Feb. 1981: 256) suggested: 'the volume of process [for summons] submitted is the most important measure of the probationary constable's ability'. *Police* magazine (Vol. 8, Feb. 1976: 6) talked of 'the old and long established practice of senior officers keeping a league table of arrests and summons'. In the late 1980s the new Operational Support Units (or Admin. Support Units in some forces) are being promoted by the Audit Commission and the Home Office; all contain the potential to read an officer's work-rate from a computerized account.

solute or 'truthful' reflection of what was occurring. In the Newcastle city area the high statistical returns for offences of being 'simple drunk' or 'drunk and disorderly' seemed at the time merely to reflect the hard drinking style of the local populous. Now, I see it was as much a result of the way we dealt with the offence and how we manipulated it for our own purposes. Our arrests for drunkenness usually topped a local 'league table' and were said to be a result of the strength of the local beer. Our simplistic and somewhat folksy functional analysis laid the blame on the local brew known as 'lunatics' broth', which later took on the name of a radio programme of the time, becoming known as 'Journey into Space'. In turn, the media reported the arrests, the court cases, and the drunkenness figures, thus reinforcing the durability of this disposition and giving this one deviance a statistical relevance I now suspect bore little relationship to its real incidence.

Drunkenness, as I have said, is not a 'crime' and perhaps should not really be featured here. However, the way this one offence was used by the system to sustain and enhance institutional values gives an insight into how the police create symbols of significance and in turn generate the *habitus* to reproduce an unthinking practical mastery. In effect, regardless of whether the statistical fiddling is for a crime or an offence, it all depends on its use to the institution.

Drunkenness was always work for the uniformed officer and not the detective. At the time the two main offences were created by the 1872 Licensing Act: (*a*) being publicly drunk and disorderly, and (*b*) being publicly drunk and incapable (simple drunk). In the city a constant turnover of drunks was processed, appearing at court on the following morning, or on the Monday morning following weekend revelry. Mostly the drunks were arrested after 10 p.m.[33] by the nightshift (10 p.m.–6 a.m.) constables and their numbers rose inexorably each weekend from payday, which was then on a Thursday or Friday.[34] Once again this perception of disorder occurring at weekends supported the ideology of power

---

[33] Public houses closed at 10 p.m. at that time, while licensed clubs selling intoxicants until 2 a.m. were still an event for the future.

[34] Wages for the working classes were invariably paid in cash on a weekly basis at that time. Traditional nights in the pubs were therefore Thursday, Friday, and Saturday.

which presented the 'dangerous classes' as being responsible for regular weekly mayhem, and directed control through a system of almost instant justice.

For reasons of judicial and practical expediency, the results of this drunken behaviour in the city was a quick court appearance and a fine, which could be paid off immediately. Meanwhile in the villages and towns of the adjacent county force, the drunk (who was often well known) would most likely be summoned for a 'common-law breach of the peace', and not for an offence of drunkenness. The reasons for this reveal another form of practical mastery which local 'polises' still hold to, but rarely articulate.

First, in the county area the courts often sat only once a week or less often, and so the accused was invariably released—not bailed to the following day—and summoned to come to court at a future date. Then there was the sentence, which as I have said, was usually a small fine in the city. 'Conduct likely to cause a breach of the peace' has no punishment other than an agreement to a 'binding over to keep the peace'. This 'common law binding over' created a powerful threat to the rural miscreant for perhaps twelve months, and made it suitable for the county constabulary to use in their dealings with regulars from their own 'dangerous classes'. The binding over carried the threat that any future reoccurrence would also incur punishment for the original event, and kept the offender 'in his place' for twelve months (again the spatial metaphor indicates the significance of social space). Of course, this threat was all but useless to hang over the heads of the huge and floating population in a city.

Some twenty years later I found the same logic still firmly in place. In the bridewell we had used 'drunk and disorderly' as a 'bread and butter charge', with as many as thirty or forty logged and lodged in the first three hours of any Friday night. In 1981, however, I found that in areas only a dozen miles from the bridewell it was still the practice to prefer charges of 'breach of the peace' rather than 'drunkenness'. I was somewhat bemused by this when I was posted to South Shields subdivision (an ex-borough area with a peculiarly insular population and no incursion of young people in the numbers which occurred each weekend evening in the city). I queried the practice and was wearily put right by a time-served veteran sergeant who had spent all his service in 'the borough'. On my first day in the subdivision, he had asked about my antecedents and responded to my history of city-based policing by letting me know I was extremely suspect. Now, he sadly set about explaining to this intruder what, for him, was the natural order of things (he probably saw my academic activities as a reason for my practical inability!), and with a certain amount of head-shaking at my naïvety, explained:

a binding over to keep the peace in the sum of £100 keeps the young buggers in order. You just have to go to a spot of bother at 'the Hill' [a local council house neighbourhood] when the bloody animals are going wild, and say to one of them 'you're facing a £100 fine to start with if you are brought in tonight, or in the next twelve months . . . so fuck off home right now!' That gets the little sods off quietly . . .' (From fieldnotes)

Such specific practice begins to reveal hidden aspects of policing in the small town with a regular clientele of known offenders, and shows that the high number of drunks in the city (just up the road on the other bank of the Tyne) can be skewed by the first of a number of factors which are not always easily accessible to any objective or outside analysis of statistical returns.

The second reason for a quick court appearance in the city concerned the 'reward' of time off. At this time the bulk of the weekend drunks appeared at court on Monday morning accompanied by the arresting constables, who came to give evidence of the offence. These nightshift constables, often in the middle of a two-week nightshift, were compensated for attendance at court by a system of time off, and were credited with $5\frac{1}{4}$ hours time off in lieu.[35] Paid overtime was still a future event and it was not until the mid-1970s that such overtime could be recompensed by 'time off' or cash.

Some officers built up a huge reservoir of hours through 'five and a quarters', which they were then allowed to take off when manpower levels permitted, or it suited 'the job'. At the time, officers only got three days off per fortnight, and this 'time off' helped to give extra days away from the rigours of constantly changing shifts. As drunks were more easily come by than burglars, this arrest category was used by some to build up huge

[35] Since that time Acts of Parliament have simplified some procedures and today such offences can be heard without either the accused or the officer being present, unless the case is to be contested. As a result many officers now attend court only on rare occasions, for guilty pleas still predominate for minor offences.

'time off' quotas, and a drunk had come to be referred to as 'a five and a quarter' long before I joined and took on the language of the institution or learned that it was normal parlance for the patrol constable to ring the divisional station from his beat box requesting them to 'send the van, I've got a five and a quarter here'.

As a result of this trading in time off, drunkenness achieved a status well beyond its importance in relation to other classificatory disorders. Although it was only an offence, and often the forte of the dosser or the more incoherent and inept members of the 'dangerous classes', it had a meaning attributed that did not match any of the other hierarchical indicators. The relative ease it presented for an officer to create a bank of 'time off' led to its wilful inflation in the figures, and seriously skewed the incidence of this type of offence in just one police area.

Certain officers were renowned for their capacity for such arrests, and I recall one religiously inclined member of one shift with a reputation for high arrest quotas for 'drunkenness' being openly derided by his colleagues. On our shift, where 'real polising' meant 'thief-taking', we would look through the Record Book and Charge sheets after the weekend and dismiss the work of our contemporaries:

Look at this dross. With 'A' Shift on nights you can be sure there'll be a bundle of five and a quarters. It's dangerous to even have a smell of the barmaid's apron when that lot are on. They're a right bunch of five and a quarter merchants; not a real thief-taker among them.

This reproduced conversation shows we viewed those who sought out the drunks as 'merchants', trading in 'time off'; for they were not 'real polises' dealing with 'real prigs' or 'real crimes'. Their activities were not inconsiderable, however, and they turned 'drunks' into a useful commodity and were largely responsible for the inflation of the figures which kept the city near the top of the league for such arrests for many years.

In 1983 in South Shields, in a company which included a senior detective who had started out with me in the city in early 1958, I described local practice and the reasons for preferring 'breach of the peace' to a 'drunkenness' charge. Turning to him, I asked bluntly, 'What's a five-and-a-quarter?' He laughed, while the rest of my audience (all policemen) looked blank. 'It's a drunk', he acknowledged, even though it was then some twenty years since the 'time off' system had changed along with the need for evidence in such cases to be given in person. We chuckled over 'famous five-and-a-quarter' merchants of the past, while our colleagues sat this one out; for they had started their road to the practical mastery of 'doing the business' in other parts of the force, and had learned other structures of significance.

Our returns for drunkenness in the late 1950s were therefore a peculiarity of our isolated practice, for this one specific incidence of disorder was always an idiosyncratic version of one reality; and this continues today. Drunks, as I again discovered in the bridewell in the late 1970s, were still being dealt with by arrest and charged under the old Licensing Acts, while in adjacent divisions the preferred course of action was still to release them and then summons for 'breach of the peace'. The practices of city officers still revolved around an understanding that the floating population is best dealt with by arrest, a quick court appearance, and a fine; while the regular contacts of rural police officers with the small town offender maintains their belief that he is best dealt with in an alternative way. Such practices are easily reproduced by new generations of 'polises',[36] but are just not apparent in the statistical record.[37]

Crime in the 1950s and 1960s: action and inaction

Techniques for surveillance of the body social (Foucault 1977) and especially the visible acts of the dispossessed were so well developed by this time that the uniformed brokers and detectives could easily deal with the traditional 'prig' targets and their petty

---

[36] From 1974, and the last police amalgamations, until at least 1983 when I left Northumbria, Sunderland Division continued to deal with all juveniles by summonsing them for all crimes, while the other half-dozen divisions regularly used a system of arrest, charge, and bail. Sunderland was following a precedent, allegedly set many years before by one despotic Magistrates' Clerk, which was specific to that area. General arrest statistics are therefore also objectively invalid, for any attempt to compare categories for any location requires that meanings surrounding the underlying practices be explored.

[37] Across the country there are great discrepancies in cautions for such offences as possessing cannabis, ranging from 42% cautioned in Lincolnshire, 25% in Merseyside, 5% in Manchester and 0% in Dorset and West Mercia (1986 HO figures). ACPO says the HO studied why regional variations were so great, but came up with no satisfactory answers. I suggest they need to hire an anthropologist!

crimes. These disorders were the sort which irritate rather than destroy the fabric of society, but are dramatized to ensure all realize just how effective the institution is in preventing social chaos.

Always the major criterion for action lay in the visibility of the incident, for surveillance of the 'dangerous classes' focused on those activities which were not just unsettling, but were perhaps capable of leading to mass public dissent. As a result, calls for the police to mediate in such invisible crimes as domestic dispute, for example, have always been unpopular. 'Domestics' hold low status in any hierarchy of 'real work', and even though the domestic brawl is a major factor in the statistics of murder and manslaughter, it is unlikely to generate social rebellion.

In practice the police have always felt there is little they can do to resolve the complexities underlying many domestic problems, which may only erupt into the public eye after years of hidden tension. Usually the police move into action only when the friction moves from behind what I have often heard called 'the semi-detached surburban façade', or when the 'domestic' victim ends up in the hospital casualty unit. Traditionally, what went on in the Englishman's castle was of no concern to the police. Indeed, any assault might well be ignored and the tension temporarily resolved in practice by tempting the inevitably drunken husband or boyfriend out into the street and then settling the issue by arresting him for being drunk and disorderly in public (which unlike the assault, does not require an injured person to make a complaint.)[38]

On my first 'domestic', I failed totally to understand the structural forms of the drama, and ended up pleasing no one. I separated bruised wife from drunken husband by arresting him

[38] Of course at this time another hindrance to the pursuit of any assault charge lay in the legal point that wives could not be compelled to give evidence against their husbands. That they were 'competent' but not 'compellable' was a legal point we had drummed into us at training school, until it became axiomatic that wives would always renege. Jean Renvoize (1978) attests to this difficulty which the police experience in dealing with domestic violence, recounting how in 1973 the Citizens' Advice Bureaux received 25,000 enquiries relating to wife battering, and yet wives (who may have limbs broken, jaws fractured, or faces slashed and bruised) often refuse to support a charge or appear at court against their husbands. No wonder, she implies, the police only reluctantly intervene in 'domestics', for they remain structurally invisible, marginal in the extreme, and the police literally 'do not see them'.

for the traditional offence, but the next day in court, I was attacked (literally) in the witness box by his wife. Wielding her handbag, she shouted to the magistrates that she would not have called the police if she had known I would arrest 'him'—pointing to her now somewhat insignificant spouse in the dock. Subsequently, I learned the traditional practice of taking the husband in the van to some other distant part of the city (or better still across the river and into Gateshead Borough area) and then abandoning him to walk home and sober up. Only a small percentage of the really argumentative or disorderly domestic cases would be arrested for drunkenness, and many late night pedestrians then were the result of police vans dropping off the remnants of the domestic violence some miles from home. Of course the actual percentages of 'domestics' resolved at the house, temporarily resolved by creating a late night pedestrian, or turned into an arrest statistic for drunkenness can never really be known, for this practical mastery fulfils an alternative agenda to that suitable to the statistician.

This unrecorded system of dumping the male side to a 'domestic' some distance from the scene obviously failed to resolve any long-standing social problem, which was inevitably much too complicated for the police to solve. Furthermore it again manœuvred the statistical record, by presenting another limited police version of reality and no doubt hid many aspects of the true nature of domestic violence. And of course the system also helped to swell the drunkenness figures, which, as we have seen, were already skewed by local practice!

This one example of a negative presentation of the 'crime' of assault was symptomatic of a belief in a settled and somewhat uneventful social milieu, which reigned at the time, while the current obsessions with certain 'crimes' and statistics for such villainy as acid house parties, vandalism, and football hooliganism may well indicate how society today represents its lack of certainty and well-being. In other words, I suspect that the idea of crime itself is widely used as a 'root metaphor' (Turner, 1974: 23–59) and taken on as an archetypal symbol which can either be used to illustrate feelings of social confidence or a singular lack of that commodity. Hough and Mayhew (1983) for example, in the *British Crime Survey*, point out that the present and somewhat unjustified 'fear of crime' is a socially reproductive state, like the concept of well-being and social confidence. They even suggest an optimistic social etiquette of the kind I suspect existed throughout the 1950s could be re-created.

No doubt such states of social calm and certainty are complex and multi-vocal constructs which are influenced by other considerations than 'crime'; but if crime is used extensively as a symbol or root metaphor of how a society feels, then the lack of media attention and the low public profile it enjoyed in the 1950s was perhaps a major factor in producing a perception of social comfort and security which is unlikely to be easily reproduced today.

Unchanging structures: the strength of the detectives

The day-to-day acts of crime I was directed to investigate as a young detective were, in the main, committed by local 'prigs' on members of their own socio-economic class. The corner-end general dealer's shop, now largely vanished, was where the young 'prig' learned his burglary trade. Its disappearance means the 'prig' has had to look to other resources, such as the increased presence of the motor car and its contents. Again, the new toughened steels and alloys together with recently developed electronic surveillance and alarm systems have virtually eliminated the once common safe-breaker or 'peter man'. In my early days some of our main targets were 'jelly men' who attacked the vulnerable Victorian safes which still inhabited many office premises, and I recall celebrations when we recovered caches of gelignite stolen from quarries, or arrested well-known 'prigs' for possessing detonators or other means of blowing a safe. Today this form of 'crime' has been replaced by the street 'hoist' or 'blagging', and by the 'tie-up merchant'. For 'real prigs' still attack cash at its weakest point, but now jump the courier at the bank door or hit the unprotected home and tie up those who are rumoured to hold cash—often from undeclared tax evasions.

The lack of mobility I have mentioned above was a major factor in restraining the areas of operation of both the 'prig' and the detective. Even in a city where social fluidity seemed to prevail, there were villages within villages where local knowledge on individuals was easily acquired. Essentially an industrial community of workers who returned home when the pub shut at 10 p.m. and rose early to be at the factory gate for 7 a.m., there is little wonder I was instructed to suspect the 2 a.m. traveller.

Furthermore, in this environment female employment was still the exception and many dwellings maintained at least one female member in the home. One consequence of this and the community activity it generated was that the morning or early afternoon house-burglary of the 1980s in the deserted dormitory estate was then a rare event.

The relative ease with which the detectives controlled this local villainy left them plenty of time to develop a strong social life which largely revolved around 'bennies'[39] and a deep knowledge of the local licensing trade. A tradition of hard drinking and complete familiarity with the haunts and dives of 'the patch' was well established. These detectives were certain of their élite position in the organization, and with their extensive knowledge of local practice and social form, they were the 'big men' of police society.

Film or television writers and novelists have all recognized the power in this role, for oppositions of 'good versus evil' ensure that the detective embodies the potential of symbolic transcendence for the voyeur or reader. These basic structural binaries underpin many of the institutional practices of the most dramatic sections of society (e.g. the church, the law, the military, politics, etc.) and in consequence, those associated with them often have an archetypal role to play, in which they are required to incorporate extremes of fantasy, ritual, and mythology. The police, the crimes they pursue, and even the criminals who commit these crimes all come to have massive symbolic power; while the detective enjoys something verging on 'hero' status; for as Jung (1964) tells us:

the hero figure is an archetype, which has existed since time immemorial . . . Archetypes have their own initiative and their own specific energy . . . These powers enable them both to produce a meaningful interpretation (in their own symbolic style) and to interfere in a given situation with their own impulses and their own thought formulations . . .

---

[39] All the 'big' detectives of any standing had a 'bennie' or benefactor, whose function was to buy the beer for the detective and his company. 'Bennies' formed a solid part of the entourage at any CID 'do' and in return for being allowed to be a part of this special 'insider/élite' group and sharing the melodramatic aspects of the detective's life, they seemed to be content to buy the beer. In 1978–9 I chaperoned a new chief superintendent who had joined us from a Midlands force on his first visit to one of the divisional Christmas CID dos. The fact that the beer was free and the spirits were 10p each left him open mouthed with amazement. The raffle prizes—all donated—took an hour to distribute and the 'bennies' were thick on the ground.

The first detectives I encountered in the 1950s clearly fitted this description, for they were worldly-wise men who considered the learning gained in 'the university of life' to be the only grounding necessary for dealing with the extremes of behaviour they experienced. They were mostly cynical and hard-bitten men who were fully conversant with the local political nuance and the machinations of the police committee. All of them manipulated their workloads with practised ease, ensuring their formidable social life was not to be interfered with. They alone determined what was to be recorded as a crime and what would not. In effect they determined the presentation of social order and acted as the conscience of social integrity. My first instruction on my first day as a cadet on the CID front desk was given to me by a seasoned detective, who often left me to 'hold the fort' for long periods while he adjourned to the nearby pub: 'remember kid, nothing is stolen unless I say . . . everything is "lost", so send them all downstairs to lost and found property'. This meant innumerable petty crimes of larceny or theft became 'lost' property—unless of course there was a possible 'body'. By such straightforward omissions in recording, the incidence of 'crime' was kept artificially low and although the victim still reported the 'crime' and saw the particulars written down on a message pad, the lost property register or some other document, it never became a crime statistic. How the report was 'recorded' was considered immaterial to the injured person, but was crucial to the institutional presentation of social reality. It was simply not something the public needed to know about. Whether the report was eventually counted as a crime in the annual lists, or was omitted to present an acceptable level of local villainy was of no public concern. It was how things were!

This manipulated presentation of an unchanging moral order was reflected in a range of unchanging pre-war bodily symbols which reassured and also reasserted this conservative mode of thought. Even in the 1960s when fashion was undergoing cyclonic changes, senior detectives still dressed as if for a 1930s newsreel, and were required to wear three-piece suits in dark or formal colours. Some still wore the 'Anthony Eden' black Homburg of pre-war officialdom, and although a softer trilby was now acceptable to go bareheaded was unusual. Even though the counter-cultural movement of the 1960s had enormous influence on the use of colour, and many conventions were being swept aside, the young detective was still required to wear his hair short and would almost certainly buy a dark suit and trilby hat on his transfer to 'the department', just as I did.

In the late 1950s, at the time I was learning that 'crime' could as easily be recorded as 'lost property', I recall a time-served detective sergeant being sent home to change into 'something suitable'. He had turned up for work in a Harris Tweed jacket, cavalry twill trousers, brogue shoes, and the inevitable trilby hat, but was then unexpectedly required to attend the High Court at Quarter Sessions. For such an occasion this was entirely the wrong dress (too informal).

Even today, when such rigid conventions have been under assault for more than two decades, detectives still present a public demonstration of the bodily control and conservative order demanded by the institution, reflecting Umberto Eco's observation (1987: 194) that 'thought abhors tights', so that containing clothes direct the individual towards the exterior aspects of life and away from any interior reflexivity, which loose and informal wear tends to encourage.[40] In effect external constraint and a formal covering is a means of hiding the true potential of these 'heroes' to straddle the margins of anti-structure which they meet in their daily exterior lives.

This peculiarity of 'style' allows the detective and his kind to be easily recognized, so that when I called in on a CID 'occasion' on my way home from university in 1976, wearing very casual university clothing, I became intensely aware that not only was my dress visibly out of place, but that it was problematic for many of my companions at the 'do'. At the same time, I found the intense

---

[40] In a humorous article in the *Justice of the Peace* magazine (30 April 1983), Eric Crowther discusses some of the unwritten rules expected by the courts in relation to 'Dress and Modes of Address'. He tells of a stipendiary magistrate in West London who refused to listen to a solicitor who was wearing brown suede shoes. 'I cannot *see* you', the stipend declared, 'your footwear is more suitable for the golf course.' Crowther also recalls a passage from *Smugglers' Circuit* by Sir Denys Roberts (1954) where an inappropriately dressed barrister was also told, 'Miss Lasalle, I cannot *see* you.' Social acceptability in many professions still depends to a large extent on being *seen* to conform to such niceties of style, and perhaps only then on professionalism and expertise. In the police I can think of many very competent officers whose 'style' prevented them from achieving high rank, for dress and presentation are often all that is needed to meet the criterion of suitability.

uniformity of their dark, formal suits to be almost overpowering. By this time, of course, the teachings of anthropology were beginning to influence my ability to stand back and reflect on the ways that a culture demonstrates and restates its preferred forms. In some ways my bodily marginality on this occasion began to reveal to me the ways in which the symbols of identity I had grown up with and lived as 'natural' could be used to illustrate some truths about the social structures of policing. Since that time I have continued to test the unwritten police rules about dress and style, in order to reveal where the boundaries of social unnacceptablity and structural discomfort lie. Some of these have been outlined during the course of the analysis, while others have been used to reveal to close colleagues just how arbitrary police constructs of 'order' can be.[41]

A continuous conformity to this model of acceptable dress stretches back across my police career and is little changed today. In consequence it makes for easy recognition of CID status, to the extent that detectives easily identify unknown colleagues at venues such as the railway station barrier when other forces arrive on visits. I clearly recall my first 'collection' at the barrier in Newcastle in the early 1960s, when I recognized two detectives from London as 'being typical Ds'. I last played this game at Birmingham Airport in 1988 when waiting for officers from the Royal Ulster Constabulary, again spotting my contemporaries without difficulty.

Thieves can also recognize this style and spot the tiny nuances

---

[41] In March 1988 I had considerable fun at Police HQ in West Mercia on 'Comic Relief' charity day, when the whole country seemed to wear outlandish clothing and don the red nose of the clown for charitable collections. I tested this anti-structure to the limit by wearing a plastic nose, the Comic Relief tee shirt, and a hat with parrot on the top, while my somewhat daring chief superintendent went 'so far but no further'. Collecting money in the CID wing of the building, accompanied by a detective sergeant and typist, I came on a detective superintendent who was visibly shocked. He paid up but was clearly embarrassed at this spectacle of 'senior rank without dignity', muttering 'I never expected to see this sort of thing at Police HQ; and from a superintendent as well!' Later on the detective sergeant worried about the possible repercussions this might have on his security of tenure in the department. The display of 'undress' we had exhibited was a talking point for some days and afterwards the sergeant ruefully mused over what I had been doing: 'you were using the whole day weren't you to see how far some people would go, and what the reactions would be . . .' This developed into what I found to be a fruitful discussion on the limits of conformity and the role of the court-jester in presenting authority with its own limitations.

of CID dress, deportment, and demeanour. The distraught 'prig', described above, who had failed to note he was under observation by the 'finger' on the shoplifting squad kept on repeating 'he didn't look like a "jack" did he?' But then this 'jack' was a new breed and failed to conform to the unwritten code that says some groups will adhere to a specific style, the meaning of which Hebdidge (1979) suggests can be essential in defining 'social place'. In this case he had discarded the detective's suit for tee shirt and jeans, and the neatly laced and polished shoes for trainers.[42] Life in such a squad moves the detective to the margins of respectability, for 'the department' continues to have a symbolic style that is both formidable and enduring. As a direct statement about their perception of reality, it reflects a presentation of order which is condensed into such symbols as dress, the length of hair, and physical form. In their obsessive conformity, they hide many of the swirling manipulations which are a constant feature of their world, and although the detectives rarely articulate it, they are well aware of the somewhat bizarre and arbitrary nature of the 'crime' and 'disorder' they struggle to contain; but any acknowledgement of this could mean they might also have to recognize the nature of their own somewhat narrow and pedantic cultural world. As a result, these careful nuances of conformity and style continue to programme the detective's outward appearance, ritually repeating the structural binaries of cleanliness and dirt, and thus linking him to homologies of order and disorder which are embodied in this archetypal hero.

In the 1950s and early 1960s the detectives easily made enough arrests and obtained sufficient admissions or 'guilty pleas' to suggest to any casual observer that they were in command of those recognizably anti-structural elements in society which the powerful and well-connected had agreed were to be controlled. To maintain this manufactured reality the manipulation of 'crimes' was made on an almost daily basis, while the classificatory differ-

---

[42] As I have shown above, in defining the place of women in police society and in descriptions of bridewell life, these symbols of bodily correctness abound and indeed are an everyday obsession. At my first superintendents' conference in West Mercia in 1984, I was introduced by the chairman to my fellow senior officers. Having failed to recall my name, he directed them to me by the red shirt I was wearing, and linked its political connotations to my origins in the 'far North-East of England'.

ences between crimes and offences was continually used to redefine the official version in a manner suitable to these practitioners. Undetected crimes could be classifiably reduced to
offences when the occasion demanded (e.g. arson to malicious
damage), or be simply lost from the account altogether (e.g. written off as accidental and not criminal). The record of what was
eventually recorded as crime was carefully controlled, and there
was little scope for anyone to deny the figures the police provided.
Nor did there seem to be any will to deny or challenge the version
of reality generated by the detectives, which proclaimed to all that
crime figures were low and detections high!

Then again, few senior police officers in the small forces could
afford to create any new 'crime wave' at this time, for no extra
finance would have been available from the unchanging local
budgets to deal with any spurt in crime statistics. Furthermore,
any sudden or significant change in the established pattern of low
crime and high detection rates would suggest there had been some
strategic change to the social face of a locality which was unlikely
to be reflected elsewhere.

Finally, and not without significance, any large increase in
'crime' numbers could have meant that the style of the detective's
life became untenable. Their not inconsiderable social life might
have been seriously interfered with. Had the manner of recording
crimes suddenly been changed, these detectives, as the maxim
puts it, 'would have needed to run faster merely to remain in the
same place'. Indeed, when changes in recording techniques and
philosophies did occur (as we shall see), many of the old guard in
'the department' went to the wall, for they could not easily adapt.

Nearly every crime department I encountered at the time was
engaged in the practice commonly known as 'cuffing'. This, in
effect, means hiding or eliminating the incidence of reported
crime from public scrutiny by tried and trusted means. At many
police stations, as I have mentioned above, the crime book was
locked away and only the detectives were allowed to record crime,
in an effort to stop uniformed 'wollies' putting in certain types
of crime. Detectable crimes were always welcomed, while those
which might result in 'a body' or had been committed against
some important local person, would be recorded to 'avoid the
wheel coming off'. However, many run-of-the-mill minor crimes
were often only collated on message pads or some other rough

record, and then only kept on the pad until it was suitable to ditch them. Once assessed as 'dead' and unsolvable, with no chance of 'the wheel coming off', they were consigned to 'File 13' (the waste-paper basket). Again this metaphoric language, as Crick (1976) suggests, builds up the unconscious beliefs and modes of thought, revealing the ideology of the user. In this case the generic term 'cuffing' is taken from the magician's trick of concealing the truth up the sleeves or cuff, so that the dramatic mode is once again invoked. It is significant that 'cuffing' has historical precedent, and has long been known to police hierarchies:

General Order 1732 [Shropshire Police, 19 April 1939]. It has come to the notice of the Chief Constable that particularly in one Division, all cases which should be reported as crimes in accordance with instructions are not being so reported to this Headquarters and the Chief Constable takes a serious view of this matter.

The rule is that anything 'which savours of a crime' must be reported on a Crime Complaint Force, and to this rule there is no exception.

The rule is rigid, so rigid that if it comes to the knowledge of the Chief Constable that any single case has not been reported to the Chief Constable, the Constable concerned will be punished and the Section Sergeant will be reduced.

The Chief Constable (or Deputy) is the sole authority for writing off any case as an 'occurrence'.

This order obviously refers to 'cuffing' (by constables) over fifty years ago, in a period when many contemporary commentators innocently tell us that 'crime' figures were low. Twenty years later, and some 200 miles further north, on Tyneside, 'cuffing' had a long established history. Despite the dire warnings of the chief constable of Shropshire, it seems obvious that the acquiescence of many senior officers in such trickery is necessary. They had come up through the ranks and must have known of such practices, for they would have had to follow the normal strategies in order to succeed; and in effect it was impossible for them not to know of the practice. However, just as we are aware of the magician's sleight of hand and only complain when the trick goes wrong, so 'cuffing' was the order of the day everywhere, but could never be acknowledged.

As a CID aide in 1963, my first detective chief inspector used occasionally to declare 'a Queen's birthday amnesty', when we could 'file the blueys in the hothouse'. This instruction allowed detectives to burn some (blue) crime reports which could not be solved. These *had* been recorded and numbered, but could not be closed as 'Unsolved—file for reference' because the detective superintendent of the day (known as 'God') refused to accept that further enquiries could not be made that would eventually produce a culprit.[43]

Even by this time, however, my force had diametrically changed its style from that of my cadet days in 1955, and we began to record every 'crime' reported. Our new bosses had looked around and passed down the message that any claim for extra typists, new desks, more men, vehicles, and all the other facilities we now understood were possible, would require a burgeoning 'crime' rate to help the argument for more finance. But having swelled the crimes by 13,000 in four years (as I have reported above) the tradition of pursuing these unsolvable or 'dead crimes' had not changed, so at times we had to resort to the 'Queen's Birthday amnesty' and 'lose' the unsolvable crime reports in the CID fireplace (for these were the days of the Edwardian police stations, where central heating had not yet removed the fireplace and chimney).

It was during this period when the social changes of the 'swinging 60s' were sweeping a number of institutions, that the crime recording techniques of many forces were adjusted to meet newly revised opinions on the amount of villainy and social dissent that was abroad in this worrying and chaotic period. As a root metaphor and prime symbol of social malaise, 'crime' was an obvious category for some political manœuvering to reflect this social uncertainty; and the police were quick to see its potential. Almost overnight in some forces the detectives were encouraged to record as much crime as possible, although in others where the influence of social change perhaps had less pronounced effect, the 'cuffing' continued unabated.

---

[43] In Newcastle at this time, a crime was first written out on a 'crime complaint' form, and later had a blue crime report attached detailing all the aspects of the incident. This was numbered and after initial enquiry, was submitted through the hierarchal machine towards 'God'. He would then mark it up for 'supplementary report' within 14 days. Eventually, after three or four of these 'supplementaries' showed all the possible enquiries, the detective hoped the 'crime' might be marked 'file for reference', especially when he considered it as 'dead' from the outset (i.e. unsolvable) and perhaps had even written various mythological lines of enquiry on the 'supplementary' report to satisfy 'God'. However, if 'God' then sent the crime back for yet more enquiries and a further 'supplementary' in 14 days, it could easily become a choice candidate for the 'hothouse'.

On training courses and on visits to other forces I met contemporaries who still 'cuffed' a substantial proportion of the crimes reported, and who still published low incidences of crime and maintained artificially high detection rates. In one nearby borough force each detective had two separate baskets on his desk. One was for those crimes which would be recorded, while the other was for lesser items of no political import, and these lacked the crucial 'crime number' to turn them into an official statistic. This basket would be cleared every month or so and the papers disappeared into 'File 13' if they continued to be undetected. In 1965, this force, only a few miles from my own, averaged 60 per cent detections while we had a celebratory drink if we managed to achieve 30 per cent. In their force, the crime book was still locked away each night to prevent uniformed men recording 'silly' crimes and each morning the overnight messages were assessed to ensure that only those reports which fitted a narrow criterion for action were numbered. The rest were listed in a 'rough book' just in case, and then went into the 'pending File 13' basket.

Such practices created bizarre and diffuse representations of reality and must produce great difficulties now for any criminological assessment of long-term changes in crime patterns, for the official record is at times a bizarre creation of history which depends on many socio-political factors, some of which I will unravel below to show the peculiar and arbitrary whimsy of the drama.

In 1966, on my first detective training course at the Regional CID Training Centre at Bishopgarth, Wakefield,[44] I was billeted

----

[44] It is essential for a detective to get onto one of these courses, for it is one of the main passports to full admission into the department. Enormous amounts of police culture are informally imbued at Wakefield, as detectives tell continual tales of 'doing the business'. So that various techniques in relation to 'write-offs', 'clear-ups', and other manipulations of the statistical record become an integral part of being on the course. I attended three courses there between 1966 and 1973. Colin Sampson, later chief constable of West Yorkshire and heavily involved in the Stalker affair (see Stalker 1988), was commandant at the Training School during this period. And although I have suggested above that it is almost impossible for senior officers to remain unaware of the detailed history and practices of 'cuffing' and manipulation, certain men, even in such an environment as a detective training school, seem to remain insulated from this practical mastery of 'doing the business'; for as Stalker (ibid.) infers, some senior men (such as Sampson?) given charge of a major investigation, appear to have no real understanding of the realities of carrying out a crime enquiry.

with two detectives in a public house on the north side of the city. One was from a Lancashire borough force and the other was from Leeds city police. Both were still 'cuffing' furiously, and the Lancastrian told us in deadly seriousness that his force had set an 80 per cent detection rate as a norm. He was aghast when I told him we had now settled for a force target (unacknowledged and unwritten, of course) of about 40 per cent, and that in my city centre division with a floating population and less chance to 'follow up' a crime, we considered 35 per cent was a 'good month'. As on all CID courses the interminable talk was about 'the job', and I learned from the other detectives on the course, who ranged from Devon to Northumberland, that many varied systems of bending and fiddling the detections existed across the country. For 'cuffing' and fixing the detection rates was the order of the day.

Until the early 1960s then, crime was not promoted as a public problem. Its dramatic negotiation and subsequent non-existence was, I believe, a metaphorical representation of the well-being and security which was prevalent across society. In effect, its absence was an institutional manipulation and mythological reality which society seemed quite willing to accept as a reflection of their own certitude.

Within the police, it was accepted that this bizarre social drama was not only suitable, but was normal and natural, for no one had stepped forward seriously to question or prevent it. Indeed it had been passed on through generations and was approved activity, for anyone who had failed to follow the dictates of the system would not have lasted long before 'being given the big hat' and sent back to uniform. The transformation of an actual level of deviancy (which we were well aware was unknowable) into another official perspective was part of how order was defined. And the support for this view stemmed from a self-generating, reproductive pragmatism essential to preserve the structures of police power, hierarchy, and control.

Such an unquestioning acceptance of police practice is now unimaginable (see Clarke and Hough 1980 and Reiner 1985 on the whole question of police effectiveness), but there is still a need for social enquiry to break through defensive structures and reveal how practices such as the sleight of hand described above, have been varied, revised, and handed on for new generations. The praxis which the police have developed in reconciling their claim to follow the rule of law with the pragmatic necessities of 'doing the business' must still be questioned, for they are structurally a potentially authoritarian institution which remains largely hidden. As Pauline Morris (1978) argued, the significance of 'crime' to the police organizational framework, as well as the social context of its commission, needs deep and urgent analysis, because 'in the past 20 years very little has emerged concerning the philosophy (as distinct from the technology) of law enforcement.'[45]

It might seem that today with the expansion of educational opportunity and communication techniques, a new social awareness and enlarged political consciousness would foster greater reluctance to accept official versions of events, and such use of 'crime' would become unsustainable. Yet it is my belief that such a manipulated idea of crime has been annexed to an ideology of social decline and disintegration. This has then been used as a metaphor of increasing disorder and been set against a mythical golden age when society allegedly enjoyed a crime-free era without dissent or disorder. The police have had a major part in creating this ideological stance, for as we shall see, the enormous symbolic value that a 'mythology of crime' has for the organization continues to be structured by these practical masters, who know the style and social etiquette of the times. This requires that the drama of statistical juggling continues to be malleable and ever changing; and ensures the use of an idea of crime continues to hold centre stage in the imagination.

---

[45] The many 'open days' at police forces around the country are a clear example of the way this technology is used to diffuse any enquiry into the philosophies of policing; for on these comfortable occasions the public are encouraged to clamber around police cars or motor cycles and watch the mounted section go through a routine. Inevitably police dogs jump through hoops or chase 'villains' with padded arms, while tea and biscuits are available after a visit to the cells. The 'Crime Prevention' caravan promotes locks and bolts and 'neighbourhood watch'. Meanwhile, an unsolicited magazine, *Law Enforcement Technology International* (Vol. 1, No. 1, May 1984) arrived on my desk throughout my last sojourn in 'Police Research', to support Morris's contention that the philosophy of policing goes largely unchallenged. This 70-page glossy is crammed with articles promoting armoured vehicles, CS gas, pistols, rifles, tactical lighting systems, night vision intensifiers, tracked robots, fibre-optic surveillance systems, riot gear, and the like. There is nothing on the philosophy of the use of such technology in such a publication, nor does it feature on the 'open day', for it remains the weaponry of the closed and militaristic system Germann envisaged (1977).

MULTIPLYING CRIME: A CHANGE OF DIRECTION

British Society as a whole is changing rapidly. The accepted order of things . . . is no longer accepted as in even the recent past. Many consider some of our institutions archaic and in need of reform. This view is fuelled by the loss of Empire and poor showing in the list of advanced industrial societies. Disrespect for those in authority is already considerable and is increasing at an accelerating rate.

This quote from an unnamed civil servant (Knight 1984: 299) reflects a widely held perception that disorder and lawlessness has been growing inexorably in recent years, and everyday conversations are filled with axiomatic statements about 'steep rises in crime since the last war' which in time become self-fulfilling. Images sustaining this idea of a 'disintegrating society' have consistently been used by senior police officers to expand their budgets and to increase manpower levels. Since the mid-1970s the amalgamated forces have systematically enhanced the use of crime as a measure of 'success' and have used the idea of crime waves to imply an ever increasing scale of 'busy-ness'. Escalating crime has therefore become a prime symbol of a declining nation theory, which not only helps to justify the extension of such power structures, but often supports their very existence. By implication, such expansion is necessary to combat the structural decline, for this can only be fought off and checked by police vigilance, and it follows that the battle can only be effective if the institution is allocated the staffing and the scientific weaponry necessary to engage in the war against an expanding criminal world. To paraphrase Douglas (1987: 92), institutions like the police can only think about such problems by suggesting solutions which lie within their limited range of experience, and which in this case means the demand for a further expansion of existing systems of control and authority.

By the mid-1970s the smaller forces had been swept away in a series of amalgamations. Budgets swelled as increases in staffing occurred and the use of new technology expanded. Specialist units proliferated and computers began to create the hard data necessary to justify this expansion. Every officer now had personal radio with immediate links to the Police National Computer, while even the smaller sections in some forces had access to computerized systems. Futhermore, Unit Beat Policing had created a vast infusion of transport, so that in places foot patrol had become almost a memory.

However, even as the numbers of police officers doubled, so the expansion was offset by losses to this proliferation of specialist units, as well as to extra allocations in such basics as Annual Leave and Rest Days; to the extent that many subdivisions and sections now parade fewer officers for each shift than they did some twenty years ago. In this situation the potentiality of new technology has been increasingly used to offset a reduced number of patrol officers, although whether this is an acceptable alternative to the system of the 1950s, when large numbers of foot patrols operated without technical assistance or the back-up of specialist units, is always going to be open to question; for there is no correct formula.

What is apparent is the obvious symbolic potentiality contained within these organizational and technological changes to reflect the uncertainty of society, while the institutional changes heralding an expansion in the police power base could be more easily justified if a perception of rampant crime could be sustained. To this end the police enhancement of crime statistics by simply and assiduously recording what had previously been hidden from sight was most effective. Inevitably this created further social pressure, as these symbols of a disintegrating world were fed to the public through the Press and PR departments which many forces were in the process of installing or expanding. The politics of power thus ensured that this one measurement of police success became the prime metaphor by which many of the newly amalgamated forces were to be sustained, for as Finnimore (1982) points out, 'Chief police officers continue to congratulate themselves on a small decrease of a particular type of crime (or a small increase in the clear-up rate), whilst the opposite trend is reported (almost) apologetically'. Of course the use of such an arbitrary and variable category of social behaviour as a basis for expanding their empires has brought problems for the police, and to some extent they have unleashed a tiger they now find difficult to control. As John Alderson (1979: 7), then chief constable of Devon and Cornwall warned, such an emphasis on crime as a structural marker could only lead into a dead end: 'Trapped as they are in the world of criminal statistics as proof of their efficiency, the police need to break out and to seek other measurements of their success'. However, no real change has occurred and the influence of the crime figures on the police mind has continued to expand in the last decade. As we shall see, it remains a prime symbol of success or failure, and is endlessly manipulated to sustain institutional practices.

By the 1970s, it seemed the 'cuffing' of crimes might have all but disappeared. Everything now had to be recorded and crimes previously lost from view became glaringly visible. In consequence their numbers appeared to escalate alarmingly, while percentage detections dropped as the 'undetectable' or 'dead crimes' which once would have ended in 'File 13', were now 'put on the books'. At the 'sharp end' the detectives grumbled about increases in workload, but understood that these changes were essential to the style of the amalgamated forces, with their powerful, political management structures. It was tacitly understood and cynically voiced that

we're creating bloody figures to prove we are busy and under pressure and give the impression of escalating crime, so we can justify the bloody amalgamations and all these computers and the technology needed to contain the expansion of 'crime' that we have created in the first place . . . (From fieldnotes: conversation with det. sgt.)

This bitter recognition that the loss of 'cuffing' had changed the face of policing has also been matched by an understanding that other factors have moved the debate on policing almost into another plane. And although detectives are clearly traditionalist and naturally resist changes, they accept and make enormous use of these changes in the direction of crime to project a new imagery of their own place in the drama on to the public consciousness.

These realities have been combined with a media explosion in the reporting of crime, which has seen the emergence of a range of celluloid supercop detectives in which heroes fight to stem tides of crime or battle to maintain a wholesome way of life against a range of out-and-out criminals, militants, striking workers, seditious dissidents, and the gullible do-gooders of society who would let a glorious past founder and dissolve. Again the dramatic mode is apparent in this exaggerated presentation of a criminal justice system, in which the police make valiant efforts to effect a symbolically perfect, but inevitably unstable world of good and evil. During this period, the secular ascendance of these arbiters of correct behaviour has given the law and its practitioners an increasing precedence over some traditional areas of authority. I doubt it is merely accidental that in recent times we have seen an awesome kudos accorded to a host of media detectives or to some chief constables. Nor is it mere chance that the senior officer often has precedence in the public mind over the previously omnipotent church and its bishops and priests. Today the pronouncements of senior policemen fill newscasts, while the views of the chief constable are often sought before those of the church leader on many occasions; for these secular heroes hold out a promise of a 'crime-free' paradise here and now, in keeping with the hedonistic style of the times.

In effect, crime has become transformed into a major metaphor of all that is evil, to be taken on by a range of symbolic warriors engaged in battles against such devils as the 'drug fiend' or the 'callous burglar'. Like other recent symbols of evil such as General Galtieri or Arthur Scargill, these enemies can be defeated by the archetypal hero (Jung 1964), exemplified for this morality drama by the persona of the detective. Using the metaphors of warfare, the crime-busting detective bids to save the nation, while encompassing what Francis Huxley (1956: 250) has called 'the hero myth', in which he pursues 'a spiritual adventure, making plain the function of the mind itself [as a drama of images] . . . [which is] thus literally acted out and becomes a rite'. On a less metaphysical level, the practices surrounding crime recording procedures have (to echo John Alderson 1979), trapped the detective-hero, turning this symbol into an illusory construct and the spiritual adventure into a sour journey of 'bending and fiddling'. For as Whitaker (1979) suggests,

Criminality is now just a question of degree . . . the law has made criminals of us all . . . A number of offences have only recently come to be regarded as crimes, either by the law itself, or by members of the public whose educational and socio-cultural standards have risen. Violent behaviour formerly used to be taken for granted much more than it is today. Similarly, assaults or cases of vandalism which used never to be reported in slum communities may now feature in the statistics.

The changing nature of the drama has meant that manipulations to the counting and recording techniques have now become a structural necessity, for continued increases in the record of crime help to justify the billions spent on the criminal justice system, but prevent any real move towards an alternative social formula. Some of the fluctuations in the detection rates reflect aspects of these changes, but need to be carefully scrutinized to reveal hidden areas in the agenda. Having irrevocably lost a 'golden age' when an 80 per cent detection rate could be claimed without question, the subsequent era of expensive amalgamations and expansions in manpower and technology was justified by the presentation of a world in disarray; but as detection rates dropped to 30 per cent or less this created alarm and by the 1980s most of the forty-three forces were returning an average of about 40 per cent detections, to show they were only just staving off the mayhem which threatens society.

In effect the changes in direction of recording and counting crimes are statements about pressures on the police, but are also a reflection of one mythological reality which these archetypal detective-heroes use to meet the demands of their own culture. Constantly they bemoan the madness of this world in which they operate, often referring to its governing principles as being determined by the 'statistical rat race'. However, it is one they have willingly helped to create and sustain over the years, for it has served them well by ensuring a continuity in their own structures of power.

MULTIPLYING CRIME:
THE EFFECTS OF RECLASSIFICATION

Classificatory oscillations in the concept of disorder have a long and notorious history. Between 1660 and 1819, over 180 new capital offences became law, nearly all to protect property rather than human life. Hughes (1987: 29) asks, 'why must forgers hang? Because the increase of paper transactions . . . banking and business —cheques, notes, bonds, shares . . . had made property of all sorts more vulnerable to forgery.' Again, the Waltham Black Act drafted to suppress minor agrarian dissent in 1722–3, prescribed the gallows for over 200 deeds considered reprehensible. Hughes (ibid. 29) tells us, 'one could be hanged for burning a hut, a standing rick of corn, or . . . a pile of straw; for poaching a rabbit . . . or even cutting ornamental shrubs'. The process continues, and the way that two offences have been recently upgraded to be reclassified as crimes follows long precedent in responding to events by enhancing both the symbolic and actual relevance they are given in law. Two crimes which have gained a new semantic value by such reclassification are *vandalism* and *car theft*, for both have moved up the scale of infamy in the recent past, creating an image of burgeoning 'criminal' activity and sustaining a belief in the theory of a disintegrating society. Both car theft and vandalism had been actionable, but until the recent past were not classified as crimes, since when they have almost certainly helped to generate a statistical picture of increasing disorder and villainy.

Sometimes it almost seems as if damage to property did not occur until the early 1970s, when the term 'vandalism' took on a significant place in the popular imagination. Statistically there was little or no recorded crime in this category until a change in the law and an administrative reclassification occurred. Then, the reaction to vandalism took on all the trappings of a classic 'moral panic' (Cohen 1973), and seemed clearly to reflect the uncertainties of the times.[46]

In police terms there is no such classification as 'vandalism', for the crime is recorded and known as 'criminal damage'. An idea of 'vandalism', however, has been subsumed into the public consciousness, incorporating a wide range of behaviour. As a Home Office report (Clarke 1978: 2) suggests, 'Vandalism, taken here as approximately equivalent to the legal category of criminal damage, may as a result become mixed up in people's minds with general worries about hooliganism and breakdowns in public order'. 'Vandalism' can therefore incorporate the high spirits and noise of young people, especially when defined by the elderly and those whose standards of normality were set before extensions in the licensing hours or the amplification of music occurred. As Bottomley and Coleman (1980: 83) suggested:

part of the problem lies in the fact that the legal and statistical categories used for official purposes have a vagueness and ambiguity that renders them open to misunderstanding on the part of the general public and

[46] In these panics there often lurks the idea that crime has genetic origins and is without socio-cultural influence. This idea surfaced in the Handsworth riots of 1985, when the event was denied a socio-economic basis by certain political commentators, and was said to be 'inherently criminal'. The police have willingly used this genetic concept to define their opposition as 'animals', for it is always easier to wage war against a non-human enemy, who is evil by nature.

allows a measure of flexibility to the police in allocating a particular incident to an official category.

Using this vagueness and ambiguity, the police have—at times— set out to hide crimes or promote them depending on the dictates of the social climate or structural need. And in the recent past they have reinforced their hegemonies by using a 'potential threat' concept, linking this to a statistical expansion in the record of such categories as vandalism.

For 103 years until 1964, the control of vandalism was defined by the Malicious Damage Act of 1861 which proscribed a range of maliciously destructive acts. Certain kinds of damage of a treasonable classification, such as 'setting fire to Her Majesty's ships of War (afloat or being built)' or 'unlawfully and maliciously setting fire to any mine of coal, cannelcoal, anthracite or other mineral fuel' (section 26) reflect the preoccupations of society in the mid-nineteenth century and the definition of hooliganism in that era (Pearson 1983). Such deeds were among a list of classifiable crimes which were only triable on indictment at the High Court, and by the start of my career were rare events. However, the 1861 Act also catered for the general day-to-day incidents of malicious damage, and lumped them together under section 51 of the Act, creating an 'offence':

If any person wilfully or maliciously commits any damage to any real or personal property whatsoever, either of a public or a private nature, and the amount of damage does not, in the opinion of the court, exceed £100 . . .

This £100 qualification became the crux of the matter of crime or offence, and was provided for by the Criminal Justice Administration Act of 1914. In effect crimes over £100 were to be tried only at the High Court, i.e. at Quarter Sessions or Assize, while offences under £100 were triable at the lower or Magistrates' Courts. A classificatory difference between crimes and offences was therefore created by this £100 definition and the place of trial.

Anything above £100 was to be recorded as a crime committed and a crime detected or undetected. Under £100, the act of damage was to remain an offence and had lower status and a totally different form of recording. In my early career all undetected offences of damage were automatically assessed by the patrolling constable as being less than £100. This was still a considerable sum, and as we quickly learned, we could not afford to have this type of undetected crime on the books. Detectives would have looked askance on anyone foolish enough to record a crime, and even if arrests were made for acts of malicious damage where the value was over £100, efforts were usually made to reduce this to £99 19s. 11d. or less, simply because of the mode of trial.

As crimes (over £100) could *only* be tried on indictment, the cost was an inhibitor which the small forces of the time could not easily ignore. Usually the category was manipulated and *detected* crimes of malicious damage might be translated into offences such as 'attempted shopbreaking' or 'storebreaking with intent to commit a felony'. These also were classifiable crimes but *could* be tried summarily at the Magistrates' Court. Of course, by the same token, *undetected* offences of malicious damage were never recorded as crimes of attempted shopbreaking, for this would have left a potentially undetected crime on the books.

Again the classification of offences was used in other ways and many crimes were written off as unsolved offences of malicious damage, thus reducing the numbers in categories such as 'attempted housebreaking', which under its current legal designation of 'burglary' continues to alarm society today. Many attempted housebreakings at that time were written off as offences, and reduced in classificatory terms to lessen the image of mayhem and disorder. [47]

In my early days on foot patrol, the 'writing off' consisted of merely writing up a résumé of the damage in the 'beat book', and perhaps asking the early shift to call round and tell the owner of the damaged premises that the matter was under attention. The statistical record of such offences was therefore negligible, and in 1965, for example, the Newcastle City Police Annual Report lists the indictable crimes of malicious damage, but has no record for the offences under £100, other than a number of those offenders

---

[47] Unitl the 1968 Theft Act, various acts of breaking and entering were separately categorized, e.g. shopbreaking, housebreaking, storebreaking, warehouse-breaking, burglary, etc. The new Act consolidated all of these into one classification of 'burglary'. Under the 1916 Larceny Act all of these 'breaking offences' were hierarchically arranged with some triable on indictment and others triable summarily. All were classifiable crimes however, and were to be counted as such; unless they were 'written off'.

who appeared at court; in other words the numbers of *undetected* offences under £100 went unrecorded. The report shows:

| Malicious damage (i.e. over £100) | Crimes recorded: 5 Crimes detected: 2 |
| Wilful damage (i.e. under £100) | Persons dealt with at court: 89; convicted:, 77; otherwise dealt with: 2; withdrawn/dismissed: 10 |

These figures clearly reflect the perceptions of the times and show the artificially low figures produced by 'cuffing' and 'writing off'.

Then in 1971, at a time when many police forces were actively seeking to record more crimes to justify their expanding budgets and new technology, the law and classification relating to damage was amended. The 1861 Malicious Damage Act was replaced by the Criminal Damage Act 1971 and the deed changed from being malicious or wilful to being 'criminal', while trial on indictment at the High Court was no longer necessary.

Overnight the drama was enhanced, for a 'crime' was to be recorded if property valued in *excess* of £20 was damaged. Immediately a new dimension to the act of vandalism was added, for the detectives had a new crime on which to impose their own criteria of value, while the amalgamations could be more easily justified as the previous neglect surrounding 'malicious damage' was swept away, and crime figures soared. 1971 was also the year in which Britain moved to decimalization while inflation increased as oil and fuel prices rose, and charges for services and repairs to property began to escalate. Now even minor incidences of damage cost more than the £20 which differentiated crimes from offences. The smallest broken window could cost more than £20, although this might easily be assessed at less than £20 if there was little or no chance of a 'body'! In an eighteen-month period on one subdivision in the early 1980s I noted many occurrences of Minor Damage offences recorded on the incident log, and the following is a typical example of this modern system of 'cuffing':

Minor Damage

PC Robinson reports slight damage to the house 114 Acacia Avenue (4 beat) between 6 p.m. and 11 p.m. 17th. Window broken in kitchen at rear, value £13, isolated incident . . . no attempt to gain entry. Attention of resident beat officer directed . . . (From fieldnotes)

Whenever I questioned the value of this offence, which had been carefully 'written off' by indicating that no attempted entry had been made (which would have turned it into a crime of attempted burglary), I saw the same rueful grin as I was told it was probably a 'guesstimate'. One detective inspector, in an adjacent subdivision to mine, described it as 'the land of £15 windows. There must be more "isolated incidents" of under £20 damage to windows here than anywhere else in the world . . .' (from fieldnotes). Of course if a 'body' materialized for these offences, then the value could easily be adjusted to just over £20, by accounting for labour and the rising cost of putty. This ensured that a 'detected crime' could now be claimed, even though the culprit would be subject to an identical charge of 'criminal damage' regardless of the value. Only the recording methodology and returns from the Statistical Departments to the Home Office were changed to indicate the power broking that was was unfolding within the institution.

By 1974 the incidence of criminal damage in Northumbria Police area had risen to 2,431 crimes recorded, with 951 crimes detected. By 1981 the Force Annual Report shows 7,875 crimes recorded, while 1,378 persons were proceeded against for lesser offences of damage under £20. Of course the 1981 force boundaries are not comparable with the pre-amalgamation days of 1965 when the five crimes in the annual report were a reflection of the structural invisibility of the category; but the incredible rise is as much about a sematic belief in rampant 'vandalism' and in consequence has been taken up and reproduced in the statistical return. This has become increasingly sophisticated, but still remains malleable. The average cost of each of the 7,875 'crimes' of criminal damage in the 1981 report was put at just over £300, although that figure is skewed because major fires at two schools accounted for almost half of the total £2.4 million cost of 'vandalism'. In the main, incidents of damage are for very small amounts; as the chief constable pointed out in his report (Northumbria Police 1981: 32): 'Inflation accounts partly for this increase, bringing some of the less serious "offences" into the recordable "crime" category . . .'. In the ten years between the implementation of the Act and this report, the police were not slow to use the effects of inflation to their statistical advantage so that an offence valued £5 or £6 in 1971, could easily have become a £20-plus 'crime' by the end of the decade; but only if it were suitable!

Other official reports have helped foster an illusion that this increase is a real and is a faithful record of a new event:

of the major indictable offences (crimes) recorded by the police in the United Kingdom in the decade 1969 to 1978, the category showing by far the fastest rate of increase, from 14,700 to 140,500 was criminal damage, which is almost certainly underreported.

This Home Office Research Bulletin (Rees 1981) only speculates on the underreporting and has little material to explain the semantic changes which caused 5 crimes in 1965 to become 2,431 in 1974 and 7,875 in 1981. It fails to make any comment on the structural relevance which the creation of this 'crime wave' has had for the amalgamated police units; nor does it reflect on how the police could ever reverse the process. Having unleashed the tiger, the police are unlikely to set out to show it has been tamed and poses no threat, for the social style of the times demands a scenario of society in decline, with the traditional institutions of discipline and order under threat of being overwhelmed.

Occasionally some critical comment on the 'wave' of vandalism has tended to concentrate on this economic factor which generates 'crimes' simply because inflation moves 'offences' across the £20 margin and upgrades them:

the trouble is that a 1971 directive from the Home Office suggests that only damage which costs more than £20 to repair should be recorded in the figures, and that sum hasn't changed ... Since inflation has rarely been out of double figures ... a number of cases which 10 years ago would have been considered trivial were now logged in official records. The apparent increase was but an artefact of inflation ... (*Guardian*, 6 September 1980)

... in these inflationary days, an arbitrary limit, such as £20 tends to confuse those figures that are compiled: an act of damage to the value of £19 one year would not be 'crimed' but the following year the same act would be included in the criminal statistics since the cost of making good would be well over £20. The effect is the artificial inflation of the crime returns in step with monetary inflation ... (HO Protection Against Vandalism: HMSO 1975)

Economic determinism is, however, only one reason for this 'crime wave'. Its newly created semantic relevance was also enhanced by its political and legal elevation at a specific point in history which was crucially relevant to the police, and yet is largely invisible to the analysts who focus on this £20 category as *the* determining factor. Since 1971, every new police officer has learned that every act of 'criminal damage' is a possible 'detection', albeit of a minor nature, and the idea of vandalism is now axiomatically linked with the street visible, dangerous punks, skins, louts, and other hooligans who are firmly lodged in the police mind as the enemies of society and the institution. This recent addition to the *habitus* of policing means that almost 7 per cent of all crimes in Northumbria (over 5,000 in 1981) and 10 per cent of the crimes in West Mercia (over 4,800 in 1986) now hold a firm symbolic place in the police and public imagination.

At the time 'criminal damage' started to be used to generate structures of significance in the police mind, most of the newly amalgamated forces were setting out to present a 50 per cent detection rate as their norm.[48] This helped foster the idea that the amalgamations had been successful, that increasing expenditure on technology and manpower had been needed and was well spent, and furthermore created the hard data needed to prove that the police were (just) able to stem a rising tide of crime.

An examination of the Annual Reports from forces across the country in the early 1970s reveals that many were now claiming detection rates of 50–55 per cent. This is in clear contrast to the impossibly high figure of 80 per cent or more which some small forces had been claiming only a dozen years earlier; and yet these figures were well up on the 30–40 per cent rate which had become the norm when the forces began to record as much 'crime' as possible, for reasons I have outlined above.

Subsequently, changes in police priorities and the social perception of rampant disorder created other pressure for statistical manipulation, so that by the mid-1980s most of the forty-three forces lowered the 50 + per cent norm again and began to show a 40 per cent detection rate as they once again set out to suggest 'their backs were against the wall'. Yet as the 1980s drew to a close, a slight reduction in the 'crime' figures occurred for the first time in years, while the detection rates began to rise again towards the 50 per cent level they had settled at briefly a decade earlier. It would be speculative, as yet, to suggest this might be yet another dra-

---

[48] It could be a mistake to include the Metropolitan Police in such a review of detection rate norms. The Met. have always presented their circumstances to be specific and continue to produce very low detection rates to illustrate their embattled situation.

matic production of the institution, used to offset some of the increasing public dissatisfactions with certain police practices, and therefore nothing more than another political manipulation appearing at a suitable time in police history. However, time and social transition will subsequently allow this statistical change to be assessed for any such possibility.

Of course during this time, the 'offences' under £20 have still been treated with disdain, for they are irrelevant to the discourse. Mostly they go undetected and have little or no credibility, for when a 'body' does emerge, they will inevitably be manipulated above the crucial figure of £20. The Standing Committee Report on *Protection against Vandalism*, acknowledges their structural relevance to the police wholly depends on whether they can be classified as crimes:

the returns we asked for, and were freely given from the police forces . . . revealed fairly accurate information on the frequency of damage to the value of £20 or more, which is religiously recorded and afforded some degree of investigation . . . but there were totally and admittedly inadequate records of minor damage . . . (ibid. 4–6)

Indeed, while collecting material on 'crime stats.' in both Northumbria and West Mercia, I found the reports of damage under £20 to be very haphazardly recorded. Throughout 1985/6, when Headquarters Stats. rang my subdivision each month to obtain the numbers of under-£20 damage incidents, I witnessed the lack of significance this category has for 'the troops'.

On one occasion I recorded what I had seen happen many times when the monthly call for the stats. came through:

STATION CONSTABLE. Headquarters Stats., Sir, asking for the 'under £20 damage' figures for last month.
ME. How do we collate them?
SC. We don't Sir, I go through the message pads and try to come up with a number.
ME. But this is only one station on the subdivision. What about the other two? Who collects them?
SC. Don't complicate things Sir; I look up the number we gave them last month in the returns and then either add a few or take a few off depending on whether its been busy or not. They're happy, and no one seems to do anything else, I've checked the other divisions and its the same system there. (From fieldnotes, 1986)

Later in 1986, when I was in an HQ department which incorporated the stats. department I spoke with the Force Stats. Officer about the figure of 3,970 offences of 'damage under £20' which had been returned to the Home Office on form Crimsec 1(A), as a subsidiary part of the 'Return of Notifiable Offences' for 1985. In contrast to a detection rate of over 45 per cent for 'real crimes', I noted we claimed a 'clear-up' of only 187 offences (4.7 per cent). However, it turned out this was merely the numbers who had appeared at court for 'damage under £20' offences, for the system had no means of including figures for those cautioned or not proceeded against.

I described how the figures were collected on division to the stats. officer and how vague and insubstantial the returns were that the thirteen subdivisions phoned back to her office. Inured by dealings with detectives as they tried to bend figures and improve the 'clear-up' rate, she agreed the 'under-£20 damage' figures were almost mythological, suggesting that the whole thing was 'totally meaningless'. However, I believe their very lack of precision or accuracy is, in fact, meaningful. For they clearly reveal how the idea of crime holds centre court in the police mind, relegating all other aspects of the drama to the margins. In Northumbria, with 7,616 'crimes' of damage over £20 in 1982 and 8,259 in 1983, I noted, 'every crash of glass requires resources are directed to the event as the rage to secure a 50 per cent detection rate is played out; for every "prig" offender caught must be "squeezed" to extract the maximum number of "coughs" to support the statistical proclamation of police effectiveness'.

Such an operational response was difficult if not impossible to create before the technological revolution in policing occurred, and it seems to me to be no mere chance or coincidence that saw this reclassification of an offence into a crime occur just at the time when society was expressing concern about a perceived social decline and was equipping its police with the technical wherewithal to impose more control and prevent the deterioration.

Again, just as the offence of damage became a crime at a significant point in social history, so the reclassification of 'taking motor vehicles without consent' was another factor in amending the view of social calm and equanimity. In the main, a large number of vehicles are simply taken, used, and then abandoned. Only a small percentage are stolen and are never seen again. Many are taken by the 'dangerous classes', and a considerable amount of car theft rests with the teenagers from the lower socio-economic echelons, who may strip parts from the vehicles for resale or take items from the vehicles they 'borrow'. The Larceny Act of 1916, not unexpectedly, had little to say about the motor vehicle. By definition, larceny required the appropriated article to be *permanently* taken and the owner be deprived forever. A borrowed vehicle hardly fitted this legal requirement and not unnaturally the 1916 Act failed to anticipate the proliferation of the car or its temporary use by the 'dispossessed' to supplement unavailable late night transport. By 1930, however, the taking of motor vehicles was acknowledged in a Road Traffic Act (section 217) and an offence was created of 'taking a motor vehicle without the consent', universally known in police circles by the acronym TWOC.

For thirty-eight years, offences of TWOC were committed and recorded with varying degrees of accuracy. No crime of theft of the vehicle was ever considered until the taking began to have a look of permanency; and the Home Office instruction was that a crime would only be recorded seventy-two hours after a vehicle was taken. Subsequently a 'no crime' would be recorded if the vehicle was later found abandoned. In many forces the seventy-two-hour rule was ignored and a crime was only recorded after some considerable time, if at all.

As I have described above, until the late 1950s society was essentially immobile. The police and their 'prig' opponents both operated on foot, and as I have shown the small forces had few vehicles in which to chase and catch offenders. Again figures taken from the Newcastle City Police Annual Report (1965: 72–3) show how few crimes of larceny of vehicles or offences of TWOC were recorded. In the case of TWOC no record was kept unless there was an arrest; and whereas 'crimes' of larceny relate to numbers of vehicles stolen, 'offences' of TWOC relate only to 'Persons Proceeded Against', and give no indication at all of the numbers of cars which had been 'borrowed' for an hour or two:

Larceny of motor cars	Crimes recorded 25	(1964: 20)
	Crimes detected 8	(1964: 8)
Larceny of m/cycles	Crimes recorded 74	(1964: 46)
	Crimes detected 46	(1964: 4)
Larceny of commercial vehicles	Crimes recorded 2	(1964: 2)
	Crimes detected —	(1964: 1)

Taking motor vehicles without consent: Persons arrested 190 (174); persons convicted 176 (162); otherwise dealt with 7 (7); withdrawn/dismissed 7 (5) (figures for 1964 in parentheses).

At this time, in the early 1960s, I worked a beat adjacent to the River Tyne, which separated our city force from the Gateshead borough force. If I saw a car crossing one of the bridges from Gateshead, perhaps driven erratically by a gang of youths and I suspected the car had been TWOC, I then had to run to my police box and phone my local station. By the time I had relayed my story the car might well be two or three miles away, and unless taken from our force area there was every likelihood we would have no record, for even links with adjacent forces were somewhat tenuous and our insularity meant we were often unwilling to make more than a token gesture to the events occurring in our despised, 'small-time' neighbours.

If the vehicle had been taken from further afield, perhaps for example from York only eighty miles away, it would be some days before it might be circulated to force level and not at all at beat level. Records were handwritten, there was no telex transmission and manual entries in 'Stolen Car books' were made up daily from the local records from the force and the immediate surrounding areas. Even in the force 'control room' the extended records of stolen vehicles were only culled from the *Police Gazette* after they had been collated by Scotland Yard, and posted from London, and were then kept in numerical and alphabetical order on cardboard strip indices. Even if the vehicle *was* recorded, the possibility of catching it was limited by our own lack of vehicles, or knowledge as to its route or present whereabouts. There was no personal radio to link patrolling officers and the force was so small that by the time this TWOC had travelled three miles, it was out of our area and a problem for someone else. My first arrest for TWOC was something of a rarity for foot patrol, but quickly lost its value when it was discovered that the motor cycle had been taken from a neighbouring force area and was not one of ours. In keeping with the style of the times, the arrest preceded the eventual report of a stolen vehicle, which only arrived some hours after this offence had been cleared up.

Just as there was always a tendency to upgrade the arrest classification of any malicious damage into a crime when circumstances (and a 'body') made it suitable, so the occasional arrest for TWOC was readily available for compromise. Many forces always preferred a charge of larceny of the petrol used during the illicit journey as well as the offence of TWOC. This use of the fuel met the criteria of 'permanently depriving the owner' of the petrol and in consequence was a 'crime' created and detected. Needless to say, the hundreds of cars taken and abandoned were never recorded as *undetected* crimes of larceny of petrol. To have done this would have negated the logic of the system.

In 1968 the Theft Act replaced the 52-year-old Larceny Act and a section included to take account of the TWOC. This was now to be called 'Taking motor vehicles or other conveyances without authority' and all reports were to be recorded at once and classified as crimes. Again it is tempting to suggest this upgrade of semantic position in a ranked order of disorder was structured by changes occurring within the new, enlarged police units. Prior to this time any reclassification of TWOC as a crime could only have increased the undetected crime statistics, for the means to even imply that such activity could be controlled were just not available. From 1968, however, the technology and organizational changes necessary to control this disorder were not only at hand, but had to be implemented and justified if the amalgamations were to make any sense.

Now, if we replay the same incident I have just described where the possible stolen car is driven erratically over one of the river bridges, it is possible to follow the consequences of social and technological change on police practice. Today, the foot patrol only has to call his control on personal radio for a 'vehicle check', to learn from the police national computer whether a vehicle is suspect or stolen anywhere in the country. Stolen cars are immediately input to the data banks and a constable, perhaps in an inconspicuous position, can be told that the vehicle he is observing has been reported stolen from a town perhaps fifty miles away, which might now still be well within his own force area. It is then a relatively simple operation to direct enough cars and men towards the offenders, set up the chase, and make the 'capture'. This exciting activity further generates a belief that this is prime police work, and it is hardly surprising that a number of young 'prigs' have been killed in spectacular car chases throughout the 1970s and 1980s, for it is now essential that the police 'capture' all possible 'TWOC merchants'. For those who take vehicles must also be 'squeezed dry' and contribute to the detection rates by admitting their involvement in other TWOCs or petty thefts of property taken from the vehicles they borrow. What does *not* change is the fact that those 'captured' for this 'crime' invariably still come from the 'dangerous classes'.

In the three years 1978–80, over 13,000 'crimes' of TWOC were recorded each year in Northumbria Police area. These made up nearly 20 per cent of all recorded crime in the force and the detections claimed in this category ranged from 46 to 54 per cent over the three years. Yet a decade earlier just 100 permanently taken vehicles were recorded as crimes.

Again it would seem that only changes in radio techniques, the input of vehicles, and the use of national computers serving the amalgamated superforces have made this reclassification possible and given this 'crime' requisite status within the police mind. And again a lightly veiled social challenge is contained within these escalating figures, for they pose a threat of rampant disorder and growing lawlessness, which presents the police with a perfect opportunity to pursue a conflict model of action. Such a format operates best when society faces what Victor Turner (1982: 108) has called its 'redressive phase' in the 'processual structure of a social drama'. As Turner tells us:

[when] redressive agents and the instruments they have at command— courts, parliaments, councils, assemblies, armies, police . . . have lost or are losing their authority, legitimacy or efficacy in the eyes of the group members . . . the response to crisis may now emerge . . . A clash between conserving and reforming parties . . . as the representatives of the 'ancien' and 'nouveau régime' confront one another . . . Much depends upon the size and scale of the group and the degree to which its social and economic division of labour has advanced. Such factors determine what modes of redress are applied or devised . . .

The three or four young 'prigs' in a TWOC (or TADA—Take And Drive Away) are now 'manna from heaven' to the section or subdivisional CID. Using classic techniques, the detectives can often split up and play one off against the other to obtain 'a bagful of clear-ups'. These can considerably ease the pressures on a local CID office, which may have a spate of undetected burglaries to set them against in order to make up the expected monthly or quarterly detection rate norms.

After leaving the bridewell and on my first day out and about as a subdivisional inspector I was 'being shown the parish' by a young constable when we somewhat fortuitously came across and arrested three young men with a large bunch of duplicate keys as they were in the act of taking a car. This produced fifty-seven detections of TWOCs and the theft of small items taken from the cars. The 'capture' was greeted with delight back in the bridewell, but the joy tailed off rapidly when it became obvious that most of the detections would be for an adjacent division. However, their detectives were very happy, for a little 'roll-up' like this can be kept back for next month's figures, or even beyond that if the detection rate is already at an acceptable level. A successful detective inspector is therefore one who can manage his 'crime' and the detection rate, and manipulate his subdivisional return to fit within an understood norm.

Reclassification of these two offences of 'damage' and 'TWOC' into crimes means that by the early 1980s in Northumbria there were well over 20,000 extra 'crimes' each year. So that even though the 'incidence of loss of authority and legitimacy or efficacy' (to requote Turner), may have contributed to the amount of dissent and disorder occurring, I believe that the *ancien régime* has been smoothly replaced by a *nouveau* model which has clearly determined which 'modes of redress are [to be] applied or devised' (ibid.), as the social schism of the 'redressive phase' is played out. These new crimes now make up almost 25 per cent of all the recorded crime in Northumbria and clearly have an illusory aspect to their make-up, even though they now form a firm basis for a continuation of a redressive 'moral panic'. In 1979, in a 3″ banner headline, the *Newcastle Evening Chronicle* reported 'Vandalism Soars', warning that 'startling new figures [are] to be presented to the police authority'. In the same report, however, the police reassuringly set out to show they still hold the balance in the battle with the hooligans, 'prigs', and vandals, by confiding that 'the detection rates are reasonably static'.

REDEFINING BEHAVIOUR: THE POTENTIAL FOR
FURTHER 'CRIME' WAVES

In the political turbulence of modern society there is always the possibility that social control will swing to a more authoritarian line and be more systematically imposed. The classificatory changes I have just outlined above in relation to TWOC and vandalism, reflect some recent schisms occurring in the social formation, and the police have not been slow to use such occasions as a means of expanding their hegemonic role.

And even though there has been some concerted action to ensure that the exercise of police power remains at an acceptable level and involves a suitable degree of accountability to the public at large, the police—and the governments they serve—seem inexorably to be expanding their controlling activities. During the recent past the police have clearly demonstrated their willingness to act as an organ of political power, for they are aware that radical change or any *nouveau régime* which gained prominence might well seek a new direction in the flow of power, and the controllers of today could as easily find themselves becoming the controlled of tomorrow. It is therefore clearly within the police interest to maintain the existing power structures.

Indeed, as Turner (1982) has consistently shown[49] the expansion of such redressive measures are part of an eternal social drama, encompassing social disjunction, conflict, struggle, crisis, and eventual social change. Those involved in this continually fractious business seem to be inherently aware that any schism in the continuity of a social system also holds the potential for power to be enhanced, allowing them to pursue even further idiosyncratic definitions of what is to be classified as disordered or 'criminal'.

The way that the police think of and use the concept of power is conservatively structured, tempered by respect for the known traditions and qualities, and even when not directly advocating further control tacitly invites us to stick with the known systems of restraint rather than be tempted by any radical alternative. As the old maxim warns, 'better the devil you know than the devil you don't'. In the circumstances, any police assertion of a non-political stance is clearly a nonsense, and the political bias and leanings of my colleagues has been plain to see during the whole of my career. On an individual basis and with few exceptions, my

[49] Turner's 1982 volume quoted here is in direct continuity with his earlier works (1957, 1967, 1969, 1974), each of which illustrates aspects of the dynamism contained in the unfolding nature of the social drama. All of these works have had a seminal influence on this analysis.

colleagues have tended to fall well to the right of centre and their political philosophies generally show a marked preference for some of the extremes of conservative political ideology. Indeed I have many fieldnote entries of instances when colleagues have included me in a conversation and axiomatically assumed I shared their markedly right-wing perception of world events.

At the 1984 Conservative Party Conference, the Police Federation sponsored MP, Eldon Griffiths, unconvincingly argued 'the police are not Conservative', and a few months later at the Bramshill Scholars' Annual Reunion dinner and AGM, I listened to the almost transparent bigotry of this élite group of police intellectuals, as they showed their political allegiances and threatened to boycott the next annual dinner of the association if the leader of the Labour Party was asked to attend as guest speaker. Of course I should have not have been surprised, for across the years I have consistent evidence of fear and suspicion of liberal views and an almost generalized hatred of active socialists.

The defensiveness exhibited by some chief officers symbolizes this conservatism most clearly, and even though it is apparent they now enjoy more power than at any other time in police history, they inevitably reject out of hand any suggestion there is a need for greater police accountability. Invariably such demands are identified as being a political tactic by hostile elements interested only in gaining the control which, of course, they currently enjoy. In a 1982 speech James Anderton, the chief constable of Greater Manchester, revealed the true nature of the threat posed by such demands:

A quiet revolution is taking place around us and the prize is political power to be wielded against the most cherished elements of the establishment, including the monarchy. It is as much the duty of the police to guard against this as it is to guard against crime. I sense and see in our midst an enemy more dangerous, insidious and ruthless than any faced since the second world war ... (Reported in the *Guardian*, 17 March 1982)

Here the use of metaphorical enemies, and the invocation of the mythological aspects of monarchy are allied to a symbolic appeal to fight another Second World War, and introduces some possible new areas for the archetypal policeman-hero to fight off ruthless, dangerous, and insidious antagonists.

By implication, the concept of crime is clearly set to be extended here, for there are conceptual treasons abroad. Again, invoking the spirit of Turner, we might even anticipate such treasons to be manifest at such times when society is suffering schism and social crisis. And indeed the extreme language used by Anderton—'guarding against insidious enemies within our midst' —is the very stuff of heightened social tension, as society moves towards the provision of more redressive controls. Such emotional rhetoric can also be found in some of the calls for enforcement of the recently rediscovered 'crimes' of criminal blasphemy and 'libel' for the evidence tends to suggest that the police and the conservative politicians they serve are now generating the belief systems necessary to sustain the pursuit of a new range of 'crimes'. In such a social milieu the grave possibility exists that even contradictory thoughts and alternative beliefs could be proscribed and become criminal acts, for this is a time when civil liberties are under attack, when the possibility of a Bill of Rights has been denied, when a new Official Secrets Act looks to set to prevent the availability of basic information on how the country is being run, and when an increasing centralization of state controls has been achieved at the expense of local democratic powers.

Along with this the police, as Ian Will (1983) suggested, seem to be moving inexorably towards national organization which can only lead to their administration under a central minister for policing, with little or no say for locally elected representatives. In such a world the style of policing has every possibility of becoming even more repressive, while calls made by the likes of Anderton for a 'Commissioner's Standing Committee established as a cabal of police top-liners more likely to speak with one voice' (quoted in Will ibid.)[50] could well become the reality. One has to question whether it would then perhaps become a classificatory 'crime' of sedition or disaffection for activists in the Campaign for

---

[50] Roger Birch, the chief constable of Sussex as the 1988 ACPO president followed Anderton in proposing that the 43 forces be brought together in a small number of regional units (*Police Review*, 18 Nov. 1988), while Sir Peter Imbert chose the 1989 Police Foundation lecture to make a radical proposal (obviously with HO approval) for a national, centrally funded crime unit, outside any local control or financial involvement (*Police* magazine, June/July 1989).

Nuclear Disarmament or the Green Party to express opposition to government policy on the expansion of nuclear power?[51]

In the first instance it seems likely there would be further extensions to the basic controls of the population, and we might, for example, follow some American states in making 'juvenile curfew breach' into a crime; for their model of deviance is often used to predict UK trends. Yet even the basic material in their statistical indices clearly illustrates crucial differences between the British and the US social experience. In Britain the count is of 'crimes' reported, recorded, and detected, while American crime statistics are based on a count of arrests. The 'Total Estimated Arrests for Crime' are published in the *Uniform Crime Reports for the United States* by the Department of Justice. In the 1981 report the grand total of arrests for the previous year is shown as 10,441,000, a figure based on 'All reporting agencies and includes estimates of arrests for unreported areas'. As their 'Crime Trends' statistics 1971–80 are said to be collected from 3,806 different police agencies (ibid. 202), it is worth speculating on how many estimated crimes are included for 'unreported areas'. If their recording techniques are as disparate as those which occur within the handful of British police forces then any relevance in the American model for this country must be tenuous, for the American concept of crime indicates further differences in the style and history of the two cultures, though there are indications of what might be used in any redressive phase in Britain. Part 1 offences or serious crimes in the USA largely mirror classified 'crimes' in Britain (e.g. homicide, rape, robbery); however some are incomparable. For example, 'Manslaughter by negligence' is one of eight 'Part 1 Crimes' and seems somewhat akin to the non-accidental, industrial death which in Britain would be the province of the Factories Inspectorate. But then, as the report (ibid.) tells us, 'this crime is not included in the statistical returns'.

A further 21 categories are listed as Part 2 Crimes. Again many are similar to the Home Office Standing List of Crimes for

---

[51] At a Senior Officers' Mess night in 1986, I listened as Sir Lawrence Byford, the Chief HMI, carefully avoided showing political allegiance in outlining a list of current police problem areas; but then completed his list by including 'those misguided groups who favour nuclear disarmament'.

England and Wales, e.g. forgery, fraud, and embezzlement, but others say more about American society than anything about a universal code of infamy. Category 17 of the Part 2 Crimes includes 'statutory rape and offences against chastity, common decency, morals and the like'. One can only speculate on whether the British police might turn a blind eye to any new 'crime' of 'breach of chastity, common decency and morals', or whether James Anderton's calls for the flogging or castration of prisoners in specific situations would stimulate a response to such incidents! Suffice to say, the 1980 return indicates there were some 67,400 'estimated arrests' for this 'Part 2 crime' in the USA.

Category 19 in the report lists 'crime' arrests for 'Gambling—promoting, permitting or engaging in illegal gambling', while Category 23 concerns 'crimes' of 'Disorder and Breach of the Peace'. Neither are recordable crimes in Britain, though they are offences; but there are, as yet, no parallels with Categories 28 and 29. The former relates to 'Curfew and Loitering Laws—Offences relating to violation of local curfew or loitering ordinances where such laws exist',[52] while the latter relates to 'Runaways—Limited to Juveniles taken into protective custody under Provisions of Local Statutes'. In the UK, C. H. Rolf has suggested (*Police Review*, 9 April 1982: 693) that a Criminal Justice Bill proposal to allow the courts to order young offenders to stay at home, was too simplistic, for it 'fails to account for the reality of the home environment, which too often is the prime cause of the anti-social activities of the juvenile'. However, in line with an expansion in other measures for surveillance of the dangerous classes (Foucault 1977) and the desire for the gaze of the controlling institutions to become even more all encompassing, it seems inevitable that 'curfew breach' (like the use of identity cards) will be pursued by government and supported by their agents of control in the

---

[52] I had a graphic example of the influence of curfew controls when we visited a licensed pizza house in Newcastle with young people on a school exchange. We were about to leave my 17-year-old son and the American visitors in the restaurant disco, when a huge 6′ 4″ youth amused us by worrying about how he was to get back to his hosts without breaching curfew, and asking 'what time is juvenile curfew here?' Back in his county, curfew for juveniles was strictly enforced at 10.30 p.m., and any breach resulted in a visit to Juvenile Hall—and no doubt created a 'crime' arrest statistic along the way!

police.[53] Such controls, along with measures such as 'electronic tagging' of those on bail, seem set for the statute books, no doubt providing a new crop of offences or crimes to ensure that the adversarial, class conflict model of society is maintained; for, as Rolph (1982) recalls: 'a New York Police lieutenant once told me that the city's curfew for its delinquent under 16's was just another way of swelling the crime figures'. Of course for police purposes this juvenile curfew would be a useful statute to enact to help maintain the image of growing lawlessness, for the American Uniform Crime Reports (1981) indicate some 66,703 arrests in one year for 'crimes' of curfew and loitering violations, while 143,598 were arrested for the 'crime' of being 'runaways' (Category 29).[54]

Perhaps there is just a possibility that British society will turn out to be really seditious and even refuse to accept that such behaviour is 'criminal' or needs to be controlled. As Manning and Butler (1982: 342) suggest in an analysis of police responses to ambiguous behaviour: 'It is essential that the police are aware of their own limitations and also the limitations of law enforcement strategy to solve society's problems'. In a survey in the West Midlands police area which suggested the problem of litter in the streets was of considerable concern, Manning and Butler (ibid.) report that if the police had carried out vigorous law enforcement, it is likely it would have been a disaster. While accepting that depositing litter is an offence, the public did not expect the police to prosecute such matters. In a similar rejection of a proposed curfew law in 1982, which would have been difficult to implement, the Probation Service objected to enforcing such a regulation and becoming 'soft cops'. But of course, their concern was at least five years too late in one respect, for I had noted in the

---

[53] It can be no accident that the first group proposed to be subject to ID surveillance were 'football supporters', who have become *the* symbolic 'hooligan animals' of the era.

[54] It is difficult to objectify the statistics contained in the American Report, for p. 191 contains 'Estimated arrests' for 'unreported areas' and the 'Total Arrest Trends' listed on p. 194 show different totals for categories also listed on p. 191. Perhaps any real significance lies in their ambivalence, for we are told: 'because of rounding, items may not add to totals'; and '*estimated* arrests in 1980 exceed the Total *actual* arrests by some 4,400,000'.

bridewell that the 'prigs' had no doubt about the controlling role of the probation service, and often referred to them as 'soft cops'.

The fallacy of accepting statistical material or accounts of 'escalating crime waves' is clearly illustrated by my examples of vandalism and car theft, which say more about social history, the practices of policing, and the philosophies of control than about 'crime' itself. The mistake of predicting future trends by using American crime patterns is indicated by their 'curfew' and 'run-away' crimes, and by arbitrary cultural factors which tend to invade all crime systems:

One outstanding example of the pervasiveness of the status offender in the US juvenile criminal justice system is that of Salt Lake City, a Mormon community, where local laws reflect Mormon beliefs. In that city, approximately 1,000 juveniles are arrested each year for [the crime of] unlawful possession of tobacco. (Thorpe 1981: 10–13)

Greenwood *et al.* (1977: 84) also see the folly in attempting any comparative use of these 'American Uniform Crime Reports'. Any relevance to our own cultural patterns, it is pointed out, is remote; more often than not they merely

illustrate the futility of attempting to use either arrest rates or clearance rates as measures of performance for comparing police departments. Evidently it is impossible that departments in the South Central portion of the United States are at the same time, the best in the country and the worst in the country, but interpreting arrest and clearance rates as performance measures appears to lead to this conclusion.

And yet the pursuit of such an interpretive drama is exactly what the police in the UK have systematically undertaken for decades, by symbolically loading the crime statistics to support their practices and ideology. Meanwhile, a stream of outsiders and academics, although realizing the whole thing is less than accurate, have been kept ignorant of how the finer detail of the drama is played out. This can be illustrated by one example in my fieldnotes concerning a research officer who came into the police from industry. Early in his sojourn in the research section of the force, he was set to assess crime administration, as new forms for recording crimes were to be introduced. Returning from a three-day study of a divisional system he despondently shook his head, shocked by what he had seen:

its all about figures and how to bend them; its about illusion and presenting a front to the outside world, as well as playing games inside the
organisation . . . its got nothing to do with what is really reported as a
'crime' or what is detected, although I suppose it has a bizarre reality and
a sort of mad logic all of its own . . . (From fieldnotes, 1984)

This researcher's recognition that the crime administration system, employing dozens of people and costing thousands each year,
was in fact built and devised for a self-generating, hegemonic
expansion caused him to reappraise his own situation as a new
civilian inside the closed institution. In many ways his self-
analysis matched the reflexivity found in the post-modern anthropology of today, which recognizes that the interpretive strategies
of anthropologists are influenced and impacted upon by their own
history, relations of power, and other subjective factors (Clifford
and Marcus 1986). In his own hermeneutic appraisal of this situation, this civilian employee (trained in management studies) was
forced to abandon his own preference for an empirical, quantitative methodology, to move towards a more communicative and
dialogical epistemology in the reflexive genre (Scholte 1987: 35).
Subsequently we spent hours discussing the possibilities of presenting what he called aspects of the 'psychology of policing' to
the organization, or of including a reflexive account in the report
on what he had found.

In this mood of 'autobiognosis', however, he acknowledged that
being a 'despised civilian' and new to the institution, he would obviously fail to create any real structural change. His terms of reference, although matching the political demands of Home Office
Circular 114/83 for enhanced efficiency and effectiveness, were in
direct contradiction to the modes of thought he found entrenched
in the 'crime recording' systems. His aim to achieve administrative simplicity, he felt would inevitably be diluted by an overriding
reverence for the inculcated systems of belief and skewed practice.
As he said, 'I now began to see why the "bending and fiddling" of
"crimes" and the "criminal statistics" has such importance'. And
indeed they are essential to sustain the institutional hegemony,
which he described as 'a system defined by devices'.

It is little wonder then that the police have been reluctant to admit the academic, the outsider, or the skilled civilian to penetrate
the secrets of the system, for ideally the 'gaze' or surveillance

undertaken by the controllers must remain on the 'hooligan' population, and should not be directed inwards.

COUNTING CRIMES: BENDING AND
FIDDLING THE ACCOUNT

Even as commentators on crime statistics acknowledge, they have little objective value as a true reflection of the complexity of social events, so the criminal justice system massively invests in the idea of crime to support its practices. Undue significance continues to be given to crime figures, reinforced for an ill-informed general public by apparently authoritative sources, so that this prime symbol of the procedural drama becomes endlessly and simply regurgitated, and even headlined by an alleged quality press: 'Crime Fall hit by Rise in Sex and Violence' (*Guardian*, 15 December 1988). As a result, the idea of crime has come to achieve a significance comparable to those ritual metaphors which Turner (1974: 55) attributes with the power of being able to 'instigate social action ... condensing many references [and] uniting them into a single cognitive and affective field'. Today the statistical record is still as mythological as it was in the 1950s, yet it has assumed what Ditton (1979: 23) describes as an almost 're-ligious significance'. Hard data has become sacrosanct, so that reflexive enquiry into policing becomes even harder to justify, simply because of this reverence for a quasi-mathematical truth. Furthermore, philosophical research might easily penetrate the inherent deceptions in the metaphor, for in effect the current need to formulate corporate plans, management strategies, and other trappings of this 'business enterprise' still rests largely on the use of this manipulated falsehood.

In such a world, the measurement of a continued expansion in crime becomes a self-evident factor in the institutional mentality, for the institution cannot contemplate its reduction or contrac-tion, nor can it be expected to set out to dismantle itself. The mythology therefore quickly becomes reality, as the idea of crime turns into hard fact and the primacy of the construct is recreated at every turn. In 1980, when a Higher National Certificate in 'Police Studies' was set up at Newcastle Polytechnic, the module on 'Crime and the Criminal' was again introduced by using this idea of a knowable crime return, and attributing an objective nature to the idea of crime statistics:

it is essential to place 'crime' in quantitative terms . . . [and for the student to explore] the continuing upsurge in recorded crime since the second world war . . . which coincided with a chronic shortage in [police] manpower . . .

This predetermined belief in a world where crime has exploded since the Second World War is set to deny the student the chance to explore an alternative reality, while the stated 'chronic shortage of manpower' pre-empts any real opportunity to analyse reasons for the expansion in policing, except to set them in a predetermined mould, for the introduction to this module seems determined to replicate an overwhelming faith in a numerical truth. [55]

By the 1970s, the newly amalgamated forces began to reverse the claims of the 1950s, when the small forces were indicating an era of social calm and tranquility. New crimes such as TWOC and criminal damage, as well as the wholesale recording of much of what had previously been 'cuffed' seemed to take the executive by surprise and the root metaphor of social stability began to run amok. [56] By the middle of the decade, the forty-three forces were more or less united in presenting a public picture of soaring 'crime' as the prime indicator of their problems. However, by returning a mean 50 per cent detection rate, they also implied that the rising tide of disorder was valiantly, but only just, being held back by these newly consolidated units. [57]

During the 1970s as recording techniques were polished and

[55] Braudel (1981) suggests the growth of a belief in the supremacy of statistical numeracy is increasingly being used as a determining basis for everyday structures of action and ideology.

[56] Skolnick (1966), Lambert (1970), McCabe and Sutcliffe (1978), Bottomley and Coleman (1981), and Farrington and Dowds (1984) all attempt to show how variable police recording techniques have influenced statistical returns of 'crime'. Farrington and Dowds (ibid.) recognize that 'car theft' and 'criminal damage' statistics have had the marked effect I have set out to demonstrate above, and theirs is one of the few studies to detail the crucial influences of these recent changes in classification.

[57] In the 1977 Northumbria annual report, crimes were reported to have increased by 15.1% on the previous year, while the detections at 49.5% were 2% lower than in 1976. The 1978 report indicated another 2.9% rise in crimes recorded and detections at 51.2%. Suffolk reported their 1979 detections at 56.4% and Hertfordshire claimed 54%, while in 1980 South Yorkshire police had 51.16%. By the early 1980s it was noticeable that many forces were now claiming just below 50% and in doing so appeared to reflect the pressures in society, as unemployment and social *Angst* increased. By 1981 Kent were regretting a drop to 47% detections, while Northumbria reported another 9% increase in crime and only 49.6% detections.

sharpened, some particularly specific practices were employed by detective departments to ensure their detected crimes remained at 50 per cent of those recorded. At this time the Home Office 'Instructions for the Preparation of Statistics relating to Crime' (1971) allowed 'crimes' to be detected not only when someone appeared at court and was convicted, but also:

(*a*) when a person is charged and acquitted;

(*b*) when 'crimes' are 'taken into consideration' after conviction;

(*c*) when there is some practical hindrance to prosecution, e.g. if the suspect dies or if the victim and/or key witnesses are unwilling to give evidence;

(*d*) when a person admits a crime and is cautioned or is under the age of criminal responsibility, i.e. 10 years;

(*e*) when a person who is already serving a custodial sentence admits a crime but it is decided that 'no useful purpose would be served by proceeding with the charge'.

It is apparent that in (*c*), it becomes possible for a dead man to provide a detection, while in (*b*), the minor theft from a shop taken into consideration (TIC) can be set against an unsolved robbery to provide a 50 per cent detection rate. In (*e*) above, the prisoner can 'clear his slate' and perhaps give the divisional 'clear-up' team 'fifty for nowt' (fifty detections for little or no effort). As Skolnick (1966) suggests, such admissions are 'a valued commodity for exchange, a substantial part of the police administrative process and a major indicator of success'.

Let us look briefly at each of these categories in turn.

Crimes detected when a person is charged and subsequently acquitted

At the time a person is charged with any crime from petty theft to murder, the normal practice is for the Officer in Charge of the case to submit a supplementary crime report and be awarded a detection. Any subsequent acquittal might follow months later after remands, adjournments, and trial; but the detection stands. Indeed the traditional party that detectives always hold on any murder inquiry always takes place on the evening of the 'arrest and charge', not on conviction or acquittal; for the case is 'wrapped up' on a charge and only the protracted file preparation follows. By the time the case is heard, many months will have elapsed and detectives on the case will be dispersed to other duties. The crime is detected, however, even if the accused is acquitted.

After conviction, a person can ask for other crimes to be TIC

The accused agrees he has committed a list of crimes, signs to that effect, and these are considered before sentence is passed. In recent years the TIC is a disappearing commodity for exchange. It is often said now that 'only the insane or the first-timers will have TICs', for the simple acquiescence of the 'prig' to an exhortation to 'come clean lad, get it off your chest and you'll feel better with it out in the open' seems to be vanishing, along with the processes of law that went with it. It is now understood that 'only a fool admits TICs ... with a list of TICs against you, you'll get more bird ...' (Fieldnotes: bridewell 'prig'). However, there are still times when the recovery of a horde of stolen property from parked cars or shops makes one initial arrest into a statistical gold-mine. As one detective said: 'just give me one milk-token thief, or a car-badge-juvenile each month, and everything will be all right'. One juvenile crime file which crossed my desk as I first drafted a seminar paper which was used as a basis for this section, had 134 TICs for the theft of trivia from stores. The injured persons—Woolworths, Boots, and the other High Street multiples, as well as the times and dates of the offences, were carefully arranged to allow each to stand as separate crimes, rather than be counted as one series of crimes which would have reduced the numbers of detections dramatically (and which I will discuss in the next section when I outline aspects of the 'counting rules'). Mawby (1979) found that 40 per cent of crimes in Sheffield were cleared up by TICs and other indirect means, while Lambert (1970: 43) rightly understood the search for TICs had played a main part in the game, and was a major symbol of police success: 'this dependence on getting offenders to confess to maintain a success rate, has ... important consequences for police administration'. These 'important consequences' are just that! They are crucial to the institution and cause some detectives to have few qualms about bending the rules. The quest for detections is as basic a task for the detectives as it is to 'nail' or 'fix' the 'prig', for it forms a homologous place in the maintenance of position and esteem.

Detected crimes all carry a potential for enhancement of the detection rates. Each detected theft of a social security giro cheque, for example, can hold out the possibility of producing at least two further 'clear-ups'. The initial crime of theft might be followed by a second of forgery when the thief signs the giro with a false name purporting to be the person named on the cheque; while a third could be a 'deception' created when the cheque is presented at the post office—or 'three for one'. The stolen television or video from one crime of burglary, if sold to a second-hand dealer can become a second crime of 'criminal deception' (i.e. the assertion by the thief that he had authority as owner, to sell the goods). Always the ability to have these recorded as separated detections will depend on the skill of the detective and on the diligence of the Force Statistical Officers to search out these attempts to double or treble up one event, an activity which is contrary to the Home Office instructions issued on the 'counting rules'. Of course undetected thefts of giro cheques or television sets are never recorded as two or three crimes committed; not until a 'body' materializes!

Ditton (1979: 39) quotes from the *Newcastle Evening Chronicle* (5 February 1977), when a 17-year-old appeared before the local Crown Court and asked for 31 TICs:

Judge Roderick Smith rapped Northumbria (Police) for abusing the system where an offender appears in court and has other offences considered. When a 17-yr-old youth appeared before him, the judge was asked to take 31 other offences into consideration, after the youth had been convicted of taking a car without consent. The youth's counsel said the other offences were nearly all for trying to take cars. Judge Smith said: a lad tries to get into 50 different cars, gets into the fifty-first, appears charged with it and 50 other offences to be taken into consideration. All it can be thought to be doing is to improve the detection rate of the Northumbria Constabulary. It is an abuse of the system whereby other offences are taken into consideration. I keep on saying it—no one takes the slightest notice of what I say. Except in this case, these 31 offences will not be taken into consideration.

Even if the accused reneges on his admissions in court (which happens regularly) or the judiciary refuse to allow the TICs, it is still possible for the detective to submit them with the statement of admission taken during the investigation and claim to his senior officer (who may well have been through the same situation), that the crimes were almost certainly committed by the accused, and to ask they be recorded as 'detections—no useful purpose to be served in charging the offender with these and taking him back before the court'. The criminal record of the accused will not show any subsequent account of them, but the crimes can be accepted by the senior officer to be written off as detections in the Home Office returns.

Other more dubious means exist for fiddling TICs and I have listened as detectives discussed ways of 'making one or two for nowt'. One such fiddle was described:

you get a young juvenile admitting say 5 crimes. You have the five typed up onto 5 separate TIC forms (where there is space for 3 or 4 to be listed). Get the juvenile to sign each and submit the necessary papers to the court. Wait until the case is over and all the papers are in, and then add perhaps one crime to each sheet from the lists of undetected rubbish. No one is hurt, the sheets and the supplementaries go off to HQ and the division gets another half-dozen rubbishy crimes solved, and even the kid's record only shows the original five TICs. The detection rate is better, everyone is happy . . . (From fieldnotes)

The incidence of getting 'two for one' in cases of theft and the subsequent 'deception', or 'theft' and 'going equipped for stealing' (widely used against car thieves) became so prevalent at one time, that a force instruction was issued in an attempt to prevent its occurrence; however, other ways of making 'crime' still occur. I was told of the cautions imposed for 'a theft of a tin of biscuits' passed around a schoolyard which became one theft and several crimes of handling stolen property; while the ten cigarettes stolen from the corner shop became one crime of theft and nine schoolyard 'handlings' of one cigarette. These 'cautioned' crimes (about which I say more below) like TICs, have to be submitted to the HQ stats. department at irregular intervals to avoid the scrutiny which sets out to confound attempts by the detectives to record *series* crimes (claim one detection), as *individual* crimes (claim each detection separately).

It is not always easy for the civilian clerks in stats. departments to spot duplications when handling many thousands of 'crime' reports, and although end totals are often computed, it is curious how slow some forces have been in setting up computerized systems which allow easy cross-reference to culprit, crime-type, and other factors that reveal attempts to get extra detections. By 1983, Northumbria had spent millions on a massive command

and control system, but still manually recorded many aspects of 'crime reporting'.

Often it is only luck when the stats. departments spot the duplication, as they chance to see an unusual name of an injured person (or accused) reappearing on new crime reports submitted weeks after the initial record has been catalogued and filed. It was by such a chance that the stats. clerks spotted a theft of a bicycle by three young men acting together had become three separately numbered crimes of theft of a wheel, theft of a wheel, and theft of a frame committed by three individuals. It was a similar chance that revealed one theft of a table from a public house committed by five men had been recorded as five separate detected 'crimes'— two of theft of the table and three of 'handling stolen property': 'sometimes they blatantly duplicate and put the same crime through two or three times with separate numbers, hoping we'll not tie them together' (Crime stats. clerk: from fieldnotes).

Practical hindrance to prosecution: death of witness or suspect or unwillingness of an essential witness

If the suspect to a murder commits suicide after committing the crime, then a detection is almost certainly assured. However, even the burglar who dies while waiting trial can be a source of detections and the counting rules allow any admissions made to be classed as detections, provided a senior officer agrees. The reluctance of a witness to appear in assault cases, which is especially prevalent in the domestic dispute, can also be a steady source of 'No Further Action' detections, and the incidence of detections following an NFA decision in minor assault cases never pursued to prosecution must be considerable.

Admissions by those under the age of criminal responsibility and those cautioned by the police

When a child under the age of 10 years admits crimes or a person agrees to be cautioned rather than prosecuted (often used for juveniles between 10 years and 17 years and for first offenders), the crimes are classed as detected. These can be a great source of detections, and fiddles to extend on these can be considerable.

Most of these manipulations again concern ways in which 'series' crimes can be separated out (and are discussed below in the next section on the counting rules), while others relate to crimes which might not even exist and offenders who are invented because of this demand for detections. One middle-ranking detective of my acquaintance created crimes which had not occurred and which were then admitted by juveniles who were similar inventions of the mind. These mythical juveniles were then cautioned or were allegedly under the age of criminal responsibility, allowing for 'detections' without a court appearance. Two or three such 'crimes' per week (about 1–2 per cent of his subdivisional totals) gave his subdivision a healthy detection rate and may well have helped him in the 'promotion stakes'.[58] Picking fictitious injured persons from the voters' register can be hazardous, however, especially when it is out of date and a crime clerk recognizes the name of a relative who died some two years previous! Of course, on his own 'detection' and fall from grace, his actions were not recorded as a 'crime' of 'criminal deception', although his disciplinary punishment of a 'return to uniform duties' again supports my point about the status of the detective in comparison to 'uniformed patrol'. Another detective was not so lucky; Roger Anderson was gaoled for six months for forgery and perverting the course of justice for much the same sort of activity (*Daily Mail*, 25 March 1980):

he gave himself less work by reporting the arrest of imaginary people for crimes that never happened . . . In files for which he was responsible fabrications are two a penny, and almost every document one turns over is false in one way or another . . . The worst thing he did was to invent defendants for real crimes, because the real criminal may have escaped being brought to justice . . . the court heard that Anderson invented a man called Mensell to admit a fictitious offence of indecency and then had him pleading guilty to real offences of stealing women's clothing. When Mensell was due to appear in Court, Anderson had him conveniently killed in a motorway accident . . . Nobody suffered as a result of these offences. Nobody could suffer because the people named in the offences were wholly fictitious.

---

[58] 'The promotion stakes' is another phrase used constantly within police culture, and is a further indication of the way that policing is considered to be a metaphorical game of chance, lodged in a drama that is enacted by participants skilled in the use of manœuvres such as the juggling created by the 'bending and fiddling' of crime figures.

Those in custody who admit crimes and no useful purpose would be served in proceeding with a charge

A person serving 'time' for crimes such as theft or burglary can, as I have suggested earlier, be regarded as socially dead and will not usually be prosecuted for other minor crimes he admits. However, he is still a prime source of detections, and after sentence will almost certainly be visited in prison by a 'clear-up squad' or 'prison visit team'. Their sole task is to follow up convicted 'prigs' and get them to 'cough' as many previously unadmitted crimes as possible. At a time when the TIC has largely disappeared from the scene, the prison visit write-off has taken off as a valuable source of detections, and today 'prigs' often ask for a visit and willingly 'clear the slate' and 'cough' outstanding crimes.

Using his potential for detections as a commodity for exchange as Skolnick (1966) suggested, the convict gains information about his family or contemporaries, and earns some time out of his cell away from his fellow inmates. In addition he solidifies contacts with detectives who will, no doubt, remain his adversaries in the future. He has access to cigarettes and may ask for family favours on the outside, while the detectives can clear perhaps fifty or sixty burglaries or other crimes, which are then written off as detected. The veracity of these 'coughs' can, at times, be somewhat suspect and there are clear indications that not all the crimes submitted as prison visit write-offs might stand up to close scrutiny. Stories of detectives who have left prison with blank statement forms signed by the inmates, which then have admissions of fifty or sixty 'rubbish crimes' written in, are not unknown. On other visits the 'prig' has allegedly run his finger down the lists of outstanding crimes and agreed to take 'some rubbish', as long as each was less than, say, £50 or £60 in value. He then gets on with the real business of making some 'snout' (enhancing a supply of tobacco or cigarettes), talking to the detectives about 'jobs', friends, relatives, and life on the outside.

Occasionally prison visit or 'clear-up' squads have fallen from grace when their bending and fiddling have come unstuck and the admissions by prisoners have been found to be less than accurate. In 1981 the chief constable of Northumbria denied his officers had given prisoners money, tobacco, and cigarettes to admit crimes they had never committed, but it was reported in the *Newcastle Journal* (10 September 1981) that

he did not deny that five officers had been returned to uniform duties
. . . after a detective constable submitted false statements which led to the
clearing up of several crimes . . . That officer together with a Sergeant
and two other detective officers from the same Sub-Division were transferred to other duties.

Following other disclosures in the national press that crimes were
being falsely admitted, some forces dispensed with special units
for 'clear-ups' altogether, leaving the responsibility for visits on
the officer in charge of each case. In addition, in the same way that
questionable dealings with informants resulted in the issue
of rules of conduct, so the rules relating to prison visits were
tightened up and a list of 'reasons for interviewing persons serving custodial sentences' was issued. At a subsequent Senior CID
conference I attended, however, it was agreed it was impossible to
discontinue the practice if for no other reason than because of the
numbers of detections the 'write-off' system produced.

In 1982, a detective inspector about to submit forty-nine burglaries valued at £37,000 as prison visit write-offs complained
over a coffee in my office about the institutional desperation for
detections which subsequently hit the lowest ranks when this
political need forced the constables to 'fiddle'. At the time he
was submitting this list to HQ asking they be recorded as 'No
Further Action Detections—offender in custody and the court
is unlikely to vary the sentence'; he shook his head somewhat
woefully, saying:

What are things coming to Malcolm? . . . I can't charge him with any of
them; the first one we charge will be the last detection we get this way
and the figures would plummet. This 'prison visit' system is a scourge;
it's a sickness and yet everyone plays the game until the bloody wheel
comes off.

Such admissions have played a major part in the detection figures
in the recent past. After the Northumbria system of prison visits
was developed, the resulting detections rose from 2,700 in 1974,
to 20,500 in 1980 and in one division in 1980 40 per cent of all
detections were cleared up in this way. These 'subsequents' or
follow-up detections have other idiosyncratic properties and it is
always likely that recorded crimes and the detections may appear
seriously out of synchronicity. For example, crimes from one
year, say 1989, can be detected by a prison visit in 1990 and be set

against that year's record of crimes committed, so that detections may well exceed crimes committed, especially in the early part of the year. Another colleague in the CID described how his divisional commander had triumphantly called him in to expose a 'fiddle' that he had spotted: 'I see we've had a dozen indecent assaults this year yet we've got 16 detected in this month's figures [February]: how do you account for that?' My detective friend told me he had to explain 'to that fool of a commander' how 'subsequents' from prison visits had accounted for the majority of the sixteen detections and that out of the dozen reported so far, 'we'd be lucky if we had one or two cleared up'. He went on to describe how the commander had not really understood the whole concept of 'subsequents' until it 'had been spelled out to him in words of one syllable'. 'But then', he concluded, 'he's never been in the department so he obviously knows nowt.'

A similar hiccup or degradation of the system occurred when a good run of early detections from prison visits gave one division a 170 per cent detection rate for house burglary in the first two months of the year. Of course, it was then necessary to hold some back and submit them as the year progressed to ensure the figures matched the expectancies of the hierarchies or some commanders, who often do not seem to understand the nuances of 'doing the business'. It is common for detectives to be asked to hold some detections back until next month if the figures are satisfactory, or alternatively to be asked by the detective inspector to 'pull out any "keepy-backs" you've got tucked away this month, we're running a bit short . . .'. At other times the detective inspector will tell his men, 'Its all right this month, I've got a few in the drawer which will see us out.'

Some years after all this has become regular practice in many county forces, it seems that the Metropolitan Police will belatedly follow the shire forces in taking on the prison visit system. The *Police Review* (14 December 1984: 2406) reported:

Frank Dobson, the Labour M.P. asked the Home Secretary when he expected the clear-up rate for crime in the Metropolitan Police area to match that of the West Midlands [The West Mids. rate at the end of 1983 was 35.8 per cent; the Met. figure was 17 per cent] Mr. Dobson also asked what steps were taken by the Metropolitan Police to study training methods in Forces with higher clear-up rates . . . Giles Shaw, for the Home Secretary, said there were regular exchanges to study the . . .

methods of other Forces and that the Met. has examined the investigative methods ... He said that an experiment is now taking place in which convicted prisoners are interviewed about unsolved crimes.

It seems hardly surprising that detectives have become cynical about this 'numbers game'. One 'clear-up squad' detective I had worked with as a young CID officer in the 1960s, revealed the inherent irony generated by the system when I visited his station in 1981 and met him for the first time in three or four years. He showed me into the 10′ square office he shared with his partner; and asked me:

'What do you think of this? 1,500 recorded detections from this room this year, for this division.'

'What percentage of those are genuine?', I asked, with a grin on my face. '50 per cent?'

He assumed a look of mock horror and outrage, placed his hand on his heart, then laughingly said, 'You're being generous, aren't you!'

Both he and I understood these statistical truths were a relative commodity, for the success of the unit was always measured in terms of its 'clear-ups' for the record of detections. The resulting cynicism manifest in our exchange, I would argue, occurred in part because of an unspoken acknowledgement of the obvious complicity which some chief officers and senior detectives play in this scrabble for an acceptable crime figure, for many have engaged in similar practices themselves as they have struggled up the hierarchies, on what Graef (1989) calls their 'obsessive quest for promotion'. And during the amalgamations and the growth in these hegemonic empires, which these statistical 'waves' of crime have helped generate and sustain, these same men have willingly ensured that such practices have taken a deep hold in the collective consciousness of the culture. However, in true hierarchical fashion and in keeping with the current refusal of senior figures in other executive corridors of power to accept responsibility when the 'wheel comes off' or fiddling of the account is revealed, it is left to those at the bottom end to take the discipline and punishment. On more than one occasion when a figure-fiddling exercise was exposed or went wrong it was the firm conviction of those in the department that the buck stopped with the detective sergeant or occasionally the detective inspector, while beyond that rank 'you were safe'.

By the late 1970s the use of 'crime waves' to indicate 'busyness' and a 'backs to the wall' mentality forced the Home Office to introduce controls under the 'Crime Counting Rules'; and in Northumbria we invented the naïve simplicities of 'Manpower Provisions', based on the fallacy that crime statistics alone could determine the deployment of manpower. It was proposed to allocate men to divisions solely in relation to their returns of crimes reported. No other measure such as population density, social factors, economic opportunity, road mileages, dispersal of communities, housing types, or any other influence which might have weighted 'crime' was to be included; and no other aspect of police work was to be added to the equation. Only crime was to be used, and each geographical division was to receive its slice of the available manpower dependent on how much crime it recorded.

The result was obvious, for each divisional commander simply ordered his section and subdivisional heads to record all the crime possible. Someone, of course, had to come bottom of the table or list, and when one subdivision reported a 2 per cent drop in crime, and its neighbour had risen by the same amount, it seemed the commander might have to lose 40–50 men from his establishment. Of course this loss would mean his reduced manpower would probably record even less crime in the following year and his subsequent allocation would drop again. The cumulative effect was that by 1980 one subdivision was calculated to need so few men that it was jokingly said the superintendent would be driving the panda, acting as foot patrol, serving as counter clerk, and logging in the prisoner which he would have to go out and arrest!

Elsewhere, a population drift into a new town caused crime to be displaced as residential patterns changed, so that detectives were sent out to find the unreported 'dark' crime in an effort to keep the divisional figures up. Many small shops do not report the petty shoplifting that goes on, for a variety of reasons, not the least because a court appearance as a witness could well close the shop down for half a day. Two sergeants concentrated on this area and were able to come back with several dozens of detections for thefts from shop (usually committed by juveniles and children under the age of criminal responsibility). These deeds had previously been resolved at the store counter by mediation and discretion, but as detected crimes they helped ensure the division could claim its share of the manpower in the following year, and of course helped add to the 'crime wave' that inexplicably was rising year by year at the time. Not unnaturally only detected crimes were really welcomed, for although the commander might want more crimes recorded, the detectives could not afford to jeopardize their system or their career prospects by having a surge in crime and fewer detections. It is only a short step from this type of exercise which has hierarchical weight behind it to the situation I have outlined where someone decides to record 'crimes' which have not happened, and are committed by 'offenders' who do not exist, but who allegedly have been 'cautioned by a senior officer'. For only two or three such detections per week can make a considerable difference to the acceptability of divisional statistics.

When the exercise had been running for three years, I was able to have some influence on its discontinuity, for it was again going to take forty men away from a quieter division and redistribute them. At this time I was in Research and Development and we were able to show that such a measurement of resource allocation was somewhat simplistic,[59] by forecasting that one subdivision would soon have no men at all. As a result, 'Manpower Provisions' was abandoned for three years until I was at a quiet subdivision, when another new superintendent in research[60] reintroduced it on the direction of chief officers, and our division suddenly lost twenty-one officers from its authorized establishment.

THE COUNTING RULES

Almost inevitably the 'crime wave' which the police found to be so useful an indicator of productivity became untenable to other sections of society, and political measures were introduced to curtail the expansion which the control industry had enjoyed. By 1979 the Home Office became obliged to impose a formula to

[59] The desire to deal in such simple statistical 'truths' has a profound influence. As Southgate (1984) pointed out, any hermeneutic exploration of ideas and attitudes is at odds with the accepted methodology of training. Most police courses deal in facts rather than ideas and policemen are less than ready to acknowledge emotions, feelings, and perceptions, for they cannot comprehend such abstractions as having a factual reality.

[60] During my bridewell days, this unpopular senior officer acquired the nickname 'nasal spray' = 'a little squirt that gets right up your nose'.

suggest that less crime was occurring. If properly instituted, this measure would present a less dramatic appearance of disorder and social unrest to the public, for the moral panic and the unleashed tiger were becoming difficult to contain as the forty-three forces trawled up an increasing surge in crime, and then skilfully manipulated the detections to show their efficacy in holding back the tide of mayhem.

Walker (1971: 24–5) has shown how multiple crimes can be generated from one circumstance, making similar points to those I included earlier in my hypothetical case study:

> an advertiser causes a fraudulent advertisement to appear in 16 issues of *The Times* and defrauds 80 people; a father has sexual intercourse with his daughter 10 times before his 'crime' comes to light. A cashier pockets small sums of money each week . . . a burglar breaks into a hotel and takes property from 10 guests. How many crimes and involved in each case . . .?

Again the answer, as Ditton (1979: 21) indicates, has got to be: 'as many as you want (to react to) . . .'.

By 1979, the police were better practised at recording the 'crimes' they wished to react to, and especially those with 'a body' to sustain the detection rate, and in that year the Home Office introduced measures in an attempt to curtail the multiple recording of crimes, such as those described above by Walker (1971). Detailed rules were issued to the police in a document: *Crime Statistics: Counting Rules for Serious Offences—Home Office Requirements*, which set out to ensure that such 'multiples' were recorded as 'only one continuous, or "series crime"...'. These directives were made under Sect. 54 of the Police Act 1964, and their implementation was agreed by ACPO.

The main requirement in the Rules concerns the way numbers of crimes are to be recorded and counted. Only the most serious offence (i.e. crime) in any series of offences will be counted. In other words, in my earlier hypothetical example the 'prig' would statistically have committed only the one crime of rape; i.e. the most serious. Severity is to be determined by the sentence and the Counting Rules set out the penalties for each, in order to determine the most serious:

> At the beginning of each of the three categories (Violence against the person, Sexual offences, Other offences) is a section listing the offences in

that part in order of maximum penalty. This is to assist in determining the most serious offence to be counted where several offences are committed in one incident. (Counting Rules, Para. 2(2): 5)

However, in the event of my hypothetical incident ever occurring, it is unlikely the police would only count one crime. It is almost certain they would count one in each of the three sections at least, and the detectives would be sure to try to count many more by the use of administrative lacunae in the local recording processes.

Offences (crimes) which are reported separately by the public, we are informed by the Counting Rules, can be counted separately and allowed to stand as individually numbered crimes when they are cleared up, even if it becomes apparent they form a part of a continuous series. However, the Home Office urge that 'serious consideration must be given, at the time the offences are reported, to the possibility that they are part of a continuous offence' (Counting Rules, Para. 3(2): 6). For over a decade now, these 'continuous' offences have been a source of great dispute, argument, and manipulation by some forces in their efforts to maintain their inculcated presentations of social reality. Some stats. departments seem to be less than scrupulous in allowing separately counted series, while others fight continuous battles with the divisional detectives as they set out to bend the Counting Rules to their favour. On one occasion in 1987 I heard a superintendent (an ex-detective) propose the use of the Force Statistical Officer on a management project, away from the immediate assessment of crime reports. Outlining the value of this move to management services department, he grinned mischievously as he added 'and it'll do wonders for the crime figures'. For stats. officers are adept at spotting attempts to get 'associated offences' (as the continuous series is also known) recorded separately, and thus getting 'three or four for one'.

Futher changes in the Counting Rules since 1979 seem to reflect the political use of 'crime' as a mirror image or metaphor of social unrest or socio-political dominance, and not surprisingly in these circumstances, they tend to have been accorded only a token acceptance by detectives who understand these changes have a political nuance which lies well outside their daily experiences of dealing with 'prigs'. In the circumstances it should come as no surprise to find they have had few qualms about bending the rules to suit their own needs, for their *habitus* of success, promotion, and status is built on their ability to maintain a suitable 'detection rate'. It is therefore almost a given fact that their interpretation of the Rules will follow and support the existing modes of thought upon which the police system is built.

In my hypothetical example, the youth who took the milk tokens from fifty doorsteps might well have committed fifty crimes, or only one, depending on whether the crimes were reported and recorded separately or in a series. Initially, in 1979, the Rules directed such thefts were associated offences and would be recorded as one continuous crime. If (and this is unlikely) all of these thefts were reported, and no immediate 'body' was anticipated, a detective had different options open to him, depending on his ability to play out the nuances of the system. He could:

(*a*) record fifty separate *undetected* crimes immediately, if he was foolish enough to try to convince his Detective Inspector that he never considered for one moment that these were a series of thefts committed by one person.

(*b*) record one continuous *undetected crime*, following the instructions in the Counting Rules to the letter.

(*c*) hold them back for a few days to see if a 'body' was forthcoming.

Option (*a*) would earn him few favours, especially if the fifty crimes remained undetected. Option (*b*) is more attractive, for if the crimes remained undetected he only needs one detection from somewhere else to maintain a 50 per cent detection rate. The third option has attractions, for if the detective finds a culprit, he can then record the fifty as separate crimes, and have 'a nice little roll-up'. Of course he can only allow them to lie unrecorded for a short period, for 'if the wheel comes off' to reveal he has not immediately recorded them, he can be disciplined. However chances are often worth taking, as the following incident illustrates:

... a youth has been brought in for shoplifting in the town centre and is searched. The gaoler turns out his pockets and milk tokens tumble out everywhere ... We phone the division from which they have been stolen and a detective from the 'clear-up' squad comes down. He arranges to see the youth and his father at his divisional station in two days' time to 'sort out this little business'. By then, he will have recorded these as perhaps 70 separate undetected thefts after he has knocked on a few doors. Then he will 're-arrest' the kid when he comes in, which will allow these 70 to stand as separate 'crimes', even though it is 'now apparent' that these form part of a continuous offence. (Bridewell fieldnote)

Even if the juvenile is cautioned in this case, it matters not! The counting system is irrelevant to the court proceedings or to cautions. It is merely how crimes are counted for the statistical returns, and the whole transaction is best understood if we note how the detective describes this incident as a 'little business', in which—it could be said—he enhances his capital in the form of statistical returns.

Early in 1983 the Counting Rules were amended once again. Milk tokens or milk stolen from doorsteps of individual houses was now to be construed as 'having remained in the constructive possession of the house'. Such thefts were therefore to stand as separate crimes, having spent the previous four years as continuous offences. In February of that year, I recorded my conversation with a stats. clerk who had just had an argument with a detective friend of mine:

STATS. Your friend has just had words with us. He's not very pleased. He put two crimes through, one for theft of 80 pints of milk and one for 50. I told him that he now had to put in 130 separate crimes ... and he's not amused!
ME. Why is that, aren't they still a continuous offence?
STATS. Not any longer.
ME. Weren't they detected?
STATS. Of course not, why do you think he was annoyed?

I then went to the detective inspector on my subdivision, described the same event, and asked him how he would resolve it:

'That's easy', he told me, 'you have to argue that as the householders have not paid for the milk, it is not in their constructive possession and still remains under the constructive possession and ownership of the milkman, so only one crime has been committed against him. Mind you, are you sure that he's not just making sure he gets 130 recorded and has a body tucked up his sleeve to produce in a couple of days?'

'Bouncy' cheques from a stolen cheque book, however, are still to be considered as 'associated' or 'continuous' offences and only one crime of criminal deception should be recorded regardless of the number of cheques issued. Such paradox in the Rules offends the sense of order which detectives operate by and cheque book deceptions are one of the crimes which stats. departments recognize detectives may well attempt to fiddle to get extra 'clear-ups'. The practice is simple, and the detective with a 'body' for ten 'bouncy' cheques might well try to put in ten separate crime reports, each separately numbered to indicate ten crimes committed and ten crimes cleared up. To avoid the stats. clerks spotting each is part of a series which should only count as one crime, he will submit the individually numbered crime reports over a period of days or even weeks, hoping they will be 'lost' in the deluge of reports submitted. If the ten reports are submitted over a month or two, they may well be hidden among 20,000 others that have arrived during that time. As the injured persons will be different on each report (e.g. Woolworth's, Boot's the Chemists, Marks & Spencer, Comet, Dixon's, etc.), the only way the stats. clerks may have of spotting the ten are a series is to check the arrested person or culprit on each report and compare each one against the other. Some stats. department clerks have developed elaborate indices to spot these attempts by the detectives to make ten detections when the Rules only allow one.

Crimes recorded are also defined in the Rules by peculiar temporal measures which specify that an 'occasion' affects the way a crime is to be counted. In burglary, robbery, theft, handling stolen property, fraud, forgery, and criminal damage, the police are instructed to 'record one offence for each victim on each "occasion". An "occasion" is classed as a 24 hour period'. At a CID conference in 1982, those present were reminded that when a series of thefts occurred against the same person with more than 24 hours between each, separate crimes should be recorded, and the copies of the Counting Rules in the stats. departments are sprinkled with bizarre examples of 'continuous offences' and 'separate occasions'. Many of these have been defined by the Home Office or been added to by the clerks as they have consulted the Home Office over some specific ruling, such as page 45 of the Rules, for Rape, Classification 19/1:

A   Four males rape three girls   Count 3 offences.
     twice each on the same
     occasion.

B   Two males assist a third to rape   Count 1 offence.
     a woman.

C	A male rapes a girl, detains her against her will and rapes her again later.	Count 1 offence.
D	A young person having temporary charge of young children on several occasions admits to having committed 2 rapes on one young child and 1 on another and several indecent assaults and gross indecencies.	If the 2 rapes were on separate occasions count 3 offences. Count the indecent assaults separately if the children were unwilling. Gross indeceny (offence 74) is not countable.

For the extremely unusual crime of 'sending unworthy ships to sea', the instruction is to 'record 1 offence for each initial sending, irrespective of the number of intermediate ports the ship calls at'. At p. 26 of the Counting Rules for 'Assault Occasioning Actual Bodily Harm', Classification 8/6, the stats. officers have added:

a husband assaults his wife on a number of different occasions	Count 1 offence for each occasion.

Under Rule 8, 'Aggravated Burglary in a Dwelling' (Classification 29), there are a number of examples of how to count crimes, which 'also cover classifications 28, 30 and 31'. A number of examples are given, such as:

F.	A wounding (classif. 5/1) occurs in the course of a burglary.	Count 1 offence of wounding and no burglary.
	A wounding (classif. 8/1) occurs in the course of a burglary.	Count 1 offence of burglary and no wounding.

In these cases, the classification of which crime is to be counted is dependent on the degree of injury in the wounding. When the wounding is categorized as more serious it supersedes the burglary in the rules.

At example L, the stats. clerks have added the following comment:

L.	Four huts on a building site are burgled; there is a perimeter fence.	Count 1 offence.
M.	As example L, but with no perimeter fence.	Count 4 offences.

Here the perimeter fence affords what is known as 'protection', thus creating only one 'crime'. When I have asked detectives how they would record the incident, they all respond by asking the question which determines their practice: 'is there a body?' If there is not, then there *is* a perimeter fence. If there is a 'body' then any fence is conveniently ignored and they claim four crimes detected. Thefts from cars on car parks will often be statistically determined in a similar manner.

Under 'Other Criminal Damage' (classification 58, p. 92), where the heading instructs: 'One offence for each occasion and offender/group of offenders', the stats. clerks have added several examples, such as:

A.	A group of offenders damage several different properties on their way home from a party.	Count 1 (continuous) offence because the rule is 1 offence for each occasion and offender/group offenders.
B.	An offender damages garden sheds in several roads on several occasions.	Count each date as 1 offence unless the incidents occur within 24 hrs of each other.

Stats. officers invariably acknowledge that the whole system is played out as a big game, and when the Rules were once again amended in the early 1980s, a stats. officer (who had been on the Working Party considering the amendments) told me that as they came away from the meeting they were asking themselves how long it would take detectives to find loopholes in the new instructions in order to maintain their practices.

At page 80 of the Rules, under classification 53/2 'Obtaining Pecuniary Advantage by Deception', the stats. clerks have added examples which clearly acknowledge these attempts by detectives to obtain statistical advantage:

C.	A person has obtained money by deceiving a number of people in a variety of ways; this is not discovered until he is interrogated for some other offence.	Count 1 offence for each method of deception that is substantially different.
D.	A self-employed motor cycle dealer forged 140 insurance cover notes with intent to defraud 3 separate insurance companies. He also dishonestly obtained cash from 134 persons	Count 1 offence of forgery (Rule 9). Do not count the dishonest obtaining of cash since forgery is the more serious element in the incident.

by falsely purporting to have
arranged insurance cover.
These offences were
'discovered' when the offender
asked for them to be taken into
consideration in court.

F. It is discovered that money was   Count 2 (continuous) offences as
illegally drawn each week from   each Pension book provided the
2 Pension books, one issued by   means of committing a continuous
the D.H.S.S. and one by the   series of deceptions.
local County Council, the true
recipient having died 15 years
earlier. A total of 1560 offences
are presented at Court.

The 1,560 offences 'presented at court' in example F and the 134
offences which were 'discovered' when the offender asked for
them to be taken into consideration in court are obvious attempts
by detectives to swell their detection rates, and I know of many
other occasions when such 'series' crimes became separate
'occasions'.

Throughout the pages of the Counting Rules similar examples
emphasize how crime generally relates to minor offences, such as
damage to sheds or the theft of trivial items; for rape and aggravated burglaries are thankfully still rare events. And although
by the early 1980s Northumbria was claiming well in excess
of 100,000 established crimes each year, we might well wonder
how many single crimes were recorded as series, or vice versa,
and how many actually occurred or were being submitted for
misrecording?

In this illusory world which has long dealt in the rituals of
'cuffing', 'creating', 'keepy-backs juggling', 'fiddling', and 'bending', I suggest the way that crime recording is manipulated
means that any statistical reality is best considered as a reflection
of the semantic values of a xenophobic and defensive institutional
system, largely enacted for the benefit of those inside the organization. Meanwhile the theatre surrounding the Counting
Rules remains relatively unknown as an aspect of a ritualized
drama played out for limited public consumption by skilled actors
who operate in a world of 'clear-ups', 'roll-ups', and occasional
'cock-ups' when 'the wheel comes off'.

OTHER TIMES, OTHER PLACES: SAME BENDING, SAME FIDDLES

In July 1986 Constable Ron Walker of Kent Police 'went public' in the *Observer* (13 July 1986) detailing various ways in which the Kent detectives had swelled their detection rates:

one division had increased its clear-up rates from 24.4% to 69.5% ... methods used included taking down a random selection of car numbers, obtaining the names of the owners from PNC [Police National Computer] and then persuading an offender to admit stealing the cars ... A statement in which an offender admitted 54 burglaries some of which occurred two years earlier was written down in 60 minutes although it included details of addresses and property stolen. (*Police Review*, 6 March 1987)

At this time I was one of thirteen subdivisional commanders in West Mercia Police, with a team of detectives skilled in 'doing the business'. Their immediate reaction was that Walker had 'lost his marbles in going public', especially as he had gone to the Metropolitan Police with his tale of administrative corruption. For it was axiomatic to my CID colleagues that the Met. are perhaps the best of the lot in the field of 'massaging events'. As my detective inspector cynically commented: 'You'll see; that man is really pissing on his fritters.'

Three years later PC Walker was still on 'sick leave' and although West Mercia, along with other forces, had carried out immediate internal inspections of the recording systems, not a lot had changed. Crime and Counting Rule recording practices continued to be manœuvred to suit the institutional need, while prevailing systems survived more or less intact. And even though a long enquiry was carried out under the guidance of the Police Complaints Authority into the Kent practices and recommended some disciplinary charges, PC Walker moved into a sort of structural limbo at the time of writing (*Police Review*, 16 September 1988).

In November 1986, following a quick internal inspection of the force systems, which reported that all was well, a visit to all our divisions was arranged for the assistant chief constable (operations) who was accompanied by a detective superintendent from HQ. All the senior staff on our division were present and I later wrote up a long fieldnote, from which the following is an extract:

... the meeting is to discuss 'current crime' and Divisional strategies. I am forcibly reminded how all of those present have different perceptions of what 'crime' is all about. The Detective Inspectors have a different reality to these HQ politicians ...

The meeting has an agenda but a crucial item is missing ... afterwards in the canteen it is agreed the visit has had two main thrusts, one of which has been left out of the circulated agenda.

The first concerns the increase in house-burglaries on the divison. Both subdivisions are about 100 up on last year at this time (but compared to the adjacent division in the West Midlands force we have no h/burglaries at all; in the first 10 months they have 3,049 while I have just over 400 but only a slightly smaller establishment). During the meeting I point out that our apparent increase is merely over two ten-month periods, Jan.–Oct. 1985 and 1986, and that comparative analysis on such a data base is relatively unsophisticated. If we look at variations in this small sample or include the 1984 and 1983 figures then some altogether different patterns emerge. The ACC doesn't want to hear this however, and even gets a bit angry. Later on a Detective Inspector says its the first time he has heard him swear.

The non-agenda item relates to the 'Kent' figure fiddling and the recent whirlwind visit by Ch. Supt. *** who has looked at our detections and found us to be whiter than white! Our prison visit 'write-offs' I think are relatively 'clean' (as far as I can tell), but the system is hardly used in some divisions and the Force only makes occasional use of it in comparison to Northumbria. The ACC then mentions that there is value in going to an Injured Person, even months later, and telling them we have someone in prison who admits their 'burglary', and who is now serving a sentence (albeit for a different crime). I look across at the Det. Inspector, who grins. We have just done some research which suggests that we perhaps tell 25% of IPs whose 'crime' is cleared, and then only tell those whom it is 'comfortable' to tell ... We do not tell them if it is likely to get difficult, e.g.

— those who are cautioned. According to the Crime Admin. Inspector, the IPs often get quite upset and won't accept the 'caution' decision, even though it is not within their power to have any say. 'They enter into lengthy telephone calls or correspondence and fuck the system up. So we don't tell many of them.'

— those where we decide to take no further action. Again it is too difficult to explain to the IP. 'They don't understand Attorney Generals' Guidelines, the Crown Prosecution code, the evidential sufficiency criterion (i.e. 50% plus chance of winning), or the 'public interest' concept; and they just cause trouble if they are informed.

— those whose crimes are admitted on prison visits. Sometimes if it is suitable we do inform the IP, but again it is often too difficult to

explain to the public, who just don't understand the business of dealing an NFA agreement in return for 'clear-ups'.

It is obvious that the ACC is oblivious to the fact that we don't tell 75%
of the injured persons that their case has been cleared up. The Crime
Admin. Inspector tells me that all the Divisions pursue the same policy
because of the problems which occur when we do try to tell the public,
for they 'want their culprit to be boiled in oil and not to be cautioned or
dealt with as an NFA.'

The ACC then staggers the detectives, by asking: 'How about seeing
offenders who receive a non-custodial sentence, e.g. probation or a fine,
to get them to "clear their slates" with a view to a "No further action—
detection"?' Anyone admitting a serious robbery might have to go to
court, he warns, but otherwise, 'I think we could offer a guarantee of
NFA'. The CID are shocked, but the ACC tells us that our 'write-offs'
are low in comparison to other Forces in the 'family' in the CIPFA
stats,[61] and the HMI has pointed out that we could increase our percentage 'write-offs'.

If our prison visit write-off situation was being played according
to the rules, and no flagrant creation of admissions had been
revealed, then the same can hardly be said for 'NFA detections'.
In a 1983 Amendment to the Counting Rules, the Home Office
defined eleven occasions when an offence (i.e. a crime) will be considered to be cleared up:

Notifiable Offences Recorded by the Police   *Crimsec 1A–2*

Offences Recorded as Cleared Up

An offence is cleared up when:

1. a person has been charged or summoned for the offence (irrespective of any subsequent acquittal);
2. the offence has been taken into consideration by the court;
3. the offender has been proceeded against in another police force area
   for the offence;
4. the offender dies before proceedings could be initiated or completed;
5. the offender has been cautioned by the police;

---

[61] In this age of a 'value for money' criteria for many public services, the increasing use of such markers as the CIPFA (Chartered Institute of Public Finance
and Accountancy) figures of force comparisons has been noticeable. West Mercia
is now included in a 'family' of six other allegedly comparable police units, i.e.
Sussex, Essex, Devon and Cornwall, Staffordshire, Northants, and Humberside.

6. the offender is ill and is unlikely to recover or is too senile or too mentally disturbed for proceedings to be taken;
7. the complainant or an essential witness is dead and the proceedings cannot be pursued;
8. the guilt of the offender is clear but the victim refuses, or is permanently unable, or if a juvenile is not permitted to give evidence;
9. the offender admits the offence but it is decided that no useful purpose would be served by proceeding with the charge;
10. it is ascertained that an offence has been committed by a child under the age of criminal responsibility;
11. an offence is admitted by a juvenile of the age of criminal responsibility and police take no action other than reporting the particulars to a local authority for action under the Children and Young Persons Act 1963 Section 1.

On the advice of the Home Office, a twelfth category had been added to the Rules. This was a variation on Rule 9 which allowed an NFA 'clear-up' when the offender admitted the offence and 'no useful purpose would be served in pursuing a prosecution'. However, the extra dimension to this NFA detection 'clear-up' rule is that it does not even need the offender to admit the offence, it only requires that 'there is sufficient evidence to charge the offender but the police prosecutions department, the DPP or a senior police officer decides that no useful purpose would be served by proceeding with the charge'. As a subdivisional commander during 1985 and 1986, I found I was authorized to 'mark off' crimes as 'detected NFA'. Once I had appended my signature to this decision, the detection was more or less assured and I found I was processing about 10–15 per month in this category. My concern became aroused when I read one file of evidence where the denial by the accused was so strong and the evidence so weak, that I set out to read an exact intepretation of the Counting Rules. No copy of the Rules existed then on the subdivision and no one in the CID had a copy of this Amendment to the Counting Rules (January 1983) listed above. Eventually I obtained one from HQ and a copy of the 'sufficiency of evidence' criteria set out in an Attorney-General's guide-line of 1983, which required that we had more than a 50 per cent chance of winning before proceeding with prosecution. At this time, some 2–3 years after these changes had been implemented, the chief inspector in charge of prosecution decision-making on the division had never even heard of them and I therefore began to make a note of files submitted to me in this category, e.g.

> Theft: a 17-year-old local villain for perfume valued £20. We would undoubtedly get a Not Guilty Plea and the only evidence is that he was in the shop near the perfume counter, and ran off when asked what he was up too. The theft could have occurred any time over a period and cannot be 51% attributed to him, but as we will have to NFA it anyway, why not ask for it to be an NFA detection—after all, as the officer in charge has said in his covering report, there is no doubt that he is guilty!
>
> Criminal damage to a car, value £300 by a 29-year-old. We have a motive, but no real evidence. We may have about 40%, but we do not have 51%, however the officers in the case are convinced of guilt and ask for a 'detected NFA'.

It seems such practice was the result of a long history in the force of taking cases that perhaps only had a 40 per cent chance (if that) to court and bluffing a way through. As a subdivisional prosecutions sergeant pointed out, 'the magistrates were on our side and we often got a guilty plea out of the unrepresented idiots we dealt with'. Such practice had ground to a halt in 1983 when a force-wide prosecuting solicitors' department was instituted many years after they had been the norm in other police areas, and the force was now having to grapple with the unwelcome phenomenon of prosecuting solicitors who demanded sufficient evidence to justify the charge as required by the Attorney-General's guide-lines and withdrew a case when it was not forthcoming.

A good proportion of the NFA detections I marked off in my twenty-two months on the subdivision would no doubt have gone to court in the past and made a conviction. Now they were claimed under Rule 12 (above) and one case in my fieldnotes illustrates the significance of these 'clear-ups':

> I have marked up a file 'NFA detection' during my first days in the sub-division for 3 offences of burglary. The accused is a 25-yr-old professional with a long criminal history. A guilty plea is not anticipated! I read the file and discuss it with the Det. Insp. and the detective in the case. There is a little evidence and a lot of suspicion, but not enough to give it a go at court. Weeks later, I track down the 1983 revised Counting Rules and the Attorney-General's Guide-lines which require a 51% chance before we can decide to take no further action, but claim a detection. Now, on the inspection following Ron Walker's 'bursting the

bubble' in Kent, Chief Superintendent *** scours our NFA detection files and rightly declares this one to be invalid. The rest are accepted even though some are very 'iffy', and we are told these three burglaries will have to be reclassified and remain on files as 'undetected'. But too late! I speak to HQ's stats. and find that there is now no way of declassifying them, for they have long since gone into the returns to the Home Office.

At this time, in 1986, the force had claimed 1,261 detections in this category 'NFA—other than by Prison Visit'. Across the thirteen subdivisions the numbers varied from 255 to 29. My own subdivision claimed 105 detections in this category, and the total statistical return at the end of the year showed:

    (*a*) 1,003 crimes cleared by TICs;
    (*b*) 1,876 crimes (previously reported) cleared by cautions;
    (*c*) 1,261 crimes cleared by NFA—other than by 'prison visit write-offs';
    (*d*) 1,372 crimes (not previously reported) cleared by TICs;
    (*e*) 693 crimes (not previously reported) cleared by cautions;
    (*f*) 269 crimes cleared by prison visit write-offs;
    (*g*) 1,138 crimes (not previously reported) cleared by prison visit write-offs.

TOTAL: 7,612

    (*h*) 5,021 crimes cleared, charged at court;
    (*i*) 230 crimes cleared, further charged at court.

TOTAL: 5,251

12,863 crimes cleared in total.

A further 5,627 detected crimes were yet to be broken down into the nine categories. However, by using the percentage norms indicated above, we could expect some 3,319 of these to fall into categories (*a*)–(*g*) and many of these to be NFA detections. In effect this means that some 10,931 crimes will be cleared by TICs, prison visit write-offs, cautions, and NFA decisions out of the total 18,490 detections for the year. Much deliberation on the creation of this 59 per cent of the overall detection rate goes unseen, just as it did in 1955 when I started out, but it still continues as an essential prerequisite for the detectives, and is seen as a marker of their ability to 'do the business'.

Some of these 'crimes' raise questions. Why, for instance, had 1,138 detections obtained by prison visit write-offs not been previously reported? At a social occasion, where I voiced this question at a time when I was surrounded by detectives, the various possibilities were outlined:

(i) the public had not bothered—i.e. the 'dark' figure.[62]
(ii) the detectives had 'cuffed' them for a time, knowing they would eventually be admitted when the suspect was sentenced. Had they then not been admitted, they could have vanished forever or have reluctantly been put in as 'undetected' crimes.
(iii) they had never occurred at all, but were figments of the imagination and were 'found' by detectives using electoral rolls and telephone directories to create unwitting injured persons. (From fieldnotes)

This led to a discussion on the unexpected problems caused by the creation of divisional Crime Operational Support Units (Crime OSUs) for the centralized administration of all 'crime papers' and a short-lived attempt to send letters to all injured persons telling them of the progress of their crime and the results of any case. As I have outlined above, many difficulties occurred because IPs were incensed by the decision-making processes; however, another problem came to light in relation to 'previously unreported clear-ups' (listed at (d) and (g) above). One of the detectives involved in the Crime OSU system told those present: 'injured persons began ringing or writing into the Unit saying they knew nothing of the crime they were allegedly the aggrieved party in. It became very embarrassing; and the OSUs had to stop sending the letters out.' This was an instance when some very experienced negotiators of the statistical drama, with their own deeply entrenched methods of purveying a suitable truth, were

---

[62] At the beginning of 1989 the Counting Rules were amended once again, so that these 'previously unreported' admissions obtained on prison visits could no longer be claimed as detections, but would be recorded as 'No Crimes'. Five months later a detective described how a dozen unreported thefts from shops could still be used to advantage at specific times, such as at the end of the year. Submission of the crimes with the information that the 'offender has been reported', but omitting the fact that he was in prison, had the effect of immediately enhancing detections for the end of year returns. Subsequently these were reclassified as 'No Crimes' after submission of a supplementary report in the new year, when the fact they had been obtained by prison visit write-off was revealed, and these new 'No Crimes' would then be set against the record of actual crimes.

suddenly left stranded by the introduction of a new computerized system which was set up as if the whole game was played out according to the Rules. On such occasions rapid adjustments have to be made to avoid revealing the bizarre realities of a historical system which PC Ron Walker seemed, somewhat naïvely, to believe he could adjust. While similarly deploring the fiddling, others have kept their heads beneath the parapet by anonymously declaiming against the demands of the system:

Tell the Truth about Crime

Once again it is the time of the year when forces publish their January/ July figures of reported crime and detection rates. You can read it in all the papers: 'Crime Down—Detections Up', or 'Neighbourhood Watch Works'. In my force and in particular my division, I am instructed to 'cuff' minor crimes, including burglary and assaults, where there is no chance of detection. I 'cuff' more crimes than I record at a rate of eight to one. We are always demanding more men and resources, yet we do this. If the true figures were published this country would have a major heart attack. Why do we do this? So that some promotion-mad detective inspector can go to his boss and say 'Look what a good DI I am', and then his boss goes to his boss, and so on. Finally the chief constable can say: 'I've got the best detection and clear-up rate in the country ...'

Name and Address Supplied

(*Police Review*, 19 August 1988: 1766).

How Crime is Being Cuffed

I write in answer to the letter 'Tell the truth about Crime' (PR Aug 19). I do not know what force the author belongs to, but I agree with everything that was said. I know that cuffing crime does go on in my Force. For example, crimes that should be attempted burglary are often recorded as criminal damage. Burglaries are sometimes crimed as theft, particularly if there is little chance of detection. Other crimes go unreported. Crime figures are adjusted basically to appease 'superior officers' and enhance promotion prospects. But who really benefits? ... The Police prides itself on honesty and does not easily tolerate corrupt or improper practices, yet we put up with 'crime cuffing'.

Name and Address Supplied

(*Police Review*, 2 September 1988)

After a lifetime's experience of this drama of manipulation I find little has changed in the basic facets of the exercise or in its centrality to the structural process of publicly claiming effective success. In the middle of 1988, at a time when I was writing fieldnotes on the rituals of retirement I was then experiencing, I also noted:

I listen as 'Val' from Stats. seeks advice from the head of the department about a crime, a burglary, recorded, established and detected. Now, some 3 months later the divisional detectives have submitted another 'detected crime' of 'theft of a key' used to commit the burglary. 'It's two for one under the rules' she is reminded, and the second crime is returned to the division to be deleted and the number to be reallocated to a 'real crime'. . . . I have visitors from another Force with me in the Stats dept. at the time. 'Val' has a pile of such 'crimes' to check back with the originating officers —all seem to be attempts to get an extra 'handling' along with a 'theft', a fraud/deception after a credit card theft, and so on—a stream of attempts to get two for one which the rules don't allow . . . I wonder how many of the 5,000 plus 'No crimes' we have had a couple of years back are from such doubling up? The difference between initially *'recorded'* crimes and the eventual return of *'established'* crimes is quite considerable and must be largely a matter of rule intepretation . . . a Detective Sergeant rings while we are there. He has 250 admissions of theft from motor vehicles but has no injured persons, no report of crimes and no property recovered. He is advised he can have those he can prove, i.e. produce an injured person for, but he has none and asks what he should do. Later when I tell a Detective Sergeant about this call, he laughs sadly at this naïvety. 'You don't ask, you find IPs. The number of times I've been put down as an IP or M— S— has, . . . i.e. someone who won't create problems if they inadvertently get an IP letter—but then you ensure they are down on the Crime Report as having been informed personally.' The message is that in such a situation you don't look a gift horse in the mouth and you invent IPs to meet the admissions—but not 250—just enough to meet the numbers necessary to hit the divisional, subdivisional or section norms.

These statistical games are sustaining dramas. They are about 'various regimes and discourses of truth' (Sheridan 1980: 222 on Foucault) which can be lived with; about those the institution can handle openly and those it cannot face. And they occur not just in Northumbria, Kent, or West Mercia, but across the organization. In July 1988 I had the opportunity to assess a new presentation by Cheshire Police in relation to its own statistical truths, when a 60-page analysis of 1987–8 crime was recommended to West Mercia by HM Inspector of Constabulary. I was asked to comment on the document and among the points in my report, I noted that:

It's thick (60 pages) and if this is an average month then it is 720 pages per year and what analytic skills lie on the Div/Sub-Div to ask of each graph 'okay what does this mean; can we influence it?' Otherwise it will end up like many other publications as so much drawer-liner . . .

. . . If there are statistically significant aspects where are they addressed and analysed? e.g. very low figures for the categories on pages 3, 5 and 6 for Feb. '87—result of very bad weather? Beyond police control? Who remembers now? P. 4 shows marked drop in June—but no explanation? P. 6 very high Dec. '87 figure for criminal damage = Xmas mayhem, or result of manipulations of detections and write-offs for the end of year returns? . . .

. . . Many of the graphs are straight line graphs and are the equivalent of 'statistical background noise' which looks as if it is the norm and will occur regardless of police action; but as the whole document is only a comparison of equivalent months for 1987 and 1988 who can say? With only this comparative data what significant trends can be assessed? This obsession in the service with a 'this year/last year' evaluation makes much of the data somewhat 'skin deep'. . . As a result, on many of the 60 pages the straight line graphs show nothing significant yet add to the bulk. Across a 6–7 year period, however, the data might have shown relevant trends . . .

. . . Then there are the detection rates! It makes interesting reading to see that Cheshire don't use an end of the year 'adjusted figure' for their detected crimes, but show them monthly. As a result, the 'subsequents' from previous years—usually from prison visit write-offs—give the sort of bizarre results shown on p. 14, where in March 1987 there was a 117% detection rate for 'burglary in a dwelling', but only 4% in April, and then 90% in May. On p. 24 the monthly 'detected' rates for 1987 show 144%, 154% and 111% for 3 months out of 12. This sort of statistical assessment renders any credibility as being at least suspect!

And yet this document was being recommended to us by the adviser to chief officers, as a valid way to put out data to the force, even though it was again telling a story which was only one very skewed representation of an institutional truth.

This inability to handle real truth and separate it from an organizational truth causes continual difficulties, which is especially ironic in an organization tasked with implementing law through a system of adversarial trials of truth telling! In February

1987 a young detective constable revealed the gulf which exists between the two categories when he described his promotion board with the chief constable and other senior officers to an understanding canteen audience. This somewhat serious minded young officer regretfully told them:

> you have to toe the party line and I had to tell them the lies they wanted to hear about our unqualified belief in neighbourhood watch, about the usefulness of special constables, and about our keen support for crime prevention and community affairs schemes, such as teaching the unemployed to drive . . .

The laughter this produced repeats the message that such games, like the counting rules, are part of a drama played out for limited public consumption. In this world where an official presentation and the realities of canteen culture both rely on mythology, the 'clear-ups' remove structural dirt and ambiguity, for the idea that crimes can be *cleared up* reasserts a belief in a world where disorder can be brushed away to restore structural purity and where incongruity can be cleaned up to re-create a perfectly ordered universe in which hierarchical principles reign undisturbed. The unending nature of this drama generates the status given to those with the ability to 'do the business', and ensures that the 'bending and fiddling' remains unseen and invisible. Senior detective officers are totally cognizant of the dramatic practices surrounding this use of 'crime' and understand that because its presentation is largely symbolic, such myths require the maintenance and continuity of a closed system, with rewards for those who sustain its many illusions. Revelation of this mythology by an insider, such as PC Walker or the academic researcher, will threaten the integrity of the closed world, for it reveals how the whole fabric is built on precepts which at times seem to border on the farcical and produce a system which might well be considered to be morally unsupportable or philosophically indefensible.

A continually unspoken need to sustain the magnitude of this myth helps reinforce an obsession with an oft-mentioned idea of the 'dignity of the job', which means that although many grumble in private or send in anonymous letters to *Police Review*, few proclaim openly about the true nature of the game. At a CID conference in 1980, I watched with interest as a newish detective inspector shocked the company when he openly complained how 'the political need to appear to be swamped with work at this time, means that all "crimes" were now being recorded and no longer were being cuffed'; so that

in consequence between 1976 and 1979 there has been a rise of 15,000 minor crimes in our force, and even in the first six months of 1980 we are 6,000 crimes up on last year, even though the Home Office Counting Rules have reduced some by introducing continuous offences and denying the practice of getting two detections for one incident as in the past.

He went on to point out to the conference that Northumbria therefore had 21,000 extra crime reports on which detectives were still required by Force Orders to show times and dates of visits to the scene, and that detectives were making fictitious entries, saying each crime had been visited when it was patently obvious it was impossible for this to have occurred. The system, he complained, was making liars of detectives and he asked that when no visit had been made to a scene of crime, then this should be recorded as such on the crime report.

This frank admission of a functional problem in what is a largely symbolic system was difficult for some to handle. I watched as senior CID officers from ACPO rank down to detective inspectors grappled with this statement that the system was built on a foundation of creative inaccuracies and deceptions. Everyone present knew that it was impossible for all the scenes of crimes to be visited, just as we all knew that many of the 21,000 crimes could be added to those for 'criminal damage' and 'car theft' which had not been crimes only a decade previous. But how could this be admitted or acknowledged, for the mythology had to be maintained? The structure of the police social world and its interlocking ideology and practice requires that the foundation remains inviolate, for an institution which is set up to impose control and define order for society relies heavily on acquiescence from its ranks. They are not required to subject it to any really close examination or philosophical scrutiny, even when they are posted to departments involved in the evaluation of its practices; for in the final analysis when the order comes to 'jump', the response must be 'Yes sir, how high Sir?'; and never 'Why Sir?' This detective inspector had transgressed this basic tenet and improvidently reminded the conference that the 'King's New Suit to Clothes' (to paraphrase Hans Christian Andersen) was a dramatic symbol, which did not really exist until it was produced and directed for an accepting audience.

This mythological disorder of crime has been dramatized and pursued in fashionable, yet archetypal settings. Its use as a meta-phor of 'masculine' activity or 'real' policework is directed along well tried and tested lines, which are not confined to one police force nor contained by any specific period of social history. In effect police ideology is sustained by the concept of crime at every turn, for the criminal-justice system is a theatre of make-believe with more than a touch of farce to its systems of production and presentation, and it is difficult for those who are sustained within its structures to admit this to themselves, never mind to the out-side world. Many have carved out powerful roles and personae for themselves within the organization, and for these participants to admit to the dramatic or mythological nature of many of their practices would be to interfere seriously with an instilled belief in the dignity of their office and the sanctity of their role in the idea of law.

As a result, open admission that 'bending' or 'fiddling' occurs, or any revelation that arbitrary 'cuffing' and 'trade-puffing' of crime reporting and recording has been standard practice across decades, is, I suggest, a structural impossibility. It is little wonder then, that anthropological research is largely unknown, or that the insider who pursues reflexive analysis will become marginal and remain largely muted, for the system promotes an uncritical reverence for institutional practice, for tradition, and for the doctrines of precedent as part of its belief in 'the dignity of the job'. To admit that 'bending' and 'fiddling' the account is the norm would be to acknowledge the fact that irreverance, disorder, and potential chaos sustains an institution which is allegedly geared to prevent its occurrence. Such a world is not one that police *habitus* is structured to contend with or even acknowledge; for any admission could easily reverse the direction of the applica-tion of power.

6

Conclusion

In the months since I retired and have been compiling the material for this book, I have become crucially aware that although I have been heavily engaged in the pragmatics of writing, I have simultaneously been involved in what I have decided can only be a deconstruction of an identity. Shedding the institutional framework and the heavy constraints of a disciplined organization after thirty-three years, like the snake sheds his skin, has been another culture shock equivalent to my move into university, and my return to the bridewell. During this time I have dreamed regularly (in full colour) of situations where I am in half or partial uniform, often, for example, in police tunic but civvy trousers, and without epaulettes on the jacket or buttons and badges of rank. In these dreams, in which I was often with ex-colleagues from the distant past, I somehow was aware that I was now standing outside my police identity, but had still to throw off the last vestiges of it. At the 1989 Association of Social Anthropologists annual conference on the subject of autobiography and anthropology, the anthropologist Paul Spencer, who had given a paper entitled 'Indulging in Automythologies', urged me to write down and record these dreams which seemed to symbolize my coming to terms with a radical change of status and deconstructed life style.

The new understanding I was experiencing, like this account, is yet another part of my own 'autobiognosis', which is a term coined by the elder statesman of anthropology Sir Raymond Firth at the same conference in an attempt to cover some of the facets of an 'insider-biographical' analysis of social events, which the ethnographer himself has lived, analysed, written about, and come to reflect upon in the course of events. Paul Spencer in his paper (which at the time of writing remains unpublished but which will perhaps be included in the eventual ASA volume from the conference) urged caution on those who pursue this process of autobiognosis:

In this paper I wish to consider personal anecdotes told and elaborated before an audience as a form of fragmented autobiography. Erving Goffman (1969: 28–40) [in *The Presentation of Self in Everyday Life*] has drawn attention to the element of performance in such presentations, with role play and the manipulation of reality to create an effect. In this way a contrived self-language is built up which inadvertently may even captivate the teller, hence my title ['Indulging Mythologies']. The aim here is to discern the relevance of exaggeration in recalling episodes of ones past for an insight into autobiography, and ultimately even the record of history itself ... Autobiography gives a uniquely personal insight into the process of history, but may view the memories of earlier times through the distorting lenses of later life.

Throughout the drafting and rewriting of this book, I have been conscious of my own distorting lenses and what Spencer (ibid.) describes as the moulding caused by the social construction of ageing, as I have relived my own history and created the account. This, in turn, I have found has also been part of the process of deconstruction of a previous identity, for I have had to recall my own manipulations in the past, such as the skills I achieved in the negotiation of crime classifications as a means of enhancing detection rates, or my own practice as a young detective taking part in such games as listing the real but largely ineffectual 'prigs' to be given the bullet in our canteen charades of who would receive the shots from a six gun if we were ever really tasked with the job of clearing the city of its crime. I have had to face the fact that even to achieve the rank of superintendent I have necessarily played some rather silly institutional games at times, and exhibited all of the stereotypes I have described above, as I have complained about our losses to maternity leave caused by too many women, or laughed with the lads at a 'do' at a sexist joke. Consistently I have replicated the narrow bounds of the police modes of thought successfully to create and present an image of being the total 'insider', while for almost half my police service I have wrestled with the knowledge that I was standing outside my immediate self, reinterpreting my own past and living what might best be termed a new *communitas* of understanding.

My whole working life therefore seems to have been split into two distinct parts by the anthropological experience of reflexive analysis, making the second half a long and unbroken, interpretive occasion, and during which I still had to fulfil all the disciplined and controlled requirements of life in the various ranks I was progressing through. Perhaps I no longer had access to or could achieve the intense personal excitement I had felt in the early 1960s when I captured a 'prig' and secured a roll-up of detections out of one set of circumstances, although I found I could still spot the potential of such an occasion in the bridewell and relive part of the intense, adrenalin-filled moments. But now I found that analytic curiosity was the stimulant, and in the recognition of the binary patterns, the homologies, and transformations across the various forms of cultural expression I found a similar thrill; for I now understood the deep structures that generated the intensity of actions I had once merely lived with.

I recall a long telephone conversation I had in 1981 with the anthropologist Shirley Ardener, when she rang to ask if I had anything in my fieldnotes on 'police wives', which was an area I had not previously even considered. Denying I had any material on the matter, I found I began to pour out examples of this unacknowledged world in which these women 'enjoy' a peculiar role married into the job (Young 1984), and realized how the anthropological mode had now made it possible for me to understand the way the whole culture of policing fitted together as a paradigmatic chain of thoughts, resolute beliefs, and well-defined, but often inarticulated practices. Here then was my new field of chase and capture!

Yet I was still enough of a 'real polis' to be influenced by my early indoctrination, and at the same time as I pursued the analysis of events I found that my eagerness to be part of the team that kept the Bromsgrove subdivisional crime detection rate above that of our neighbours in Kidderminster in 1985–6 was still as charged with intensity as when I had been a city centre detective; and I was certain of my own superiority over neighbours in Gateshead or Northumberland. However, this was activity now tempered with the crucial awareness of what we were about, and what cultural power games we were indulging in. That my *habitus* was still firmly in place, however, was brought home to me in the two years I spent as subdivisional superintendent, when I experienced intense pleasure as my detective inspector (Mick Bullock) and his detectives invited me to their private departmental dinners and celebrations yet denied access to others of higher rank; and turned out in full strength for my own 'leaving do' after my two years as an honorary member of their department.

During the late 1970s and the 1980s I gained several close friends in Northumbria, West Mercia, and other forces, who have (perhaps) been touched by the inquisitive nature of the anthropological method I have pursued, and some have even read Mary Douglas, Michel Foucault, Shirley Ardener, Stan Cohen, and the like. Working in police research departments for over half of the last decade, a range of 'ex-polises' and detectives have spent a twelve-month or two-year secondment often taking on board some of the ideas I have put about. I have seen my analysis of events and the seminar papers I have given them to read (when they have asked to see them) come as something of a jolt, as they in turn have undertaken some navel-gazing and been forced to reconsider the cultural practices which, like me, they had once considered to be natural. The odd one or two have even said that the reflexive style I presented had rubbed off onto them and irreversibly changed their understanding of what it was the organization was about, and what they themselves were up to. And seeking, in typical police style to catch this, nail it down, and classify it, they have wanted to know how to define or place such activity:

We have daily discussions (and arguments) about the problems of research, the difficulties of the organization handling change, the conservatism and resistance of those in positions of power and influence. Chief Superintendent X (who has been a strong traditionalist but is now tasked to head research and has just been on a management of change course) is now in the process of standing the world on its head, challenging every precept he has previously taken on board as gospel.

He asks me how I define our role, and using a white board and markers I draw a model of us (research dept) sitting between the King (the chief constable) and the common herd (the divisions and their personnel). I suggest we are the equivalent of the court jester, licensed to think the unthinkable and challenge all the dearly held beliefs of the culture; able to tell the herd that their systems and styles are inept, hopeless, out of date, and in need of renewal. At times, we can use swingeing language in this task, for we are licensed to state the unacceptable and be protected from the wrath of the herd. We are also licensed occasionally to tell the King he has no clothes on, or is wrong, for we are also his conscience. However, we should be wary about how we approach this part of the bargain, for if our message is too painful for the King to digest, then sitting at the apex of power he can merely chop off the jester's head, or send him into limbo in some suitable dungeon (or punishment post) and acquire a new model. (From fieldnotes: December 1987)

One or two of my working colleagues who have become close friends now have the problem of living with their own newly acquired perceptions of the deep structures of policing. They, like me, have acquired the knowledge that policing remains a highly visible yet carefully concealed business, which at one and the same time is perhaps the most symbolically apparent of the systems of social control, but carefully keeps many of its practices hidden from scrutiny. Their new-found wisdom and reflexive awareness is a problem which has been mine, for in such a self-sustaining world of carefully delineated practice, the intrusive critical eye must be deflected; and it remains axiomatic that the King or the controller retains the high ground of power, thus ensuring that the authoritarian gaze is imposed by him and not levelled on him (Reiner 1989). My erstwhile colleagues therefore have joined me in accepting that there is a measure of complicity (overshadowed by the discipline code) which ensures that any 'inside' revelation will be kept to a minimum; for the publication of any research will inevitably reveal warts on the face of the organization and fly in the face of the cardinal rule of an institution of power which demands that any commentary on its activities will emanate from the top and in general is not supportive of radicalism or massive structural change.

The strength of this institutional thinking, which seems to me to have only changed in minor ways throughout my three decades inside police boundaries, holds out the distinct possibility that the 1990 'Plus' programme of the Metropolitan Police Commissioner, Peter Imbert, will run aground. This new regime, talked of as a version of *glasnost* and *perestroika*, is designed to tackle the crisis in public confidence indicated in the Wolff Ollins (1988) report on the Met., but because of the strength of beliefs at canteen culture level, and even in the management ranks, it could well achieve the same fate as the similar attempt by Imbert's predecessor, Sir Kenneth Newman, whose 'little blue book' on management change (described above) was destined to sweep the force onto a new level of thinking, but is now just a memory and so much waste paper. Sir Peter has set out to meet the criticisms in

the Wolff Ollins report on force deficiencies by similarly challenging management styles and bringing about a consensus involving
the lower ranks in the debate ('Forces of Change', *Guardian*, 21
February 1990). However, my own experience suggests that such
attempts at radical change will always fail, for as a researcher I
have recognized that the place of the analytic jester in the police is
still one charged with a potential for disaster, for he disturbs the
hegemonic mode by which the society is sustained. As another of
my former research colleagues told me recently in relation to yet
another Force Review he is involved in:

The problem is deciding what the Chief really wants. There is a political
reality which is very apparent, but also an agenda that is not even
acknowledged. As you used to say, 'it's largely illusory and about
maintaining the illusions'. The real problem [we have] is to guess where
the hidden agenda lies, for the stimuli for the project seem to have come
from a recent Audit Commission report that was critical of the operational roles and excessive rank structures in [another force]; but we can't
be sure if the Chief merely wants to anticipate a similar thrust by the
Audit Commission at our force and, as a result, is making token gestures
about looking at the force organizational structure, or has had a radical
change of heart since 1986 when he said he wouldn't change the existing
organizational format or the divisional layout. (From fieldnotes, 1990)

Talking through four or even five possibilities that may or may
not lie in the hidden agenda, we eventually acknowledged that in
the best traditions of the service there is no means of the jester
asking the chief to put all his political cards on the table, for the
culture is still firmly based on rigidities of thought that ensured
my early (1958) reports all ended, 'I am, Sir, Your obedient
Servant', while thirty years later any contentious conversation
between a subordinate and a senior officer is still likely to be
prefaced by the phrase 'with respect, Sir'. Furthermore, as we
acknowledged, a large number of the reports travelling up the intensive police rank structures still reflect this unquestioning subservience by including such phrases as 'I respectfully submit this
report for your consideration'.

In this event, it is likely the chief constable will be presented
with various options ranging from a possible radical readjustment
of the force (which will be unacceptable and is definitely not
supported by the chief superintendents) to what I defined during

my years of police research as being 'our basic task of merely tinkering with the edges of the fabric of the institution'.

For as I have found, and hopefully demonstrated above (and as Foucault (1978) suggests),[1] the ability to pursue any discourse on such a cultural system cannot be separated from considerations of power and its continued implementation.

[1] See also Parkin (1982: xlv) and Sheridan (1980: 113–34).

References

ADAMS, SIMON (1988), 'Institutions are Created for the Purpose of Resisting Change: that's their main function', Unpublished paper prepared for Police Staff College, Bramshill Fellowship.

AKEROYD, ANNE V. (1980), 'Whither Social Anthropology—Apply and/or Die, Unpublished paper for ASA/SSRC Conference on Employment of Social Anthropologists, London, 25 June.

——(1984), 'Ethics in Relation to Informants, the Profession and Governments', in R. F. Ellen (ed.), *Ethnographic Research*. Academic Press, London.

ALDERSON, JOHN (1979), *Policing Freedom*. MacDonald & Evans, London.

——(1980), *Public Office*. Granada TV, 20 June.

ARDENER, EDWIN (1973), 'Some Outstanding Problems in the Analysis of Events', Paper presented at the Decennial Conference of the ASA and published in *The Yearbook of Symbolic Anthropology*, ed. E. Schwimmer. Hurst, London.

——(1975a), 'Belief and the Problem of Women', and 'The Problem Revisited', in S. Ardener (ed.), *Perceiving Women*. J. M. Dent, London.

——(1975b), 'The Voice of Prophecy: Further Problems in the Analysis of Events'. The Munro Lecture, Edinburgh, 24 April.

——(1987), 'Remote Areas: Some Theoretical Considerations', in A. Jackson (ed.), *Anthropology at Home*. ASA 25, Tavistock, London.

ARDENER, SHIRLEY (ed.) (1975), *Perceiving Women*. J. M. Dent, London.

——(ed.) (1978), *Defining Females: The Nature of Women in Society*. Croom Helm, London.

——(ed.) (1981), *Women and Space: Ground Rules and Social Maps*. Croom Helm, London.

ARENDT, HANNAH (1958), *The Origins of Totalitarianism*. Median New World Publishing Company, New York.

BAILEY, VICTOR (1981), *Policing and Punishment in the 19th Century*. Croom Helm, London.

BALDWIN, JOHN and MCCONVILLE, MICHAEL (1977), *Negotiated Justice: Pressures on Defendants to Plead Guilty*. Martin Robertson, Oxford.

BARKER, DIANA L. and ALLEN, SHEILA (1976), *Dependence and Exploitation in Work and Marriage*. Longman, London.

BARNES, J. A. (1981), 'Ethical and Political Compromise in Social Research', MSS quoted in Akeroyd (1984: 154).

BARTHES, ROLAND (1983), *Barthes: Selected Writings*, Introduced by Susan Sontag. Fontana/Collins, London.

BBC TV (1988), *A Policewoman's Lot*, 10 November, BBC 2.

BECKER, HOWARD (1963), *Outsiders*. Free Press, New York.

BENEDICT, RUTH (1967), *The Chrysanthemum and the Sword: Patterns of Japanese Culture*. Routledge and Kegan Paul, London.

BENNETT, TREVOR (1989), 'The Neighbourhood Watch Experiment', in *Coming to Terms with Policing*. Routledge, London.

BENTHALL, J. (1976), *The Body Electric: Patterns of Western Industrial Culture*. Thames and Hudson Academic Press, London.

—— and POLHEMUS, T. (1975), *The Body as a Medium of Expression*. Allen Lane, London.

BENYON, HUW (1988), 'Regulating Research: Politics and Decision Making in Industrial Organisations', in A. Bryman (ed.), *'Doing Research in Organisations*. Routledge, London.

BIRD, CATHY (1987), *Register of Policing Research 1986–89*. The Police Foundation, London.

BLACKING, JOHN (1977), *The Anthropology of the Body*. ASA 15, Academic Press, London.

BLOCH PETER B. and ANDERSON, DEBORAH (1974), *Policewomen on Patrol*. Police Foundation, Washington, DC.

BOTTOMLEY, A. K. and COLEMAN, C. A. (1980), 'Police Effectiveness and the Public: The Limitations of Official Crime Rates', in R. Clarke and J. M. Hough (eds.), *The Effectiveness of Policing*. Gower, Farnborough.

—— —— (1981), *Understanding Crime Rates*. Gower, Farnborough.

BOURDIEU, PIERRE (1973), 'The Berber House', in M. Douglas (ed.), *Rules and Meanings*. Penguin, Harmondsworth.

—— (1977), *Outline of a Theory of Practice*. Cambridge University Press, Cambridge.

BOX, STEVEN (1971), *Deviance, Reality and Society*. Holt, Reinhart and Winston, London.

—— (1983), *Power, Crime and Mystification*. Tavistock, London.

BOYLE, JIMMY (1977), *A Sense of Freedom*. Canongate, London.

BRAUDEL, FERNAND (1981), *The Structures of Everyday Life: Civilisation and Capitalism, 15th–18th Century*, Vol. i. Collins, London.

BRYANT L., DUNKERLEY D., and KELLAND G. (1985), 'One Of the Boys', in *Policing*, Autumn.

BULMER, RALPH (1967), 'Why is the Cassowary Not a Bird? A Problem of Zoological Taxonomy among the Karam of the New Guinea Highlands', in *Man* (NS) 2: 5–25.

BURMA, JOHN R. (1965), 'Self-Tattooing among Delinquents: A Research Note', in M. E. Roach and J. B. Eicher (eds.), *Dress, Adornment and the Social Order*. Wiley, New York (also in *Society and Social Research*, 43 (May 1959), 341–51).

BURRIDGE, KENELM (1969), *New Heaven, New Earth*. Blackwell, Oxford.

BURTON, FRANK (1980), 'Questions of Violence in Party Political Criminology', in P. Carlen and M. Collinson (eds.), *Radical Issues in Criminology*. Martin Robertson, Oxford.

BUTLER, A. J. P. (1984), *Police Management*. Gower, Farnborough.

CALLAN, HILARY and ARDENER, SHIRLEY (eds.) (1984), *The Incorporated Wife*. Croom Helm, London.

CAPLAN, PAT (1988), 'Engendering Knowledge: The Politics of Ethnography', in *Anthropology Today*, 4, Nos. 5 and 6, Oct. and Dec.

CARSON, W. G. (1970), 'White Collar Crime and the Enforcement of Factory Legislation', in *British Journal of Criminology*, 10: 383–98.

CASTENADA, C. (1970), *The Teachings of Don Juan: A Yaqui Way Knowledge*. Penguin, Harmondsworth.

CHAPLIN, JOCELYN (1988), *Feminist Counselling in Action*. Sage Publishing, London.

CHATTERTON, MICHAEL (1973), 'Sociology and the Police', in J. C. Alderson and P. J. Stead (eds.), *The Police We Deserve*. Wolf, London.

——(1976), 'Police in Social Control', in *Control without Custody*. Cropwood Papers, Cambridge Univ. Institute of Criminology.

——and ROGERS, M. C. (1989), 'Focussed Patrol', in R. Morgan and D. Smith (eds.), *Coming to Terms with Policing*. Routledge, London.

CHEATER, ANGELA P. (1987), 'The Anthropologist as Citizen: The Diffracted Self?', in A. Jackson (ed.), *Anthropology at Home*. Tavistock, London.

CHIBNALL, STEVE (1977), *Law and Order News: An Analysis of Crime Reporting in the British Press*. Tavistock, London.

CLARKE, R. V. G. (1978), *Tackling Vandalism*. HO Research Study No. 47, HMSO.

——and HOUGH, J. M. (eds.) (1980), *The Effectiveness of Policing*. Gower, Farnborough.

CLIFFORD, J. and MARCUS, G. (eds.) (1986), *Writing Culture*. Univ. of California Press, Berkeley, Calif.

COHEN, ANTHONY P. (1984), 'Producing Data', in R. F. Ellen (ed.), *Ethnographic Research*. Academic Press, London.

——(1985), *The Symbolic Construction of Community*. Ellis Horwood Ltd., Chichester.

——(1986), *Symbolising Boundaries: Identity and Diversity in British Cultures*. Manchester University Press, Manchester.

COHEN, STANLEY (1973), *Folk Devils and Moral Panics*. Paladin, St Albans.

CONKLIN, J. E. (1977), *Illegal but not Criminal*. Spectrum, New Jersey.

CONLIN, SEAN (1980), 'Development and Anthropology', Unpublished paper for ASA/SSRC Conference on Training and Employment of Social Anthropologists, London, 25 June.

CORNWALL, HUGO (1987), 'Fraud: the billion pound racket that we all but ignore', in *Police*, Oct.

COWARD, ROSALIND (1984), *Female Desire*. Paladin, St Albans.

COX, B., SHIRLEY J., and SHORT M. (1977), *The Fall of Scotland Yard*. Penguin, Harmondsworth.

CRICK, MALCOLM (1976), *Explorations in Language and Meaning: Towards a Semantic Anthropology*, Malaby Press, London.

——(1982), 'Anthropological Field Research, Meaning, Creation and Knowledge Construction', in D. Parkin (ed.), *Semantic Anthropology*. ASA 22, Academic Press, London.

CRITCHLEY, T. A. (1967), *A History of the Police in England and Wales 1900–1966*. Constable, London.

CROFT, JOHN (1984), 'Crime, Punishment and Penal Policy', *Criminal Law Review*, Sept.: 531–6.

CROWTHER, ERIC (1983), 'Dress and Modes of Address', *Justice of the Peace*, 30 Apr.: 280–3.

CUCCHIARI, S. (1981), 'The Origins of Gender Hierarchy', in S. B. Ortner and H. Whitehead (eds.), *Sexual Meanings: The Cultural Construction of Gender and Sexuality*. Cambridge Univ. Press, Cambridge.

CUMBERBACH, D. (1984), 'Community Schemes are mere P. R.', *Guardian*, 13 Sept.

DEAN, MALCOLM (1983), Two articles on 'Discrimination in the Police', *Guardian*, 28, 29 Dec.

DIAMOND, STANLEY (1964), 'Nigerian Discovery: The Politics of Fieldwork', in A. Vidich, J. Bensman, and M. Stein (eds.), *Reflection on Community Studies*. Wiley, New York.

DICK, CRESSIDA (1985), 'Implications of the Miners Strike', *Police Review*, 18 Oct.

DITTON, JASON (1977), *Part Time Crime: An Ethnography of Fiddling and Pilferage*. Macmillan, London.

——(1979), *Contrology: Beyond the New Criminology*. Macmillan, London.

——and WILLIAMS, ROBIN (n.d.), 'The Fundable—vs—The Doable: On the Logical and Administrative Inability of Official Funding Bodies to Buy Authentic Qualitative Research'. Unpublished paper given to the British Sociological Society.

DOUGLAS, MARY (1957), 'Animals in Lele Religious Symbolism', *Africa*, 27: 46–57 (reprinted in *Implicit Meanings*).

——(1966), *Purity and Danger: An Analysis of Concepts of Pollution and Taboo*. Routledge and Kegan Paul, London.

——(1972), 'Self Evidence'. Proceedings of the RAI, (reprinted in *Implicit Meanings*).

——(1973), *Natural Symbols: Explorations in Cosmology*. Penguin, Harmondsworth.

——(1975), *Implicit Meanings: Essays in Anthropology*. Routledge and Kegan Paul, London.

——(1987), *How Institutions Think*. Routledge and Kegan Paul, London.

DUBE, L., LEACOCK, E., and ARDENER S. (eds.) (1986), *Visibility and Power: Essays on Women and Development*. OUP, Delhi.

ECO, UMBERTO (1987), *Travels in Hyper-Reality*. Picador edn., Pan Books, London.

EDHOLM, F., HARRIS, O., and YOUNG, K. (1977), 'Conceptualising Women', *Critique of Anthropology*, 3, No. 9/10.

ELIADE, MAURICE (1958), *Death and Rebirth: The Religious Meanings of Initiation in Human Culture*. Harper & Row, New York.

——(1960), *Myths, Dreams and Mysteries*. Fontana, London.

ELLEN, R. F. (ed.) (1984), *Ethnographic Research: A Guide to General Conduct*. Academic Press, London.

EVANS, PETER (1977), 'The Tribal Nature of the Police', *The Times*, 10 Nov.

EVANS-PRITCHARD, E. E. (1951), *Social Anthropology*. Routledge and Kegan Paul, London.

FARIS, J. C. (1968), 'Occasions and Non-Occasions', in M. Douglas (ed.), *Rules and Meanings*. Penguin, Harmondsworth.

FARRINGTON, DAVID P. and DOWN, ELIZABETH A. (1984), 'Why Does Crime Increase?', *Justice of the Peace*, 11 Aug.: 506–9.

FAVRET-SAADA, JEANNE (1980), *Deadly Words: Witchcraft in the Bocage*. Cambridge University Press, Cambridge.

FIELDING, NIGEL (1989), 'Constraints on the Practice of Community Policing', in *Coming to Terms with Policing*. Routledge, London.

FINNIMORE, PETER (1982), 'How should Effectiveness of the Police be Assessed?', *Police Journal*, 55, No. 1 (Jan.–Mar.).

FIRTH, RAYMOND (1973), *Symbols, Public and Private*. Allen and Unwin, London.

FLAHER, PAUL (1982), 'Police Studies: The Discipline of the Future', *The Times Higher Education Supplement*, 25 June.

FOUCAULT, MICHEL (1967), *Madness and Civilization*. Tavistock, London.

——(1970), *The Order of Things: An Archeology of the Human Sciences*. Pantheon Books, New York.

——(1977), *Discipline and Punish*. Allen Lane, London.

——(1978), *I, Pierre Rivière, Having Slaughtered my Mother, My Sister and My Brother*. Peregrine Books, London.

——(1980), *Power/Knowledge: Selected Interviews and Other Writings*, ed. C. Gordon. The Harvester Press, Brighton.

FURLONG, MONICA (1973), *The End of Our Exploring*. Hodder and Stoughton, London.

GEERTZ, CLIFFORD (1975), *The Interpretation of Culture*. Hutchinson, London.

GEERTZ, CLIFFORD (1976), 'From the Native's Point of View', in K. H. Bassy and H. A. Selby (eds.), *Meaning in Anthropology*. Univ. of New Mexico, Albuquerque.

GENET, JEAN (1967), *The Thief's Journal*. Penguin, Harmondsworth.

GENNEP, ARNOLD VAN (1960), *The Rites of Passage*. Routledge and Kegan Paul, London.

GERMANNN, A. C. (1977), 'Law Enforcement: A Look into the Future', *Police Journal*, Oct.: 340–7.

GLC POLICE COMMITTEE (1984), Report on Metropolitan Police, referring to percentages of women in the ranks of the Metropolitan Police.

GOFFMAN, ERVING (1961), *Asylums*. Penguin, Harmondsworth.

——(1963), *Stigma; Notes on the Management of Spoiled Identity*. Prentice-Hall, New Jersey (Pelican edn., Harmondsworth, 1968).

——(1969), *The Presentation of Self in Everyday Life*. Penguin, Harmondsworth.

——(1975), *Frame Analysis*. Penguin, Harmondsworth.

GORNALL, M. (1975), 'The Changing Role of Women in the Police Services of Britain and America', *Bramshill Journal*: 38–44.

GOWARD, NICOLA (1984), 'The Fieldwork Experience', in R. F. Ellen (ed.), *Ethnographic Research*. Academic Press, London.

GRAEF, ROGER (1989), *Talking Blues: The Police in their Own Words*. Collins Harvill, London.

GREENHILL, NORMAN (1981), 'The Value of Sociology in Policing', in D. Pope and N. L. Weiner (eds.), *Modern Policing*. Croom Helm, London.

GREENWOOD, P., CHAIKEN, J., and PETERSILIA, J. (1977), *The Criminal Investigation Process*. D. C. Heath, Lexington, Mass.

GREER, GERMAINE (1971), *The Female Eunuch*. Paladin, St. Albans.

GRILLO, RALPH (1980), 'Anthropology made Useful: Some Comments', Unpublished paper for ASA/SSRC Conference on Training and Employment of Social Anthropologists, 25 June.

HM CHIEF INSPECTOR OF CONSTABULARY (1985), Annual Report for 1985.

HALFORD, ALISON (1987), 'Until the 12th of Never', *Police Review*, 9 Oct.

HALLPIKE, C. R. (1969), 'Social Hair', in *Man* (NS) 4: 256–64.

HAMBLY, W. D. (1925), *The History of Tattooing and its Significance*. H. F. and G. Witherby, London.

HARRISON, FRASER (1982), *Strange Lands. The Countryside: Myth and Reality*. Sidgwick and Jackson, London.

HASTRUP, KIRSTEN (1987), 'Fieldwork among Friends: Ethnographic Exchange within the Northern Civilization', in A. Jackson (ed.), *Anthropology at Home*. ASA 25, Tavistock, London.

HAY, D., LINEBAUGH P., and THOMPSON, E. P. (eds.) (1975), *Albions Fatal Tree: Crime and Society in 18th Century England*. Allen Lane, London.

HAYES, E. NELSON and HAYES, T. (1970), *Claude Levi-Strauss: The Anthropologist as Hero*. MIT, Cambridge, Mass.

HEBDIDGE, DICK (1979), *Subculture: The Meaning of Style*. Methuen, London.

HEILBRUN, CAROLYN, G. (1979), *Reinventing Womanhood*. Gollancz, London.

HENRY, STUART (1978), *The Hidden Economy: The Content and Control of Borderline Crime*. Martin Robertson, Oxford.

HERTZ, ROBERT (1973), 'The Pre-Eminence of the Right Hand', in R. Needham (ed.), *Right and Left*. University of Chicago Press, Chicago, Ill.

HESS, A. and MARRINER, D. (1975), 'On the Sociology of Crime Cartoons', *International Journal of Criminology and Penology*, 3, No. 3.

HILTON, JENNIFER (1976), 'Women in the Police Service', in *Police Journal*, 49: 93–103 (and *Police Review*, 17 Sept.)

HOBBS, DICK (1988), *Doing the Business: Crime Culture and Detective Work*. Oxford University Press, Oxford.

HOLDAWAY, SIMON (ed.) (1979), *The British Police*. Edward Arnold, London.

——(1982), ' "An Inside Job": A Case Study of Covert Research on the Police', in M. Bulmer (ed.), *Social Research Ethics: an Examination of the Merits of Covert Participant Observation*. Macmillan, London.

——(1983), *Inside the British Police*. Blackwell, Oxford.

HOLDEN, PAT (ed.) (1983), *Women's Religious Experience*. Croom Helm, London.

HOLY, LADISLAV (1984), 'Theory, Methodology and the Research Process', in R. F. Ellen (ed.), *Ethnographic Research*. Academic Press, London.

HORTON, CHRISTINE (1989), 'Evaluating Policing', in R. Morgan and D. Smith (eds.), *Coming to Terms with Policing*. Routledge, London.

HOUGH, M. and MAYHEW, P. (1983), *The British Crime Survey*. HO Research Study. No. 76, HMSO.

HUGHES, ROBERT (1987), *The Fatal Shore: A History of the Transportation of Convicts to Australia 1787–1868*. Collins Harvill, London.

HULSMAN, L. H. G. (1977), 'The Causes and Manifestations of Recent Trends in Juvenile Delinquency: Their Impact on Policies of Prevention, Treatment and Rehabilitation of Offenders', in UN Conference report, *New Approaches to the Treatment of Young Offenders*. United Nations European Social Affairs Div. 1979.

HUTTER, BRIDGET and WILLIAMS, GILLIAN (eds.) (1981), *Controlling Women: The Normal and Deviant*. Croom Helm, London.

HUXLEY, FRANCIS (1956), *Affable Savages*. Rupert Hart-Davis, London.

——(1970), 'Which May Never Have Existed', in *Claude Levi-Strauss: The Anthropologist as Hero*. MIT Press, Cambridge, Mass.

HUXLEY, FRANCIS (1976), *The Raven and the Writing Desk*. Thames and Hudson, London.

IFEKA, CAROLINE (1983), Review of S. Ardener (ed.), *Women and Space: Ground Rules and Social Maps* in *Man* (NS) 17, No. 4.

IRVING, BARRIE (1983), 'Research into Policy Won't Go', Unpublished paper given to the British Psychological Society.

—— (1984), *The Police Foundation Annual Review*, 1983–4. Police Foundation, London.

—— and McKENZIE, IAN (n.d.), 'Interrogating in a Legal Framework', in R. Morgan and D. Smith (eds.), *Coming to Terms with Policing*. Routledge & Kegan Paul, London.

JACOBI, JOLANDE (1967), *The Way of Individuation*. Hodder and Stoughton, London.

JAMES, ALLISON (1979), 'When is a Child not a Child? Nicknames: A test case for a Mode of Thought', *Working Papers in Social Anthropology*, No. 3. University of Durham.

JAMES, LESLIE (1978), 'Penology and Party Politics', *Justice of the Peace*, 11 Mar.: 144–5.

JONES, J. MERVYN (1980), *Organisational Aspects of Police Behaviour*. Gower, Farnborough.

JONES, SANDRA (1987), 'Policewomen and Equality: Formal policy—v— Informal Practice', reported in *Police Review*, 27 July as 'Not Yet One of the Boys'.

JUNG, CARL G. (1940), *The Integration of the Personality*. Routledge and Kegan Paul, London.

—— (1964), *Man and his Symbols*. Aldus Books, London.

—— (1967), *Memories, Dreams and Reflections*. Fontana, London.

KERSWELL-GOOCH, C. S. S. (1980), Policewomen's Uniform: The Unconsidered Handicap', *Police Review*, 12 Dec.

KNIGHT, STEPHEN (1984), *The Brotherhood*. Granada, London.

KOLIG, ERICH (1978), 'Aboriginal Dogmatics: Canines in Theory, Myth and Dogma', *Bidrajen Tot De Taal Land-en-Volkenkunde*, 134: 84–115.

KUPER, ADAM (1973), *Anthropologists and Anthropology: The British School, 1922–72*. Allen Lane Penguin Books, Harmondsworth.

LAKOFF, ROBIN (1975), *Language and Woman's Place*. Harper, Colophon Books, New York.

LAKOFF, GEORGE and JOHNSON, MARK (1980), *Metaphors We Live By*. University of Chicago Press, Chicago, Ill.

LAMBERT, JOHN R. (1970), *Crime, Police and Race Relations: A Study in Birmingham*. Oxford Univ. Press, Oxford.

LAMFORD T.G. (n.d.), 'Bramshill: The Way Ahead', in *Bramshill Journal*.

LEACH, EDMUND (1958), 'Magical Hair', *Journal of the RAI*, 88: 147–64.

——(1964) 'Anthropological Aspects of Language: Animal Categories and Verbal Abuse', in *New Directions in the Study of Language*. MIT Press, Cambridge, Mass.

——(1970), *Levi-Strauss*. Fontana, London.

——(1976), *Culture and Communication*. Cambridge University Press, Cambridge.

——(1977), *Custom, Law and Terrorist Violence*. Edinburgh University.

——(1982), *Social Anthropology*. Fontana, London.

LEIBOW, ELLIOTT (1967), *Tally's Corner: A Study in Negro Street Corner men*. Routledge & Kegan Paul, London.

LÉVI-STRAUSS, CLAUDE (1966), *The Savage Mind*. Weidenfeld and Nicolson, London.

——(1967), 'The Scope of Anthropology', in *Current Anthropology*, 7(2): 112–123.

——(1968), *Mythologiques III: L'origine des manières de table*. Plon, Paris.

——(1969), *Totemism*. Pelican, Harmondsworth.

——(1973), *Tristes Tropiques*. Jonathan Cape, London.

——(1976), *Structual Anthropolgy II*. Allen Lane, London.

LEWIS, ROY (1976), *A Force for the Future: the Role of the Police in the next 10 years*. Temple Smith, London.

LOCK, JOAN (1986a), 'Grantham's Other First', *Police Review*, 6 June: 1192–3.

——(1986b), 'Pioneer of Women Police', *Police Review*, 28 Nov., 5 Dec.

——(1987), 'Not Yet One of the Boys', *Police Review*, 27 Feb.

LUSTIG, ROBERT (1983), 'Policemen in the Dock', review of the Policy Studies Institute. 4 volumes, *Observer*, 20 Nov.

McCABE, SARAH (1980), 'The Police and the Public', *Police Journal*, 53, No. 4, Oct/Dec.

——and SUTCLIFFE, FRANK (1978), *Defining Crime: A Study of Police Decisions*. Oxford Univ. Centre for Criminological Research, Occasional Paper No. 9. Blackwell, Oxford.

MACCORMACK, CAROL and STRATHERN, MARILYN (eds.) (1980), *Nature, Culture and Gender*. Cambridge Univ. Press, Cambridge.

MACDONALD, MARYON (1987), 'The Politics of Fieldwork in Britain', in A. Jackson (ed.), *Anthropology at Home*. ASA 25, Tavistock, London.

MACDONALD, S., HOLDEN, PAT, and ARDENER, SHIRLEY (1987), *Images of Women in Peace and War: Cross-Cultural and Historical Perspectives*. Macmillan, London.

McNEE, SIR DAVID (1977), *Annual Report of the Commissioner of the Metropolitan Police for 1977*.

MAGUIRE, MICHAEL (1974), 'Criminology and Social Anthropology', *Journal of the Anthropological Society of Oxford*, 5, No. 2: 109–17.

MAGUIRE, MICHAEL (1980), 'The Impact of Burglary upon Victims', *British Journal of Criminology*, 20, No. 3, July.

——(1982), *Burglary in a Dwelling*. Cambridge Studies in Criminology 49. Heinemann, London.

MANNING, P. K. and BUTLER, A. J. P. (1982), 'Perceptions of Police Authority', *Police Journal*, 55, No. 4 (Oct./Dec.)

MARK, SIR ROBERT (1973), *Annual Report of the Commissioner of the Metropolitan Police*. Metropolitan Police, London.

——(1977), *Policing a Perplexed Society*. Allen and Unwin, London.

——(1978), *In the Office of Constable: An Autobiography*. Collins, London.

MARS, GERALD (1983), *Cheats at Work*. Allen and Unwin, London.

MAUSS, MARCEL (1935), 'Les Techniques du corps', *Journal de psychologie normale et pathologique*. 32 (translated B. Brewster and published in *Economy and Society*, 2/1, Feb. 1973: 70–88).

MAWBY, R. (1979), *Policing the City*. Gower, Farnborough.

MAY, DOREEN (1978), 'Paying the Price for Equality', *Police Review*, 12 May.

——(1979), 'Women Police: The Early Years', *Police Review*, 9 Mar.

——(1981), 'What Price Equality', *Police Review*, 6 Mar.

METROPOLITAN POLICE (1985), *The Principles of Policing and Guidance for Professional Behaviour*.

MISHKIN, BARRY D. (1981), 'Female Police in the United States', *Police Journal*, 54, No. 1.

MORGAN, ROD (1989), 'Policing by Consent: Legitimating the Doctrine', in *Coming to Terms with Policing*. Routledge, London.

——and SMITH, D. (eds.) (1989), *Coming to Terms with Policing*. Routledge, London.

MORRIS, PAULINE (1978), 'Police Interrogation in England and Wales: A Critical Review of the Literature'. Prepared for the Royal Commission on Criminal Procedure. Unpublished version.

MORRIS, TERENCE (1985), 'The Case for a Riot Squad', in *New Society*, 25 Nov.

MORRISON, CATHY (1982), 'Cartoon Coppers', in *Police Review*, 22 Oct.

MYERHOFF, BARBARA G. and MOORE, SALLY (eds.) (1977), *Secular Ritual: Form and Meanings*. Royal Van Gorcum, Amsterdam.

NEEDHAM, RODNEY (1963), Introduction to E. Durkheim and M. Mauss, *Primitive Classification*. Routledge and Kegan Paul, London.

——(ed.) (1973), *Right and Left: Essays in Dual Symbolic Classification*. Routledge and Kegan Paul, London.

NEWCASTLE CITY POLICE (1965), Annual Report for 1965.

NEWMAN, SIR KENNETH (1988), 'Police Management: The View from the Top', unpublished paper given at Conference on 'Management in the Police Service: Innovation and Evaluation', Bristol University.

NORTHUMBERLAND CONSTABULARY (1957), Centennial Handbook, 1957.
——(1958), Force Standing Orders.
——(1960), Force Orders, Section 6: Conditions of Service and Instructions for Policewomen, Cadets, Police Reservists and Special Constables.
NORTHUMBRIA POLICE (1977), Chief Constable's Annual Report, 1977.
——(1980), Force Standing Orders, Sect. 2 Para. 27.
——(1981), Chief Constable's Annual Report, 1981.
OKELY, JUDITH (1975a), 'The Self and Scientism', *Journal of the Anthropological Society of Oxford*, 6, No. 3.
——(1975b), 'Gypsy Identity', in B. Adams, J. Okely, D. Morgan, and D. Smith, *Gypsies and Government Policy in England*. Heinemann, London.
——(1978), 'Privileged, Schooled and Finished: Boarding Education of Girls', in S. Ardener (ed.), *Defining Females*. Croom Helm, London.
——(1983), *The Traveller Gypsies*. Cambridge Univ. Press, Cambridge.
——(1987), 'Fieldwork up the M.1: Policy and Political Aspects', in A. Jackson (ed.), *Anthropology at Home*. ASA 25, Tavistock, London.
ORTNER, SHERRY B. (1972), 'Is Female to Male as Nature is to Culture?' *Feminist Studies*, 1: 5–31 (reprinted in M. Z. Rosaldo and L. Lamphere (eds.), *Women, Culture and Society*. Stanford Univ. Press, Calif., (1974).
——and WHITEHEAD, H. (1981), *Sexual Meanings: The Cultural Construction of Gender and Sexuality*. Cambridge Univ. Press, Cambridge.
ORWELL, GEORGE (1951), *Animal Farm*. Penguin, Harmondsworth.
PACKARD, VANCE (1960), *The Hidden Persuaders*. Penguin, Harmondsworth.
PARKIN, DAVID (ed.) (1982), *Semantic Anthropology*. ASA 22, Academic Press, London.
PARTRIDGE, ERIC (1972), *A Dictionary of Historical Slang*. Penguin, Harmondsworth.
PEARSON, GEOFFREY (1983), *Hooligan: A History of Respectable Fears*. Macmillan, London.
PHILLIPS, D. L. (1973), *Abandoning Method*. Jossey-Bass, San Francisco.
PIRSIG, ROBERT M. (1979), *Zen and the Art of Motor Cycle Maintenance*. Corgi, London.
POCOCK, DAVID (1973), 'The Idea of a Personal Anthropology', Paper presented to the decennial meeting of the ASA, Oxford 1973. Unpublished.
POLHEMUS, TED (ed.) (1978), *Social Aspects of the Human Body*. Penguin, Harmondsworth.
POLICY STUDIES INSTITUTE (1983), *Police and People in London*. Vol. i, Smith, D. J., *A Survey of Londoners*; Vol. ii, Small, S., A Group of Young Black People; Vol. iii, Smith, D. J., *A Survey of Police Officers*;

Vol. iv., Smith, D. J. and Gray, J., *The Police in Action*. London, PSI (see also Smith, D. J., and Gray, J.).

POOLE, ROGER (1969), Introduction, to C. Lévi-Strauss, *Totemism*. Penguin, Harmondsworth.

POPE, DAVID WATTS and WEINER, N.L. (eds.) (1981), *Modern Policing*. Croom Helm, London.

POWDERMAKER, HORTENSE (1967), *Stranger and Friend*. Secker and Warburg, London.

PUNCH, MAURICE (1979), *Policing the Inner City: A Study of Amsterdam's Warmoesstraat*. Macmillan, London.

PURCE, JILL (1974), *The Mystic Spiral: Journey of the Soul*. Avon Books, Thames & Hudson, London.

PYRAH, GILL (1979), 'Policewomen', *Listener*, 25 January.

RADZINOWICZ, SIR LEON and KING, JOAN (1977), *The Growth of Crime: The International Experience*. Hamilton, London.

REES, TOM (1981), *The Concept of Crime*. HO Research Bulletin No. 12.

REIMAN, J. J. (1979), *The Rich Get Richer and the Poor get Prison*. Wiley, New York.

REINER, ROBERT (1978a), *The Blue Coated Worker*. Cambridge Univ. Press, Cambridge.

——(1978b), 'The New Blue Films', *New Society*, 30 Mar.

——(1978c), 'The Police Federation Conference', *Police Journal*, Jan.: 22–3.

——(1980), 'Forces of Disorder: How the Police Control Riots', *New Society*, 10 Apr.

——(1985), *The Politics of the Police*. The Harvester Press, Brighton.

——(1989), 'Where the Buck Stops: Chief Constable's Views on Police Accountability', in R. Morgan and D. Smith (eds.), *Coming to terms with Policing*. Routledge, London.

REITER, R. R. (ed.) (1975), *Towards an Anthropology of Women*. Monthly Review Press, New York and London.

RENVOIZE, JEAN (1978), *Web of Violence: A Study of Family Violence*. Routledge and Kegan Paul, London.

RICHTER, DONALD C. (1981), *Riotous Victorians*. Ohio Univ. Press, Columbus, Ohio.

RICOEUR, PAUL (1981), *Hermeneutics and the Human Sciences*. Cambridge Univ. Press, Cambridge.

ROBERTS, SIR DENYS (1954), *Smugglers' Circuit*. Methuen, London.

ROLF, C. H. (1982), 'Personally Speaking', *Police Review*, 9 Apr.: 693.

ROSALDO, M. Z. and LAMPHERE, L. (eds.) (1974), *Women, Culture and Society*. Stanford Univ. Press, Stanford. Calif.

ROSS, ROBERT R. and McKAY, BRIAN (1980), *Self Mutilation*. Lexington Books, Lexington, Mass.

SALMOND, ANNE (1982), 'Theoretical Landscapes: On a Cross Cultural

Conception of Knowledge', in D. Parkin (ed.), *Semantic Anthropology*. ASA 22, Academic Press, London.

SARSBY, JACQUELINE (1984), 'The Fieldwork Experience', in R. F. Ellen (ed.), *Ethnographic Research*. Academic Press, London.

SCARMAN, LORD (1981), *The Scarman Report: The Brixton Disorders*. 10–12 April 1981. HMSO (and Pelican, Harmondsworth, 1982).

SCHILDER, PAUL (1950), *The Image and Appearance of the Human Body*. Internal Universities Press, New York.

SCHOLTE, B. (1987), 'The Literary Turn in Contemporary Anthropology', *Critique of Anthropology*, 7(1): 33–47.

SCUTT, RONALD and GOTCH, CHRIS (1974), *Skin Deep: The Mystery of Tattooing*. Peter Davis, London.

SEWBERRY, JANE (1975), 'Fair Cop', *Guardian*, 17 Oct.

SHAPLAND, J. and HOBBS, DICK (1989), 'Policing Priorities on the Ground,' in R. Morgan and D. Smith (eds.), *Coming to Terms with Policing*. Routledge, London.

SHERIDAN, ALAN (1980), *Michel Foucault: The Will to Truth*. Tavistock, London.

SHERMAN, L. J. (1975), 'An Evaluation of Policewomen on Patrol in a Suburban Police Dept.', *Journal of Police Science and Administration*, 3, No. 4, Dec.

SHROPSHIRE POLICE (1939), General Order 1732: 19 Apr.

SIMEY, MARGARET (1988), *Democracy Rediscovered: A Study in Accountability*. Pluto Press, London.

SKOLNICK, J. H. (1966), *Justice without Trial: Law Enforcement in a Democratic Society*. Wiley, New York.

SMITH, COLIN (1978), 'The Bramshill Scholar: An Assessment', *Police Journal*, Apr.: 136–70.

SMITH, DAVID J. and GRAY, JEREMY (1983), *Police and People in London*, Vol. iv, *The Police in Action*. The Policy Studies Institute, London (see also under Policy Studies Institute).

SMITH, DAVID R. (1981), 'An Examination of Non-Verbal Cues by which Police Officers Perceive Potential Criminality', Unpublished B.A. dissertation, Liverpool University.

SOUTHGATE, PETER (1980), *Women in the Police*. HO Research Study No. 10, HMSO London (also in *Police Journal*, 54, No. 2, Apr. 1981).

—— (1984), *Racism Awareness Training for the Police*. Research and Planning Unit Paper 29, Home Office, London.

SPENCER, PAUL (1989), 'Indulging Automythologies', Paper given to Association of Social Anthropologists' Conference on Autobiography and Anthropology, York.

SPEIGAL, J. and MACHOTKA, D. (1974), *Messages of Body*. The Free Press, London.

STALKER, JOHN (1988), *Stalker*. Harrap, London.

STEAD, P. J. (1980), 'The Nature of Police Command', *Police Journal*, 58, No. 4, Oct./Dec.: 303–13.

STEER, DAVID (1980), *Uncovering Crime: The Police Role.* HMSO, London.

SULLIVAN, P. K. (1979), 'The Role of Women in the Police Service: The Effects of the Sex Discrimination Act 1975—A Comparison of Respective Positions', *Police Journal*, 52, No. 4, Oct.–Dec.

SWARTZ, J. (1975), 'Silent Killers at Work', *Crime and Social Justice*, 3, 15–20.

TAMBIAH, S. J. (1969), 'Animals are Good to Think and Good to Profit', in *Ethnology*, 8, No. 4: 424–59.

TAYLOR, IAN, WALTON, PAUL, and YOUNG, J. (eds.) (1973), *The New Criminology.* Routledge and Kegan Paul, London.

——————(eds.) (1975), *Critical Criminology.* Routledge and Kegan Paul, London.

TEMPLETON, HARRY (1980), 'Don't Be Afraid of the Sociologist', *Police Review*, 25 Apr. : 904.

THACKRAH, J. R. (ed.) (1985), *Contemporary Policing: An Examination of Society in the 1980s.* Sphere, London.

THOMPSON, E. P. (1968), *The Making of the English Working Class.* Penguin Books, Pelican edition, Harmondsworth.

——(1979), 'Law and Order and the Police', *New Society*, 15 Nov.: 380.

——(1980), *Writing by Candlelight.* Merlin Press, London.

THOMPSON, JOHN B. (1981), *Critical Hermeneutics: A Study in the Thought of Paul Ricoeur and Jurgen Habermas.* Cambridge Univ. Press, Cambridge.

THORPE, DAVID (1981), 'States of Justice', Social Work Today, 12. No. 48.

—— SMITH, D., GREEN, C. J., and PALEY, J. H. (1980), *Out of Care: The Community Support of Juvenile Offenders.* Allen and Unwin, London.

TOBIAS, J. J. (1967), *Crime and Industrial Society in the 19th Century.* Batsford, London.

TURNER, TERENCE (1977), 'Transformation, Hierarchy and Transcendence: A Reformation of Van Gennep's Model of the Structure of Rites of Passage', in B. G. Myerhoff and S. F. Moore (eds.), *Secular Rituals: Forms and Meanings.* Royal Van Gorcum, Amsterdam.

TURNER, VICTOR (1957), *Schism and Continuity in an African Society.* Manchester Univ. Press, Manchester.

——(1967), *The Forest of Symbols: Aspects of Ndembu Rituals.* Cornell Univ. Press, Ithaca, NY.

——(1969), *The Ritual Process: Structure and Anti-Structure.* Aldine, Chicago, Ill.

——(1974), *Dramas, Fields and Metaphors: Symbolic Action in Human Society.* Cornell University Press, Ithaca, NY.

——(1977), 'Variations on a Theme of Liminality', in B. G. Myerhoff and S. F. Moore (eds.), *Secular Rituals: Forms and Meanings*. Royal Van Gorcum, Amsterdam.

——(1978), 'Comments and Conclusions', in B. Babcock (ed.), *The Reversible World: Symbolic Inversion in Art and Society*. Cornell Univ. Press, Ithaca, NY.

——(1982), *From Ritual to Theatre: The Human Seriousness of Play*. Performing Arts Journal Publications, New York.

US DEPT. OF JUSTICE (1972), *Marihuana: A Signal of Misunderstanding*. First Report of the National Commission on Marihuana and Drug Abuse, Washington, DC.

——(1981), *Uniform Crime Reports for the United States for 1980*. Federal Bureau of Investigation, Washington, DC.

WALKER, NIGEL (1971), *Crimes, Courts and Figures: an Introduction to Criminal Statistics*. Penguin, Harmondsworth.

WAMBAUGH, JOSEPH (1976), *The Choirboys*. Weidenfeld and Nicolson, London.

WARNER, MARINA (1985), *Monuments and Maidens: The Allegory of the Female Form*. Weidenfeld and Nicolson, London.

WEATHERITT, MOLLY (1986), *Innovations in Policing*. The Police Foundation and Croom Helm, London.

WEBB, E. J., CAMPBELL, D. T., SCHWARTZ, R. D., and SECHREST, L. (1966), *Unobtrusive Measures: Non-Reactive Research in the Social Sciences*. Rand McNally, Chicago, Ill.

WEST MERCIA CONSTABULARY (1983), Chief Constable's Annual Report, 1983.

——(1987), Force Order, week ending 28 Nov.

WHITAKER, BEN (1979), *The Police in Society*. Methuen, London.

WHITEHEAD, ANN (1976), 'Sexual Antagonism in Herefordshire', in D. L. Barker and S. Allen (eds.), *Dependence and Exploitation in Work and Marriage*. Longman, London.

WILL, IAN (1983), *The Big Brother Society*. Harrap, London.

WILSON, GORDON (1978), 'Communication in a Disciplined Society', Unpublished M.Phil thesis, Durham Business School, Durham University.

WILSON, IRENE (1981), 'Political Awareness in Policing, in D. W. Pope and N. L. Weiner (eds.), *Modern Policing*. Croom Helm, London.

WINCH, PETER (1958), *The Idea of a Social Science and its Relation to Philosophy*. Routledge and Kegan Paul, London.

WOJTAS, OLGA (1982), 'A New Research Centre is Set Up', *The Times Higher Educational Supplement*, 25 June.

WOLFF OLINS, PUBLIC RELATIONS CONSULTANTS (1988), *A Force for Change*. Report on the 'Corporate Identity' of the Metropolitan Police (reported in *Police Review*, 30 Sept.).

WRIGHT, PETER and GREENGLASS, M. (1986), *Spycatcher*. Heinemann, Richmond, Victoria.

WYLES, LILIAN (1952), *A Woman at Scotland Yard*. Faber, London.

YOUNG, MALCOLM (1977), 'An Examination of some Aspects of the Developing Perception in a Local Community of Non-medical Drug Use as a Marginal, Anti-structural Deviant Behaviour', Unpublished BA dissertation, Univ. of Durham.

——(1979*a*), 'Pigs 'n Prigs: A Mode of Thought, Experience and Practice', *Working Papers in Social Anthropology*, No. 3, University of Durham.

——(1979*b*), 'The Symbolic Language of Cannabis', in *DYN, The Journal of the Anthropological Society of Durham*, 5.

——(1979*c*), 'Ladies of the Blue Light: An anthropology of Police-women', Unpublished seminar paper, University of Durham.

——(1984), 'Police Wives: A reflection of Police Concepts of Order and Control', in H. Callan and S. Ardener (eds.), *The Incorporated Wife*. Croom Helm, London.

——(1986) 'An Anthropology of the Police: Semantic Constructs of Social Order', Unpublished Ph.D. thesis, University of Durham.

——(1989), Review of 1989 ASA Conference on 'Anthropology and Autobiography', in *BASAPP Newsletter*, No. 3, summer.

Index